VENGEANCE IS MINE

VENGEANCE

MACMILLAN PUBLISHING COMPANY   NEW YORK

IS MINE

Jimmy "The Weasel"
Fratianno
Tells How
He Brought
the Kiss of Death
to the Mafia

Michael J. Zuckerman

COLLIER MACMILLAN PUBLISHERS   LONDON

Macmillan Publishing Company
866 Third Avenue, New York, N.Y. 10022
Collier Macmillan Canada, Inc.

Library of Congress Cataloging-in-Publication Data

Zuckerman, Michael J.
   Vengeance is mine.

   Includes index.
   1. Fratianno, Jimmy, 1913–   . 2. Mafia—
United States—Case studies. 3. Crime and criminals—
United States—Biography. I. Fratianno, Jimmy,
1913–   . II. Title.
HV6248.F68Z83   1987   364.1'06   [B]   87-5495
ISBN 0-02-633640-5

Macmillan books are available at special discounts for bulk purchases
for sales promotions, premiums, fund-raising, or educational use.
For details, contact:

Special Sales Director
Macmillan Publishing Company
866 Third Avenue
New York, N.Y. 10022

10 9 8 7 6 5 4 3 2 1

Designed by Jack Meserole

Printed in the United States of America

For Matthew, my son, who gently
reminds me, whenever I forget,
why we bother to create anything.

Contents

Preface

Aladena "Jimmy the Weasel" Fratianno has cut a wide swath across the U.S. justice system. But his view and recollection of how these events unfolded—the court battles he joined on the side of the Justice Department or on behalf of those civil litigants able to pay his fees—have not always been the same as mine or others who attended and studied the cases. Indeed, Fratianno's view is colored by his somewhat distorted sense of self-importance. And so it is necessary to offer some explanation of what is truth and what is fancy in these pages.

In researching for this book I have conducted more than 300 hours of formal interviews, about one-third of those with Fratianno himself, either face-to-face or over the telephone. The rest of the interviews have been with federal prosecutors, FBI agents, local authorities, private investigators, newspaper editors, publishers, columnists and reporters, and some defendants and defense lawyers. More than 10,000 pages of court records, testimony, police and FBI reports, newspaper clips, and Justice Department reports were also reviewed. And then there were a few dozen hours of videotape testimony and my own notes from covering Fratianno's testimony in three cases I wrote about as an investigative reporter for the Gannett newspapers in New York.

In short, the material in this book has been verified to the best of my ability. Where there is any uncertainty—a disputed fact or event—the recollection of that matter is presented from the perspective of one of the participants. In most instances, dialogue has been reconstructed to reflect the nature or sense of the time, place, or event and is not intended as a verbatim recounting of what was said. However, in every critical instance of dialogue, the conversations presented do reflect the precise substance of what was said.

In some instances it has been necessary to rely solely on Fratianno's recollections for matters that the Witness Security Program, Justice Department, FBI, or other institutions have been constrained from verifying or commenting upon.

On the cases he testified in, Fratianno's recollections are limited to his own time on the witness stand or his preparation for trial.

Descriptions of the investigations that led up to indictments and the preparations for those trials have been provided by others.

Those who have been associated with Fratianno have been highly cooperative. Where possible, the views of defendants or those Fratianno testified against have been sought, but frequently without response. One such nonresponse came from attorney William Marchiondo, who Fratianno testified against in a libel suit in Albuquerque, New Mexico. Marchiondo not only declined requests for an interview but said he would file a suit if his name was mentioned here. This is brought out not to harass Mr. Marchiondo, but rather to illustrate a point; Fratianno has cut to the nerve in more than one instance.

But that was one extreme. Many defendants and defense attorneys have gone out of their way to be cooperative. The only intentional alteration of fact presented in these pages is designed to protect the security of Fratianno, his wife, and his family. In some instances locations or a name has been changed. There are no clear photos of Fratianno in these pages—the reason for which will become clear in the final chapters.

Several people deserve special thanks for their encouragement and assistance. At the risk of boring most readers:

First and foremost, Nathaniel (aka "Nick") Akerman and Lisa Helmrich, whose interest, guidance, and critical support has been instrumental.

Jim Henderson, former chief of the U.S. Organized Crime Strike Force in Los Angeles, for his time and infinite patience.

Clarence Newton, a rare individual, whose friendship and interest has been a source of strength to Jimmy and me.

Jean Fratianno, whose unique view of life, often brittle or scattered, provided a refreshingly different perspective from her husband's.

Jon Standefer and Bill Hume for sheltering a lonely traveler, keeping me honest, and offering direction and detail.

Edward Whalen, who probably knows everything worth knowing about Cleveland.

Jim Ahearn, the FBI supervisor who had the rare ability to bring Jimmy in from the street and the even more unique quality of standing by Jimmy when needed.

Norman Ostrow, a defense attorney, who is proof that there are two sides to every story and who is the best tour guide the Southern District courthouse in Manhattan has ever known.

Phil Fox, Nick Lore, Ron Hadinger, Doug Roller, Bruce Kelton, Carmen Marino, Tom Vinton, Rudolph Giuliani, Howard Safir, Bud McPherson, and a host of other federal and state investigators and prosecutors, many who asked that their names not appear in these pages, who provided a wealth of information and much of their valuable time.

Steve Rodner, whose legal advice and sincere care for his craft—and my best interests—were invaluable.

John Quinn, editor of *USA Today* and executive vice president/chief news executive of Gannett Co. Inc., whose support and corporate understanding were greatly appreciated.

Brad Blanton, David Colton, Eileen Colton, Mungo, David Greenfield, Karen DeWitt, Susan Clurman, Robert Deutsch, and Phil Lerman for their advice and encouragement at critical moments.

Ned Chase and Dominick Anfuso, my editors, who believed in this project, supported it, and minimized my anguish by applying their considerable talents.

Thea and Stanley, who never understood why I was bothering with this project but remained steadfast supporters throughout.

Tara, who patiently endured myriad moods brought on by daily frustrations and victories and had the foresight to appreciate the importance of personal gratification.

It should be noted that this book makes no attempt to tell all of Fratianno's remarkable life. For those interested in a detailed account of Fratianno's life prior to entering government service, I recommend *The Last Mafioso*, a highly accurate biography of Fratianno's life of scams and philandering, by Ovid Demaris, who has provided valuable assistance to this project.

VENGEANCE IS MINE

Prologue

Q. Would you please state your name?*
A. Aladena James Fratianno.
Q. Have you used a name, a first name, other than Aladena, sir?
A. James, yes.
Q. When did you begin to use that name?
A. When I was ten years old, eleven years old.
Q. Why did you begin to use that name?
A. Well, years ago—when you used to go to school they'd have a roll call, and the name sounded like a girl's name. So I used to get in fights and they'd laugh. I just changed it to James.
Q. Mr. Fratianno, do you have a nickname?
A. Well, yes, I do.
Q. What is that nickname, sir?
A. The Weasel.
Q. Can you tell us how you acquired that nickname, sir?
A. Yes, sir. I lived in a neighborhood where there was all Italians. And there was a policeman that was assigned to that area. We used to steal fruit, apples, and he'd chase us and kick us in the fanny. It went on for a few years.

   As I got to be around fourteen, fifteen years old, it was the fifteenth of August, the holidays, and I hit this guy with a tomato—in the face with a rotten tomato. And he started chasing me and I was going in and out of cars. And the older guys says, "Look at the weasel run."

   So this policeman, when he made his report he says, "These guys called him a weasel." And that name just stuck with me ever since.
Q. When were you born?
A. November 14, 1913.
Q. Where were you born?
A. Italy.
Q. When did you come to the United States?
A. I was five, six months old.

*Testimony of Jimmy Fratianno, May 12, 1981, in a deposition for the defense in a libel suit brought by attorney Vincent "Louie" Todisco against the *Sacramento Bee*. The questions were asked by Hamilton P. Fox III. The transcript has been abridged for its use here.

Q. Are you now a citizen of the United States?

A. Yes, sir.

Q. Where were you raised?

A. Cleveland, Ohio.

Q. Mr. Fratianno, have you ever belonged to a criminal organization?

A. Yes, sir.

Q. What is the name of the criminal organization to which you belonged?

A. La Cosa Nostra.

Q. What does that phrase mean in English?

A. It means "Our Thing."

Q. Is that sometimes referred to as the Mafia?

A. Well, we never call it that. Newspapers called it the Mafia. We never called it that.

Q. Will you tell us what the purpose of La Cosa Nostra is?

A. The purpose is to make money.

Q. What means of making money does La Cosa Nostra employ?

A. Anything you can think of: legitimate business, illegal business, illegal activities, gambling, labor racketeering. They do everything.

Q. Have you, sir, been involved in any killings?

A. I think eleven . . . nine occurred in the years of forty-seven to fifty-three and the other two in the seventies.

Q. Of those eleven killings, how many did you actually participate in?

A. Five.

Q. The nine murders that occurred in the late forties and early fifties, were you ever prosecuted for any of those murders?

A. No, sir.

Q. Referring now to the two murders that you were involved in in the late 1970s . . . were you prosecuted?

A. No, but I was indicted.

Q. Did you enter a guilty plea?

A. Yes, sir.

Q. Aside from murder, what, if any, other crimes have you committed?

A. Gambling, loan-sharking, extortion, murder.

Q. What offenses have you been convicted of?

A. I pled guilty to robbery in 1937; 1954 I was found guilty of conspiracy to extort; 1968 I was found guilty of making a false report; 1970 I pled guilty to violating the Public Utility Code. In 1971 I pled guilty to conspiracy to extort.

Q. What kinds of persons are allowed to become members of La Cosa Nostra?

A. Well, you have to be Italian.

Q. Who decides if a person can become a member of La Cosa Nostra?

A. Well, number one, you've got to be proposed [by a member]. The boss decides if you're to become a member, the boss of the Fam-

ily. . . . Sometimes you have to do something significant, like kill somebody . . . to prove you're the right person to get in.

Q. Now, when a person becomes a member of La Cosa Nostra, what, if
any, initiation ceremony is carried out?

A. Well, I can tell you about the one that I attended, and they're all more
or less the same. Some vary. Some have big dinners. You know, just
variations. But the basis [*sic*] are all the same.

When I got initiated it was late forty-seven or early forty-eight. There
was five of us. They brought me in first. I think at the time we had fifty
to sixty members, and maybe forty to forty-five were present. They had
a long table. The boss and underboss would sit on one side; the *capos*
on the end. There was a gun and a sword in the middle of the table
crossing each other.

The boss would . . . we would all stand up. We would hold our hands
together, and the boss would rattle something off in Sicilian. That would
take maybe two or three minutes.

After that they would prick your finger with a sword or with a pin to
draw blood. And they take you around to each member, introduce you,
and you kiss them on the cheek. That's the initiation.

Q. What, if anything, had you done to qualify for membership?

A. Well, the time I got made, I don't know if I did anything significant, but
I know a few months later I did something.

Q. Was that a murder . . . ?

A. Yes.

Q. You used the phrase just a moment ago, "made." What does that mean?

A. Well, you're a "made guy." That means you're a member of the organization.

Q. In what city were you initiated?

A. Los Angeles, California . . . a winery on Western Boulevard.

Q. How is it possible to resign from La Cosa Nostra?

A. You can't resign. You go in alive and go out dead.

Q. Is that a rule?

A. That's the law.

Q. What, if any, other rules are there that are imposed on members of La
Cosa Nostra?

A. I was told that you couldn't deal in narcotics; you could never talk to an
FBI agent; you could never talk to any officers of any kind; you can't go
on a grand jury and tell the truth; you can't testify in no way. You can't
fool around with anybody's family. They say that the Family comes first.
If your wife is dying and they need you for something, you have to leave
her. These things they all tell you when you're initiated.

Q. Are you aware of any other members of La Cosa Nostra who have testified
for the government?

A. Yes, one person. Joe Valachi.

Q. You mentioned a rule about secrecy. What is that rule called?
A. They call it *Omertà*. It means silence.
Q. If membership in the family is secret . . . [i]s there a special way in which made guys, as you put it, are introduced to one another?
A. Yes . . . well, like when they take me to introduce me to somebody they say, "Jimmy, I want you to meet so-and-so; he is a friend of ours," *amico nostra*. When they say "a friend of ours" that means a made guy.

Mace Ebhardt cuts the deck and begins tossing cards across the dining room table. It has been a long day spent cloistered in a plush Washington, D.C., residential hotel, rooms reserved by the Justice Department as a safe house for its prized informants. With nightfall, the curtains have been drawn tight, the door double-bolted, and Mace has left his guard post to come inside. On the floor by his chair sits a tan Samsonite briefcase containing a 9mm Uzi.

Since early morning, Jimmy "The Weasel" Fratianno has sat for hours at a time, sprawled across a deep chocolate-colored sofa, nearly motionless yet often emotional, recounting the challenges, triumphs, and disappointments of a unique life. Breaks in his monologues have been provided by searches through a dog-eared address book for names of FBI agents and prosecutors—his promoters and protectors—or by the cooking frenzies in which he enlists the help of anyone around to cut, peel, dice, pound, or clean while he seasons and supervises. Food is his passion, he says, the most important thing in life.

Inside of a couple of hours, Jimmy has dominated the otherwise luxurious accommodations, filling the suite with his presence. Permeating the air are rich kitchen smells—tomato sauce and *pasta e fagiola* bubbling in large caldrons; hot Italian sausage, green peppers, and onions simmering in heavy oil; meatballs browning in garlic. Cluttering tabletops are newspapers with horses and football teams marked for the next day's wagers. Court documents that he has been reviewing for an upcoming trial are spread across chairs. And teacups filled with the spent juice of chewing tobacco grace kitchen counters and coffee tables.

It wasn't until his seventieth birthday, in 1983, that Fratianno began to realize his age. His once proud, sturdy shoulders had stooped and now sloped downward along his sides. And with greater frequency his thin lips fail to make connections to his usually agile mind, though given time the mind still wins out.

His disproportionately large hands, which some have described as inherently evil, have begun to age, and are not as powerful as they were in the days when he squeezed the life from his victims. But the two diamond rings he wears sparkle as brightly as ever.

The blue eyes, set behind heavily tinted designer-framed glasses, are incredibly deep and dark, seemingly without end; a pair of parallel black holes, drawing and capturing anyone in his company.

And since entering his seventh decade, he has taken to wearing a gold, hand-crafted crucifix inlaid with diamond chips.

But age hasn't brought fatigue to Fratianno. Hours of sedentary inaction are contrasted by sudden flurries. When there's a job to be done, he has to do it that instant, and anything that stands in his way is struck with a hail of fury, a voice that thunders with power but is trimmed with whining emotionalism.

He is—as he likes it—the center of attention; his every whim has to be satisfied, every demand met. Despite his bell-bottom jeans and styled haircut, this tough-talking, rehabilitated mob kingpin seems every bit a period piece, a 1950s mobster drawn directly from central casting for the government's big push on organized crime prosecutions. It is his unique presence, a sense of authority and self-assurance, that draws people to him and has brought him celebrity status.

Jimmy Fratianno—Aladena Tony Fratianno, his baptismal name—is capable of charm and élan. His most admirable characteristic is his sincere devotion and loyalty to friends and family. But he is not by nature warm or likable. He is too vile a personality; his past acts are too repugnant, his expectation too grandiose. Everything experienced in his company is colored by his past—the murders, robberies, pornography, and all variety of scams that only an adolescent mind could conceive and a child's morality could abide by.

And yet they have all found themselves attracted and, indeed, exhibit sincere warmth and caring for him. The prosecutors and lawmen of the United States—in whose hands we have entrusted the protection of society, the most conservative bastions charged with preserving the status quo—genuinely like Fratianno.

But a deeper inquiry will find that nearly every one of those who has used Fratianno in pursuit of justice or known him well has "sensed" something alarming. Most say it is something they had never experienced before: evil. In his eyes or his hands. An eerie feeling that permeates as he leaves you laughing, genuinely engrossed, by a tale of how he murdered this guy or got away with extorting money from that guy. A feeling of self-disgust that you are attracted to him.

Yet these feelings are largely overlooked, for Fratianno has served his purpose well. In a seemingly endless tour of courthouses and hearings that began in 1978, he has lived up to his advanced billing as the government's most potent tool against organized crime—the crown jewel of WITSEC, the Witness Security Program.

For most of his life, Fratianno had been a prolific small-time hustler and top mob enforcer, while at the same time an enthusiastic La Cosa Nostra figure who had gotten around to knowing firsthand many of the mob's major U.S. enterprises. Cloaked in the imprimatur of power as acting boss of the Los Angeles Family in 1975, he was able to hobnob and deal directly with the nation's most powerful crime bosses.

He has established, to the satisfaction of juries, a legal premise debated for decades: There *is* a secret society known as La Cosa Nostra that is dedicated to making money through any legal or illegal means at its disposal.

And from witness stands in many major American cities, Fratianno has proven himself a reliable, unshakable witness or informant against the luminaries of La Cosa Nostra—"Our Thing"—and its fringe elements, including corrupt associates and financiers of the Teamsters, businessmen, and the powerbrokers of Las Vegas.

But rarely, in his court appearances or in private, do his mouth and eyes surrender more than he wants known. There is always the sense that something is being held back, that some half-truth dangles in the air. He answers crisply with "Yes, sir," "No, sir," and "I don't recall, sir"; at times volunteering unsolicited explanations from the witness stand or engaging defense lawyers in parries and thrusts of wit while rarely sustaining a scratch.

His cunning, agile mind has easily mastered courtroom technique: a source of bounty, say prosecutors; a perverse threat to our justice system, argue defense lawyers.

As the cards hit the glass tabletop, Jimmy once again launches into a detailed account of his last few weeks as an honored member of the American ruling mob class—before the contract on his life, before he turned to the government for protection in late 1977.

"You see, I was going to turn anyway. You know what I mean. I had a good suspicion in August and September that they [La Cosa Nostra] wanted to clip me," he says, reaching to collect his cards.

His square thumbs toy with the edges of the cards, sensitizing his fingers to the deck, like a safecracker using sandpaper to gain a finer touch. His attention is distracted momentarily by Ted Koppel sorting out President Reagan's get-tough stance on communism. Jimmy has little interest in international affairs—he rarely reads anything but the sports pages, *Time*, or *TV Guide*—but he enjoys a good fight. "Kick the Communist bastards' asses."

"Now then, in the fall, all these things started happening. All these guys calling me with ideas about why I should go to Chicago with them. To do them a favor or saying that I can straighten out my troubles if I'll talk to [Joey] Aiuppa [the boss in Chicago]. Well, these dirty cocksuckers, I knew right then and there that there was a contract on me. I'd get to Chicago and I'd disappear."

These thoughts go to the core of Jimmy's rage over his current life—friends double-crossing him. Jimmy becomes animated. He rocks in his seat. His arms swing back at his sides.

Mace, Jimmy's federal bodyguard, has seen this too many times and rolls his head back, staring at the ceiling, awaiting the explosion to come and the seizure to pass.

When angered—as he has become recalling the mob's efforts to waste him—Jimmy's age becomes most apparent as he reaches to muster a force, a presence, that's been lost, causing him to resort to a grating, whining tone of voice and physical flailing to punctuate his conviction.

Jimmy sets his cards face down on the table.

"Well, you know, these dirty cocksuckers. This is my racket," he says jabbing his chest with his thumb. "There's no way I'm going to Chicago. In the old days I might have gone, to try to straighten out these motherfuckers before they could clip me. But now is different. Now they owe me a little respect. I've been making money for all of them. And besides, I know these cocksuckers aren't going to listen to reason. They want me dead."

He walks to the kitchen muttering obscenities. He stands by the stove, lifting lids and peering through rising steam to be sure everything is simmering properly. There is enough food to get him through the next three days in Washington while he meets with federal prosecutors on a case against the bosses of New York City's five crime Families. He'll also see the directors of the Witness Security Program and Justice Department to complain about funding.

He returns to the table and sits in silence, erect, his hands folded one in the other on the table, like a schoolboy. He reaches into a pouch of Big Red chewing tobacco, packs a chaw, and lifts his cards. Seeing the tirade has passed, Mace throws the first card and the action shifts to Jimmy, who's sitting on his left. Jimmy barely looks at his cards, or the card Mace has tossed on the table, and draws from his hand. Fratianno is an old card shark. At one time he was making $50,000 a night in Vegas, hustling at casinos. He not only believes in cheating and card counting, he sees them as essential parts of the game. Without an edge on the other players, what's the point of bothering? Gambling is a fool's passion; always have the odds rigged.

As the game progresses, Jimmy is registering somewhere in his head the face of every card played in a carefully honed matrix built around the elimination of each card played. More importantly, Jimmy plays the faces seated around the table, carefully sensing every nuance of a person's presence and, either at a card table or on the street, turning their weaknesses and strengths to his advantage.

The name of the game is "31." Each player holds three cards and draws from the deck or the discard pile. The object is to draw to 31, or as close as you can, before knocking or having your opponent knock. Cards are worth their face value, picture cards are worth 10, and aces are either high or low.

The stakes are usually a dime a hand. It's Mace's game and his rules; U.S. Marshal rules, keeping the wagering low so the game can run endless tedious hours into a night of guard duty. But Mace knows better than to gamble with Jimmy—a losing proposition—so tonight the loser cleans the dinner dishes.

Mace Ebhardt knows a lot about Jimmy. He has become Jimmy's constant companion on his frequent trips to Washington for meetings with Justice Department officials, lawyers, the FBI, or state lawmen.

A quiet and meticulously handsome marine pilot and Korean War vet, Mace has gained a reputation among his U.S. Marshals Service colleagues as one of the few men who can tolerate large doses of Jimmy's constant demands and complaints. Since becoming involved with Jimmy in 1981, his blond hair has gone to white, but his golf game has improved.

Jimmy screams and Mace nods. Jimmy complains about his wife's problems with the program and Mace quietly offers advice. Jimmy rants that the spaghetti sauce has been covered for too long and Mace mimics his charge as he goes to uncover the pot. Anything Fratianno can dish out seems to roll off Mace's back. And Mace knows better than anyone that there comes a time when you just have to tell Jimmy "No"—it's the only way to win his respect.

They genuinely care for each other.

"Jimmy's not so bad," Mace confides. "He's just noisy. You should see some of the other characters on this detail."

Jimmy says of Mace: "He's the only one of these marshals who understands. Most of these worthless motherfuckers treat me like any other witness. As if I were some scumbag-doper-biker-trash like ninety percent of the guys on this program."

But Mace freely cautions anyone meeting Jimmy for the first time: "Just always remember who you're dealing with."

Jimmy sees himself as unique. And, indeed, he is. In his years in the program, he has set new records for the most time in protection, most money, and most testimony. The Witness Security Program was never designed to carry someone for the balance of his or her natural life. It was intended as a way station, providing a year or two of support and protection while a witness completes testifying, and then it assists in the transition to a new identity and occupation.

For Jimmy, though, it has become a seemingly permanent condition. At a time of life when most men are reconciling their retirement, Jimmy Fratianno is involved in a new career: living in leisure and secrecy, and surfacing every few months to assist in prosecutions.

So far, he has testified in fifteen criminal trials, sending thirty-seven men to prison. He has provided leads to dozens of investigations; testified before scores of grand juries, congressional hearings, a presidential commission, the Pennsylvania Organized Crime Commission, and the Nevada Gaming Board. Frank Sinatra, Teamsters presidents Roy Williams and Jackie Presser, Chicago's mob boss Joseph Aiuppa, and New York's top mob bosses Frank "Funzi" Tieri, Paul Castellano, Carmine "Junior" Persico, and Gennaro "Gerry Lang" Langella have each been stung by Fratianno's tongue.

He has lived in at least eleven different places, including winters in various Caribbean resorts, changed his name and identity more than a dozen times, and with new cases cropping up every few months he contemplates ending his life in this insulated gravy train.

The government has paid for Fratianno's business travel; his home, utilities, phone bills, and one car; his family's medical needs; and provided $1,350 a month in cash for him and his wife. The total cost exceeds half a million dollars.

Jimmy says the pay is not enough. His view is reminiscent of the scene in a grade-B gangster movie, where the guy taking the fall for his "boss" is assured that his family will be taken care of while he's away. Fratianno expects the government to pick up *all* his expenses.

He says he's flat broke. All the money he has made since turning state's evidence—more than $300,000 from interviews, his biography, and testimony in civil cases—is gone. From 1978 to 1983, while he and his wife were separated for security reasons, he claims he had to supplement the government's limited room and board payments to her. He also had been sending money to help support his mother-in-law and his out-of-work brother-in-law. And there's a long list of incidentals bleeding him dry. "I mean, my wife's dry cleaning bill runs something like $150 a month."

The government has pushed him to be self-supporting, to start a small business, but he says he's too old to start over. And besides, with all the notoriety from his testimony, people are always recognizing him. Having a business to go to every day would just make him a sitting duck.

"When I started making my deal with the government," he said, "I thought there was only going to be the one case. But then these prosecutors start coming around to where they're keeping me in San Diego and Texas. First there's one more case, then another, and another. Now it's like every fuckin' week there's another FBI or U.S. Attorney getting me in deeper. This thing has boomeranged."

Fratianno rails at the suggestion that he's making a livelihood from testifying, that he's a professional witness providing the government any service for the right fee:

"See, you got it all wrong. I'm doing this for one reason: to protect my life. I'd be a dead motherfucker if they told me, 'Here, that's it, you're on your own.' Right now I have no money. I have no place to go.

"You know what a professional witness is? A professional witness is a guy who makes a practice of something and he's the best at it— like a professional golfer. I don't call myself a professional witness. If I did, my testimony wouldn't be worth two cents."

Generally unflappable, this is one topic that gets Fratianno's mouth moving faster than his mind. It is an attack that has been used against him at trials, where defense lawyers argue that the government has "made a pact with the devil," and the devil is an expert witness, knowledgeable enough in courtroom technique to avoid having his lies detected.

"You know why they call me a professional witness? It's because they never catch me in a lie. You know what I mean? They can't shake up my story and that aggravates them. It's because when you're telling the truth it's pretty fuckin' hard to shake up your story."

And he insists he wants to get out of this agreement—as soon as he can raise enough money.

"You think I want to testify for the rest of my fuckin' life? My one intention is to get through these cases and get the fuck out of here. I despise going into those courtrooms. I don't like sending people to jail.

"Everytime I go into a courtroom my stomach turns a little. I'm betraying a trust, *Omertà,* the silence. But all I did all my life was give away money and kill for those dirty cocksuckers. Well, sure I'm betraying a trust, but they forced me, by trying to clip me."

His only pleasure comes from knowing that some of those who turned on him will end up in jail. He recalls how after his best friend, Johnny Roselli—a top Las Vegas and Hollywood operator, who Jack Kennedy drafted for a botched assassination of Fidel Castro—was killed by the Chicago outfit, "I kept my mouth shut." But now Fratianno has had his revenge; he testified against Aiuppa who Jimmy believed, as boss of the Chicago mob, bore some responsibility for Johnny's murder.

"What did Roselli ever do? It's the same with me. They were just fuckin' jealous. They killed him for what? They cut his fuckin' legs off and stuffed him in an oil drum! So I can look right at them. I can look a guy like Aiuppa right in the fuckin' eye. Sure, I don't like being there. But that's what I got to do."

The deal Fratianno carved out with the government offers both sides great opportunities. Fratianno gets protection and money—"not enough money"—and the government has information and testimony it couldn't possibly get any other way.

"I'm not asking for sympathy because I'm getting fucked in this deal. But don't say I'm walking away either. I did twenty fuckin' years of my life in jail. That's a lifetime. Do you know that?" His voice grows shrill and cracks.

"People kill four or five guys and they get out of prison in eight or ten years. The average murderer in California does four, maybe five, years for second degree." His mind is beginning to play with numbers just as fast as he spits out the words. "Well, I did twenty years in prison and I did eight in this motherfucker. All right? So that's twenty-eight years. I only killed five guys, so they owe me. I've got to kill at least one more guy to get even," he says, breaking into a broad grin.

Fratianno lived fast for the months he led the Los Angeles Family of La Cosa Nostra. While it enabled him to make a giant impact— expanding operations in gambling, loan-sharking, and pornography— it ultimately left him with powerful enemies.

Dominic Brooklier and the hierarchy of his Los Angeles mob were sent to prison in June 1975 on a federal conspiracy charge. In their absence, Brooklier authorized Fratianno, who had been living in San Francisco, to become acting underboss for Los Angeles, the number-two man for West Coast operations, working in concert with the acting boss, Louis Dragna. But when Fratianno found Dragna, a millionaire ladies' dress manufacturer, suffering from a bad case of cold feet, he took it upon himself to play the role of number one in L.A., the boss—a title of nobility by his reckoning. And, as the weeks and months passed, he found it necessary and comforting—in order to achieve his goals of enriching himself and the Los Angeles Family— to introduce himself as the boss, sometimes neglecting to mention his partnership with Dragna.

During the next eighteen months, he initiated some potentially profitable deals, generally conspiring with or taking orders from Dragna. A few times he visited with Brooklier in prison to fill him in.

Fratianno did not make a lot of money, but—and this was more important to him—he made friends and gained influence. His name was circulated in every mob stronghold in the United States; he made sure of that by traveling the length of the country, to towns and cities he had never seen before, to introduce himself and proclaim his respect for the ways of La Cosa Nostra.

By 1977, he had initiated deals, arranged investments, or fought turf wars in New York City; Hollywood, Florida; Cleveland; Las Vegas; San Francisco; Albuquerque, New Mexico; Palm Springs; and a number of smaller spots in between.

But fortune couldn't help being followed by fame. His name was appearing regularly in news accounts on mob activity. *Time* reported his presence at Sinatra's Westchester Premier Theatre concerts in New York in 1977, while the *Los Angeles Times* followed him to dinner at the city's finest restaurants.

As opportunities presented themselves, Fratianno began making unilateral decisions about the Los Angeles Family—a small enterprise compared to the Families on the East Coast. He initiated one new member, sought others, and was arranging long-term investments. It was inevitable that when "the old man," Brooklier, got out of prison he would take offense at Fratianno's free-wheeling style.

By January of 1977 Brooklier was back in control. And by June, when he sent word out to the bosses of La Cosa Nostra families in other cities that Fratianno had been "misrepresenting himself," all the new friendships dissolved. He tried straightening things out with his partners and colleagues, but no one would listen.

By that time, most of Fratianno's newfound friends had troubles of their own. His sudden notoriety and headlong rush toward fortune had brought increased pressure from the law. And Fratianno's lack of discretion in choosing friends who didn't know enough not to discuss business on the phone proved fatal to many.

By December, Fratianno would be indicted or a target in five criminal cases: murders in San Diego and Cleveland, a pornography-extortion caper in Los Angeles, a bankruptcy fraud in New York, and gambling charges in San Francisco.

During Brooklier's absence, Fratianno had never doubted himself. He assumed that because he was aligning mob operations in San Francisco and Los Angeles with those of other cities, the network of mob bosses would see the good he was doing and come to his defense, or, at the very least, allow him to keep deals he had made and leave Brooklier's territory.

It was faulty thinking. The other bosses recognized their own vulnerability in Fratianno's actions. They would never abandon Brooklier.

In the fall of 1977, Fratianno made repeated attempts to have "sit-downs" with Brooklier. He was not turned down in these requests for meetings, he was ignored. He was treated as if he were already dead.

Fratianno began seeing demons. He envisioned cabals, bent on his death, forming everywhere. Lacking money to flee or to mount a defense in the charges pending against him—"I could have beaten every one of those charges"—and convinced his life was in jeopardy as long as he walked the streets, Fratianno cautiously began his relationship with the government.

It has taken years, but Fratianno is convinced he has nothing to be ashamed of. He believes he never broke any of the rules of La Cosa Nostra; they gave him no opportunity to explain himself and no options. Now they deserved whatever they got. He is still an honorable man.

Throughout the card game at his Washington, D.C., hotel, Jimmy, without prompting, persists in his recollection of those last days. Much of it is the kind of stuff he only admits during sleepless nights when he reassesses his actions, when he thinks about what he would do if he could just live a few critical days of his life over again. But in the light of day he never acknowledges such introspection.

On the last hand of the night, Mace, who has listened in silence to Jimmy's stories, knocks with 30. "Just give up, Jim, and go start the dishes."

Jimmy's out-of-practice fingers lift the second card off the deck and is caught before he can slide the card into his hand. He calculated that the top card was unlikely to be the ten he needed to win. The card he drew in his uncertain sleight of hand was an eight, giving him 29 points and a loss.

Like a kid caught in a lie, Jimmy wails and quickly reaches over to flip the top card, which should have been his—it's a ten.

"Give me a fuckin' break. The ten is my fuckin' card. I should have won the hand . . . " and so on and so forth, hollering to beat the band, disrupting several sleeping hotel patrons who have the front desk calling to silence the hysterics.

Indignantly, Jimmy tosses his cards on the table. Still protesting that he had been cheated, he struts off to the kitchen, rolling up his sleeves.

1

Final Days

JIMMY FRATIANNO was a walking dead man, and he knew it. By early November 1977, his Moss Beach, California, home had become a fortified camp in preparation for a siege. There was no hysteria, just precautions: the drapes were drawn; antique furniture and over-stuffed chairs blocked windows and hallways; outdoor floodlights burned all night; a loaded shotgun, rifles, and automatic handguns were strategically placed; and empty grocery bags lined the floors of the usually immaculate house.

The dark days of autumn at a beachfront community provided privacy. But still the TV played silently—even through his beloved Sunday football games—so Jimmy could listen for movement outside. The only sounds were the lapping of ocean waves and an occasional noisy motorcycle on Highway 1 heading toward San Francisco, 20 miles to the north.

For the first time in his life Jimmy was packing a gun. Made guys, guys with the organization, don't carry guns: For one thing, there is no way for them to get a permit, and for another, packing an unregistered, unlicensed piece makes them easy marks for any detective looking to cash in on a cheap hustle.

But at this late stage of the game Jimmy had abandoned a lot of the rules; there wasn't much left to lose or do—except to finger the Bauer .25-caliber automatic in his suit jacket while he paced, sat, or thought.

What does a walking dead man think about? If you're Jimmy

15

Fratianno you think of ways to make a deal, a way to escape. You never consider what you may have done wrong or how to make it right again. Regret is never a consideration; "wrong" and "right" are never factors in the process of deciding on action. The act is all there is.

If you're Jimmy Fratianno, you never worry. The lack of wrinkles in his skin, his youthful head of thick hair, a self-assured bounce in his arrogant swaggering stride, and his gregarious spirit are proof, he says, of a man younger than his years; the result of never worrying about problems but acting on them.

As he approached his sixty-fourth birthday, he still displayed the outlook of an adolescent. Everything in his experience was one-sided; the truth of any matter was always totally subjective. He rationalized every misdeed to the point of having no social conscience, making him nearly incapable of realizing any wrong on his part. As a result, he never understood why there was a contract on his life—"petty jealousy" was the best reason he could muster.

His refusal to ever look back, a lack of consciousness combined with a pragmatic cunning, is what makes Fratianno a survivor.

But for the first time in his memory Fratianno saw no way out; neither his slick tongue nor coercion could save his neck. In the thirty years since his initiation into La Cosa Nostra, Jimmy had never been scared. He could handle himself. He had gained the reputation as the mob's West Coast enforcer during the 1940s and 1950s and knew all the ruses. The Los Angeles Police Department gave him credit for at least sixteen murders—none of which the L.A.P.D. could prove—and countless extortions. His reputation was so fantastic that he became the subject of suspicion in more crimes than any person could reasonably commit in a lifetime.

He was more than the mob's buttonman. He also was a moneymaker, legitimately building a fortune in highway construction in the 1960s and later losing it over a petty fraud charge during a "clean up California" campaign by then Governor Ronald Reagan.

Jimmy Fratianno had done it all. But he had never been the target of a murder contract and he always had either money or well-placed friends to help him through tough times. Now he had run out of old friends and money; even his "crew" of hard-working buttonmen had all but abandoned him—Brooklier had seen to that.

Brooklier, convinced that Jimmy was building his own power base in an attempt to take control of the West Coast, had sent out word that Fratianno had fallen from grace, that he had been insubordinate and would soon "be taken care of."

In early November, Fratianno sent Mike Rizzitello, his closest lieutenant, back East to seek help from Russell Bufalino, a friend and the boss of the Pittston, Pennsylvania, Family. Rizzi returned with advice: Jimmy should go to see Joey Aiuppa, boss of the powerful Chicago Family, to "straighten himself out."

"He's trying to lay a trap," Jimmy snapped at Rizzi. "I thought he'd say fight your way out, which you're supposed to do anyhow. I knew that, but I wanted to hear it from him."

By sending Rizzi to see Bufalino, Jimmy felt he had probably turned his last trusted, able-bodied soldier against him. Bufalino must have told Rizzi that things had gone too far, that Rizzi should make peace with the Family in power, and as a sign of good faith he would have to help kill Jimmy. Fratianno was disappointed, but he understood what Rizzi was doing; hell, he would have done the exact same thing.

Losing Rizzi hurt. He was the kind of man Jimmy liked to have on his crew; a big, tough-talking guy not afraid to follow up on his threats, but possessing enough street smarts to know which way the wind was blowing.

Rizzi—Michael Rizzitello, an enforcer for New York's Crazy Joe Gallo in the 1960s and a suspect in several mob assassinations—had been Jimmy's constant traveling companion during the past two years. He probably would have been the *consiglieri,* or underboss, in Jimmy's new West Coast order, but he traded allegiances to become a *capo* under Brooklier.

Days swept by as Thanksgiving approached and Jimmy was unable to stay his execution. Days after Rizzi's attempt to get him to Chicago, a call came from Marshall "Johnny Marshall" Caifano, an old friend, asking Jimmy to meet him in Chicago and then fly to Las Vegas to introduce him to casino operator Benny Binion. "You dirty cocksucker, you're in on this, too? You know Benny as good as I do."

Jimmy scrambled around trying to raise enough money so he could flee, but he was unable to get a loan or collect the $70,000 he had put on the street as shylock—loan-shark—money. In a panic, he met with the head of the Mexican Mafia in Los Angeles, arranging to have Brooklier and his top aides—Sam Sciortino and Jack LoCicero— "clipped."

It was this last attempt at salvation, perhaps more than anything else, that made Jimmy realize there was no way out. Even he recognized the irrational acts of a desperate man; thinking he could kill the entire L.A. leadership was ludicrous. Others would take their places and the other La Cosa Nostra families in the U.S. would never stand for such wholesale slaughter.

Friday, November 18: Jimmy was pacing the kitchen in silence. His gun sat on a Formica counter next to a freezer bag filled with gnocchi. Frank "Skinny" Velotta, the last mate on a sinking ship, had moved in with him weeks earlier and was taking abuse. All else may be lost, but a man still has to eat—and eat well.

"You've got the flame up too high," Jimmy scolded as he dipped a crust of bread to taste the nearly ready spaghetti sauce and, still chewing, turned to the ringing phone.

Lifting the wall phone with one hand, he reached over and grabbed the .22, stroking the barrel with his thumb as he slipped it in his pants pocket.

"Yeah."

"Hey Jimmy. How you been?" Rizzi asked.

"What's up?"

"We've got to talk."

"So talk," Jimmy said—if he could only fire off a few rounds into the phone.

"No, I mean this is hot. There's no way. I'm on a pay phone in L.A. Go out and I'll call you in fifteen."

Rizzi was trying to get Jimmy out of the house to a pay phone he used for sensitive calls.

"Mike," his voice rising in a loud whine, "there's no fuckin' way I'm stepping out tonight. It's going to have to wait."

"Jesus, Jimmy, you have some broad there or what?"

"Forget about it. Give me a call in a couple days or something," Jimmy said.

"I'll be in Frisco in a few days, I'll talk to you then."

"Yeah, so long," he said, dropping the receiver back on the wall. Skinny looked up from the sports page. "What was that all about?"

"Nothin'. Just Rizzi."

Go to a phone booth? After dark? This guy had to be out of his mind. Who did he think invented that routine? These guys had no originality at all. They had to be idiots. It was the same routine Jimmy put together so they could clip Frank "The Bomp" Bompensiero in

San Diego last February. But these guys lacked Jimmy's finesse for a clean hit: you had to woo a guy, make him think he was your best friend, take him to dinner or get him a free trip to Vegas, get him to go to the phone booth a couple of times without anything happening. And then, after you have him all warmed up and confident, boom, you clip him.

Go to a phone booth after dark!

Dinner and the rest of the night were spent largely in silence. Jimmy spent a lot of time standing around, staring into space, his hands buried deep in his pockets. He called on an inner reserve and calm overtook his mind as he got down to some serious planning.

By sack time he had reached a conclusion: "I'm going to shut this place down—you know, move all the furniture into storage—and take an apartment somewhere."

Skinny thought for a moment. "Hey Jimmy, that's going to cramp my style. You know, the two of us in some small fuckin' apartment."

"Hey man, I don't need you. Your wife's in town, go live with her. I don't need nobody baby-sitting me."

"You sure, Jim? I mean . . ."

"Sure, I'm sure. I've got something working that I haven't talked about and I'm better off working it alone right now. I'll give you a call if I need you." Jimmy was winging it. He had been considering a move like this for a while. He had even looked at a furnished apartment on Nob Hill in San Francisco, but beyond that his plans remained uncertain.

Velotta shrugged, rubbed his balding head in wonder, and made off for the bedroom, mumbling something about it being all right with him.

About an hour later, as Jimmy prepared for the next morning, circling moving and storage companies in the Yellow Pages and puffing his way through his last fat Havana of the day, the phone rang. "What the fuck, at one in the morning." Walking toward the phone he shot a look outside, peering through the drapes at the front lawn and scrub evergreens frozen motionless in the floodlit yard. Skinny came into the living room, a pump-action shotgun perched on his hip.

"Yeah," Jimmy said, grabbing the phone after ten rings.

"Hi, honey," the sweet plaintive voice sang in reply.

Jimmy chuckled with genuine boyish delight. "Hey babe. I've been missin' you; how are you?"

After a nine-year courtship, Jean—a stunning blond, at forty-one, twenty-three years younger than Fratianno—married him at a Reno,

Nevada, wedding chapel in April 1975. It took sixteen months before Jimmy started going off on what she calls "one of his emotional benders," and by January 1977, she had moved to their Palm Springs condominium, seeking a divorce.

The last time they had seen each other was in July in Palm Springs, and it ended in one of their regular screaming bouts over money. If Jimmy was capable of killing out of anger, Jean would be dead several times over. But at the same time, they were utterly devoted to each other.

Just after 1 A.M. that November morning, she awoke from a sound sleep "sensing" something was wrong with Jimmy and decided she had to see him. Recovery from a heavy bout with alcoholism had imbued in Jean a keen ability to follow her senses and chalk it up to divine order. Jean was a little skittish, a little off-center, but her instincts were sound.

"I'm fine, but I'm worried about you," she told Jimmy. "I want to come home."

"No, babe; listen, there are all sorts of things going on and this . . . well, really bad. I don't think—"

"I don't care, Jim. The Lord wouldn't have put this in my mind tonight if it wasn't the right time. There's something wrong and I want to be there with you. You need me there. I'll be in on Monday, on the evening flight," and the phone line went dead.

Jimmy was stunned. She comes swooping in here from nowhere, after months, with all this "Lord" shit and expects to just pick up again. What a dizzy broad. And in the middle of all this bullshit! He was stirred at that moment by two genuine emotions: fear she might get hurt, and a burning desire to make love to her.

He fell back on the couch, relit his cigar, and weighed the options. He could pick her up safely at the airport; he just had to be certain he wan't being tailed. They wouldn't go home. They'd spend the night at a motel and he would send her off in a cab for the first flight the next morning. It would all work—and he was as excited as a schoolboy. Jimmy had been with scores of women and he still felt Jean was the best he'd ever known; she knew how to let a guy make love to her, and it made him feel like a million bucks.

Jimmy prefers her in subdued lighting. In such light she is striking; dark skin and West Coast bleach blond hair, shapely legs, and firm breasts. She walks with the fluid confidence of an athlete, a bright smile, self-assured handshake, and warm voice. She wears a lot of pinks and whites to accentuate her tanned, girlish good looks. She could pass for her late twenties.

In slightly better lighting the picture is different. She's clearly in her forties, but no older. Her darkened skin is desert-wrinkled and worn, and her hair shows the dryness of years in peroxide or ultraviolet rays; there are telltale signs of cosmetic surgery. Here she looks her age and less like a West Coast beach kid. Her habit of sleeping in isn't as sweet as the carefree teenager she portrays, the person she sees herself as. No, her sleeping in, in a person of this age, in this light, suggests a character who has felt more pain, one who finds sleep uneasy. Her voice is capable of brightness, but she shrieks more often than she laughs. Her physical agility permits her to curl up fully in an easy chair, but it's hard to tell if Jean Fratianno is just comfortably athletic or scared.

In any case, she has a striking presence—strong, often bitter, always sexual.

Like Jimmy, she was born to relative wealth and good taste. Growing up in Cleveland, Jimmy's father had a coal and ice delivery business and owned a couple of small apartment houses. During the Depression they always had a new car and didn't lack for anything.

Her father, a Mobil Oil executive, provided what she calls an upper-middle-class income that permitted them to live comfortably in San Pedro, on the Palos Verdes Peninsula near Los Angeles, and enabled her to receive a private education at St. Anthony's.

She concedes that marrying a man so much older was a quest for a father figure. After serving as a navy lieutenant in World War II her father had gone to work for Mobil and was away at sea for months at a time directing oil tanker operations. Her mother was a strong, eccentric woman who was hard to get close to or win approval from. So it was only during her father's brief visits that she found the warmth she needed as a child.

Jimmy, too, was rarely home—off hustling around the country or doing time in prison. But when he was there he was generous, giving, and loving, and aware of her every need except one: her need to feel secure in his fidelity.

She was always insulated by Jimmy; first as his mistress, being kept in an apartment a few blocks from where he and his first wife, Jewel, lived in Sacramento; and later, after he was divorced and they were married, refusing to tell her about his business. She would have been appalled to learn about his involvement with pornography, but her suspicions of his dealings with the mob didn't bother her.

In the years immediately preceding his becoming the acting underboss in L.A., Jean had read news accounts describing Jimmy in polite, libel-proof terms as "alias Jimmy the Weasel," "allegedly a crime kingpin," or "the reputed boss of West Coast mobs."

Made guys keep their families in the dark. Certainly the wife, kids, and neighbors know they're involved—you can't hide a thing like that—but their exact role is impossible to determine. But Jean wasn't going to play the "old-fashioned Mafia wife" who sat home silent, professing ignorance. She was always prying: picking up the extension phone to eavesdrop; going through his papers. It was "just a yearning" to know what was going on, she had explained.

Piquing her curiosity were hints that he was seeing other women. Nothing enraged Jean more than Jimmy's philandering. In fact, one time, when a writer claimed Jimmy was cheating on his wife and cited unconfirmed old L.A. police reports to describe Jean as a former jet-set call girl, she called the author demanding to know who the other women were—never mentioning the call girl allegation.

After they had separated, early in 1977, Jean had made up her mind to find out who Jimmy was dating. She had known the man too long to be suspicious without reason, and she wanted the satisfaction of a name to which she could direct her hatred. She couldn't take it out on Jimmy; she still loved him.

She spoke to some of Jimmy's friends without results and even tried, without success, following him around for a while. But after a few days of watching him go through his daily routine, Jean spied two men in an undistinguished Chrysler, apparently doing the same thing. She realized she had been wasting her time: Why do this kind of work when the FBI was already doing it for her?

She decided to trade up with the FBI, offer them what little she knew in return for their telling her who Jimmy was dating. This was not entirely untested territory for Jean. Agents had been cozying up to her as long as she had known Jimmy. Some scored better than others, but none had ever gotten anything of substance for their trouble.

At the end of a day-long Palm Springs shopping spree in May 1977, Jean dropped a dime at a phone booth and called the FBI. Agents came right out to see her and convinced her to travel to L.A. to meet Jack Barron, supervisor of the FBI's Organized Crime Squad.

In a flash she was being ushered into an office where Barron looked her up and down admiringly and commented, "Hey, you aren't at all what I expected."

"Why, what were you expecting?" Jean asked with a gentle smile, taking a chair at the side of his desk and crossing her legs.

"Can't rightly say," he said, watching her claim her seat. "But you're something special."

Barron, a fast-talking agent who had been tracking the wise guys for twenty-two years, knew as much about Jimmy Fratianno as anyone in law enforcement. He knew Jimmy was running street operations for the L.A. Family, that he had been the acting underboss, and that he had somehow fallen into disfavor.

Special Agent Robert John Barron, one of the FBI's most flamboyant, knowledgeable, and accomplished agents in the field of organized crime, was coming close to retirement and was saving a place in his trophy case for Fratianno's carcass.

A year before Jean's visit, Barron had targeted Jimmy in POR-NEX, the FBI's pornography sting operation in Los Angeles. A team of agents posing as Forex, a porno dealership, had drawn out Jimmy's crew. The mobsters were caught on tape recordings threatening the pornographers unless they paid $20,000 up front and $500 a week tribute. But Jimmy had evaded direct involvement in the shakedown.

Barron's pursuit of Fratianno had gone from professional zeal to personal rage after Frank Bompensiero's execution on February 10. They never intended to get Bomp killed—but they lost control of the situation. Barron was convinced that Jimmy had set up Bompensiero's murder, which greatly annoyed Barron since for the past eleven years "The Bomp"' had been Barron's most productive informant.

In fact, Barron and Special Agent Jack Armstrong had used Bompensiero—most say they burned Bomp—to draw the L.A. Family into the sting. They had told Bomp that there was a new porno outfit in town, Forex, and had urged him to have the Family take a look at it. When the subpoenas came down, Brooklier and Fratianno traced their knowledge of Forex back to Bomp and three months later he was gunned down near a pay phone outside his San Diego home, a cigar clutched in his fingers and change scattered along the pavement.

There was one more incentive in Barron's desire to see Fratianno permanently off the streets. Just as surely as there have been running rivalries between the 49ers and the Rams, the Giants and the Dodgers, UCLA and Cal Tech, between Northern Californians and Southern Californians, there was a deep-seeded rivalry between the FBI

office in San Francisco and the one in Los Angeles. The two offices
frequently fought turf wars over how to divide their jurisdictions,
which office takes precedence when a crime is committed in one area,
but the suspect was already under investigation in the other? Now
Barron envisioned a coup. Neither of the other two offices had ever
been able to close the lid on Fratianno. He saw himself on the verge
of a good bust, a personal vindication, and a team victory.

Jean played her best dumb-blonde routine in Barron's office: She
claimed she was worried about Jimmy, he had been acting oddly, all
those strange men he was meeting with in San Francisco and all those
trips to L.A., Palm Springs, Murietta Hot Springs, and the Westchester Premier Theatre in New York. And he wasn't telling her what
was going on. However, if she could just learn the names of some of
the women Jimmy was keeping company with, well, maybe she could
use her wiles to find out something for the FBI.

Barron played the caring public servant: He was worried about
Jean's safety and Jimmy's well-being. Without offering details, he told
Jean that Jimmy was keeping her in the dark to protect her, that she
should stick by Jimmy and try to help him along. And, Barron said,
she should call at least every Tuesday—just so the FBI could be sure
she was all right.

Jean was driven home to Palm Springs by an agent who collected,
copied, and returned a pile of Jimmy's papers. Among them was a
photo, which, when it landed on Barron's desk, seemed more a conversation piece than anything else.

There, in full color, was Frank Sinatra—who had long denied any
association with La Cosa Nostra—smiling, his arms outstretched around
two operators of the mob-financed Westchester Premier Theatre in
New York State. Flanking them were a variety of La Cosa Nostra
luminaries, including Fratianno, notorious mob boss Carlo Gambino,
and Paul Castellano, destined to become Gambino's successor.

Jean called Barron regularly offering the best she knew—which
really wasn't of great value. She even called Jimmy on several occasions in an unsuccessful attempt to develop more information. But
what she wanted in return she never got: the names of the women
Jimmy was messing around with. Throughout 1977, while living in
Palm Springs, Jean contemplated a divorce. She even spoke to a
lawyer, Kenny Gale, about it.

Gale had been a friend of Jean's family long before she had known
Jimmy. But he and Jimmy had hit it off and the two men had used

their positions to do favors for one another—Jimmy getting Gale the royal treatment in Vegas and Gale writing to the parole board on Jimmy's behalf in the early 1970s.

"Jean, I like you and I like Jimmy. Why don't you give it some time, try to patch it up," she remembers Gale telling her. "And besides, I'm up for a state judgeship and if I do anything for you it would put a damper on my case."

Maybe Gale and Barron were right, she thought. Maybe she should stick by Jimmy, try to get through these rough times. She had the Palm Springs condo in the old Biltmore Hotel and Jimmy was sending her money. In time, maybe they could work things out.

Anticipating Jean's arrival, Jimmy spent the weekend taking care of business, renting the furnished apartment, hiring the storage company, and carrying a few bags over to Nob Hill. On Sunday he watched the 49ers take a 23-to-10 beating at the hands of the Rams, and sent Skinny out to pick up his winnings—about $4,600—on the rest of the weekend's action.

He had refined his plans: As soon as he saw Jean off to the airport he would spend Tuesday afternoon driving around, making sure he wasn't being followed, and then go up to Nob Hill and never return to Moss Beach.

The new apartment, in a modern high-rise, would be a lot safer. There was a doorman and heavy security in the garage. He wasn't going to give anyone his new phone number—well, maybe one or two people.

The Nob Hill neighborhood was safe, too. A quiet residential area. No made guys lived up there or had any reason to visit. He had spent a few hours acquainting himself with the area after signing the sublease—seeing which streets were one-way, taking down the numbers and locations of pay phones, looking in on markets and restaurants. He could be holed up safely in there for months.

After lunch on Monday, Skinny loaded three large suitcases into Jimmy's Cadillac. Fratianno inspected the car for bombs, closed the trunk, and flipped a switch on the dash that electronically double-bolted it shut.

"You stay here for a few days, till the movers get through, and then I'll give you a call at your place, maybe Thursday," Jimmy said.

"Wait a minute. You mean this is it. You're not coming back?"

Skinny had thought Jimmy was loading up for another trip to his apartment—wherever that was—and would return with Jean that evening.

"No, I told you. I have something working. I'm not sticking around."

"I guess that means I'm not going to have to straighten things up or nothing. Shit, I wanted to see Jean."

"I tell you what," Jimmy said, already behind the wheel and pressing the remote control to open the garage door. "I'll send her your regards."

Jimmy was cruising. Nothing he liked better than sitting behind the wheel of a car seeing the sights. Jimmy could live in a car if it were big enough, and there was always a good Italian restaurant within driving distance. He cruised for two hours making sure he wasn't being tailed—by either the FBI or the mob.

Despite the No Parking signs, Jimmy parked on the concourse in front of the terminal and walked in looking for Jean. She saw him first. He looked tired but seemed calm enough. As always, he was looking natty in a well-tailored brown pin-stripe suit; red tie; and matching breast pocket handkerchief. She was glowing with warmth as she came up to him, dropped her bag, and grabbed him for a long kiss. He kept his eyes open.

"I was worried about your coming, but I'm glad you're here, babe," he said, planting his right hand in his suit jacket while carrying her bag in his left.

"I love you so, honey." She was entwined in his pocketed arm, resting against his shoulder as they walked out to the car.

"So you're still driving the pimpcar," she commented as he opened the passenger door and pitched her bag in the backseat. It was a fully loaded, 1976 white Caddy with a blue vinyl top, sunroof, and red pin striping.

"Yeah," he said and chuckled. "It's kind of becoming my signature, you know, like the cigars."

As he moved the big car into airport traffic at dusk she cooed, "Oh, honey, I can't wait to get home."

He paused. "Well, babe, we're not going home."

Jean was startled. "I don't understand. What are you talking about, Jimmy?"

"Jean, just believe me. We can't go home. Let's put it that way."

"Jimmy, what are you talking about? I want to go home. I want to sleep with you in our bed. Where do you think we're going to stay? At one of your hoodlum friend's houses?"

"No, Jean, I've chosen a motel. Fuck, we just can't go home, and that's the end of it." He hadn't thought all this through beforehand, and now he could see she was revving up for a fight. He didn't want to tell her the whole story—it would probably scare her.

"Look, Jimmy. I told you I was coming in to see you because I wanted to come home. Remember me telling you that when I called? And going home means going to my house, with all my things, and having you there. I'm not going to take any of your bullshit. Get this car on the highway and let's go." She was screeching, pounding the padded dashboard with her hand, and pressing her face into his view as he steered out of the airport complex.

She kept up her rant. "I know you're in some trouble. I understand. But I don't care. I don't care. I don't care. You hear me? You've got to act normal if you're going to straighten this shit out. And normal people go home with their wives."

"You motherfucker, you don't understand nothing. They're trying to clip me. You get that. These jealous, dirty cocksuckers are trying to kill me, and if you happen to be around when it goes down, well, that's your bad fuckin' luck."

He was sorry as soon as he let the words slip out—a wife isn't supposed to know that kind of thing—but she knew how to press all the right buttons to get under his skin. She was going to be scared to death.

Without losing a beat, Jean responded. "I don't care who's trying to kill you. I'm here to protect you. God won't let anything happen to you or me," she said, assuring him that God wouldn't have put her there if it was Jimmy's time.

Jimmy swung the big Caddy into the lot of one of the less distinguished airport motels.

Jean was still hot. She kicked the door open, climbed out, and punched the vinyl roof. "Shit, I've never gone first-class with you. A fucking dump of a motel."

She stood by the car as Jimmy checked them in under the names of Jean and Jimmy Russo.

They got into the motel room and, with hardly another word, climbed into bed.

Except for a brief break for dinner, Jean and Jimmy spent the rest of the evening in the motel alternately talking and making love. More precisely, when they weren't locked in passion, Jean did the talking while Jimmy smoked cigars and listened. She talked about God and divine order and how this was a time for Jimmy to reflect on his past and plan for the future; his final years during which he should seek peace with himself and the Lord.

Jean had found Jesus on the floor of a seedy desert motel room. About eight months earlier, she had been on a drunk and collapsed in front of a 15-inch color TV in some nameless motel. She faded out with the TV reception around 11 P.M. When she came to, there was Oral Roberts commanding "Jesus loves you. Jesus wants you. Yes, you lying there drunk on the floor of that motel room," and he was pointing right at her. She spent the rest of the night crying and praying, first with Roberts, then with the "Star-Spangled Banner," and finally with the test signal. She has regarded herself a recovering alcoholic and born-again Christian ever since.

Jimmy listened to Jean's pleas for him to find religion and rehabilitate himself. He protested at certain points that Brooklier and Aiuppa and the rest didn't give two damns about what the Lord intended, and unless he did something to straighten things out they would determine his fate: "God helps them that help themselves, right?"

She assured Jimmy that God wasn't ready for him yet and wouldn't have sent her to him at this point if there wasn't still some good he had to do in this life; it was up to him to turn things around.

Jimmy was contemplative. He had been touched by religion in his life. He believed in God, although he wasn't a church-going man. He believed that when your time comes, God calls, and there's no point in worrying yourself over it.

When he was in the tenth grade, Jimmy had contracted pneumonia and lapsed into a coma when his fever reached 106. Two weeks later, his family doctor proclaimed the boy on the brink of death. Two nuns, his parents, and the parish priest gathered at his bedside for the last rites. When the communion wafer touched his lips, the boy opened his eyes, gazed at the gathering, and proclaimed, "I'm better."

It took another week for him to regain full consciousness, but by then he had contracted pleurisy, his left lung had filled with pus and was pressing against his heart. To relieve the pressure doctors cut open his back and, without the aid of anesthesia, hacked out a piece of rib to insert a tube in the lung. It took more than a year of bed rest, with the tube draining pus from his lung, to regain his strength. During this time Jimmy decided that if he couldn't play softball or run track there was no point in school. Until then, he had envisioned a softball scholarship and law school—he would have contemplated a track scholarship, but there was this other local kid, Jesse Owens, who always left Fratianno in the dust.

Jimmy always believed his recovery was a miracle, that divine intervention had saved his life. So Jean's discussion that night about God's role in whether he should live or die now was not beyond his range of comprehension. The pneumonia was the result of nature, nothing he had done could have avoided it, and in his view, the efforts now of others to kill him were similarly not of his making. But he couldn't sit and wait, he had to make something happen.

Exhausted from sex and talk, Jean, cast in her role as Angel of Mercy, mentioned something about a government program. "I don't know much about it, but they can protect you, honey. I'm sure you could get them to pay for everything we need."

Jimmy sputtered something about it all being bullshit.

They fell asleep at sunrise.

Later that day she finally convinced Jimmy to take her back to Moss Beach, where Velotta was delighted to see her and she was shocked by the condition of her beloved home: dishes piled high, furniture in disarray, guns everywhere. She spent the day cleaning, slept there that night, and awoke the next morning with a realization that Jimmy was right: There was danger in the house. She took Jimmy to the side of the house, to a big aboveground gas tank, and told him, "That's how they're going to kill you. They're going to blow up that tank while you're in the house. You must get out of here."

That afternoon, as they drove back to the airport, Jimmy spotted in his rearview mirror a camper truck with out-of-state plates. His efforts to shake it off failed. Two men sat in the pickup, both with dark glasses.

"Get down," he said grabbing the back of Jean's neck, forcing her to the floor of the car.

"What the hell are you doing, Jimmy," she hollered, trying to press herself back into her seat. "They're not going to kill you with me here."

Jimmy threw his weight behind his arm and pounded her head to the hump in the floor between the driver's and passenger's seats. "Where do you get these fuckin' ideas? They won't kill you? They'd kill you in a hot fuckin' minute if they had to to get to me. Don't move."

The Cadillac picked up speed. The camper kept pace. For the

first time Jean was frightened. If Jimmy was scared—something she had never seen—it was obviously time for her to be scared.

He let go of her long enough to pull the .22 from a compartment he had fashioned behind the fold-down cushion beside the driver's seat.

"Oh, honey, don't start shooting at them unless you're sure," Jean pleaded from under the dashboard.

"Hey, don't even fuckin' breathe down there," he ordered. "What you want me to do? Wait till they take a few shots at me?"

He began looking for a break in the highway median divider. He would take the U-turn and then peel off a few rounds at the pickup as he passed it heading in the opposite direction.

When he looked back again the camper was gone.

They were both too distracted or rattled for long goodbyes at the airport. Just a quick kiss, and Jimmy pulled away as Jean scampered into the terminal. She changed her scheduled flight—she thought that was a wise thing to do to avoid detection—and stayed away from people as much as possible while waiting to board.

Jimmy took a circuitous route to Nob Hill. He would try to retain some semblance of a normal life from this hideout—seeing his girl-friends, meeting people for business. But how long could he continue like this, peering through curtains, staring into the rearview mirror, staying away from his routine haunts, watching his remaining funds dwindle?

He thought of copping a plea on one of the charges pending against him and hiding out in prison for a couple of years, where he would not be a threat to Brooklier. Having already spent more than seventeen years of his life behind bars he knew how to do prison time: you just relax, forget about the outside world, forget about your family and friends, throw out the calendar, exercise, sleep, and think about your next meal. But he was getting too old for all that.

What he really needed was money, a bank roll, a meal ticket. Jimmy Fratianno understood better than most the power and prestige associated with money. If you have money, even a Rockefeller won't flinch at being associated with you, even if you got your hands dirty making it. It is the ultimate root purpose in life; it is what gave his longtime associates a degree of control in the U.S.; it is the life's blood of places like Las Vegas, where he and his cronies have always reigned—let the Rockefellers have New York, we have Vegas. In Jimmy's view, money is what makes guys like Sinatra and John Roselli respectable enough for socialites and presidents to pal around with. In Jimmy's mind, money is freedom—even in a prison cell.

As he spent his final days on Nob Hill, Jimmy had a recurring thought: He could walk off the streets and into the waiting arms of the FBI. They could protect him, pay him, and perhaps best of all give him the opportunity to go into a courtroom and get revenge on each and every one who had betrayed him.

Jean's thought about going into the Witness Security Program was nothing new; he had already been considering it as an option—a rather unpalatable option, but one to be considered if all else failed. The problem was would they ignore those murders he had committed and never been charged with? He would certainly have to tell them everything and somehow get it all absolved. "I didn't kill no innocent people; these were all gangsters I fucked with"—he figured that might be his best argument.

And there was still a matter of honor: How to justify breaking *Omertà*. At what point, he wondered time and again, would Brooklier, Aiuppa, Rizzi, and the rest "force me" to abandon that honor? How much pressure would there have to be? How close would they have to come to clipping him? How certain would he have to be that there was no other direction to turn?

He finally decided the stakes weren't high enough—yet.

Jim Ahearn was balanced on a gossamer-thin line. He had been playing both sides from the middle, holding back the floodgates from a series of indictments in order to orchestrate control of Fratianno. Letting the bad guys get close enough to scare Jimmy the Weasel, but not close enough to kill him; secretly giving him limited protection while Fratianno continued as an active member of organized crime. All the while fanning the flames of Fratianno's concerns with every form of bullshit he could conceive in order to build distrust between Fratianno and his cohorts.

And he wasn't doing it all by the book either. Ahearn wasn't going to break the law, just bend the laws and the FBI's rules as far as he had to to win Fratianno's trust. You can't always go by the book when you're dealing with organized criminals. They're too knowledgeable; they know how to work the law to their advantage to avoid detection, how to use the pretense of "innocent until proven guilty" to thwart justice. Every so often you have to get down in the trenches with the bad guys and play at their games to capture them.

No. James F. Ahearn, assistant special agent in charge of the FBI's San Francisco office, was skirting the rules, playing a long shot. And just as certainly as time was running out for Fratianno, it was running out for Ahearn. He was fearful Fratianno would be killed, arrested by some other jurisdiction, or flee before he could be brought in from the cold. And Ahearn was trying to make it just as cold as he could without inducing frostbite.

It was Fratianno who initiated the FBI's invovement. On Friday, August 12, 1977, he had called retired FBI agent Larry Lawrence at home in San Francisco. The two men had known each other since 1973, when Lawrence began plying Fratianno for information in a traditional game of good-guy, bad-guy rapport. The way it works is that the agent cultivates the relationship, paying guys like Fratianno some monthly cash for what they know is largely useless information, banking on the hope that over the years, something significant may emerge. The mobster, for his part, provides some dated information, or perhaps something of little value about someone he doesn't like, and accepts the cash, viewing it as an easy scam that doesn't violate *Omertà* but which could come in handy later as insurance; an escape hatch in times of trouble.

That August Fratianno had sensed trouble and decided to cash in his insurance policy. Lawrence protested that he was no longer with the Bureau and was no longer paying for information. Jimmy told him to shut up and listen.

He told Lawrence that he had just returned from Cleveland, where he had attended the funeral of Tony "Dope" DelSanter, a childhood friend who, like many of his childhood pals, had risen to a position of prestige in La Cosa Nostra. In the past that is where his tale would have ended, but this time he kept talking.

He said that during the wake one of his cronies, James "Jack White" Licavoli, boss of the Cleveland Family, had pulled him aside and shown him a set of documents: copies of FBI confidential informant files complete with names and reports on the informants. One described a meeting between Bompensiero and Joey Aiuppa, for which Bomp was the apparent snitch. The document was marked with the code number "SD-1064." Another document identified as an informant Tony Hughes, a business partner of Jackie Presser's, then an international vice president of the Teamsters and destined to become their president. Licavoli told him that the Cleveland outfit had a woman in the FBI office who was slowly gathering up the names of all the snitches.

Lawrence didn't ask too many questions and Fratianno didn't volunteer, but the clear implication was that Fratianno feared his name could turn up in that informant file. Lawrence was shaken by Fratianno's story. He told Jimmy that if his information about a leak was accurate it would be the first case of its kind in the Bureau's history; it would get top priority and he might be asked to meet with other agents.

"You do whatever you want with the information," he told Lawrence. "Just keep my fuckin' name out of it. I have family in that town." Lawrence felt pretty much the same way; he was retired and wanted no more dealings with the FBI or Fratianno, but he couldn't make any promises.

"Well, if I got to get involved I don't want to talk to any agents, only the fuckin' boss, the guy at the top or else forget about it," Fratianno told him.

Lawrence rushed Fratianno off the phone after having him promise to call the next day, Saturday. He then called Special Agent Chuck Hiner, who in turn called Ahearn at home. They arranged a meeting with Fratianno for Monday at the Sheraton airport hotel—Ahearn didn't want to lose any momentum, but he wanted some time to read everything he could about Fratianno.

Ahearn, just thirty-seven, had been second in command at the FBI's San Francisco office for about eight months. He didn't know much about the West Coast yet, but the name Jimmy Fratianno was one he had picked up. Ahearn had also read some of Lawrence's informant reports about Fratianno and felt that, with the right amount of pressure and deceit, there was a chance to develop Fratianno as a top-flight informant.

The product of New York City blue-collar stock, Ahearn grew up in Woodside, Queens, where, at fifteen, he was tossed out of Bishop Loughlin High School for poor scholarship and even worse discipline. He traveled with groups of young leather-jacketed toughs and learned the ways of city streets while his father, a city cop, walked a beat.

His brawling teen years could have broken him and left him without direction. Instead, it gave him enough savvy and toughness to get out of the gutters, through high school, and into St. John's University, where he received a degree in management while working nights as an FBI clerk.

In 1963, he became the youngest agent ever inducted into the FBI. After tours of duty investigating street crimes and mob truck hijackings in Tampa, Detroit, and New York City, he went to FBI headquarters in Washington, D.C., in 1971. He was assigned as a bottomrung administrator in the organized crime section, where he soon found himself drawn to the inner sanctum of FBI internal politics.

In May 1972, little more than a year after Ahearn arrived in Washington, J. Edgar Hoover, known to FBI insiders as "The Director" and regarded by many of them as the most powerful man since the pharaohs, died. Hoover left no successor and the Bureau was caught in a power vacuum. Wanting to avoid any repetition of Hoover's unchecked power, Congress ordered a stem-to-stern overhaul of the FBI, and gave L. Patrick Gray the post of "acting director" to re-create the agency.

Gray did some good; he also did some bad. Among the good was creating the Office of Planning Evaluation, charged with reviewing and recommending changes in Bureau policies. Ahearn was assigned to this think-tank which, among its many decisions, set a new policy about organized crime; targeting the Mafia or La Cosa Nostra as a priority, something Hoover always neglected for fear that its corrupting influence would consume his agents.

Among the bad was Gray's role in the growing Watergate cover-up. Under instructions from White House counsel John Dean, Gray had hidden a briefcase that he was told contained "political dynamite" and eventually burned it in his backyard barbecue pit at the end of the year with the Christmas gift wrappings. Gray would later confess his deed and resign from the Bureau.

Ahearn remained in Washington through 1976, waiting for the plum assignment as ASAC (assistant special agent in charge) in San Francisco. He arrived with a lifetime of training as a street-smart bullshit artist and the meticulous political grooming of the new FBI; both would prove assets.

In order to talk to Fratianno, Ahearn had to break Bureau rules. Since 1976, Fratianno was off-limits to all agents by order of FBI headquarters because Jack Barron, wanting to corner Fratianno as his own, had reported to Washington that Fratianno was the target of a grand jury pornography probe and all other agents should steer clear.

During the weekend before his meeting with Fratianno, Ahearn spoke with his boss, Special Agent in Charge Charles "Roy" McKinnon. They decided they had to move quickly to bring Fratianno under Ahearn's wing if they were to avoid a turf battle betwen L.A. and San Francisco. They would also have to bring Cleveland in on the case immediately.

McKinnon flew to Cleveland that Sunday for a meeting with Joe Griffin, the acting SAC in Cleveland, where they discussed Fratianno's story and the document marked "SD-1064"—the Bomp's informant title. Griffin, a plump balding man with a mind like a steel trap, appeared calm at McKinnon's report. McKinnon might have expected as much; Griff is a quiet guy, a man of few words, given to unemotional analysis. What he hadn't expected—and no one outside Cleveland knew—was that suspicions of a leak had surfaced several months earlier when a wiretap on the home phone of a Cleveland mobster turned into a "dry hole," a live phone line with virtually no activity.

Cleveland was already creating a paper trail, generating phony documents of apparent importance, keeping a chart of which clerks and agents handled them, and then waiting to see if any of them made it to the street. So far there had been no results. Now, with Fratianno's information confirming Cleveland's worst suspicions, they knew they had to double their efforts.

Informants are more than just well-placed sources of gossip, they are the coin of the realm in law enforcement; they are the first wedge into a criminal conspiracy. To the chagrin of defense lawyers, statements from unnamed informants, who never show their faces in court, are almost always the basis for obtaining court authorized wiretaps or Justice Department approval for undercover operations. And it is those wiretaps and undercover operations that give prosecutors nearly irrefutable firsthand evidence of crimes. If the FBI had to choose between the right to carry weapons and the right to develop informants, they would probably opt for informants.

A leak threatening informants would be bad enough in any FBI office, but it was a special danger at that time in Cleveland, where the local La Cosa Nostra was involved in a mob war, engineering daylight car bombings and machine-gun assaults on Irish gangsters and Teamsters pretenders to the well-entrenched mob throne. In May, John Nardi, a Teamsters official with dreams of taking over the Cleveland Family, had been killed. Danny Greene, head of a cocky

Irish gang muscling its way into the mob's rackets, was the next target.

It was a race with time. The Cleveland office had developed two top-flight informants who had to be protected; the leak had to be plugged before either Danny Greene or Jackie Presser were identified by the mob and killed.

McKinnon, Griffin, and Pat Foran, supervisor of the FBI's organized crime squad in Cleveland, mapped out some strategy that Sunday afternoon. It was imperative to keep developing Fratianno and try to get him back to Cleveland to pick up more information on the leak. But no reports would be filed and not even Washington would know of Fratianno's identity until the time was ripe. Griffin would open a wide-ranging racketeering investigation entitled GANGMURS and use Fratianno's information to justify using half of his 180-agent office in tackling the leak and gang warfare case.

By August 14, Fratianno hadn't even met Ahearn, yet his future was already being planned.

Jimmy swaggered into the motel room. With his right hand slung deep in the pocket of his Brione suit and his left hand holding a freshly lit 10-inch Havana, he sized up Ahearn: tall and heavyset, like a fullback, blond and mustachioed, kind of dapper. He demanded to know if he was the top man, to which Ahearn offered his credentials. Fratianno drew his hand from his pants pocket and shook Ahearn's hand.

As Fratianno told his story—and again repeated his plea to be left out of the investigation—Ahearn was impressed by just how calm the notorious mobster appeared. Jimmy denied he was cooperating to save his own skin; Ahearn didn't buy it.

"If what you say is true, this is serious business," Ahearn said. "And you've started something here that you can't just walk away from."

Jimmy looked over to Hiner for support and found none. Hiner had met Fratianno several times with Lawrence. They didn't know each other well, but Jimmy felt a little more comfortable having a familiar face in the room.

"Now just a fuckin' minute," Fratianno wailed, using the cigar to point at Ahearn. "I had a deal with Larry that my name would stay out of it. I told you, I'm only here as a favor to him and that's as far as I go. My sister lives in Cleveland and I don't need to bring any fuckin' heat on her and her husband."

Ahearn wasn't letting Jimmy off that easy. He had told Hiner before Fratianno walked into the room that when the meeting was over they would know if Fratianno was going to be an informant or if they were putting him in jail.

"Have it your way, Jimmy, but understand something: Larry's retired and can't make deals with you. And without your cooperation I have no way of convincing the Cleveland office that there's a leak. Right now they think it's a lot of bullshit. If I can't convince them there's a leak, God only knows whose name might surface as an informant next."

Jimmy was still. "But what can I do? I told you everything I know and that's all there is. Period."

"I don't know, Jim. Why don't you meet me here again tomorrow and we'll see what can be arranged. Maybe there's something else you'll recall. Maybe you'll want to talk about Bomp's murder or the Nardi thing in Cleveland."

"Oh, listen you motherfucker, you start talking about that kind of shit and I'm out of this whole thing. You know what I mean?" Jimmy said, rising bolt-upright from his chair and heading for the door.

Ahearn knew he had pushed a little too hard. "Okay, Jim, we'll keep out of the other stuff for now. Just meet me here tomorrow, same time, and we'll try to work something out."

"You're too fuckin' much, man. Yeah, I'll see you tomorrow. But one thing, don't write no fuckin' reports about me," Jimmy said, chuckling as he walked out—looking not quite as calm as when he had arrived but still swaggering with self-confidence.

Ahearn had played his bluff and it had worked—his first line of bullshit. He was convinced now that Fratianno was concerned about the leak, concerned enough that he was willing to keep meeting with the FBI. And Fratianno could rest assured there would be reports of their meetings, at least until Ahearn secured enough information to have FBI headquarters lift the hands-off-Fratianno policy.

In a series of meetings over the next several days, Ahearn convinced Jimmy he would have to travel to Cleveland to nose around for more information on the leak. Ahearn brought Foran in to meet Jimmy. Both men were satisfied that Fratianno had told everything he knew about the leak and that there was nothing more to be gained unless he went back East.

On Wednesday, August 24, Fratianno and Ahearn flew into Cleveland. Ahearn stayed out of the way while Fratianno met with the boss, Licavoli, and pumped him for information on the leak.

Ahearn stayed by the telephone in his hotel room waiting to hear from Fratianno. Griffin and Foran joined him at the hotel and they reviewed additional steps being taken by the Cleveland office, including allowing clerks and agents access to a phony list of confidential informants containing the names of Licavoli's closest allies. Griffin was hoping to use the leak to his advantage, creating distrust among the mobsters or discrediting all of the information the mob was getting.

On Friday they flew together to New York City, where Fratianno said he wanted to check with a few friends about the leak. Ahearn knew he was being conned—if there was any information about the leak it was in Cleveland, not New York—but he decided to let Fratianno run his little scam for free passage to New York.

Although Fratianno came up empty during that trip, it was still well worth the $1,210 in travel expenses Ahearn billed the FBI. Fratianno had made a giant leap. He was on his way to becoming an informant.

Jimmy, of course, had a different view. He felt he had Ahearn's confidence and protection, which he needed to keep his FBI informant jacket from getting onto the streets of Cleveland. But he also felt that he hadn't done anything to betray his friends.

Ahearn flew alone to Washington on August 29 where he met up with Griffin. They would make their case at FBI headquarters together.

Edward Sharpe, the organized crime section chief, and FBI Deputy Associate Director James Adams listened. Griffin and Ahearn recounted Fratianno's information and his potential as an informant, certainly in Cleveland's GANGMURS case and probably in Bomp's murder. They were handing their superiors a fait accompli: a violation of the hands-off-Fratianno order that could have gotten them in trouble. But Sharpe and Adams offered their blessings and countermanded the hands-off instruction.

Over the next few months, Fratianno met Ahearn at least once a week and there began a steady stream of "209's"—FBI confidential informant reports—in which Fratianno is referred to only as "Source."

At each meeting Ahearn chipped away at Fratianno's armor with any kind of reasonable lie that would increase his fears and drive a wedge between Fratianno and those he trusted. And with each meeting Fratianno volunteered a little more about La Cosa Nostra and about his own problems.

Sept. 9: Source advised that there are 15 LCN [La Cosa Nostra] members currently operating in the Los Angeles area . . . that the Los Angeles LCN "Family" during recent years has not been a strong independent group and has frequently been directed by the Chicago LCN "Family."

Source advised that during recent months he has heard that there has been some friction between Los Angeles LCN Underboss Sam Sciortino and Fratianno. Source could not explain the reason for this friction.

In his conversation with Ahearn, Fratianno had made the reason for the "friction" clear: He had no respect for Sciortino. "Jim, I'm telling you, this fat little prick couldn't earn two fuckin' nickels. He's not a good worker and he has no fuckin' brains. I could do twice the job he's doing and he knows it. Fuck, these guys are all dumb motherfuckers."

By mid-September, Ahearn was getting pressure from McKinnon and the Cleveland office for something more from Fratianno. It was time to play the big bluff: suggesting to Fratianno that his life could be in danger. It seemed reasonable to Ahearn; Fratianno was in trouble with the mob and a murder contract is the way these people settle their differences. At a meeting at the Sheraton on September 14, Fratianno was talking about Brooklier's refusing to talk to him.

"There's been no change. I can't get this guy to get on the phone with me. I've called his son, the lawyer, three or four times this week and nothing."

"You can't straighten it out if he won't talk to you," Ahearn said. "Why don't you go see him, just go to his house?"

"He's not home. The old man's been sick and he's living with his son somewhere. I don't know where the kid lives. Hey, you're the guy with all the government know-how. How would you track down this cocksucker?"

Ahearn laughed at Fratianno's clumsy attempt to enlist his aid. "Look, we have ways of doing things. But your ways and ours are different, and I'm not about to get the Bureau involved in solving your personal problems." Ahearn paused. "I'll tell you the truth though. I'm kind of worried about you, Jimmy. I'm hearing things about, well, like there could be a contract on you. I might be able to offer you protection if you'd consider—"

"Get off it, Jim," Fratianno broke in. "For one thing, if there was a contract no one would be talking about it—made guys don't talk about a contract on a guy. It just doesn't work that way. And for another thing, Rizzi and I can handle this hit, he and I can handle it. So forget about your protection."

"What makes you so sure about Rizzi? I mean, I just want you to be careful, you know. Rizzi could turn on you, couldn't he?"

"Hey man, look, I know what I'm about. Okay? These pricks don't have enough brains or muscle to clip a guy like me. Rizzi's the one who's been keeping me informed and he's the only guy in this thing capable of clipping me."

"I don't want to get you alarmed, but wouldn't it make sense for them to use Rizzi to get to you?"

Jimmy shook his head. "To be perfectly honest, I don't really know what they're up to. But I know I'm better off alone than with a bunch of agents around me. I know how these motherfuckers operate, Jim. I can take care of myself."

A few days later Ahearn learned that his fantasy about a contract on Fratianno's life was not only an effective ploy, it was the truth. On September 21 they met again and Fratianno began displaying his growing trust in Ahearn, as the FBI report indicates:

Source advised today that Fratianno was informed on 9/18/77 by Mike Rizzatelli [*sic*] that things looked bad for Fratianno . . . that Dominic Brooklier and Sam Sciortino are extremely upset.

Fratianno was informed by Marty Allen, a well-known Las Vegas and Los Angeles gambling figure, that a contract has been "let" on Fratianno's life. Allen allegedly learned of this from [Johnny] George of the Dunes Hotel [through his connections with the Chicago LCN].

Fratianno told the source that he believes a strong possibility exists that a contract, in fact, has been issued . . . and if the contract was to be carried out it would be handled by Chicago LCN members since practically no one in the Los Angeles LCN "Family" is capable of handling a contract of this type.

Fratianno speculated to the source that while he trusts Rizzatelli [*sic*] implicitly and believes he is the only one on his side, the possibility does exist that Rizzatelli [*sic*] could be used to set him up for a hit.

By September 23, Ahearn saw some movement. While Fratianno was still calm, claiming he wasn't bothered by the contract on his life, he began providing real information: the names of La Cosa Nostra members and their criminal activities, including extortions of Las Vegas casino owners and pornographers.

The meetings continued through October. Ahearn was becoming a source of comfort. Fratianno knew he could speak to Ahearn without danger. Ahearn wasn't going to kill him; put him in jail, maybe, but not kill him. Ahearn kept pressing Fratianno, telling him he was going to jail on the PORNEX case if he didn't cooperate and badgering him with questions about Rizzi.

"I'm telling you, me and Mike can handle these cocksuckers."

"What makes you so sure you can handle Mike?"

"Oh, Jim," Fratianno whined. "I made this motherfucker, I'm like his sponsor. He ain't turning on me so fast."

But in November, Ahearn finally closed the door on Rizzi and became Fratianno's closest ally. Ahearn had increased Fratianno's concerns to such a level that Jimmy was looking at everyone with a jaundiced eye, searching for proof of betrayal. When Rizzi returned from seeing Rus Bufalino and advised Fratianno to go to Chicago, it was sufficient evidence for Fratianno to begin losing faith.

During the first couple of weeks of November, Ahearn assigned a surveillance team to keep an eye on Fratianno. It was standard practice to do some surveillance on the subject of a wiretap investigation and Fratianno's phones had been tapped off and on for the past two years. No one in San Francisco except for Ahearn, Hiner, and McKinnon knew about Fratianno's true status.

One night, a surveillance unit spotted Fratianno and Velotta heading north, out of Moss Beach toward San Francisco. They also spotted another car, a red and white T-Bird, unmistakably tailing Fratianno's Caddy. They followed for a while, taking the license number of the other car and breaking off the surveillance when the car entered the city. They thought it was a city police car following Fratianno, but ran the plate to be sure.

The next morning the report on the T-Bird landed on Ahearn's desk. The car was rented at the airport to a Joey Hansen—a known jewel thief and reputed killer working in Las Vegas for Tony Spilotro, the man in charge of the Chicago Family's casino and hotel interests.

Ahearn phoned Fratianno in a mild panic. Hearing Fratianno's voice was reassuring. They met later that morning and talked about the T-Bird. Fratianno said he had spotted the car the night before, and that he and Velotta had chased it off but were unable to see who was inside. Ahearn told him that the driver was Hansen and, for added effect, that Rizzi was riding shotgun. Jimmy was silent.

Ahearn no longer had time to cajole Fratianno. He could see the events of the past few months were taking their toll: Jimmy was losing weight, he was tired all the time, and had dark rings under his eyes. They had previously talked about protection, but now Ahearn was saying Fratianno would have to come in off the streets and enter the Witness Security Program.

Overnight Ahearn had gone from developing Fratianno as an informant to making him a witness, and Fratianno was primed to cross that final line. Up until then any mention of protection elicited responses of "Go fuck yourself," or "Get out of my life." But after the Hansen affair, Fratianno wasn't quite as cocky. He listened more carefully to what Ahearn said. He started asking questions.

"What could I possibly testify to?"

"How about the Cleveland thing?"

"Jim," Fratianno said, "you keep askin' and I keeping tellin' you: I don't know nothin' about those killings except what I hear from Skinny."

"Well, damn it, tell me something. Tell me what Skinny's telling you. Maybe it will lead somewhere."

"Hey man, it's just a lot of bullshit. I don't know. Ferritto, he says this guy Ray Ferritto, a friend of ours in Cleveland, is involved. Now that's a useless pile of shit to you, isn't it? I mean, it's nothing I could testify about."

"You're right, it's not much. But Jimmy, you've got to know something about Bomp, like who ordered the hit or who got paid for the contract."

"Lookit, will you stop with this 'contract' shit. You think someone in this thing gets paid for clipping a guy? Fuck, what are you going to do, walk up to Brooklier or Aiuppa and say, 'Hey man, pay me for that murder'? In this thing, if you clip a guy, you do it because the boss told you to. And if you don't follow through on the orders, you get clipped." He continued, "We don't talk about those things, Jim. Any motherfucker who tells me that he's going to do the job on Bomp would be way out of line. Made guys just don't talk about it at all. Period." They sat in silence for several minutes. "So what am I gonna testify to?" Fratianno asked again.

"I don't know, Jimmy, but let's think about it."

Ahearn got a call from Fratianno on November 15, and they met at the Hilton that afternoon:

Source advices [*sic*] that several weeks following the murder of Bompensiero at San Diego on 2/10/77, Dominic Brooklier, Sam Sciortino, Anthony [Dominick] Longo, and Jimmy Fratianno met at the residence of Vito Musso in Palm Springs, California. Fratianno subsequently told source that during this meeting Brooklier took Fratianno aside and stated, "I took care of that thing to the south." Fratianno explained to source that he is certain that Brooklier either ordered or helped set up the Bompensiero hit.

Ahearn called Fratianno that evening. After determining that Velotta was not there, and it was safe to talk, Ahearn explained the call:

"Have I ever told you this is a two-way street?" Ahearn began.

Jimmy was in the midst of picking up around the house. "What are you talking about?"

"Well, I just wanted you to know, the grand jury in L.A. has indicted you on that Forex shakedown thing."

"Are you fuckin' kidding?" Fratianno said, tossing down a bag of laundry. "Rizzi's the one who was dealing with those guys, I never had anything to do with it. Are you bullshitting me?"

"Not at all. They have you up on extortion and racketeering along with Rizzi and LoCicero," Ahearn said.

"Hey Jim, I'm telling you, it's that prick Barron. I never had a thing to do with this Forex. Not a fuckin' thing. And they indicted me? Can you feature that?"

"I don't know, Jimmy," Ahearn said. "I just wanted you to know so you could surrender and we wouldn't have to come out to arrest you."

"I just can't believe this. You know, these guys are trying to kill me and now I have to go to court and stand there next to them to defend myself." Fratianno seemed not to have heard a word Ahearn said.

"Don't worry, Jimmy. There are ways out of this thing," Ahearn was saying. "Just come in here tomorrow to surrender and we'll work something out."

"Yeah, okay. I'll set up the bail tonight. See ya in the morning."

During the next ten days, Jimmy did a lot of thinking. Jean made her short visit and then Jimmy moved to Nob Hill. While Jimmy and Ahearn kept meeting regularly, there were no more reports filed. Ahearn was certain Fratianno was ready to complete his metamorphosis.

Jimmy was confused. He couldn't tell any longer who was the fish and who was the fisherman. Was Ahearn reeling him in, or was he reeling in the FBI? He didn't like the feeling. He must maintain control. He was willing to be an informant, but on his terms. He would offer them direction and information, but he didn't want to testify. And if he had to testify, if Brooklier, Rizzi, Sciortino, and the rest forced him into this witness program, he'd do it on his terms. He swore to himself that he would never get on a witness stand in Cleveland.

In those last few days on Nob Hill, Jimmy engaged in some rare introspection: Fuckin' Bomp. That cigar chomping old cocksucker. He had been a good friend. Why the fuck did he start informing? If he hadn't gotten them tied up with Forex he would never have been killed; and if I hadn't seen that "SD-1064" report in Cleveland I wouldn't be all hooked up with the FBI. It was like the fat little bastard was reaching back from the grave, pointing a finger at his killers.

He set his cigar in the ashtray and flipped on the TV. It was Sunday, December 4. Oakland was favored to take the Western Division title against the Rams that afternoon.

Dennis McDonald was busy, otherwise Fratianno would have been at his house watching the game. McDonald was Fratianno's lawyer and a good friend; a millionaire negligence lawyer from Montana who cared more about organized sports than organized crime and found Fratianno's involvement in La Cosa Nostra a source of amusement rather than a professional concern. Ahearn and McDonald were the only ones who had Fratianno's new number.

At home in the East Bay, Ahearn got a call from Griffin. Fratianno's information, justifying the elaborate GANGMURS probe, had come full circle and he was now caught in the web: Griffin had a warrant for Jimmy's arrest.

"I don't know, Griff," Ahearn told Griffin. "Jimmy has me convinced he doesn't know anything about those murders. He's gone out of his way to stay clear of the entire thing. This guy just doesn't want any trouble in Cleveland."

Griffin stiffened. "All I know is I have a guy here willing to testify that Fratianno was in on the Danny Greene contract, and that Fratianno was the one who introduced the hit man to the Cleveland Family. That puts your guy in the middle of this conspiracy. Now, if he's not guilty, let him prove it."

"Look Griff, I'm not entirely against having him arrested. This murder beef is just what I've needed. Coming right on the heels of this Forex thing in L.A., it could be the thing that turns this guy." Ahearn continued, "But if it isn't, if Fratianno doesn't turn around on this one, he may just beat the charges and we'll lose him as an informant. I'm real nervous about this guy, Griff. You can't pressure a guy like Fratianno, you have to make him think he's calling the shots."

They discussed ways of using the murder charges to their mutual advantage, agreeing it would be best to arrest him as soon as possible. But as an act of good faith, they decided to have him locked up in the same cell as Licavoli so he could keep scratching for information on the leak.

"Sounds pretty good. Having him in the cell might give him a little added incentive—you know, he faces the electric chair in this state," Griffin said.

"Listen, remind the prosecutors that he's already cooperated in the leak case—maybe they'll show him a little kindness . . ."

"Hell, Jim," Griffin said. "I haven't told them lawyers anything about the leak or Fratianno. It's been handled as an internal matter. As far as these prosecutors are concerned, Fratianno is just another hardass and security at my office is tight as a drum."

Ahearn called Fratianno and set up a meeting for 2:30 the next day at the airport Holiday Inn. Fratianno rushed Ahearn off the phone. He was deeply absorbed in the football game. He watched the L.A. Rams score a 20-to-4 upset victory on a 43-yard touchdown pass in the last two minutes of play and went out to dinner on Nob Hill.

It was over in a moment. Hiner opened the door and Jimmy walked into Room 222 at the Holiday Inn about ten minutes late. Ahearn was seated in a chair, his right arm crossing his gut; his hand inside his jacket gripped his "James Bond" special 9mm automatic. He knew Jimmy had been packing a gun and feared he might do something stupid. His other fear was that the sudden distortion of reality—this betrayal atop his other considerable anxieties—could leave him collapsed on the floor with a massive coronary.

Neither occurred. It was as if he had been expecting it. There was no tensing of muscles, no flailing, not so much as a curse or a sound. He just heard the words: "Jimmy, I'm sorry about this, but . . ." and his body relaxed.

As if materialized by some holography magic, other agents were in the room and Jimmy was sitting and looking at a printed form entitled "Your Rights." They must have already frisked him.

"You know what that form is, Jimmy?"

"Yeah, I know all that. You know, I've been through this a couple times before. But I ain't signing," he said with a smirk.

Ahearn read him his rights.

He was given, and agreed to sign, another form permitting a search of his car. As an agent headed out to the car Jimmy took Ahearn aside and told him about his .25 automatic hidden behind the driver's armrest.

Ahearn had choreographed every move by the book. No more off-the-record conversations; no more bullshit.

"Jimmy, this is my boss, the SAC, Roy McKinnon. I want you to understand, this is the last chance. You can, you probably should, call McDonald. He can meet us over at my office. I hope you've been giving a lot of thought to everything we've been talking about for the last few months because this is where you have some big decisions to make."

Jimmy was smiling at McKinnon—he was listening to Ahearn but he was sizing up McKinnon, the top guy.

"No, Jim," he said. "Let's just get out of here. I can call from your office." He stood and began heading for the door. He was cuffed before he could reach for the doorknob.

They left the elevator, Jimmy flanked on every side by agents, and walked in tight formation through the lobby drawing stares. Jimmy's car was parked in the fire lane near the parking lot; the hood, trunk, and doors were all open.

"Looks clean," an agent told Ahearn.

Jimmy smiled.

"Look behind the armrest," Ahearn said, never acknowledging Fratianno's wink.

Pursuant to the arrest of ALADENA T. FRATIANNO on Dec. 5, 1977, at San Francisco, California, a search of Fratianno's person was conducted by Special Agents Kenneth C. Thompson and David L. Dirkse, which included a strip search. The following items were taken from Fratianno and included all such items found on his person:

1. I.K. Sports Wire (betting form).
2. Two $20's $40
   Four $10's $40
   Three $5's $15
   Six $1's $6
                    ─────
                    $101
3. Six quarters $1.50

Six nickles   .30
Three dimes   .30
Eleven pennies   .11
(The above change was returned to Fratianno.)
4. One parking ticket, #A0089511, 11/14/73
5. One address book
6. One Metro Park
7. Three Alioto's restaurant matchbooks
8. One pen—Palace Burlesque, 53 Turk Street, San Francisco, "Best Nude Show in Town"
9. One pen—"Stardust" Hotel & Casino
10. One key—apartment (returned to Fratianno)
    One key—mailbox (returned to Fratianno)
11. One set of keys (returned to Fratianno)

By 4 P.M. the preliminaries were completed. Fratianno, devoid of all personal possessions except his diamond rings, wristwatch, eyeglasses, and some pocket change, sat alone in a windowless eight-by-eight FBI debriefing room with a long metal table and four hard chairs covered in green vinyl. Ahearn walked in, his shirt-sleeves rolled up and his tie loosened.

"Jimmy, I didn't want it to go this way, but we can't change that now. In a minute McKinnon is going to join us and from that moment on everything is on the record. You know what I mean? I'm going to be the only person you can deal with here. Is there anything I should know?"

Fratianno knew what had to be done. He knew he had to come across. He was convinced that Brooklier and Sciortino had created this situation and Dragna had been only too happy to help them. He had decided that Rizzi was an accomplice, that Johnny Marshall was involved, that Bufalino had failed him, and Aiuppa had arranged for Spilotro to send Hansen after him. Funzi Tieri, the most powerful boss in New York, head of the Genovese Family, had bought all the lies about him and told others that he was a pariah. And Paulie Castellano, head of the Gambino Family, was also part of the mix; he and the rest of them at the Premier Theatre hadn't lifted a finger to help straighten him out.

There was a lot Ahearn should know.

"What do you want to know, Jim?"

"I'm going to ask you again: Do you want Dennis [McDonald] in here. You really should speak to him before—"

"Jim, don't ask me any more about Dennis. I'll call him later to arrange bail or something."

McKinnon entered the room and took up a chair.

"How about Jean? Do you want to call her?"

Fratianno was getting annoyed with the warm-up speeches. "Jim, I can call her later. She's not important."

"In that case, I want to know about the murders. We know you've been involved in a lot of LCN murders in California, and if there's going to be any deal here we have to know the score."

Ahearn was jumping in with both feet and all Jimmy had expected were a few questions about the Cleveland case. He was prepared to say he knew nothing about Cleveland and ask what were they going to do for him if he couldn't help in that case? He wanted them to draw it out of him. He just stared.

"Okay, then, we'll start with the most recent ones and work our way back," Ahearn said. "I know you were involved at some level with Bompensiero's killing. And I know it's more than we've talked about in the past. I know you engineered the hit."

For the first time since his arrest Jimmy showed some reaction. He was stunned. He was waiting for Bomp's murder to be brought up but he didn't think they knew anything. Ahearn was conning him or else he had been holding back all these months. It really didn't matter. "Yeah, that's right. But I wasn't involved when they clipped him."

"Okay, but I know who was: Brooklier, Sciortino, and Tommy Ricciardi."

Fratianno started laughing. "You've got almost the entire cast of characters," he told them.

"So give us the rest," Ahearn said, leaning across the table toward Fratianno.

"You left out Jack LoCicero, he drove the car, and Dragna, he helped make the plans. Look, I'll tell you whatever you want to know, but I have to have some guarantees from you guys."

"We're not making deals today, Jimmy. You can tell us what you're going to want. But before we can do anything we have to hear something to make it worth our while and deliver a package for the strike force attorneys to consider. Right now your ass is in a sling and it's up to you to change that."

"Oh, fuck you. You think that these charges are any big deal? Forget about it." Fratianno was getting red-faced.

"As a matter of fact, I do," Ahearn shot back. "I think you could go to the electric chair in Cleveland or do a whole lot of years for the cases against you here in California."

"I had nothing to do with this Cleveland thing, and these guys have nothing on me in that pornography case in L.A. And that gambling case you guys have is a lot of bullshit. You think because you got a recording of me making one lousy bet I'm scared? I can beat all these charges. So don't tell me my ass is in a sling."

Ahearn was on his feet, pacing around Jimmy's chair.

"So what do you want to do, Jimmy? Go back on the street where Brooklier's jackals are looking to waste you?"

"No. But I don't want to become no witness; I'm not coming across unless you come across. Let's put it that way."

"Jimmy, if your story's good, if we can corroborate it and bring it to trial, then we can do just about anything you want. We can wipe the slate clean, we can give you money to live on and protection. What more do you want?"

"I don't want to testify in Cleveland and I want a passport under a fake name so I can live in another country," Fratianno said, delivering his top demands.

"That's a tall order. I don't know about Cleveland, but I know we can get you a passport; we're the damned government. But are you worth it?" Ahearn was once again taken by Fratianno's bravado: The man's back was against the wall and he was still making deals as if he had the upper hand.

"I can give you the entire leadership of the Los Angeles Family. They were all involved in clipping Bomp. They'd wanted him dead for years. Is that good enough?"

With a little more prompting Fratianno offered up the conspiracy, sparing the details. Brooklier ordered the killing, which was carried out by Ricciardi and LoCicero. Dragna and Sciortino each had full knowledge of the plan. It was just the skeleton of the story, but enough for now.

Fratianno had gone over the brink, where he had been hovering indecisively for months. There was no turning back even if he thought he could. A knot that had been in Ahearn's chest all day was suddenly gone, but a new tension, born of excitement from the story he had just heard, began to form. If Fratianno could deliver the entire Los Angeles Family with such ease there must be far more that they didn't know about.

There were still reams of forms to be filled out, reports to be made, and details to be resolved—months of haggling to win plea bargain agreements with prosecutors in Los Angeles, San Francisco, and Ohio—but Ahearn was confident Fratianno was going to make a deal and become a federal witness.

Ahearn told him that they would have another debriefing session the next day, before Jimmy went to Cleveland to be booked. He knew that Fratianno was just stubborn enough to refuse to cooperate in the Bompensiero case if he were forced to testify in Cleveland. He told Fratianno that the only way to get Cleveland to go along would be to show them how important Fratianno was in the Bomp case.

"This is the last question I'm going to ask you, Jimmy, and it's only because I need some idea of what we're getting into: How many murders were you involved in? Is it as many as fifty?"

"Oh, Jim." Fratianno was laughing. "You've read too many of those L.A.P.D. reports. Way far less than that. It goes a long way back, into the 1940s. It's more like, well, fewer than a dozen."

"Okay, that's good enough for now. But eventually we're going to have to know everything. If we know everything we can probably take care of all your cases, give you probation, and I'll try to do what I can with Cleveland. But if you forget to tell us something, if we go into court with you as a witness and get embarrassed by something a defense lawyer brings up . . . all bets are off. These strike force guys are deadly serious about this; they'll make a golden deal for a good witness, but if they get fucked by you they'll see that you die of old age in the joint."

"So who says I'm going to be a witness?" Fratianno said as he straightened his tie, preparing for the newsmen he knew were waiting outside the courthouse. In every photo taken of Fratianno being led into a police station, FBI office, or courtroom under arrest—and there had been more than a few—the man looked as if he was being brought to the podium to accept an Emmy rather than on his way to face criminal charges.

The morning after his arraignment, Fratianno sat in the backseat of an FBI car on his way from county jail in Oakland, where he was being held, to Ahearn's office for another show-and-tell session. He hadn't had any trouble sleeping the night before; after all the hiding he had been doing lately there was something reassuring about being held securely. Yet since breakfast he had been struggling with what he feared was coming: Ahearn would offer a deal.

There was no point in trying to bargain, he figured. He would just rush into the whole story, get the worst part of it over with, and see what they offered.

Ahearn was waiting in the same debriefing room they had used the day before. Agents Dirkse and Thompson were there, too.

"I spoke to Dennis last night and told him you would be here today. He said you'd want these." Ahearn handed Fratianno a fistful of Havanas.

Fratianno was delighted. "Anybody got a light? I'm going to smoke you guys out of this little room."

Someone found some matches and he lit up.

"Jimmy, we're going to go through this again. Either you're going to sign this form, waiving your rights, or you're going to speak with Dennis. He's on his way over—"

"Jim, just give me the fuckin' form, I'll sign it. Dennis is useless, he's no fuckin' criminal lawyer. I know what to do here better than he does. Let him wait outside."

"Okay, then. I've been in touch with some of the prosecutors on these cases here and back in Cleveland," Ahearn said as Fratianno finished scratching his name on the form. "I've told them you'd be willing to testify in some of the cases if the right thing is done for you. Now, Mike DeFeo, the L.A. strike force chief, feels that he'd want to meet with you before—"

"Jim, I don't care about that. I want to tell you about Bomp's murder," Fratianno said, and for the next four and a half hours Fratianno did just that; talking his heart out, making Brooklier's and Sciortino's roles especially clear, yet never missing the opportunity for an amusing digression.

As they parted, Ahearn gave Fratianno some final advice: From here on out, until he had a signed agreement with the government, he shouldn't tell anyone any specifics of his other criminal activities. And when he got to Cleveland, he would have to be especially careful— every word would be scrutinized.

Ahearn walked back into his office carrying a yellow legal-size pad containing a few pages of notes from the interview and called Special Agent Nick Lore in San Diego. He had been talking to Lore for weeks, checking on the progress of the Bomp investigation and trying to see if any of Lore's information could help in turning Fratianno.

"Nick? It's Jim Ahearn. We've got the Bomp killing solved."

2

Going Home and Making Deals

JIMMY sat in county jail for two more days—reading the sports pages, thinking about his next meal, and giving orders to Ahearn and McDonald during their frequent visits—while awaiting his transfer to Cleveland.

He was the center of attention and he liked that. Officials in San Francisco, Los Angeles, Cleveland, and Washington, D.C., were discussing what he could do for them and they for him. McDonald was conducting negotiations, offering Fratianno's cooperation if they would drop all the charges and provide him with protection. Jimmy was certain that news of his arrest had left Brooklier scheming how he could kill Fratianno in prison.

What Jimmy didn't like was that he had never done prison time like this before. The trick to keeping sane in the joint had always been to forget about the outside world. Right now, his only thoughts were about what was happening on the outside. He sat motionless for hours, mentally compiling lists of options. If what he was hearing from Ahearn was true, the witness program could be a pretty sweet deal: protection and money. But he wondered what they would do in Cleveland and would he get immunity for all his past crimes, including the killings. Or would he have to cop a plea somewhere down the line and face sentencing? His gut was telling him to walk away from the entire thing, just act as an informant, not a witness, and take his chances fighting Brooklier and the charges.

It really didn't matter; there was nothing he could do now anyway.

He had to wait for his trip to Cleveland to see what could be arranged. He grew more uneasy, and louder, with each passing hour.

About 2,500 miles away, in Cleveland, where the Great Lakes cities were covered in a blanket of early winter snow, Doug Roller, the federal prosecutor, was hearing about the leak for the first time. He was also hearing from officials in San Francisco and Los Angeles that Fratianno should be given "a pass" on GANGMURS in order to win his cooperation in other cases.

Roller, the U.S. strike force attorney in Cleveland, didn't like any of it. He didn't like the pressure from outside his jurisdiction. He was annoyed that he hadn't been made aware of the leak earlier. And he exploded when he learned of Fratianno's cooperation in the leak case.

"I never would have ordered an arrest warrant for Fratianno if I knew he was an informant," he told Griffin the day after Fratianno and most of Cleveland's La Cosa Nostra members were arrested on GANGMURS warrants. "One of the things he's charged with are his trips to Cleveland as part of the conspiracy and you're telling me that at least one of those trips was on behalf of the FBI in San Francisco to investigate your goddamned leak? The case against Fratianno is weak enough without this shit."

Griffin argued that Cleveland should ignore pleas from the West Coast and Washington to tread lightly on Fratianno. He urged that they use the electric chair as a bludgeon, take a hard line, and insist Fratianno cooperate and testify or face prosecution.

Griffin offered the proposal he and Ahearn had discussed: place Fratianno in the same cell with Licavoli so he could continue seeking information on the leak, letting him know they could work with him but that they weren't about to knuckle under to his demands.

Roller wasn't comfortable with Griffin's idea; he wanted to do it all by the book. He agreed that Fratianno had probably stood on the edge of the gang wars conspiracy, if not taking a direct role, but the problem now was proving it.

The entire case had been this way: a battle of wills, a constant pulling and tugging by local and federal authorities for dominance. Each side had jealously guarded sources and evidence to gain advantages. And now, just as it appeared the case was coming together, up pops Fratianno and this West Coast connection—an added player vying for some guarantees in how the case would be conducted.

Roller ultimately approved Griffin's plan as a compromise that satisfied everyone's needs—Cleveland's and California's—without jeopardizing the case. However, he set a proviso: Fratianno should be instructed not to discuss the GANGMURS case with the defendants, and if he overheard anything about their defense strategy he shouldn't discuss it with officials.

Roller left that meeting still uncertain, torn by the competing pressures for Fratianno's cooperation. His first impression was to distrust the local FBI. There was no love lost between Griffin's office and Roller; the FBI felt the prosecutor spent too much time trying to please Washington, and Roller felt the local FBI office had been toying with him—first on the leak case and now by putting him at the center of the dispute with California.

For Roller, Cleveland was a way station on his path to a more important office. He had come from the Chicago strike force office in 1975 where he had been a bit player, told that he had to "pay his dues as a tailgunner" in Cleveland if he ever wanted to run one of the strike force offices in a major city.

He had expected to do a couple of years in Cleveland prosecuting some union racketeering cases and then get out clean. No one had planned the GANGMURS investigation. But the events of the past eighteen months had drawn Roller and the FBI into one of the most extensive, and ultimately successful, organized crime probes in American history.

There was a royal funeral in Cleveland the year before Fratianno was taken into custody, a funeral befitting the leader of a great American mob empire. As much as Bompensiero's death would haunt Fratianno, so too did the death of Cleveland's great don, the debonair John T. Scalish, play havoc with that city's mobs for the next four years and eventually end up at Fratianno's doorstep.

Scalish, whose silver hair and rakish style had drawn repeated comparisons to Marlon Brando's Don Vito Corleone, died May 26, 1976, in a hospital recovery room after coronary bypass surgery. He was sixty-three. His funeral, at Calvary Cemetery, was attended by hundreds of people, many from out of state, as well as the FBI, from a respectable distance.

As the funeral party departed the hallowed soil of the gravesite, there was talk—sotto voce—among many of the mourners that Scalish, although highly regarded while he led the Family, had made a fatal mistake by never grooming a successor. When Scalish died he took his power with him to the grave. Many looked upon Milton "Maishe" Rockman, Scalish's brother-in-law and business partner, as the de facto Family boss—and the comparisons to Meyer Lansky have been numerous—but it was an impossible role for a Jew to play. And so James Licavoli, seventy-one at the time, was drafted into service as the boss, for what he hoped would be a brief period.

Licavoli, known best by his alias of Jack White, was not well-suited to the job. He had become a millionaire during the 1930s running the Jungle Inn, a Warren, Ohio, gambling club, and hadn't participated in mob enterprises since the 1940s. The stooped, balding, quiet bachelor was further at a loss, for he lacked Scalish's command, dignity, flair, and renown. Licavoli's only clear claim to power were his ties to the national mob syndicate; a blood relation to La Cosa Nostra leaders in St. Louis and Detroit.

He told Fratianno, a lifelong friend, that he thought his job would be simply to rebuild the organization and name a successor: "He [Scalish] left me with a lot of chiefs and no soldiers—not a single soldier to do the work." But recognizing Licavoli's obvious weaknesses, others were moving in to wrest control of the city's rackets, spreading the word on the street that no one had to pay off Scalish's crew anymore. Most notable among these were John Nardi, a Teamsters official with legitimate lineage—an Italian-American and nephew of a former mob underboss. Nardi wanted not only the rackets, but felt his birthright entitled him to control the largely Italian Teamsters union in Ohio, which had been run for two generations by Jews: William "Big Bill" Presser and later his son Jackie, who began cooperating with the FBI to silence Nardi and his other rivals.

To aid him, Nardi enlisted Daniel John Patrick Greene, a fearless, homicidal megalomaniac hell-bent on destroying anyone barring his way to fame and fortune—which to his way of thinking meant just about anyone associated with Scalish's regime. Their agreement, as best as it can be discerned, was that Nardi would provide the leadership and Greene the muscle; after the war they would divide the rackets and go their own ways.

In the opening battle, the first to die was the underboss, Leo "Lips" Moceri, a heartless killer and former colleague of Fratianno's; he was targeted because he was the only one of Licavoli's Old Mustache Petes capable of engaging in a war. He was also Licavoli's closest ally and one of Nardi's most outspoken enemies. Late in August of 1976, Lips Moceri disappeared. Days later, his car was found at an Akron motel, its trunk stained with his blood.

Moceri wasn't merely a colorful Cleveland native. The man was a national legend. He had been suspected of murders committed throughout Ohio and on both coasts without ever being convicted. Most important, he was respected in every American mob stronghold, making his murder an affront to Cleveland's manhood among its La Cosa Nostra brethren. It was unthinkable that such a man should be killed by an outsider; it was even more unthinkable that the act should go without grand retribution.

Bosses of the leading U.S. crime Families approved Licavoli's reign, but held Cleveland off-limits—no outside help or business deals—until they straightened out their problems with Nardi and Greene.

Licavoli, who had wanted nothing more than to establish a peaceful transition of power, inherited a divided city and a cadre of supporters thirsting for revenge, yet nearly all of them too old to fight. Surrounded by his lieutenants, Licavoli would sit in an overstuffed embroidered easy chair, beside the statue of the Blessed Virgin, in his deteriorating home on Murray Hill planning the war that would establish his authority and the Family's dominance. Killing Nardi and Greene was the first order of business.

During the following year there were numerous attempts to kill Nardi and Greene—daylight machine gunnings, bombings that backfired or were never detonated. And each failure brought further credibility to growing reports of Nardi and Greene's prowess, or else increased the belief that Licavoli's mob was merely the gang that couldn't shoot straight.

Cleveland quickly attained a dubious honor, becoming known as "the bombing capitol of America" as explosives tore through front porches, shattered windows, and sprayed car fragments into the streets. Some of the blasts struck their intended targets—combatants loyal to one side or the other—but just as frequently, those killed or injured were innocent bystanders or the bomb makers themselves.

But, on May 17, 1977, one day after Fratianno had visited Cleveland, John Nardi climbed into his Cadillac at the Teamsters offices and the car next to his exploded. Licavoli had lost several men along the way, but the primary goal had been accomplished: Nardi had been eliminated.

Now it was time to clip Greene.

At forty-seven, Greene was an athletically handsome man with curly blond hair and a trigger-fast mind to match his temper. He had been thrown out of the International Longshoreman's Union after a

Cleveland Plain Dealer exposé revealed that, as a dock foreman, he was extorting money from his dockhands and was trying to shake down management as well.

Banned from the waterfront, Greene started his own rackets in loan-sharking, gambling, and some narcotics dealing. He also created Emerald Industrial Relations, an old-fashioned protection scam. For the right price his firm could get construction workers back on the job site or put an end to destructive nocturnal raids on contractors' heavy equipment.

He made scores of enemies but seemed to thrive on their threats and hatred. Some tried to kill Greene by dynamiting his car and apartment—both times he walked away unscathed. It is known that at least three of those who failed in attempts to kill him were dead before they got a second chance.

His cavalier attitude about death and battle earned him the respect of his adversaries. Some years earlier, a bomb he intended for an enemy exploded beside him on the driver's seat, totaling his car but leaving him with only some hearing loss. And there were the legends of an empty-handed Danny Greene chasing his armed enemies through the streets, or of Danny Greene standing in front of an enemy's home, waving a lit stick of dynamite, demanding the man come out and talk with him. But physical confrontation was only one means Greene had of settling scores with his enemies; he was also an active snitch for the FBI.

Greene was quickly rising to sainthood status on the streets; an untouchable and fearless mad dog killer of folkloric proportions: the invincible Danny Greene.

Licavoli had no one of Greene's stature, but he had the luxury of time: He could select Greene's assassin carefully and choose the time of his execution.

The man was Raymond Ferritto, a slow-talking hustler and part-time burglar from Erie, Pennsylvania, an unknown face in Cleveland, whom Fratianno introduced to the mob as "a dependable worker."

Fratianno met Ferritto during the 1960s. At the time, Ferritto was running with Skinny Velotta's burglary team in Los Angeles, a band of émigrés from the Cleveland area whom Fratianno had befriended.

Fratianno admired Ferritto—he was tough and had a tenacity and temper that wouldn't quit. Rumor had it that on a good day Ferritto would down a bottle of Maalox, several Valium, and a couple of joints and still have enough rage bottled up to burn a hole in an average man's stomach.

In 1976, Fratianno invited his friend to join his West Coast Family. But the invitation was quickly revoked by Brooklier, who forbade the initiation, already fearing that Fratianno intended to take control of the Family.

Ferritto was crushed. Like so many others involved in crime and living in the shadows of La Cosa Nostra, becoming a member of the secret society had become Ferritto's lifelong ambition. He believed becoming a made guy would provide him with security in times of need and a pension fund in old age; there would always be work and money.

To quell his disappointment, Fratianno introduced Ferritto to the Cleveland Family in 1976 as someone they should consider. There were no immediate promises or offers, but Fratianno knew Licavoli was looking for soldiers, and at forty-nine, Ferritto made a good prospect. Later, when Licavoli and Dope DelSanter offered membership in La Cosa Nostra as payment if Ferritto completed the Greene murder, Ferritto jumped at the opportunity.

The better part of a year passed and Nardi was killed before Ferritto was brought back as an active member of the murder plot. In that time they had provided him with an "untraceable car"—a blue Plymouth, registered under a phony name in Ohio. But they had also taken a couple of poorly aimed shots at the Irishman themselves, and Ferritto was furious, feeling that his opportunity for being "made" was slipping away.

Dope DelSanter's funeral in August 1977 brought together all of the mob's friends from across the nation, including Fratianno and Ferritto.

The day after Dope's funeral, Ferritto met with Licavoli and several of his men for dinner at Sabbatino's Restaurant. He was hot. He ranted loudly about "these amateurs" trying to steal his contract and how they hadn't been helping him. He needed recent photos of Greene, descriptions of his cars, and someone to show him around town.

Licavoli assured him that the job was still his and that he would get the help he needed. To start with, they gave him $5,000 to cover his expenses. And as an added incentive, he was told that if he succeeded he would be given the Dope's former domain—25 percent of the rackets in Warren and Youngstown, Ohio.

In September, Ferritto began getting some help, but it was always too little or too late. He was given some old magazine photos of Greene and began receiving recordings, which Licavoli's people had made from a tap on Greene's phone. But petty factionalism among Licavoli's soldiers—this guy didn't trust that one—always delayed delivery of the tapes, making them useless in tracking Greene's appointments.

Frustrated by his comrades, yet anxious to make at least one attempt, Ferritto enlisted the aid of an old Cleveland friend, Ronald Carabbia, in building a bomb that they planned to place under the front stoop of Greene's apartment house and detonate some night when he came or left. Ferritto was climbing through the thorny hedges in front of the building when he realized the plan wasn't going to work; there were too many people, most of them elderly, talking, reading, or playing cards in the front lobby. He feared one of them would be injured in the blast. Ferritto departed Cleveland at the end of September, leaving word for Licavoli and his cohorts that he was "fed up."

Days after he had left town, Ferritto got a call from Carabbia asking him to return for one last attempt. He told Ferritto there was going to be a meeting he should attend. They had some "important new information."

On October 4, Ferritto joined the key conspirators at a fenced-in boat yard on Mosquito Lake, which was quiet with the passing of the summer season. The spot had been chosen because they feared that any one of their homes or offices could be bugged. They sat on the back deck of a cabin cruiser—someone had forgotten the key to the cabin—shivering in an early autumn chill, and listened to the latest tape; Greene was heard complaining about a loose dental filling. He had made, and later verified, an appointment with his dentist, Dr. Alfonso Rossi, for 2:30 on October 6.

It was the first time they knew with any precision where Greene would be. Ferritto, who had begun the meeting by telling them he was definitely out of the deal, was back in.

The next morning Ferritto drove the blue Plymouth to Carabbia's apartment, where they assembled the bomb, using three sticks of dynamite. To detonate the bomb, Carabbia had a remote control device, the kind used for operating large model airplanes. They packed their equipment in shopping bags and waited for the next morning.

Carabbia and Ferritto arrived a few hours early so they could be sure to see Greene drive into the medical building parking lot. Ferritto drove the Plymouth, which was to be used as the getaway car, while Carabbia followed in a maroon Chevy Nova. A two-man back-up team, who were to shoot Greene if the bomb failed, were told to leave when they began getting on Ferritto's nerves. Ferritto wanted to be clear-headed that day and hadn't taken anything to calm himself. He was beginning to wish he had.

At about 2:45 P.M., Greene drove up in a 1976 brown Lincoln Continental, parked, and dashed off, carrying his blue Adidas gym bag. Ferrito jumped from his car and drove the Nova to a space next to Greene's. He armed the bomb, loaded it into a metal box welded inside the passenger door of the Nova, and walked away.

The assassins positioned themselves across the street from the parking lot and waited for what seemed an eternity. Greene stepped from the office building at about 3:25 P.M.

As Ferritto turned the Plymouth into the street, Carabbia sat in the backseat staring out the rear window nervously fingering the detonator, its antenna extended. A young couple riding in a car along-side the Plymouth stared at Ferritto—they apparently thought the two men appeared odd. And then Carabbia hit the detonator.

A blinding explosion sent a fireball into the late afternoon sky and lifted shrapnel hundreds of feet across the parking lot. Greene's final sight may have been the bright, momentary flash of ignition, but he was dead in an instant. The frontal force of the blast pressing on Greene's chest ripped open his back and crushed his spine. His clothes were torn from his body and his left arm was cast 100 feet away. Remarkably, almost untouched was Greene's Adidas gym bag, in which police found a 9mm pistol with extra ammunition, some business papers, a list of his enemies' cars and license plate numbers, and an address book.

Ferritto and Carabbia were on I-271 when the blast cleared and had no idea if they had succeeded or failed. Carabbia would get news of their success from the radio. Ferritto drove back to Erie that evening in the Plymouth, missing the celebration in Cleveland's Little Italy but occupying himself with thoughts of how he was going to run things in Youngstown and Warren after he became a made guy.

The bomb blast was on a Thursday. By Monday chaos had set in. The local police in Lyndhurst were vying with the FBI for jurisdiction over the murder. Alcohol, Tobacco and Firearms claimed authority. Cleveland police said it was their case because it was obviously tied to the city's gang wars. The U.S. Attorney's office, the U.S. Organized

Crime Strike Force, and the Cuyahoga County Prosecutors Office were each seeking to control the prosecution. And in Berea, a suburb of Cleveland, there was a detective who claimed to have some vital information but refused to give up his source.

All things considered, Doug Roller wasn't having a good day on this October 10, the first day of the new work week. Each of the competing parties was calling his office, on the assumption that he was coordinating the case, and demanding that they get priority. Roller dealt with the problem as any self-respecting government official would have: He called for a meeting the next day with everyone present. They would sort it out together.

The U.S. Organized Crime Strike Force is a unique creature of law enforcement, an elite group of lawyers and investigators with powers as limitless as the federal government. But their domain is specialized, focusing on developing cases against criminal groups, not merely reacting to crimes. If they chose to investigate a crime—and they usually get their pick of the litter—the crime becomes a vehicle for a broader investigation into a far-reaching criminal conspiracy. The Danny Greene murder was custom-made strike force material.

But even with its extensive powers, this Goliath of the law must tread lightly through the gardens of local authorities. A criminal conspiracy may well be the domain for which the strike force was created, but a crime, such as murder, committed anywhere except on federal property is within the jurisdiction of local police and prosecutors. It takes enormous diplomacy to establish cooperation between state and federal authorities under the best of circumstances; petty jealousies, animosities, and turf battles are always present. The Greene case proved no exception.

As Roller welcomed all the players to his office, he knew full well that the Cuyahoga County Prosecutors Office was going to want first crack at the case. And he really couldn't object too strenuously—the state of Ohio had the death penalty, a potent tool for pressuring conspirators to cooperate in the investigation and the most powerful form of "justice."

"I tell you what," Roller said after hearing the views of the dozen or so men assembled in his office. "Let's establish this group as a task force. Each of you assigns a representative who will meet here every few days to compare notes and share sources. We'll see what kind of information everyone has and when the time comes to start herding people into a grand jury we'll decide whether the state or federal government takes the lead."

"The hell with that," a voice shot back. It was Carmen Marino, the assistant county prosecutor. "You know you guys, the FBI and the rest of you, always play this as a one-way street: We give and you take." The impetuous prosecutor, thirty-four years old at the time, wasn't going to budge. He recognized that this was the kind of investigation and trial an aggressive prosecutor would see only once in his career, if he was lucky. "I'm not buying it. I'll go back and talk to my boss, but I already know he wants to go in on this thing with the clear understanding that this is our case," Marino said.

"Now, how are you going to do that?" asked an agent from Alcohol, Tobacco and Firearms. "We've already got the Trojan horse, the bomb car, locked up and you're not going anywhere without it."

Marino rambled on about the death penalty and the state's rights in the case. He said that the feds would just have to cooperate with his office. But even as he pressed his argument, he knew he had played his hand too early. For the time being, he couldn't take control over the case.

The meeting broke up with agreements that the local police, FBI, and AT&F would develop a working relationship and everyone would return to Roller's office in two days. But before their next meeting a remarkable thing happened. Lieutenant Andy Vanyo, of the Cleveland police intelligence unit, answered a call he had received from Art Volpe, a Berea police detective, who said he had some important information.

Volpe began by swearing Vanyo to secrecy; he then recounted a story his daughter and son-in-law, Debbie and Greg Spoth, had told him. It seems they were driving through Lyndhurst and past the intersection of the bomb blast moments before the explosion. They saw two men in a blue Plymouth next to their car—one man driving and the other in the back, staring intently toward the parking lot and holding some kind of gadget with a long antenna. It looked strange, but they thought nothing of it for the moment. Then there was the blast and they peeled out. A few minutes later, the Plymouth was pulling up alongside them on I-271. This time they jotted down the license plate number and Volpe's daughter, an artist, immediately began making a sketch of the driver.

Upon hearing the account and description, Vanyo pulled Ferritto's picture, which he had occasion to see a few weeks earlier while working on another case. Within twenty-four hours, the Spoths picked Ferritto's mug shot from a photo array.

"That's just dandy," Marino said when he was given Ferritto's photo. "Now all we have to do is find corroboration that he was in the state of Ohio that day and then show something, anything, to link him with the murder. It's a good start, but we're still a long way off," he told Vanyo.

Vanyo's office kept after the Ferritto lead. When he ran down the Pennsylvania license on the blue Plymouth, it came back under the name Guy Mitchell—a "Joe Blow," fictitious name—but the address matched Ferritto's girlfriend.

The FBI and the Lyndhurst police were also focusing on the Plymouth. They ran the registration, looked into the Guy Mitchell alias, and checked the VIN (Vehicle Identification Number) to see who the previous owners had been. Lyndhurst conducted more than 600 interviews and almost always asked about the Plymouth. And nothing. The closest they got was that the Plymouth had been registered in Ohio, before it was registered in Pennsylvania.

And then: Paydirt. An AT&F agent reviewing the FBI's investigative reports found the elusive link. The charred and twisted license plate from the Chevy Nova, the Trojan horse, was in sequence with the Plymouth's former Ohio registration: both cars had been registered at the same motor vehicle office, on the same day in sequence. It was circumstantial, but it was enough to link the Plymouth to the Nova—and Ferritto to the bomb.

Marino ordered up a search warrant of Ferritto's home and went over to Roller's office to tell them about the tentative ID and discuss some strategy.

"I've been thinking about how we approach this thing," he told Roller and FBI case agents Bob Friedrick and Thomas Kimmell. "If we play it right, this case could go on for years. Our objective here shouldn't be just to get the people who killed Danny Greene, but to get the entire Cleveland Mafia. And to do that we're going to have to dignify Greene's killing."

So far he had pretty much stated the obvious.

"Now everyone knows he was a hoodlum. Who on a jury is going to really care if one hoodlum killed another? But we also know he was an FBI informant and one way to dignify his murder is to tell the jury that he was killed because he was informing on the mob." Striking a pose, as if holding a podium and addressing a jury, he added, "No matter how bad Danny Greene may have been, he was on our side helping you."

"Forget it," said Friedrick. "You do that and you'll spook every informant we have in this and every other case. It's just no good."

"He's right, Carmen," added Roller. "You start that kind of thing and informants are going to start fearing for their lives. You might win this case, but you'll be doing irreparable harm for the future."

"Look, we're balancing what you see as the danger to informants against getting convictions of a whole lot of the LCN in Cleveland," Marino argued. "At this point we can probably count on indicting Ferritto, but I don't care about him. I want to turn Ferritto, give him a deal, and then use him to wipe out the rest of these guys. Without this informant strategy no jury is going to care enough to convict anyone for killing a bum like Greene."

Roller just kept shaking his head. "Absolutely not. It's out of the question. Look, Carmen, why don't you wait to see if you can prove it's the motive before you start shooting from the hip," Roller scolded.

"We can prove it without you," said Marino. "We have enough to show he was an FBI informant and that's enough for any jury."

"Come off the grandstanding, Carmen. There's no way you can prove someone's an informant unless they or the Bureau admit it," said Kimmell.

"Okay, if you don't believe me, let's do this, you write down Greene's contact name and I'll write a name and we'll see if it matches."

"No, Carmen. Let's not play fuckin' games here," Roller replied.

But Marino wasn't bluffing. Among the personal items found in Greene's Adidas gym bag was his address book, which contained a phone number, 522-1400, under the name Dr. Falls. Vanyo knew that number and it wasn't a doctor's office—it was the FBI. When he called and asked for Dr. Falls, he was connected to a clerk who told him that the doctor was out but was expected a little later.

After several more minutes of dickering Marino showed his hand: "Okay, then I'll tell you what I know and can prove. The contact's code name is Dr. Falls."

Roller and Kimmell shot looks at each other.

"Oh, shit," Kimmell said, jumping up and walking out. "You son of a bitch, I'll never work with you again."

Marino turned to Roller: "Look, I have the informants and the secret witnesses. If I need searches in Pennsylvania, I can use the state police. I can make this entire case without you; so you either start coming across or we'll go at it alone. What's it going to be?" Marino asked, looking at Roller. "You talk to whoever you have to in Washington and find out what you're going to do. We need your help and support if we're going to go all the way with this case, but I'm prepared to go alone."

The next afternoon Roller called Marino to offer him the first shot at the case and the full cooperation of the federal government. But, he added, the feds would simultaneously work up a RICO case— Racketeer Influenced Corrupt Organization—and bring the entire mob under indictment. Roller was holding a list of several hundred target-witnesses he intended to drag kicking and screaming into the grand jury in what he would later call "one of the greatest abuses of the grand jury system in U.S. history."

In mid-November, Special Agent Thomas Fitzpatrick, of the FBI's Pittsburgh office, armed with an arrest warrant and a federal grand jury subpoena, picked up Ferritto, who was read his rights and asked what he wanted to do.

"Take me to Cleveland. I have some friends there who'll get me a lawyer," he demanded.

Fitzpatrick obliged, but first gave Ferritto his business card. "Here, I'll write my home number on it, too. You know, I think your friends are selling you out—and you never know when you'll need a new friend," he said, stuffing the card into the breast pocket of Ferritto's jacket.

Ferritto sat in the Cuyahoga County Jail for weeks awaiting arraignment, while his lawyer used delaying tactics to shop for a lenient judge.

Trust and patience were two things Ferritto had in short supply. And without anything to calm his nerves he was coming unglued. It figured that Licavoli wanted him to have a good lawyer to assure that he wouldn't start talking, but now Ferritto was sensing betrayal; he wasn't going to get made and he was going to end up doing time— or worse—to cover for the rest of them.

At Ferritto's arraignment, Marino made a charged argument in opposition to bail. He offered that Ferritto had a history of fleeing while on bail and couldn't be trusted in this case. And further said that Ferritto's erstwhile conspirators wanted him silenced and might kill him if he was on the street.

The judge ordered no bail.

Marino's comments about the mob wanting Ferritto dead hit home.

When Ferritto got back to his cell he asked for his jacket from the property clerk's office. He removed Agent Fitzpatrick's card and gave it to a Cleveland intelligence cop who had befriended him.

"Call this guy and tell him I want to see him. I'm willing to cooperate. But whatever you do, I don't want anyone at the Cleveland FBI involved—they have trouble keeping secrets there."

Two days later, Ferritto was in the Federal Metropolitan Correctional Center in Chicago, cutting a rough deal with the state and feds. He would testify to everything he knew. He would plead guilty in Greene's murder—but face no more than five years in prison or in the Witness Security Program. And he would deliver at least one additional big mob name to the conspiracy: Jimmy Fratianno, the one who got him tied up in this thing to begin with. No one had to coach Ferritto, he understood that the government wanted him to reach just as far as he could to implicate anyone he could.

On December 4, he signed a detailed confession and arrest warrants were immediately drawn for the Cleveland mob and Fratianno.

Ahearn had worked out the details of Fratianno's trip to Cleveland for arraignment. Jimmy would come into town in the custody of U.S. Marshals, spend a few days in a cell with Licavoli's gang, plead not guilty at his arraignment, and then be swept out again on the premise that he was awaiting trial on federal charges in Los Angeles. There were to be no meetings with authorities in Cleveland, but one would be held during a brief stopover in Milwaukee on his way into Cleveland.

Special Agent Ron Hadinger, a Cleveland native, had been appointed the official baby-sitter for Fratianno and Ferritto in the Cleveland case. He would oversee their debriefings and provide whatever hand-holding was needed. Hadinger had been picked from the Akron field office—where there was no leak—and was experienced in the affairs of organized crime.

Sitting in Milwaukee's FBI office, Hadinger immediately hit it off with Fratianno. Both men had grown up in the Collinwood section of Cleveland. The forty-four-year-old lean and soft-spoken agent took Fratianno through the evidence they had against him, including the surveillances of him in Cleveland and Ferritto's claims that Fratianno had introduced him into the conspiracy.

"It's a fuckin' lie, Ron," Fratianno said. "This motherfucker, well, yeah, I introduced him to Dope DelSanter. But back in 1975, long before anybody got clipped. I'm tellin' you this guy just kept crying to me how bad he wanted to be made and I was trying to do him a favor."

"Well, why would Ray lie? I mean, you two have been friends for a lot of years."

"He's just using me to get a good deal with you guys," Fratianno said, looking out the window at a heavy snowfall just getting underway.

"Well, Jim, this prosecutor, Marino, is a tough nut, a real ball buster. You're going to have to come up with some real good reason to have him keep you out of this case."

"What? Like testifying. I'm telling you, Ron, I have nothing I could testify to, unless you want me to lie."

"No, you don't have to lie," Hadinger said. "Jim, you were in town for Dope's funeral and you spoke to Licavoli a couple more times. We know you met him in Warren, Ohio—at the Town and Country Motel and during a July Fourth picnic. You mean in all those get-togethers you never heard a thing about their plans for killing Greene?"

"That's correct; not a fuckin' word," Fratianno said. "Fuck, they're not going to tell me anyhow. See, number one, they're not allowed to tell me anything like that. You follow me? Like if I'm going to kill somebody, I'm not going to tell them; it's against the rules."

"I don't buy it, Jimmy. Stretch your mind a little; there's got to be something in there that we could use," Hadinger said. "You know, you can't pick and choose the cases where you'll cooperate and those where you won't—it's in for a dime, in for a dollar."

Jimmy wasn't even going to try. "Forget about it, Ron. There's nothing I know that's of any use. I just know nothing about it. Okay?"

Hadinger got nowhere. He pushed every button he knew and couldn't shake Fratianno's story. He had him relate detailed accounts of his trips to Cleveland, his meetings with Licavoli, and his introduction of Ferritto to DelSanter—and he had him repeat the stories over and over again during the four-hour interview. But it was like listening to a recording: nothing changed in the retelling, right down to Fratianno's choice of words.

He ended the interview and flew back to Cleveland.

That evening the snowfall picked up, grounding Fratianno and Ahearn in Milwaukee for the weekend. There was no way to get Fratianno out of his cell again without raising suspicion among the guards and other inmates. So Ahearn and his friend, Milwaukee SAC

Ralph Hill—former head of C-1 in Chicago, the FBI's first organized crime gangbusters squad—spent the better part of the weekend at the jail, visiting Fratianno in a special hospital wing.

Hill and Fratianno shared tall tales about the old days of Al Capone, Sam Giancana, Lucky Luciano, and Vito Genovese, as Ahearn sat by plying Jimmy with cigars, wine, and Italian cold cuts.

The evening before they were to leave Milwaukee, Ahearn arrived at the jail carrying a shopping bag of goodies to find Fratianno in an unusual mood. He was quiet, as if possessed by an unfamiliar feeling he was trying to sort out. Ahearn had never seen Fratianno like this.

"You okay, Jimmy?" Ahearn asked, finding himself genuinely concerned—and a little shocked at his feelings for Fratianno.

"No. I mean, it's nothing important, Jim," Fratianno said. "It's just all the talk about these guys who made it big. Johnny [Roselli] and I used to talk that way a lot." His eyes were focusing on a spot on the cell wall. "It always brought us back to the same question: Why did we ever get ourselves in this thing to begin with? He and I could have had the world by the fuckin' balls if we'd steered clear."

Ahearn put down his bag and took a seat on the bed. "Why did you get into it? What was the appeal?"

"Money," Jimmy said without hesitating. "I was young and it seemed like there would be a lot of fuckin' money. But I was the one making the rest of them rich. At one point there in the fifties I had two booking operations running and was making $5,000 a week in vigorish [loan-shark interest] and turning a cut of everything over to these motherfuckers. And then I was clipping guys for them, too. I'm telling you, Jim, I was a fuckin' whore."

He looked at Ahearn with a blank stare for several moments. Ahearn didn't know quite what to say and so sat, looking back at Fratianno, in silence.

"Anyway, Jim, what did you bring to eat?"

Licavoli welcomed Jimmy to the Family jail cell in Cleveland with an outstretched hand of greeting; while pressing a finger of his left hand against his lips to indicate silence.

"Welcome to our little home away from home," Licavoli said. "What took you so long?"

"Are you kidding?" Jimmy said with laughter in his voice. It was good to be with his old friends, even in the joint. "We got snowed in at Milwaukee and then this fuckin' FBI comes on to me asking about Greene. Well, I told this cocksucker—"

Licavoli broke in, pressing his finger to his lips again. "Don't trust anyone," he whispered. "This place is probably wired."

They made some small talk. Licavoli took Jimmy aside. "I've arranged a lawyer for you—one of the best. But be patient, old friend, the lawyers are trying to get the right judge and it will be a few more days before we get bailed out of here."

Jimmy listened but his mind was working overtime. He was concerned that their cautious silence about the case would jeopardize his bargaining chips in Cleveland. If he couldn't get more information on the leak, there wasn't much for him to trade on.

"Listen, Jack," Jimmy said in a whisper, leading his friend toward a corner. "What the fuck am I doing here anyway? I mean, I had nothing to do with this fight of yours. Can you get your FBI leak to find out why I'm locked up in this thing?"

Licavoli's dark face soured. He grabbed Jimmy's head, one beefy hand pressing on each side of Fratianno's upper skull, and pulled him close. He whispered, "Look around and figure out who's missing and then you'll have your answer. Ferritto was picked up a couple of weeks ago; now he's nowhere to be found. The prick."

On his third day in the cell the guards came by and told Fratianno he had a visitor. When he got to the end of the jail corridor he found Hadinger waiting for him.

"Hey man," Jimmy said, looking back toward the cells. "Are you crazy. I can't be seen talking to you. Get out of my life," he said pulling away, heading back toward the cell.

"Look, Jimmy, Marino wants to talk to you. *Now*," Hadinger said in a near whisper. "And if you don't come along you're just going to leave the impression that you're double dealing."

This was the pressure the authorities had planned all along. If Jimmy was going to get anything on the leak, he would have it by now. It was time to turn tough on him.

Jimmy swaggered into Marino's office—one of a very few men who can walk with confidence in handcuffs. Hadinger unlocked the cuffs and took up a position by the door.

"Thanks for coming up," Marino began, as he extended his hand.

Jimmy ignored the gesture and took a seat. "Like I had any choice in the matter."

Despite his tough attitude, Jimmy was uneasy. This was where he would make or break his deal. It was the first time he was meeting with a prosecutor, and according to his advance billing this Marino would be no pushover.

"Where's Ahearn? I'd like to have him here," Jimmy said.

"No, Jimmy, this one is just between the two of us. Ron is here to make sure I don't trample on your rights. Now, if you want a lawyer—"

"In this town? Are you kidding? No, I don't want a lawyer. I'll talk to you, but I don't know if you're going to like what I have to say—it ain't much."

Marino was seated on the edge of his desk looking down toward Fratianno in a chair.

"I guess that's okay, because I don't think you'll be too pleased with me either," he said, hopping off the desk.

Marino spoke slowly as he paced. "Look, to be perfectly frank, I have a partner in this case, and he wants to prosecute you and see you fry in the chair. Personally, I don't give a damn if we're going to kill you or we're going to use you, that's going to be your decision. What I want to know is whether you have any information of any worth." He stopped and stared at Jimmy for effect.

"You know, you don't have to be such a hardass about it," Fratianno replied. "I'm willing to work with you guys, but I don't have much; I don't know much."

"I'm not giving you a hard time," Marino said, wagging a finger in Fratianno's face. "I just want you to understand the facts so that if we make a decision that puts you in the jackpot, well, that's your problem; you led your life, not us."

Hadinger was silent. He approved of this hard-edged approach and wasn't going to bail Fratianno out unless Marino got out of line, which was always a strong possibility.

"But I wasn't anywhere near this Nardi-Greene thing," Fratianno protested.

"Well, that's okay, too," Marino said. "You see, Fratianno, I don't give a shit about Danny Greene's murder; I've got more than enough to see the whole lot of you fry or die in prison. And as I told you, I don't care what happens to you. I also don't give a damn about Ahearn and the feds." He paused to let it sink in. "What I care about is me: What can you do for me? What I'm looking for is what you can tell me about organized crime, about LCN. Who makes the rules and who runs the syndicates? How are the Teamsters tied in? I want to know about Luciano and Capone and people like that. Who runs Las Vegas? How do you become a member and how do you get out? I want an education.

"In short, what I want is some proof that you're the genuine article. That you're not just jerking us all off. That you really know who's who and what's what, and if you get a deal from the feds I want to know that you're going to make it worthwhile for all of us. And I'll tell you something else. Before this office makes any deals with you, you're first going to plead guilty in this Greene murder. Oh, yes you are. And then I'm going to hold back on sentencing just as long as I possibly can to make sure you've done all you promised before I ask a judge to reduce your sentence."

Marino was laying it all out. He pulled no punches. "This is all so we understand each other—whether you cooperate and go free or get prosecuted and fry, either way, you walk like a man."

Fratianno believed Marino was sincere. It was the clearest picture of his options that Fratianno had been offered. He could avoid testifying in Cleveland, but he would have to cooperate in every other case the feds had to avoid being yanked back to face twenty years in the Ohio pen.

"Where do you want to begin?" Jimmy asked.

"How about with your initiation?"

Jimmy stopped for a moment to think. He had already told Ahearn about this stuff, and there was no crime involved. He would have to speak slowly: He was remembering Ahearn's warning to be careful about what he said until his deal was in writing.

Jimmy opened up with what was going to become his traveling road show: the winery in Los Angeles; the crossed gun and sword; a few words in Sicilian; kissing his new brothers; and *amico nostra*. The rules were what gave security to the organization: No drugs, don't fuck with a made guy's family, and never talk about Family business outside the Family. "You come in alive and go out dead."

The structure made this thing strong: The boss of each Family is elected and each boss in every city is co-equal with every other boss— "there's no boss-of-bosses, never has been—that's newspaper bullshit." But it is like any democracy: those with more respect are more equal than others.

Marino asked if there was any way a made guy could return to the fold after having been an informant or after testifying against his cohorts.

"You think this is some kind of fuckin' country club? No way, man. If you talk you're dead. Even later on, years later, they'd still have to set an example," Fratianno said.

He explained how his friend and sponsor in La Cosa Nostra, Johnny Roselli, had been killed because he had been talking to some congressional committees—nothing incriminating, just talk about Kennedy and Castro.

If he wanted to talk, Fratianno said, Roselli could have told them how he oversaw Chicago's interests with labor unions in L.A. and casino operations in Vegas for bosses Al Capone and Frank Nitti.

"How does that work?" asked Marino. "I mean, how does a guy like Roselli get control of a union?"

"Oh, Carmen. You can't be serious," Fratianno said, laughing. "You think these unions operate on the up-and-up? With all the loose cash they have and all the under-the-table deals to avoid strikes?" He expounded on this opinion: "Sure, lots of them are clean. But take the Teamsters. The bosses run them guys. I mean, like every city has its favorite-son candidate for head of the Teamsters and the city with the most juice usually gets its way."

"Okay, so who will be the next Teamsters president if [Frank] Fitzsimmons drops out of the picture?" Marino asked.

Jimmy leaned back in the hard-backed chair and thought for a moment. "Well, Carmen, I'd say it's between Roy Williams and Jackie Presser. Presser has Cleveland, but Williams has [Nick] Civella in Kansas City and Aiuppa in Chicago. I'd go with Williams. If Scalish were still alive, Presser would have a better chance. Presser told me that he doesn't make a move without getting the okay from Rockman, Scalish's brother-in-law." He went on to tell Marino about meeting Lucky Luciano in 1935 and running with his crowd at Hialeah—making book for Luciano's men, and eventually taking them for $24,000.

They talked about how the Jews from Cleveland had acted as fronts in Las Vegas for Italian mob money and became legitimate millionaires by declaring taxes on their income. The Italians secreted the millions they took from the casino-hotels they owned and had to live like paupers to evade the IRS.

"Dumb fuckin' guineas," Jimmy said. "Those Jews are cunning bastards, you know? They just tell the IRS they made it gambling or by selling some property to a friend, they make some fake papers and boom, the fuckin' government doesn't ask another question."

Marino shifted gears. "Jimmy, you know the two Tonys?"

Jimmy halted on this one. Up to this point questions and answers flowed freely. Now Marino was getting into some sensitive territory—asking about Tony Trombino and Tony Brancato, a pair of California thugs, shakedown artists, who were killed in 1951.

"Yeah, I knew them," Jimmy finally volunteered. "They worked out of Kansas City, a pair of really bad cocksuckers. They'd done everything from robbery to rape and murders. And they did a whole lot of things they shouldn't have, you know what I mean?"

"Yeah, and one of the things they shouldn't have done was rob that guy at the Flamingo. Isn't that right?" Marino asked.

"Yeah, you're right about that," Jimmy said, laughing.

"You know, they were killed,"Marino said.

"Everyone knows they were killed," Jimmy said, feigning boredom with the questions.

"I bet you even know when and where they were killed."

"Sure, I heard about that stuff," Jimmy answered slowly, starting to tighten up. "Why are you bringing this shit up?"

"Jimmy, did you kill them?"

"Carmen, what are you fuckin' kidding? Forget about it. I don't know where you get this stuff."

"Ron, is he supposed to be doing this?" Jimmy demanded of Hadinger.

"Come on, Jimmy, you and Moceri were in on the hit; someone wanted them dead and you were the buttons," Marino persisted.

"He's right, Carmen," Hadinger urged. "Back off a little. You're getting into areas outside your jurisdiction."

"As a matter of fact, Carmen, this might be a good time to break off. It's been a long time since I took Jimmy out of the cell; he'd better start back."

"Okay. Well, I got an education all right," he said, extending his hand.

"So we have a deal?" Fratianno asked, this time taking Marino's hand.

"It looks good for now, Jimmy. But I still want your guilty plea and then you have to sort things out in California."

"Hey, I can handle California. But we're going to have to get something in writing before I plead out for you."

"Yeah, sure. That's a ways off."

The cuffs went back on and Fratianno went back to his cell. He told his friends the FBI was grilling him on one of the West Coast cases.

Marino called Roller and told him he was prepared to let Fratianno pass in his case, after he pleaded out.

"So you think this guy is giving us the whole story?" Roller asked.

"Hell no. I didn't say that. Every one of these guys holds something back, they never know when they may need a new contract. In fact, I'm as convinced as ever that he just doesn't want to testify against his old friends. But I think he's going to make a hell of a witness for the FBI."

The next day Jimmy went to court in Cleveland where he entered a not guilty plea and was quickly shipped back West, to the federal Metropolitan Correctional Center in San Diego.

MCC San Diego is a rather inconspicuous, modern, twelve-story structure, with a white waffle-iron façade and narrow windows, adjacent to the U.S. District Courthouse. It is one of the most secure prison facilities in the United States. Inside there is a section for general prisoner population—those recently arrested, those being held without bail, and those serving out a short term. On another level are the protected inmates—those who might be at risk in general population, those who are informants or witnesses.

Jimmy, at this point, didn't fit either definition. He was clearly not fit for general population, but his deal with the government hadn't been cut yet, so he couldn't go in the protected inmates' wing. Instead, he was placed in an isolation cell and only during visits with approved nonofficials—McDonald or Jean, for example—was he permitted to be in the dayroom, where other inmates met visitors.

Keeping Jimmy entertained and in good spirits became a full-time job. Ahearn virtually moved to San Diego, taking up residence at the Executive Hotel, a few blocks from MCC, working constantly to complete Jimmy's cooperation agreement.

Nick Lore—the essential mix of mild-tempered baby-sitter, diplomat, confidant, and top-flight investigative agent—became Jimmy's guardian, friend, and confessor.

Ahearn would arrive with a box of Havanas provided by McDonald; Lore made regular visits to the Italian markets on India Street to pick up sausage and pepper sandwiches, prosciutto, and capicola.

Lore was a study in contrasts: His smart Brooks Brothers suits and sophisticated command of language softened his appearance as a small tough guy with a thick New York City accent and a map of Sicily printed on his dark face.

His understanding of La Cosa Nostra made it easy for Jimmy to warm to him immediately. Lore began his career as a street agent in New York City, where he was on a first-name basis with boss Gaetano "Tommy" Luchese; he had gone on to Washington as a supervisor on organized crime cases; in San Diego he was in charge of the Bompensiero murder investigation; and, perhaps most important, he spoke fluent Sicilian.

The only other source of companionship Jimmy enjoyed was McDonald. The two men had become fast friends three years earlier after being introduced by one of McDonald's clients. At the age of thirty-three, McDonald was already a millionaire from a practice in negligence law and investments in ranch land near his hometown of Stevensville, Montana. Fratianno was thirty-three when he joined La Cosa Nostra, and looking at McDonald now Fratianno saw the man he might have been had he gotten up from his sick bed as a teenager and returned to school.

While McDonald was familiar with Jimmy's reputation as a gangster, he had never known—and never asked—any details. Since the arrests on the PORNEX case and now on the Cleveland matter, McDonald was learning just who his friend was.

But he wasn't so much stunned by what he was learning as he was by what he was seeing; since arriving at MCC, Jimmy was losing weight at an alarming rate, he was sullen, drawn, and tired. His arrogance had been replaced by a tone of desperation, his swaggering gate had become a weary shuffle. McDonald had always thought of Fratianno as one of those remarkable people immune to stress and depression.

"That prosecutor, DeFeo, and Ahearn are telling me that you're ready to sign anything, that you're willing to cooperate fully. Is that the case?" McDonald asked.

"Dennis, I don't think I have much of a choice. I mean, I could fight the charges, but I don't know how much longer I'd last outside. These people, people who I trusted my entire life, are trying to kill me."

"Let's be honest here. I'm no criminal lawyer, but from what you've told me, I'm sure Billy Marchiondo could get you off," McDonald said, uncomfortably shifting in his seat, finding this not his idea of a comfortable place to talk with a client.

Jimmy had called his friend Marchiondo, a prominent criminal lawyer, from the Cleveland jail. The Albuquerque lawyer said he had already heard about Jimmy's problems and offered to defend him, without any mention of price, which Jimmy took to mean a free ride. McDonald, who also contacted Marchiondo, was left with the same impression.

"But even if I get off, I'll need protection, Dennis. What do I do after I'm out of here? Lookit, my only option if I'm not protected is to start some kind of gang war here and I'm too old for that."

McDonald had trouble speaking to Jimmy. He couldn't help thinking how much Jimmy was beginning to look like a caged animal.

"Well, here's the deal they're offering, and I don't mind telling you I think it stinks," McDonald began. "DeFeo wants you to combine all of your cases into one big ball and have you plead guilty in return for no more than a five-year sentence."

"Hey Dennis, no way I'm going down for five years," Jimmy protested, with a sudden spark of life.

"I feel the same way and told him so, but what do you want me to do?"

"Just tell them that I don't do five years. They're going to get the whole Los Angeles Family from my testimony. I mean, that should be worth giving me parole and no more prison time."

McDonald shook his head. "I don't think they'll budge. You see, when you go in to testify, DeFeo wants to be able to tell the jury that you're paying for your crimes; it gives your testimony more credibility if he can tell the jury you're a bad guy, that you took part in this conspiracy and you're paying for it."

"What crimes? I didn't do any crimes," Jimmy said.

"Here's what I want to do. I think we should tell them you're prepared to fight all the charges. Look, if you're telling me straight that you had nothing to do with these cases, then they won't be able to convict you. And they know that as well as we do."

"You do what you can, Dennis," Fratianno said. "But I need to get this thing straightened out. This fuckin' place is driving me nuts." There was a pause. "I've told you this before, Dennis. But I'm more convinced than ever. This has been a treacherous life—you never know who you can trust. You come along in years as far as I have and you still can't know for sure who your friends are."

"Is there anything I can do for you?" McDonald asked.

"No, I don't think so." Fratianno stopped to think for a moment. "Not unless you can figure out a way to get a few broads in here to me." He chuckled.

"Well, just keep thinking what kind of broad you'd like once we get this thing settled," McDonald said, getting up to leave. "And don't mess around with any little boys."

"Not on your life," Fratianno said, leaning in close to McDonald. "You know, I've done seventeen and a half years of hard time and never touched a punk—never even was tempted by one of those perverts," Fratianno said.

"Oh, in the meantime, I understand Jean is coming down here to see you this week. Please try to get along. I think you need each other right now."

Jimmy spent Christmas in jail at MCC. His spirits grew increasingly desperate as the negotiations moved at a snail's pace. DeFeo was in the process of transferring from Los Angeles to take over the strike force office in Kansas City.

Jean received a visit from Barron, and at his urging went to San Diego the day after Christmas to ask Jimmy to go into the program. "We can start life all over again somewhere, honey."

She looked beautiful and the thought of starting life over with her was beginning to sound pretty good. He began to picture a life, paid-in-full by Uncle Sam, living on a small tropical island.

"Babe, I'm trying to get this thing worked out so we all come out okay," Jimmy said, leaning toward her, petting her bare thigh under her skirt as they sat in the dayroom.

"Hey Jimmy, stop mauling me," she said as his fingers slipped under the trim of her panties.

"What? I'm not doing anything," he said, pulling back and crossing his arms.

She was the only one in the room protesting. Other husbands and wives, boyfriends and girlfriends, were off in the corners caressing, reaching to feel under clothes and dry humping.

"I've made up my mind to stay with you through this, Jimmy. But you're going to have to start making some changes in your life—in our life."

"Like what?" he asked, reaching for his cigar.

"Settling down and coming to terms with yourself. Jesus loves you, I just know he does. And you could be great if you'd only realize that—" She broke off as Jimmy rolled his eyes. "Okay, if that's how you're going to be, fine." She stood to leave. "To hell with you. But you're still my husband," she scolded, standing over him. "I'm going to be part of your life. And whether you're in this witness program or not, you're responsible for taking care of me. I need money to live, Jimmy. You're going to have to arrange something for me while you're in jail and this witness program would help."

"Who the fuck says I'm going to jail?" Jimmy asked.

"Be realistic for once, will you. They're going to put you away. I know it. I feel it," she said, starting to cry now and stomping her foot, remembering too late that she was wearing heels. She twisted her ankle and fell into Jimmy's lap.

"It's going to be all right, babe," he said tenderly. "I'll work it out."

By New Year's Eve, almost anything, even five years in prison, looked better to Jimmy than spending another day in MCC's isolation cell. Ahearn had him convinced that the government had made its best offer: Jimmy would plead guilty to all the cases—the PORNEX and Bompensiero murder in Los Angeles, the gambling charges in San Francisco, and the federal and state cases in Cleveland—in return for which he'd get parole after eighteen months of a five-year sentence.

McDonald opposed the deal.

Jimmy held out on two points: He wouldn't testify in Cleveland, and he wanted to know what the Witness Security Program was guaranteeing. During the first two weeks of 1978, officials came to San Diego to iron out those details.

The first meeting was with the top brass of Witness Security: Gerald Shur, who ran the program for the Justice Department, and Donald "Bud" McPherson, chief marshal for the Western states. Not too many witnesses got that kind of attention. But then the seven-year-old program had never had a witness of this caliber.

As Jimmy listened, and McDonald looked on shaking his head in disgust, Shur explained the parameters: First, they guaranteed that he would do his prison time in a "safe prison atmosphere"—what was euphemistically called the "Valachi suite," three secure rooms in La Tuna, a federal prison outside of El Paso, Texas, where Joseph Valachi had done his time.

"Come on," McDonald complained. "That's nothing more than isolation, solitary confinement. It's not like he's going to run anywhere. You could detain him in a hotel under FBI protection or in a safe house; something more pleasant than La Tuna."

But, Shur explained, this was nonnegotiable; if Fratianno was sentenced, he would do his time in a prison. And, he emphasized, even after parole, life wouldn't be easy.

"We're not offering you a glamorous life and probably nothing compared to what you're used to," Shur said. "The only thing we're guaranteeing is to keep you alive on our terms. And that means we'll take care of you and your family. We'll choose a place to relocate you, feed you, and cover your basic needs, like housing and medical, until you start making a living."

"Are you kidding?" Jimmy shot back. "You're going to put me in solitary for eighteen months, stick me in some town I've never seen before, and then put me to work? At my age? With all that I'm going to give *you* guys? Fuck that."

"Jimmy, I think you have to understand something," Shur replied calmly. "You're not giving *us* anything. You may be helping the prosecutors and the FBI, but those are other agencies. I'm not here to cut any deals. I'm just telling you what's going to be. And if you don't like what we're offering, well, I can walk out of here today without a second thought about you.

"But, Jimmy, you've got to do this for yourself. For your protection. For your family. And more than that, you should think about doing it for your country, to have something your grandkids can point to with pride."

"Oh, get out of my fuckin' life," Jimmy said, stiffening at talk of God, country, and grandchildren. "The question is what is the fuckin' country going to do for me."

And the answer was: not as much as he wanted.

As Jimmy was led back to his cell he reviewed Shur's words. Unfortunately, despite Shur's cautious warnings and efforts to avoid false promises, he had repeated a key phrase used weeks earlier by Ahearn: "We'll take care of you and your family." Despite everything else said to the contrary, those words rang in Jimmy's ears as he searched for any glimmer of hope.

On January 10, 1978, the top officials on Fratianno's case gathered in San Diego to complete the last detail of his agreement: his testimony in Cleveland. DeFeo was in from Kansas City to chair the meeting attended by Hadinger and Kimmell from Cleveland, and Ahearn and Lore.

"I'm telling you, it's just like training a dog," Hadinger argued.

"You have to pull his chain really hard, right now, at the outset—if you're weak with him now, you'll have trouble with him forever. You can't have him telling you which cases he will and won't testify in. He has to learn right now who his master is. I've done this before. I know what I'm talking about."

"I know this guy," Ahearn said. "I feel like I've spent a lifetime with him already. And I know he's just stubborn enough to walk away, to say 'fuck this,' and walk."

" 'Fuck this' and go where?" Hadinger pressed. "He's already been branded as no-good by the mob; they have a contract on him, right? And he has four trials to face. Where's he going to go?"

"None of these cases are strong enough to hold him," Ahearn said. "The only case that he could go down on is this gambling charge, and that's a nickle-dime deal; he won't get any hard time from that. And meanwhile, he still seems to have a couple of lawyer friends out there willing to mount his defense for nothing and stake him to some cash."

"So we just roll over, is that it? Buy his lie that he knows nothing about the case?" Hadinger asked.

"For now, yeah," Kimmel said, taking Ahearn's side. "We're all convinced he's lying, but we get him to plead guilty anyway. And if we don't get all these guys in the state case, we come back and push him to testify in the federal trials."

Lore agreed. "I've heard it from him two dozen times now. He says if he's forced to testify in Cleveland, he says, 'Tell those cock-suckers I won't testify anywhere—let them testify.' I believe he means it."

"I just think we'll be making a big tactical mistake," Hadinger said, upset but retaining his usual calm, smooth demeanor. "He's the only one, the connecting tissue, that can link Ferritto with Cleveland's bosses, Licavoli and [Angelo] Lonardo [underboss after DelSanter's death]. We need him in the state case to corroborate Ferritto and make the connection to the leaders."

"Look Ron. We hear you," DeFeo said. "But you're going to get a whole lot of shots at these guys in Cleveland. You have the state case, the federal murder-racketeering case, the leak, and I understand there's some narcotics case brewing. All against the same guys.

"You've done it. You've positioned yourselves to break the back of LCN in that town, with or without Fratianno. In L.A., we're looking at the same level of success—but only if we have Fratianno. Without him we're sunk."

Hadinger shrugged. He asked for and got permission from the

group to make one last-ditch attempt to talk Fratianno into testifying. It failed. Fratianno was shipped to Cleveland two days later to be arraigned again, this time on the federal racketeering charges, Roller's case.

Hadinger's report on Fratianno's trip to Cleveland said:

On 1/16/78 James Fratianno entered a plea of not guilty to the RICO violation [federal racketeering charge] for which he had been indicted. Immediately following his not-guilty plea, Fratianno requested a meeting with Cleveland Strike Force Attorney in Charge Douglas P. Roller. Fratianno advised Roller that he would be willing to plead guilty to the state and federal charges pending against him in connection with the Danny Greene . . . murder cases and further that he would cooperate fully with the FBI in connection with the PORNEX case and FRANK BOMPENSIERO murder. Fratianno, however, indicated that he would not testify for the state or federal authorities in Cleveland . . . because of his absolute fear and certainty that retribution would be taken against members of his immediate family . . . currently residing in Cleveland.

Cuyahoga County Prosecuting Attorney Carmen Marino agreed to the following: that the Cuyahoga County Prosecutors Office would accept a guilty plea from Fratianno in the Greene case without benefit of Fratianno's testimony on the condition that Fratianno cooperate fully and truthfully with the federal authorities in the West Coast cases. Marino admonished Fratianno that if his complete cooperation was not given that the Cuyahoga County Prosecutors Office would aggressively prosecute him in the Greene case.

The significance of this action and cooperation by Marino paved the way for a formal agreement between Fratianno and the Department of Justice, which will ensure Fratianno's complete cooperation and testimony in the PORNEX case and the Frank Bompensiero murder. Fratianno's singular ability to implicate the hierarchy of the Los Angeles LCN Family, including Dominic Brooklier, boss; Sam Sciortino, underboss; Jack LoCicero, consiglieri; Tommy Ricciardi, Peter Milano and Louis Tom Dragna, soldiers, adds a new dimension to the PORNEX case.

Fratianno's agreement with the Justice Department will include his willingness to be thoroughly debriefed concerning other cases that may be of interest to federal and state authorities and his providing of intelligence information concerning LCN matters throughout the country.

Two days later, at MCC San Diego, Jimmy joined Ahearn in a conference call to DeFeo in Kansas City and McDonald in San Francisco. Without fanfare, Fratianno agreed to a bare-bones cooperation agreement, which McDonald refused to sign.

That afternoon he moved to the protected inmates' wing of MCC.

He stretched out on his new bed smoking a cigar, playing a hand of gin with Ahearn.

"You know something, Jim," he said. "It's amazing. With all of the guys I've clipped and scams I've gotten away with, it all ends with me having to plead guilty in two crimes I had no part in just to save my life. Can you feature that? Some system of justice, huh?"

3

A Primer

JOE VALACHI was a crazed squeal, a stoolie, a snitch fink who was hallucinating demons when he turned federal informant. On June 22, 1962, Valachi went berserk in the federal prison yard in Atlanta, Georgia, bludgeoning a fellow inmate to death after mistaking him for a made guy who he decided was out to kill him. Valachi was diagnosed by prison psychiatrists as being in a "paranoid state" characterized by "delusions of persecution." But he was sane enough to cut a deal with the feds; he would spill his guts and they would go easy on him for the murder.

A year later, in September 1963, he was hauled up to Washington, D.C., for a coming out party, where Attorney General Robert Kennedy presented Valachi to the world by way of Senator John McClellan's Permanent Subcommittee on Investigations.

There was nothing noble in Valachi's action and nothing even significantly new in what he said, except for the details he provided. What was generally called the Mafia had been known to exist by law enforcement agencies even if J. Edgar Hoover refused to acknowledge it.

What was significant was that Valachi excited a somnolent nation into believing what they had widely regarded as a fantastic myth: A secret society with its own rules and laws of conduct built around a military code of honor and respect did exist, and it was robbing us blind.

There could no longer be any doubt—Valachi was living proof.

83

He embodied a new awareness. His name became synonymous with "The Black Hand," "The Mafia," "The Syndicate," "La Cosa Nostra." This personification was helped along by his having a name that rolled off the English-speaking tongue as easily as "lasagna"—nothing so complex as gnocchi, capicola, *pasta e fagiola*, or, for that matter, Fra-ti-a-nno.

What he provided was a history lesson on how La Cosa Nostra came to its present form, how it was organized, and who were its leaders. It was good intelligence information, but he offered nothing lawmen could use in a single criminal investigation or to attack La Cosa Nostra as a corrupt organization.

Tales of his formal initiation captured the imagination of America, which was spellbound by daily newspaper reports of his revelations. The ceremony he described was much the same as that which Fra-tianno spoke of nearly two decades later. The only difference—true to California's more laid-back style—was that Valachi was ordered to hold a piece of burning paper in his hands and recite: "This is the way I burn if I expose this organization."

He introduced America and the world to a substrata society of names that became indistinguishably mingled like alphabet soup in the Anglo mind. And in their enthusiasm at learning this once-mythic kingdom was real, Americans mistook La Cosa Nostra as a generic concept. Overnight, it seemed, every crook working in concert with another crook was a member of "the mob." According to news accounts, every city seemed to have a Family, and the nation was virtually overrun with crime *"soldati"* doing the bidding of crime "bosses."

Somewhere, the very special meaning of La Cosa Nostra was lost in translation. Americans had missed the point: La Cosa Nostra is a secret society with fewer than 5,000—recent accounts say as few as 2,500—formally initiated male members of Italian heritage, operating out of twenty-four select cities.

There are many fringe elements associated with LCN, but there is a vast difference between a made guy and an associate; membership brings with it a unique fraternal bond, exclusive knowledge of how "this thing of ours" operates, and access to a power base—none of which is enjoyed by associates.

Members enjoy the rewards of the powerful network of criminal powerbrokers that stretches across the nation. If you are *amico nostra* the usual obstacles barring a loan at a bank or union pension fund may be removed, a government contract may be more easily obtained, or a competitor could be silenced. Coercion in its darkest, most violent form is their stock in trade, which they bargain upon to control both rackets and legitimately profitable businesses.

During the first half of this century, many members of La Cosa Nostra weren't interested in participating in crimes, coercion, or wars. They sought membership as a sign of their being men of honor and respect in the community. It was insurance against being taken advantage of by other criminal alliances. It meant they had the protection of the Family in times of need, and that they were willing to help if called upon. "He's with good people" was a common expression for pointing out a made guy in New York's mob neighborhoods in the 1950s.

By the time of Valachi's disclosures, however, membership in La Costa Nostra no longer carried the same sense of honor. As crime became the primary purpose of the society, its membership changed. The brighter sons and daughters were going off to universities, spurning the old family ways, and settling into American lives. Middle-aged members were trying to remain inactive, getting into legitimate businesses, going to jail, or getting killed off. The Families were left with aging members or generally not-too-bright young turks who yearned for a life of crime.

The secret society had become nothing more than a criminal syndicate guided by a strict hierarchy, but one with little regard for the rules. Any of the rules of military-type conduct, honor, and respect could be broken if the person breaking them was powerful enough. A case of might making right as long as there was no higher authority than an individual's will.

Where membership was originally limited solely to those born in Sicily, the passage of years and gang wars had necessitated initiation of second-generation Neapolitans.

Where the older leaders, fearful of corruption and detection, had set rules against narcotics trafficking in the 1940s, the lure of enormous financial rewards became too great for younger men. By the 1970s, federal agents were intercepting phone conversations in which young soldiers were openly critical of their bosses, discussing narcotics deals and talking candidly to nonmembers about La Cosa Nostra criminal conspiracies. Clearly, the fabric of pride and honor that once ruled had deteriorated. What remained were not Italian men of honor, but common American gangsters using the secret society as any criminal conspiracy would, to insulate themselves. Their increasing lack of order and discipline made them more vulnerable to detection and prosecution. And certainly Valachi's disclosures, the first crack in the dike, created impetus for some action.

Innocent until proven guilty is a fine maxim for protecting the rights of the innocent. Placing the overwhelming burden of proof on the prosecution seems the fairest means of conducting a trial. Yet these protections of the individual in a free society are fragile concepts, easily abused by a secret society that insulates its leaders and activities by a shroud of silence enforced through threats, torture, and the killing of witnesses.

In 1965, President Lyndon Johnson created a commission to find tools capable of ferreting out these criminal conspiracies without disturbing the foundations of our judicial system. And in 1967 that commision made 200 recommendations. Of those, twenty-two dealt specifically with organized crime. They seemed radical notions in their day, but were merely an awakening to reality at the federal level.

A year later, Congress overwhelmingly passed the Omnibus Crime Control and Safe Streets Act of 1968, which included an electronic surveillance section—wiretaps and bugs—commonly referred to as Title III.

And in 1970, guided by the President's commission report, but going far beyond its recommendations, Congress cleared the Organized Crime Control Act of 1970, a sweeping document that granted law enforcement agencies powers it had only imagined.

Embodied in those two bills were the potent ingredients that, with aggressive prosecution, could break the back of organized crime by allowing law enforcement agencies to reach inside those conspiracies, to erode the insulation surrounding the leadership. While they would create a storm of controversy in the legal community, these bills provided for:

- Increased manpower, funding, and record keeping that would enable street agents to identify the bad guys and their conspiracies, largely by using informants.
- Once a conspiracy was identified, agents could use their knowledge and their informants' statements to apply to courts for Title III wiretaps and bugs, which could provide the best possible evidence: recordings of criminals making confessions of their conduct.
- A new immunity statute created a standard of "use immunity"—

while it provided that anything a witness said could not be used as evidence against them, it did enable prosecutors to grab low-level conspirators off the streets and compel their testimony before a grand jury.

- New perjury statutes relaxed former standards of proof, meaning that the bad guy who wouldn't cooperate, but walked into the grand jury and lied, could be more easily prosecuted.
- The Witness Security Program (WITSEC) gave lawmen a means of hiding cooperating witnesses and providing them with new identities to start life over.
- Increased staffing in the sixteen strike force offices and U.S. Attorneys offices enabled more imaginative prosecution techniques.
- And then there was RICO.

Going to prison used to be the cost of doing business. A few years to relax in the slam and you're back on the street again. But RICO changed that.

The formal name is the Racketeer Influenced Corrupt Organization statute. Someone must have labored long and hard to come up with that Italian-sounding acronym. Remember Edward G. Robinson in *Little Caesar*? He played the tough gangster who pulled himself up from the gutter to create a prototype underworld syndicate. His final line as he lay dying in the streets: "Mother of Mercy, is this the end of Rico?"

The stated congressional intent of RICO was to attack businesses operating under the corrupt influence of organized crime—or, as the law states, conducting a "continuing enterprise" through a "pattern of racketeering." But its application has grown—and been approved by the courts—to encompass a broad variety of uses.

The government was slow to realize RICO's potential, stumbling in early efforts to define its applications outside of formal businesses, such as corporations burdened with corrupt labor unions. The model for RICO's use in organized crime cases was established in 1980, in the indictment of Frank "Funzi" Tieri, boss of New York's Genovese Family. His specific crimes included extortion, murder conspiracy, bankruptcy fraud, and interfering with interstate commerce. Tieri became the first person ever charged as the boss of a Family, and the Family was defined as a "continuing criminal enterprise" under RICO. In effect, Tieri's "crime" was being the "boss."

There has been a furious debate in the legal community over the proper use of RICO. Criminal defense lawyers insist that criminal syndicates should not be regarded as "enterprises," that the intention of the law had been to protect legitimate businesses from racketeers, not to interpret the criminal syndicate as an enterprise.

Gennaro J. Angiulo, boss of Boston's crime Family, apparently had understood from his lawyer that he could beat RICO by arguing he never corrupted legitimate businesses. He is heard in a 1983 wiretap instructing a cohort: "Our argument is that we're an illegitimate business. We're a bookmaker; we're selling marijuana. We are illegal here; we're illegal there. Arsonists. We are everything." It was a novel approach. It didn't work.

In its simplest terms, RICO provides for forfeiture of all "ill-gotten gains" and up to twenty years in prison upon conviction. The way you get convicted is by operating a continuing criminal enterprise— the key word is enterprise, not criminal—in which you committed two separate crimes within a ten-year period.

So, by way of explanation: If Mom and Pop Jones are running a clothing store and they pay off Joe Sleeze, the electrical inspector, $10 to get their certificate of occupany in 1978, and then make false statements in an application for a Small Business Administration loan in 1986, then bing, bang, boom they're guilty of bribing a public official and mail fraud as the predicate (key criminal) acts in a RICO (AKA racketeering) conspiracy. At trial they're found guilty of the individual crimes (bribery and mail fraud) and the clothing store is determined by the jury to be "a continuing criminal enterprise," thus they are guilty of the RICO conspiracy charge. They each go off to do ten years—they got a hanging judge—and have to turn over the store to Uncle Sam.

Now, in reality, it is unlikely that the government is going to be bothered with small fish like Mom and Pop Jones—unless, of course, prosecutors are trying to build a case against Sleeze, the electrical inspector, who has been going around town with his hand out for years and whose shoddy methods have led to fires. In that case the scenario changes dramatically. If the Joneses have a lawyer willing to "rat them out," they go in, cop a plea on the bribery charge, and as a sign of good faith the government drops the mail fraud charge. The government agrees it will speak on their behalf at the time of sentencing *if* they testify truthfully at Sleeze's trial. If it turns out that Sleeze is "connected"—a made guy or has close contacts with LCN—the government might also offer to put the Joneses in the Witness Security Program.

In theory, that's how the law works. In reality, the forfeiture clause has had some problems. It's usually hard to determine just what was obtained from the profits of crime, and frequently harder to actually make collection.

RICO gradually became the darling of aggressive prosecutors. It provided not only potentially stiff sentences and, therefore, leverage to compel a co-conspirator's testimony, but it also gave prosecutors the ability to string together a collection of petty crimes or weak cases, which showed the collective impact of a continuing criminal conspiracy.

In its first seven years of operation, thirty-seven RICO cases were initiated. By 1980, there were 250 reported, and its use began growing annually in geometric progressions as prosecutors realized its potential. By the end of 1984, more than 500 RICO cases with multiple defendants had been undertaken.

Still, before any indictment, there must be evidence. With the tools provided by Congress in 1968 and 1970, prosecutors are more likely today than ever before to have the evidence they'll need for convictions. They don't need to walk into court with merely the evidence found at the crime scene and the testimony of an eyewitness.

Combining Title III wiretaps and bugs with immunity against prosecution as a means of securing testimony at trial, aggressive lawmen are able to build their cases. Using a single crime as a wedge, they can investigate and net an entire criminal conspiracy, as in the Greene case, or tempt criminals into a sting operation, as in PORNEX. Twenty years ago, the Greene case would have ended with the indictment of Ferritto and PORNEX would never have happened.

The cornerstone to building those kinds of cases has been the informant or immunized witness. It is on the informant's statements that applications are made to courts for Title III wiretaps, bugs, or video surveillances, each intercepting an average of 265 incriminating conversations.

By 1984, there were 773 surveillances installed, the vast majority focusing on narcotics transactions. During that year there were 2,393 arrests and 649 convictions—many of those arrested were not brought to trial in the same year—as a result of Title III investigations. The total cost of running those wiretaps and bugs came to a whopping $33.5 million, or $13,999 per arrest.

Like RICO and Title III, the Witness Security Program, known informally as WITSEC or witness protection, has come under close scrutiny but with far more general criticism—largely the result of problems encountered in a project as unprecedented as reinventing the wheel.

The program was originally designed to accept as many as thirty witnesses a year; these people would be placed in secure facilities to await trials or serve short sentences. After their release, the program would relocate them under a new identity and with nominal subsistence funding until they found a job.

Initially, officials realized the need for secure facilities to house witnesses and broke ground for MCCs—in New York, Chicago, and San Diego. They also advertised for, hired, and trained a small team of security agents.

No one anticipated the sudden demand that law enforcement, primarily the FBI, would put on the fledgling program. Almost from its inception, WITSEC was overwhelmed by several hundred "clients" a year and procedural snafus. In its first fifteen years of operation, more than 4,700 witnesses and more than 11,000 family members were processed, with an average of 300 new witnesses a year anticipated for the foreseeable future.

In late 1977, as Fratianno prepared to sign on, the program was still in chaos and Howard Safir, a thirteen-year veteran of the Drug Enforcement Administration, was brought in to straighten it out. The creation of the program as it exists today can be traced to the date of Safir's arrival. He was the fourteenth person to run the program in seven years but the first to cope effectively with its unique needs.

In his first two years, Safir set to work increasing the number of witness-security specialists—U.S. Marshals with the rank of inspector—from about two dozen to more than 130. He ordered up a hot line that witnesses could call from anywhere in the country if they were in trouble. Numbers of annual admissions to the program were trimmed from the 1977 high of 469 to a more manageable number of about 300. He changed an earlier policy, under which the program provided "job placement assistance," and made "satisfactory" job placement "a requirement." A roster of more than 150 corporations agreeing to employ witnesses was developed. Witness specialists were given training in everything from organized crime and evasive driving procedures to the psychological problems witnesses are likely to encounter. And new clients began receiving psychological and vocational testing and counseling.

Today, the average witness stays on the program for thirteen months, during which they receive up to $3,000 a month in subsistence funding. After that they're on their own as far as security and financing, unless they run into a problem.

With increasing frequency, the problems clients run into have been with the law. About 95 percent of WITSEC's clients have criminal records and a General Accounting Office study in 1984 found that 23 percent of all those who had ever been in WITSEC returned to crime under their new identities. While that rate is far lower than the usual criminal recidivism rate, which 1985 studies set at 61 percent, it is nonetheless a shocking circumstance for the individual who finds himself victimized by a person who would have been in prison but for the government's largess.

Perhaps the best-known example was Marion Albert Pruett. Pruett was released from an eight-year prison term on bank robbery charges after he testified against the killer of a federal prisoner. He did a stint at MCC San Diego with Fratianno in 1978. By 1979, relocated with a new identity but no more WITSEC funding, Pruett went on a criminal rampage, raping three women and killing five. He was picked up in Arkansas midway through his crime spree but was released when a federal crime computer showed no outstanding warrants or record. A couple of murders later, Pruett was apprehended, tried, convicted, and sentenced to death—in three states.

A less heinous criminal, yet one who has enjoyed greater notoriety, is Henry Hill, a mob associate whose escapades were chronicled in the 1986 best-seller, *Wise Guy.*

It was revealed in a 1986 trial that Hill, a top witness who testified in federal and state cases, including the Boston College basketball point-shaving scandal, was convicted six times on charges of burglary, assault, and drunk driving since joining WITSEC in 1980. He did sixty days on the burglary charge and got a slap on the wrist for the others.

Pruett and Hill are typical of a caste of criminals who have traded up with authorities, offering information for freedom, a stint in WITSEC, and a new identity. They never intended to straighten out their lives; they were just looking for a deal.

In total, the GAO study of WITSEC found former clients involved in at least a dozen murders and various credit card scams, robberies, arsons, extortions, and narcotics deals. They also found the program created problems for courts unable to enforce civil judgments against witnesses with new identities—everything from delinquent alimony and child support payments to failure to repay bank loans. In one six-month period, twenty witnesses were slapped with judgments in excess of $800,000.

Beyond the program's problems in dealing with criminals, there are leagues of stories reflecting its procedural difficulties: The witness who finds himself shuffled from pillar to post around the U.S., family in tow and children disoriented, unable to find a job that pays as well as his previous career; the family of a witness who doesn't exist because of a foul-up at WITSEC; a witness who is unable to get employment because the Social Security Administration is reluctant to issue new social security cards to the witnesses; or the witness who insists on attending the funeral of a parent, where anyone looking for them is bound to be lying in wait.

Even after a witness has been successfully relocated with a new name, there's the matter of finding work. Most witnesses arrive with minimal job skills but are accustomed to large incomes. If WITSEC could find jobs matching most witnesses' skill levels and income demands, the marshals, whose starting salary is about $20,000, would probably take them for themselves.

Just changing a witness's identity without leaving a trail—creating an entire history complete with birth certificate, military record, credit history, driver's license, medical record, on back to high school record and diploma—can be a nearly insurmountable problem.

Take for example the half-Hopi Indian witness who was given an Anglo identity; several years after entering the program he wanted his daughter to be eligible for native-American federal college scholarship money. Or the time Jean Fratianno's furniture arrived at her new location, where her new neighbors, who knew her as Jean Fisher, watched as movers unloaded crate after crate marked with the name "Martin," the identity she carried in her last incarnation.

WITSEC has become fodder for American exposé writers, and rightly so, for by its very nature it is bound to be plagued with problems. But the bad publicity has brought congressional hearings and some responses from government to improve the program.

To contain criminal-witness recidivism, Congress and the Justice Department have cracked down on who can and can't enter the program, ordering extensive applicant screening. The standard for admission has become one of weighing whether the need for a person's testimony is greater than the danger they pose to the community. However, it's a standard that is easily stretched to suit any situation, for the most valuable testimony generally is provided by the most heinous criminals, as demonstrated by a witness like Fratianno.

Congress also has ordered the creation of a fund to compensate victims of witnesses' crimes. WITSEC now has a twenty-two-page memorandum of understanding, a contract spelling out the WITSEC rules and regulations, that every witness and family member must read and initial before they get into the program. Any breach of these regulations, such as ignoring a civil judgment, can result in suspension of funding and protection.

The most common reason for being dropped from the program has been for breaching security, such as becoming involved with known criminals, visiting a place where the witness is known under his or her original identity, or refusing to leave an area after the cover story has been exposed.

In its first fifteen years of operation, twenty WITSEC clients were killed. But, says Safir, only after they themselves breached security.

"I wouldn't want to be in the witness program unless the alternative was being dead," says Safir. "Being in the witness program is not a reward for giving testimony. You get put in the witness program because the alternative is being killed. Yes, it's restrictive; yes, it's traumatic; and yes, it's certainly hard on family members—it's especially hard on children—but it's better than the alternative."

Some former WITSEC clients disagree with Safir; they have found alternatives other than being killed. WITSEC's restraints on its clients have caused many of the government's most potent witnesses to leave the program, fending for themselves or seeking sanctuary in customized makeshift programs created by the FBI.

Fratianno and several FBI agents complain that WITSEC sets out unilateral policy decisions, angering witnesses and dampening their interest in cooperating with the government. WITSEC, they say, is a caretaker of the FBI's courtroom gems and doesn't coordinate its activities well with the Bureau or prosecutors, delaying or complicating trials.

There is a strong territorial imperative at work here. Given their choice, most FBI supervisors would have Safir's WITSEC responsibilities handed over to the Bureau. There is deep animosity between FBI agents, who feel the marshals are nothing more than overblown summons servers, and the marshals, who feel the Bureau is dominated by egotistical, power-hungry agents.

On more than one occasion, Safir has met privately with FBI

supervisors in an effort to iron out their differences only to have the sessions end in screaming matches.

In fact, several times, tensions between WITSEC and the FBI became so great that Fratianno threatened to stop testifying for the government on the eve of major trials, requiring top Justice Department officials to step in to mediate the disputes.

Though the items Fratianno claimed essential were sometimes beyond reason, he still demanded and received no fewer than thirty audiences with Safir and officials of the Justice Department to plead his case. While he has lost more battles than he's won, the program has met his demands for increased finances, repeated changes in locations, paying for his phone bills, a period of funding for his mother-in-law, and some forms of elective surgery, such as a facelift, capped teeth, and breast implants for Jean. Among the items they have re-fused to underwrite were Jean's Cadillac, their gasoline bills, cleaning her furs, and new "security" draperies.

But Fratianno is the exception; the exceptional witness making exceptional demands. In his first eight years on the program he received more than $508,000 in funding.

Despite the social and legal issues they have raised, pleas to eradicate the tools created for law enforcement in 1968 and 1970—particularly Title III, RICO, and WITSEC—are few and far between.

The scope of the problems created by organized crime, the best-known variety being La Cosa Nostra, appear too real and threatening for society to turn back.

While the "Honored Society" has evolved into nothing more than a criminal conspiracy of sophisticated American gangsters, it has not lost sight of its primary goal: making money. Organized crime drives up the costs of industries, services, and goods for consumers through its domination of essential areas of commerce; they pervert the operation of government through political payoffs and bribery; and they threaten the lives of every citizen through drug trafficking.

Officials can only guess at the mob's cut from industries wholly dominated by organized crime, such as New York's $40-billion-a-year garment center or that city's docks, meat packing houses, construction business, and restaurants and bars.

There is no way to set a precise figure on La Cosa Nostra's tally in dollar and cents. Yet when narcotics trafficking, white-collar crime, and all varieties of organized criminal activity are added together, the lowest estimates begin at $80 billion a year and run to upwards of $150 billion a year. Meyer Lansky is said to have proclaimed: "We're bigger than U.S. Steel."

Bigger than U.S. Steel? Exxon, the Fortune 500's top corporation, reported net income of $5.5 billion on sales of $90.8 billion in 1985. The top twenty of the Fortune 500 in 1985 had net incomes of only $38.7 billion. The unpaid taxes bled from the economy by organized crime conceivably could start bringing the current $3 trillion national deficit under control by the end of the century. But taxing crime is an impossible contradiction in terms. So the next best thing is defeating them.

It took nearly twenty years, from the mid-1960s when they were first being drafted until the mid-1980s, for the resounding success of these new tools of law enforcement to become apparent. As of this writing, federal and state prosecutors, pooling their resources and applying those tools, have virtually closed down La Cosa Nostra in Cleveland and Los Angeles; indicted and convicted its leaders in New York, Kansas City, Chicago, Milwaukee, St. Louis, Pittston, Pennsylvania, and Boston; targeted and convicted crime leaders throughout the West and Midwest who held controlling interests in many Las Vegas hotels and casinos; forced the Teamsters to withdraw from Las Vegas; and initiated massive cases in union racketeering nationwide.

In every one of those cases, the common tool used by prosecutors has been the testimony of co-conspirators granted a plea-bargain deal or immunity from prosecution. And from every couple of convictions there arises another informant, another former defendant who opts for immunity or a reduced sentence in return for his information, which leads to new cases, more Title IIIs, and his testimony against others. It's a cycle of investigation and prosecution that keeps cutting deeper into La Cosa Nostra.

Many federal prosecutors are now predicting an end of La Cosa Nostra, at least in its current form, in this century. And they say the emerging crime groups—such as the so-called Jewish Mafia of the West, the motorcycle gangs, South American cocaine traffickers, and the Oriental varieties—will similarly fall as each is clearly identified.

But at what cost? At the cost of seeing a Ray Ferritto, who admits to at least one murder, or a Jimmy Fratianno, who's committed at least five or as many as eleven murders, go free after serving a minimal sentence? Is there justice in a system that uses a Fratianno to testify against white-collar criminals who have committed bankruptcy frauds, or crime bosses charged with extortions? Or, in Ferritto's case, is there justice in making a deal with the man who committed a murder while prosecuting those who hired him?

Granted, Fratianno is an extraordinary witness and has testified against so many organized crime figures and their associates that his collective testimony provides a compelling justification for the government's largess. But with a lesser witness, how is one to weigh the value of their testimony against their criminal acts and decide if they can go free under a new name? Is there a point at which the scales of justice are no longer in balance? And whose eye will make that determination?

As to the question of whether these witnesses should be believed in court, it is left to a jury to determine their value and credibility. But how well can these jurors stand up against someone who is virtually a professional witness skilled in courtroom technique? And how are they to weigh the testimony of a witness of little moral conviction, offered great incentives—perhaps his life—in return for testimony? They face a formidable task of foraging for the truth within a thicket of legal intricacies.

Booker T. Washington, when commenting on slavery, said that "You can't hold a man down without staying down with him," and graphically offered the image of the slave master climbing into the trenches, whip in hand, to keep slaves at labor. He used this image to argue that it was the lowering of their standards to maintain their society that destroyed the South.

Today, as prosecutors climb into bed with the likes of Fratianno and Ferritto, they argue that "Crimes aren't committed in church by members of the congregation and members of the choir aren't witnesses," so the government must take its witnesses where it finds them. Even if it means climbing into the trench.

A New
Crew

"I'LL TELL YA," Fratianno began. "What I really think happened with these two Tonys is that Jack Dragna, Louie's uncle, got money from Vegas gamblers to clip these guys. They'd caused trouble around that place for a long time. So he told me, 'They're out of line' and we had to clip them. And I said, 'Okay.' "

"Jimmy, just a second," Nick Lore broke in. "You mean just like that. He didn't tell you why or anything? The boss says go kill someone and you don't ask any questions. Just okay?"

"Yeah, if you want to live," Fratianno said earnestly.

Lore wasn't convinced. "Come on, weren't you curious?"

"Curious don't matter. You see, Nick, in this thing you don't ask no questions about why or what or nothing. You get an order, you carry it out. You know what I mean?"

Lore nodded. The other agents in the room, Ahearn, Dirkse, and Thompson, sat by, occasionally taking notes and adding their questions.

It was January 18, 1978. Fratianno's debriefing was beginning— an arduous task of reviewing over and over again details of his crimes. They needed to know everything about his criminal past and tap his mind for cases they could start developing.

They were up to August 6, 1951: Fratianno was a soldier, a rising star in the Family, who answered only to the boss. Jack Dragna had taken a liking to the young man, making him his aide-de-camp in recognition of his special qualities; he was bright, loyal, and possessed nerves of steel.

"So then these two Tonys shook down this guy, Sam, ah, Sammy. Shit, I can't remember his last name. Some Jewish kid. Anyway, Abe Benjamin calls me and tells me they're shaking down this Sammy, right? And the guy on the phone tells me to get them off his back. Now Abe works for me and Sammy. Sammy Lazes! That's his name, L-A-Z-E-S. Sammy Lazes is working for him.

"So I go back to Jack, met him at the Five O'Clock Club, and said—"

Dirkse recognized the name: "That was the place the boss, Nick Licata, owned. Right?"

"Yeah, right. But this is years before he was made boss. Dragna was still boss. So I met Jack and said, 'Lookit, this is a good chance for me to nail these two guys, to set them up.' And he says, 'Do what you can.'

"So in the meantime I arrange to meet with these guys in Sam London's apartment, okay? And I told them: 'Lookit you guys. You're out of line shaking these guys down, and, you know, it's no good, they belong to me, these guys. You want some money, you tell me and I'll help you get some money.' They says, 'Well, you know, we got this trial in Las Vegas, we need money for attorneys.' "

Fratianno paused, leaning forward and speaking in hushed conspiratorial tones, as he had to Tony Brancato and Tony Trombino twenty-seven years earlier.

"I said, 'Well, okay then. There's a gambling place down here where there's a big stakes card game tonight. Why don't you meet me here at about nine-thirty and we'll take a ride and see if we can get you some money. I think you can take the joint for maybe $15,000.'

"They asked some questions, and I tell them that I get a cut for setting it all up and bringing along another guy to help out. You know, I'm making out like their buddy, but it's still business, I'm getting a cut. So the thing sounds real, you know? And they say all right.

"Meanwhile, I go back to the Five O'Clock Club, and told Jack that we had it all set up and he said, 'Well, who do you want to take?' and I said Charlie Bats. Leo Moceri had a car and he was going to sort of be the back up, you see. And then another guy was around there, by the name of Procello, who'd help out.

"That night we were attending this fish fry at the club, maybe sixty or seventy people there, and this waitress is taking care of us and all. So we slip out through the back and it's maybe fifteen minutes to where I have to meet these guys. Meanwhile, in the car, I've got the tools and set of clothes to put on after I did the work.

"So what happened? They showed up, I don't remember when. Charlie and I get in the backseat and—I don't even think we said a word to them—I pull out my thirty-eight, I press it up against Brancato's head, and I shoot six times, and this fuckin' Charlie Bats just froze on me. So I said, 'What the fuck are you doing, man?' and I think he fired one shot. I think one of my shots ricocheted and hits this other Tony in the head. So I says to Charlie, 'You know, if I tell Jack you froze, you motherfucker, you're dead.'

"So anyhow, we got back and we meet Nick Licata's son and son-in-law and they take us back to this apartment where we change clothes and I wash good. Shampoo my hair and under my fingernails and all to get rid of the blood and gunpowder. I'm telling you, that fuckin' car was a mess, I was covered," he says, and he gestures his showering, shampooing, and nail-cleaning ritual and grimaces in disgust, recalling the spray of human blood and brain tissue that had covered him.

"It took maybe only forty-five minutes to do this whole operation and we slipped in the back of the club and I slipped back into my seat. No one even missed us. I mean, the waitress thought I'd been in the bathroom or something," he says, flushed with appreciation of his cunning.

"So the next morning, I know they're going to pick me up. So I set my clothes on the chair, nice. They come about five-thirty in the morning and they asked me what clothes I had on, and I show them the clothes. And they took me and the clothes downtown and booked me for murder, pending investigation."

Thompson interrupted: "Now why is it that the cops come to your door at dawn? I mean, how are they going to nail you for this job?"

"Are you kidding? I had a reputation already. The cops knew I was the only worker Jack had in those days and they were always comin' around on one case or another. Well, anyway, everybody from the club went down to the police a couple of days later and said, 'Lookit, this guy was in the bar with us until one in the morning.' You know. This waitress, a really well-built babe, she swore to it. I wish I could remember her name."

Fratianno pauses on the lost name.

"Yeah, Jim," Dirkse kidded. "Let us know if you remember it, we might be interested in looking her up."

Their joking seemed to go right by Fratianno. It was gnawing at him that he couldn't fill in the detail.

"Anyhow, about twelve or fourteen days later they release me and call me to the grand jury. This grand jury was meeting every Tuesday and every Tuesday I got hauled down there. About the third or fourth month these two detectives got this girl, the waitress, and burned her with cigarettes to make her say what they wanted. So come Tuesday, she walks into the grand jury with bandages all over her arms and I said, 'Hey honey, what happened to you?' And she told me about these detectives and I called Adolph Alexander, the prosecutor, and said, 'Hey man, what are you trying to do, frame me?' And that's when he dropped the whole case.

"After that they put these detectives on my detail and they followed me for like a year, and never got a thing," he said, seeming to conclude the story. But then, after a pause, he added for effect: "That's what they based the *Dragnet* movie on."

Lore, Dirkse, and Thompson listened as the stories of Fratianno's early days with La Cosa Nostra poured out—no hesitation, no unwillingness. They just came cascading from his mind. Vivid color and detail were available for the asking. His animated delight came with the price of admission; the hand gestures and a wide range of facial expressions evidencing concentration, surprise, anger, or terror.

Retelling the garrote murders—the strangulations of Louis "Russian Louie" Strauss, Frank Borgia, and Frank Niccoli—Fratianno summoned up all his storytelling abilities. His arms outstretched in a circle, he demonstrates the bear hug that an accomplice pressed on the victim; standing, he reaches into his pocket to remove the rope, one end of which he holds up in his left hand as he whips the length of imaginary cord in a circular motion with his right hand, entrapping the victim's neck. The other end of the garrote is handed to a third accomplice and together they each pull . . . harder . . . collapsing downward, until they were resting on the floor, beside Strauss's, Borgia's, or Niccoli's lifeless body, which was bathed in a pool of human excrement.

Fratianno tried to demonstrate the look of horror stitched to his victims' faces, but never got it quite to his satisfaction. No living soul, not even one with Fratianno's powers as a spellbinder, can re-create the look of sudden death by betrayal.

Those were his murders: the two Tonys, Borgia, Niccoli, and Strauss—two by gun, three by strangulation. Niccoli, he explained, had been a friend, but had aligned himself with Mickey Cohen, another Cleveland native, an enemy of Jack Dragna's. The other men Fratianno barely knew. But for each execution, he had befriended the victim, putting each at ease so he could stand close enough to see his eyes, hear his last breath.

He thoroughly enjoyed telling these tales without any fear of prosecution. The killings were decades old. They were mobsters. So no one really cared. He had been granted "use-immunity," so nothing he confessed to could be used against him without independent evidence—and there's scant chance of that. And besides, some might argue, confession is good for the soul.

As the stories proceeded, the agents noted something odd in how they were told. It was almost as if he were speaking in the "third person," that Fratianno was a witness, not a participant. There was always a sense of impersonal detachment; the murder was always the least of the matter, the focus was the cunning, the deceit that went into the preparation and escape.

His detachment was also apparent in his choice of words: He never "killed" anyone, they were always "clipped." The killer was never anything so graphic as a "hit man," but a "good worker." And they never used "guns" or "weapons," but rather "tools."

By the second day of debriefings, Fratianno began digressing, recounting his favorite scams, the little ones that were more entertaining than criminal; the contractors he had gotten laid as payoffs for highway construction jobs, or the days in Cleveland when the mob was running the town.

The agents found they had to allow him these digressions to clear his mind, to put him at ease before they hit him for the bigger stories.

"I'll tell ya, I had it made in those early days, before I came out West," he told his keepers. "I had it all working after I got sprung in forty-five. I did eight years on robbery, you know, and hit the streets running. All I wanted to do was make some quick money and fuck every good-lookin' broad in sight. I mean, I'd been walking around with a hard-on most of the time I'd been in prison and I felt like a mad dog in heat.

"In the first two weeks I was out, me and this friend, Frank Velenti, we hit this gambling joint, one of these social clubs in Erie, and I was working for the Teamsters throwing acid and busting heads at strikes—that was some good money. And I had a job at this Teamsters canteen, just to keep my parole officer happy, where I was switching their cash for counterfeit money I was buying at ten cents on the dollar.

"Anyway, on weekends, we'd always find a poker game somewhere and I'd take these poor motherfuckers for like a couple thousand sometimes. Forget about it; when my fingers were good, I could slip cards in and out of the deck like nobody.

"And after we left the game we'd go get these hookers, nice broads, and take them up to a hotel where we knew the owner and got the best suites for nothing; real decent places with a big sitting room and a bedroom. I'd turn all the lights off, draw the curtains and get fucked good in the bedroom. Well, then I'd tell this broad that I had to go get something in the other room and when I'd go out, me and Frank would switch places. Now in the dark there, we wouldn't say nothin' and these broads didn't know that there was a new guy in the sack with them.

"So anyway, later we'd switch again and at the end of the night, I'd pay this broad with a counterfeit ten." His rapid-fire delivery stops for the punch line: "I was getting fucked by two top-notch broads in a night for a dollar," he said, now beside himself with delight, and as proud about it as any major scam he'd ever pulled.

Ahearn and Lore were waiting in the marshals' conference room at MCC when Fratianno returned from lunch.

"It's showtime, Jimmy," Ahearn said.

"What? What happens now?" Fratianno asked, making whistling and clicking noises to clear food from between his teeth.

"Now we go over the Bompensiero killing—again," Ahearn said, handing Fratianno a half dozen of his favorite cigars. "By the way, how does McDonald get these Havanas for you?"

Biting the butt end from one, Fratianno looked for a trash can and then spat the wrapper out, hitting everything but the target. "Friends, Jim. Just friends," he said and chuckled.

"My buddy here been treating you right?" Ahearn asked, nodding toward Lore. He was trying to draw Fratianno closer to Lore, so he could fade from the daily hand-holding and return to his duties in San Francisco.

"I guess. But I really could use some decent food and a little exercise. This food is rotten and there's nothing to do around here when you guys aren't around."

"We're working on getting you out of here, Jimmy. Just bear with me for a while," Lore said. "And I'll make a run to India Street tomorrow for some cold cuts."

"Be sure you get some of that sweet sausage, Nick. And some cheeses, maybe some artichoke salad—"

"Okay, okay. Enough on the menu," Ahearn interrupted. "I'm sure Nick will see to it that you're fed. Let me tell you about the schedule. This L.A. case is getting top priority. So for the next few weeks every agent who's had anything to do with Bomp's murder or PORNEX is going to be in here grilling you. Nick and [Special Agent Bill] Fleming will be handling the Bomp murder part. And Nick and I will be around as much as we can when the others come in."

"Good, I don't care who's coming as long as you two are close by," Fratianno said.

"We will be, Jimmy. But we're not here to save your ass on the tough questions. A bunch of these guys belong to Jack Barron and they're not looking to make friends with you so—"

"I can handle them, Jim," Fratianno said with a deep chortle. "I'll make monkeys out of the bastards."

"No, you don't understand. You don't handle these guys that way. All you've got to do is tell the truth as best you can. They're not going to trip you up if you're honest. We're not in San Francisco anymore. Now you play it our way and that means every question gets an answer, no matter how much it hurts; a truthful answer."

"Jim," Fratianno whined. "Don't keep telling me that. I'm not going to tell no lies; I ain't got nothing to lie about. But I'm not going to let Barron's guys fuck me either."

"Good, just keep it all honest. Anyway, after a few weeks, maybe toward the end of February, we're going to start opening the doors, a few at a time, to a whole bunch of agents from out of town who want to see you."

"Okay," Fratianno said, with a quick, nonchalant shrug.

"Now, Jimmy, I want you to take it back to the start," Lore said. "I know you've been through some of this stuff about Bomp's murder with Jim, but I haven't heard it. So let's take it from the very top."

"Well, I knew they wanted to clip Bomp for a long time. Is that what you mean?" Fratianno asked.

"Yeah, that's fine for now," Lore said. "But let's get into what you knew and when."

"You see, Nick, he had a bad mouth, Bomp did. He was always spouting off. He didn't show the right respect for people. Like years ago, in 1947, or 1948, we used to go to the track at Del Mar together . . ."

Almost in unison, Lore and Ahearn put their pens down. They could see what was coming. Spend a few hours with Fratianno and it quickly becomes apparent that the only way to get to the heart of a matter is through the back door, letting him ramble for a while.

"So one time, we're sitting in these box seats, and I poked Bomp and pointed at this fella sitting in the box in front of us, a few rows down and said, 'Hey Bomp, lookit there, it's J. Edgar Hoover.' That's who it was. And this Bomp says right out loud, so's everyone can hear, 'Ah, that J. Edgar's a punk, he's a fuckin' degenerate queer.'

"Well, everyone turns around, including this group of agents sitting with Hoover, and I just started cursing at him, really quiet, and then walked away. About ten minutes later, Bomp got up to go to the can and I walked over to him and walking up right behind me, where I don't see him, is Hoover, and I says, 'Bomp, that's not the right way to talk about this guy, you can't call him a degenerate.' And Hoover, right behind me says, 'Yeah, Frank, what do you make cracks like that for? What did I ever do to hurt you?'

"Now I'm standing there frozen. Right? Right in the middle of these two guys. And this Bomp doesn't even bat an eyelash. Just stands there with his fat cigar stuffed in the corner of his mouth. Smiling, he looks over at Hoover and says, 'Ah, I was just bullshitting, you know how it is, having a little fun with the boys.' And Hoover, like some hurt little kid, says, 'Well, Frank, that's not a nice way to talk about me, especially when I have people with me.' "

Lore and Ahearn were trying to keep straight-faced.

"Listen, Jimmy, I don't want to get side-tracked," Lore said. "But how does Hoover know Bomp?"

"Nick, this Hoover used to come down to LaJolla every winter and he knew all the guys who hung around the track," Fratianno said. "I'll tell you about this guy; I think he liked being around the wise guys."

"Okay, we get the picture; let's get on with Bomp's murder," Ahearn said. "Do you know why they killed him, and *if* you know, how do you know?"

Fratianno thought for a moment. "Well, it's like I'm telling you, he had a bad mouth. I mean, I know they said he wasn't showing the proper respect to the Family. Brooklier told me that before we knew he was an informant. He told me, 'We're going to have to dump him.' "

"By that he meant—"

"He meant we were going to clip him," Fratianno interrupted before Lore could finish his question.

"When was that? When did he tell you this?" Ahearn asked.

"I don't remember," Fratianno said in an annoyed tone.

"Well, was it before he went to prison in seventy-five or after he got out?" Lore asked.

"Before."

"How long before?"

"A few months. Maybe less," Fratianno answered slowly.

"Well, was it winter, springtime, or when?"

"I'm not sure."

"Okay, where was it that you spoke with him?"

And then there was silence. Fratianno was thinking. Ahearn and Lore looked at each other. There was suddenly a chill on Fratianno's gleeful storytelling.

Ahearn broke the silence. "Jimmy, you're going to have to do better than that."

"I'm trying. I'm just not real good on dates. Never have been," Fratianno said, rolling his cigar between thumb and fingers.

Unlike the murder stories or the statements he had previously given Ahearn about Bomp's death, there was clearly a greater significance to this debriefing. He was going to have to stand up in court sometime and repeat this tale.

While his spirit was willing, his mind, trained to contain these matters, had trapped the words, blurred the details. A lifetime of treachery had educated his tongue; he was capable of telling tales of apparent intrigue but little significance, and he could lay down a bold-faced lie without flinching or recast an entire conversation to avoid answering a question. But if he was going to be of service to the government, he would have to start relearning, or perhaps learning for the first time, how to speak with some modicum of honesty. He was learning to let go, to trust.

This learning process made these sessions so much more difficult than they already had to be. But gradually, over two weeks, the story came out in bits and pieces, with interruptions for digressions and only in response to specific questions by as many as a dozen agents who had expertise in some area of the case.

On each occasion, the interviewers had to warm Fratianno to the story. Each began with Louis Tom Dragna, with Brooklier's approval, asking Jimmy to be "with him" in running the Family while Brooklier and Sam Sciortino were in prison. That was sometime in the spring of 1975.

Then about a month later, before Brooklier and Sciortino went off to prison, there was a private meeting at a friend's office in the Los Angeles Clothing Mart, which was not far from where Dragna's business, Roberta Company, was churning out women's wear and $10 million in annual sales.

Brooklier took Fratianno aside and asked if he was still close to Bompensiero. Fratianno told him that they were good friends and spoke frequently, to which Brooklier said, "If you don't straighten him out, we'll take care of him."

"They told me that's why they brought me in to work with Louie, because they figured I was the only one could get close enough to clip this guy. They didn't have no love for me and I didn't have no love for them. I could have done it in a minute. I had Bomp in Frisco lots of times. But I said, 'Fuck these guys,' and just let it go."

He recalled two meetings in San Pedro that summer at which he and Dragna discussed Bompensiero. The first was in front of a liquor store, the other at a Denny's. They decided to make Bompensiero the Family *consiglieri* "to relax him" and make it easier "to clip him."

It was also at those meetings that Fratianno came up with the plan "to clip Bomp near his pay phone. You know, we'd have him go out there regular for business calls. We'd set up a routine that he'd get comfortable with."

It was after the second of those meetings, Fratianno recalled, that Bompensiero phoned him and suggested that this new porno outfit, Forex, would be an easy mark for the Family to shake down. Fratianno begged off, he wanted no part in it; Forex was an unknown quantity, they could be aligned with another Family, and it wasn't worth the risk.

Fratianno said the next discussions about killing Bompensiero didn't occur until about December of 1976, after Brooklier returned from prison. They met in Beverly Hills at the law offices of Brooklier's son where the elder Brooklier privately told Fratianno, "We're going to take care of him."

And weeks later, at the home of a mutual friend in Palm Springs, Brooklier again took Fratianno aside. This time he said, "Bomp is a wrong guy and he's no good," which Fratianno translated to mean that Bomp was suspected of being an informant and would have to be killed.

"Well, by that time I was out of it. I mean, this Brooklier was a fuckin' imbecile and I wanted nothing to do with him or his schemes. And besides, Bomp wasn't no threat to me."

It was November of 1976 when Fratianno and members of the Family—Jack LoCicero, Mike Rizzi, and Thomas Ricciardi—were served with subpoenas from the grand jury looking into the PORNEX case. The agents who served the subpoenas were the same men who had posed as pornographers; the men LoCicero, Rizzi, and Ricciardi had shaken down on Bomp's recommendation.

"That's when we knew for sure that Bomp was an informant," Fratianno said.

"You knew?" Lore asked. "Or were you just speculating?"

"Nick, we knew. Lookit. Right after the subpoenas come out I called this Bomp and said, 'Hey man, what the fuck is going on here? How did you learn about this Forex company?' Now he was really rattled. He told me that he'd been introduced to them by a guy who ran a pornography store. Well, I told him it didn't look good and everyone thought he was full of shit and he raced off the phone saying he'd straighten it out.

"A few days go by, and then I get a call and it's Bomp. He says, 'Remember that thing we were talking about? Well, Bye, Bye Blackbird.' Well, this crazy motherfucker. I said, 'What are you talking about?' and he said it again: 'Bye, Bye Blackbird.'

"He wanted me to think he clipped this guy who set him up. So I called around to a few guys in San Diego and they checked it out and there wasn't no one missing. No murders. Nothing. That cinched it."

Lore shook his head. "What I'm saying, Jimmy, is that you were kind of guessing. I mean, you didn't have any confirmation that he was an informant, you didn't have an agent telling you or anything like that."

"Hey man, you'd have to be a fuckin' idiot not to put this picture together. There's no other way to figure it. Of course Bomp was an informant," Fratianno protested.

In Fratianno's recollection, he heard no more talk about Bompensiero's murder until the first week in February 1977, when he got a call at a friend's restaurant from Tommy Ricciardi. Ricciardi asked Fratianno to call Bomp and have him go to the pay phone. "I thought maybe I'd just forget about it, you know, never make the call. But then I'd be their next target. So I called and I figured that was it, they'd clip him as he left the phone booth.

"A couple hours later, just to check, I called his house. Well, I'll be a dirty cocksucker, Bomp answers the phone. I just hung up without saying a word."

A few days later Bompensiero showed up in San Francisco with a few friends—Jimmy Styles, Chris Petti, and Abe Chapman—and asked Fratianno to join them for dinner at Montefusco's Restaurant.

"Now, I didn't say nothing to Bomp. I knew this poor motherfucker was as good as dead while we were sitting there drinking wine and eating. But that was his fuckin' problem. If I warned him, it would become my problem."

It was the next night, on February 10, Fratianno recalls, while he was dining out with Skinny Velotta and a girlfriend, that news came over the radio that Bomp had been gunned down near the phone booth outside his home.

"I think all I said was, 'So, the poor motherfucker's dead. That's the way it goes,' or something like that. I wasn't about to make no confession or nothing."

Fratianno said he kept to himself for the next couple of months. It wasn't until the spring of 1977, while Fratianno was in Palm Springs trying to patch things up with Jean, that he next met with Brooklier. Sciortino picked him up at the Biltmore condo. As they drove, he recalls Sciortino telling him, "We eliminated Frank and there's more to come."

Brooklier and Fratianno had a long conversation that day. Brooklier was upset by Fratianno's misrepresentations about his running the Family. Fratianno denied he had ever made any such claims. "I told him that by telling people I was with Louie Dragna, they assumed that I was running the Family.

"Then he starts saying, 'I understand there's another faction.' You see, Sciortino is giving him this shit. He don't like me, he's threatened and wants me out of the way. So he's telling Brooklier that I was putting together a new crew to take over.

"Then Brooklier says, 'There are too many people informing' and he wanted it to stop. He made a fist and pointed his thumb down, like ordering a hit, and says, 'Things are going to straighten up around here and there will be no more of this.' So, I told him, 'Hey, what's going on here, Dom? This is a lot of bullshit. I saved your life in the forties when you was with Mickey Cohen. Jack Dragna was going to kill you if it wasn't for me. Remember that? You owe me a little respect. Now I'm telling you, there's no other faction. Dom, you're getting some bad information, you're listening to some fuckin' assholes.' Well, I think he bought it. Because he says to me, 'Well, I just wanted to hear it from you.'

"So we ironed out our differences, or at least I thought we did, and we had some nice talk. And then he told me, 'I made the call when Frank got hit.' You see, he was the one who got Bomp to go out to the pay phone."

The agents scribbled notes furiously as Fratianno rattled along.

It was during that conversation, Fratianno said, that he first realized all of Brooklier's concerns. It wasn't only that Bompensiero had been disrespectful and an informant—certainly sufficient grounds to have him killed. But it seems perhaps most significant to Brooklier that Bompensiero was shaping a new faction, a new order within the Los Angeles Family.

Since the 1930s, there had always been three La Cosa Nostra families on the West Coast: Los Angeles, San Francisco, and San Jose. The most powerful of the three had always been Los Angeles, to which San Diego was an appendage. But suspicions were running high that Bomp had been looking to create a new Family in San Diego, possibly staging a coupe and, with the aid of Joseph Bonanno, overthrowing Brooklier.

In defiance of La Cosa Nostra rules, Bomp had been in touch with Bonanno, New York's exiled mob boss, who was living in Tucson, Arizona. Bonanno had been off-limits to all La Cosa Nostra members since staging his own kidnapping in 1964 to evade a federal grand jury subpoena and to defy the bosses of the other Five Families, whose turf he had been raiding. In 1966, when Bonanno again surfaced in New York, the bosses decided to spare his life and instead banished him from the city.

During 1976, Brooklier heard reports that Bompensiero was trying to rehabilitate Bonanno, appealing to powerful mob bosses in New York, Denver, and Chicago to let him establish a new Family—an expansion team—in a neutral Southwest territory.

"Yeah, we heard from informants that Bomp was traveling around the country, talking to the bosses, plotting to get Bonanno reinstated so they could take over," Lore said.

"There may have been rumors, but there was no fuckin' plot," Fratianno said. "Look, Bomp wasn't interested in taking over in L.A. You have to be elected boss by the members and Bomp didn't have the juice for that. And Bonanno knows there's no way he's going back into action. I don't even know the guy, never spoke to him. But he

knows New York would clip him in a hot fuckin' minute if he tried
to get back into this thing.

"To be honest with you, I know Bomp used to talk like that. I
mean, he'd say things like 'I'm taking over this Family' and 'Those
guys don't tell me what to do in San Diego, this is my town.' But the
only guy who ever thought about taking over was me. I had the juice
to get elected boss if Sciortino and Brooklier weren't in my way. And
I had a really good crew, guys who weren't afraid to do a little work."

Fratianno's last piece of information on Bomp's murder was based
on a meeting in May at Bobby's Restaurant, a New York City Garment
District saloon.

"I got Ricciardi alone at the bar and asked him about that night
he'd called me. Well, he told me they could have clipped Bomp that
night, but wanted to follow him and see how long it took him and
all. Kind of a dry run. Then he tells me he was the one that clipped
Bomp and that's why he was made. He said the old bastard really
put up quite a fight and he had to shoot him a couple of times before
LoCicero and he drove out of there."

During the first wave of interviews, agents came from up and down
the West Coast, filling Fratianno's every waking hour. There was an
endless stream of agents, sometimes six or ten at a time, packed into
the MCC's small conference rooms.

They fired off questions and scribbled notes as he talked; played
him wiretaps on which he had been picked up so he could flesh out
the topics of his carefully guarded conversations; asked him to identify
people accompanying him in surveillance photos; and ran through
long lists of names, trying to establish pedigrees for every mob hanger-
on in the West and Southwest.

Fratianno told them secrets of his organization and they told him
the secrets of theirs. They traded old war stories and discussed wiretaps, undercover operations, and new areas of investigation being
opened into mob control of Vegas casinos, the Teamsters, and insurance companies.

He began arriving for what he called "my interviews" toting a
small leather-bound address book and notepad, in which he would
jot down agents' phone numbers or make notations of a matter he
wanted to bring up with authorities later. These sessions were becoming his work and he was throwing himself into it.

Sometimes he'd call Skinny Velotta or an old girlfriend—before word of his cooperation got out—to verify his story or to get some detail of which he was uncertain. But it was rare that he needed assistance. Once he overcame his initial reluctance his memory proved remarkable. Sparked by a name or incident, he would launch into his involvement or detailed knowledge of that person or affair without the slightest pause to gather his thoughts, but always taking advantage of an opportunity to digress into his favorite tales.

The agents found themselves taken by his adventures and allowed a lot of time in their schedules for these episodes. But they also came away from these meetings with more business than they bargained for.

In the first two months of 1978, Fratianno offered many road maps to the routes he or the West Coast mob traveled in recent years. Most were history lessons. Others gave a voice of authenticity to what was already suspected. Some led to investigative paths lawmen had never imagined.

He opened up about the shakedowns of pornographers and book-makers in which the Family had been involved since the early 1970s. He described the phone calls from Brooklier telling him to go to San Diego to help LoCicero take over Bompensiero's old rackets—loan-sharking, real estate, and vending machines—or to shake down casino operators, like Benny Binion at the Horseshoe Casino in Vegas.

There had been meetings he attended in New York City with the bosses of the Gambino and Genovese crime Families to plot murders of informants, loan-shark investments at the Premier Theatre, and turf battles over the control of bookmaking in different parts of the country.

They heard tales of his links to the Teamsters, how each mob Family had a favorite son in the Teamsters whom they promoted into a leadership role, and about his meetings with Jackie Presser and Allen Dorfman, who ran the Teamsters Central State Pension Fund, who assisted in his schemes for ripping off union benefit plans.

He told of trips to Chicago to see Joey Aiuppa, who had told Jimmy how the Chicago, Kansas City, Cleveland, and Milwaukee crime Families were siphoning money out of the casinos or showrooms at the Tropicana, Stardust, and Fremont hotels in Las Vegas.

He described how Tony Spilotro used Lefty Rosenthal as a legitimate front to control Chicago's interests in Vegas, and how Spilotro was paying off cops to get advance warning of grand juries convening or imminent arrests.

He snitched on San Francisco Teamsters boss Rudy Tham, a longtime friend, explaining how Tham had misappropriated union funds and used his position to get free hotel rooms, or to smuggle contraband into the city through connections on the docks.

And he told anyone who would listen that Ray Ferritto had lied about Fratianno's involvement in Cleveland's gang wars.

It was a very productive couple of weeks.

FBI agents were generating hundreds of pages of reports from meetings with Fratianno, and they were teletyping agents throughout the country about what they were learning. Lore was going back to Fratianno almost daily to flesh out some detail or resolve an apparent contradiction in his statements, which would generate yet another set of reports.

Throughout all of this there were no challenges raised to Fratianno's veracity, just searches for details of when, where, and who. Agents were just taking down his statements; it would be left to the prosecutors and further investigation to see if the stories stood up.

But ultimately the prosecutors would accept Fratianno's tales as gospel, justifying their suspicions. They would use these tales as road maps and seek evidence to support his statements, not to take them apart.

On Sunday, February 12, 1978, Fratianno began his first traveling road show, telling the mob gospel according to Jimmy Fratianno. Under the direction of Bud McPherson, chief U.S. Marshal in Los Angeles, three unmarked Chevys secreted Fratianno out of MCC, up Interstate 5 from San Diego, and into Los Angeles, where he was held overnight at a U.S. Navy base in Santa Anna.

The next morning the grand jury convened before normal business hours to hear Fratianno's version of the Bompensiero murder and the Family's porno operations. The story was essentially the same one he had been telling Lore, Ahearn, and the other agents for the past three weeks.

Two weeks later the grand jury would bring a RICO indictment incorporating the charges from the original PORNEX case, which the government had withdrawn in light of Fratianno's testimony. The new indictment would charge the Los Angeles Family of La Cosa Nostra as the racketeering "enterprise" with the pornography extortions and the conspiracy to murder Bompensiero the underlying acts. Fratianno's testimony was the key. Brooklier, Sciortino, Dragna, Rizzi,

LoCicero, and Ricciardi—all of those who had turned against Fratianno—came under indictment.

On the night of February 14, Fratianno was on the move again. Under cover of darkness he flew into Cleveland on a commercial airliner. Three cars waited on the tarmac. Fratianno, McPherson, and another marshal were permitted to leave the plane first; they were met by a team of six heavily armed U.S. Marshals who whisked him off to a county jail in Sandusky for the evening.

The next morning, February 15, in a specially arranged appearance in an old courthouse on the shores of Lake Erie, Fratianno stood with McDonald before James Carroll, the common pleas judge, to enter his guilty plea to the state's charges of conspiring to murder Danny Greene.

The courthouse wasn't open for business yet as Judge Carroll pushed and prodded at Fratianno, almost urging him not to take the guilty plea. The law required Carroll to do everything in his power to avoid a coerced plea and confession.

It was touch and go for a while. Fratianno still wasn't willing to admit any direct involvement. But he understood that the only way he was going to secure his deal for protection from the feds was to go down on the Cleveland charges.

After dancing around a while he conceded he had known about the plot to kill Greene. Carroll accepted his guilty pleas to murder, arson, and engaging in organized crime. Sentencing would be suspended until Marino filed his sentencing report.

To leave Fratianno with something to think about, Carroll added that all the charges against him could and would be reinstated if he didn't testify satisfactorily in the state or federal trials in which he was involved.

By the time lawyers for the seven remaining defendants learned of the plea bargain, at a hearing in Judge Carroll's courtroom that morning, Fratianno was already on a plane heading back to Los Angeles.

The plea sparked outrage from defense lawyers and, more importantly, a flurry of publicity, much of it inaccurate, about how Fratianno had cut his deal with the government and the "scores of murders" he was responsible for. They also reported on plans for him to appear as a witness in Los Angeles and a $100,000 mob contract on his life.

The next morning, February 16, Fratianno appeared in Federal

District Court in Los Angeles, prepared to enter a guilty plea there also, but flinched at the last moment, uncertain over the disposition of the murders and his deal for protection and funding.

Fratianno's deal with the government wouldn't be formally completed until the end of the year, but the publicity generated by his appearance in Judge Carroll's courtroom ended any lingering hope Fratianno might have entertained about returning to the streets.

Upon his return to MCC the second wave of agents began. At first just a trickle, but soon Lore was inundated with requests.

In short order, the line of agents became too long and Fratianno's frustration at being cooped up in small rooms all day became too great. Lore made arrangements for an apartment—at first an agent's home, later he rented a penthouse in downtown San Diego—where Fratianno could meet "my agents" and "my DAs," and conduct "my interviews" in a more comfortable setting.

He would be ushered into the garage at MCC under heavy guard, placed in an unmarked van, and, under escort of three marshals' cars, driven to the apartment. He got to wear his street clothes when he left MCC, but returned each evening in prison-issue overalls and workshirt.

Despite his pleas, Lore would never let Fratianno spend the night there, go out for meals, or call up an old girlfriend to come visit. Still, Fratianno was satisfied with the arrangement. He could order out for food, had the devoted attention of the agents, and every so often found someone in the group foolish enough to bet with him on a sporting event.

He was again the center of attention; a fact that wasn't lost on the other MCC inmates. Among the eight or ten inmates being held at the witness security wing in San Deigo at any given time there was always a top cat, a cock of the walk, someone the government was willing to do a little extra for, someone who was bound to draw the ire of his fellow inmates. And Fratianno was the unmistakable target during most of 1978.

After doing more than seventeen years in prison without ever getting into trouble, Fratianno seemed unable to remain at MCC for more than a week at a time without getting into fights and landing in the hole—an isolated hospital unit: the same one in which Patty Hearst had served a good portion of her prison time.

Inmate Marion Pruett was the leader of the pack. Together with

Frank Woods, Steve Thomas, and Gary Bodash, Pruett would create elaborate schemes to taunt Fratianno.

One time they set Carl, a hulking, black inmate, on Fratianno's case. They told him that Fratianno had made some disparaging remarks about blacks, which was not uncharacteristic of Fratianno. One afternoon, when Fratianno was in the dayroom playing pool, Carl came up alongside him and decked him with a sucker punch. Fratianno scrambled to his feet, raced for a pool cue, and hollered, "I'm going to kill you, you nigger cocksucker. . . ." Before he could take a swing the guards were on him and he was on his way to solitary.

Days after he returned to the security wing, guards came to Fratianno's room and told him to pack his gear; he was moving. Pruett and Bodash had sent a letter to the warden claiming Fratianno had been phoning newspaper reporters, leaking stories about MCC.

"Nick, I ain't the one using those phones," Fratianno later protested. "It's those other motherfuckers. Send them into solitary."

Fratianno was right. It was Pruett and his crew who were phoning reporters—telling the *San Diego Union*, among others, that Fratianno was being held there, a valuable and closely guarded piece of information.

By that time Fratianno was getting national attention. Reporters were relaying his cooperation to a public thirsting for Mafia stories. *Time* magazine was ahead of the pack, reporting his appearance before the Los Angeles grand jury days after he got back to San Diego.

And then there were the inmates, like Clayton Dawson, who tried to climb aboard Fratianno's high profile to gain mileage for their own cause. Dawson told agents that, a year or so earlier, he'd been offered $50,000 by Brooklier's crew to kill Fratianno and Bompensiero. Investigators weren't impressed; the story lacked detailed credibility.

When confronted with the story, Fratianno told Lore, "This guy is some piece of shit. He ain't no worker. He told me about this contract bullshit a few weeks ago and I told him, 'So why didn't you collect on it, motherfucker?' "

The resentment of his fellow inmates forced Fratianno to become a loner and pressed him ever closer to the agents and prosecutors for daily companionship and sustenance. When he wasn't being interviewed, he would spend at least a few hours a day, six or seven days a week, in MCC's conference room with Lore, eating, talking about his life, or arranging for more interviews.

There was a rapport developing between the two men. Lore was coming to genuinely care about Fratianno, and so he didn't object to running errands or extending his caretaking into weekends. He found Fratianno engaging; he had a thousand remarkable stories to tell; he was bright and had a good sense of humor.

For his part, Fratianno respected Lore, a soft-spoken, gentle soul who was a tenacious interrogator, a man with the ability to cut through all of Jimmy's bunk and go directly to the heart of a matter.

Lore understood, as few others would, Fratianno's insatiable greed, the high value he placed on trust, and the necessity to avenge betrayal among these "men of respect." In Lore's view, Fratianno wasn't co-operating merely to save his life, though certainly the Cleveland indictment, with its threat of the electric chair, and the prospects of protection and government funding for him and his family were in-centives. Lore was one of the few people who understood that it was the betrayal and the need for vengeance that drove Fratianno.

What disturbed Lore, and what he couldn't fathom, was Fratian-no's utter lack of contrition for the murders. Lore was appalled that such a bright and charismatic man could be a killer.

"Nick, in this thing you're just like a soldier, you know what I mean? You follow orders."

"Come on, it's not that simple," Lore contended. "You're telling me you don't feel one way or the other about it; it's just business?"

"I guess so. I mean, I never clipped no one who didn't deserve it. Like the time this guy was roughing up my wife, I just stepped in and broke it up; I got hit a few times and never even touched the guy. But these guys I fucked with all were gangsters; they knew what was coming."

Fratianno bristled at the question no matter how many different ways it was posed. His attitude demanded: "How could you ask such a question?"

He had always taken pride in being a "worker," having the courage to do what other men shied away from. And it had earned him respect. Yet there was a twist on reality here. Fratianno's view was that these men were at war with each other. Murder is permitted at times of war, or condoned as a means of capital punishment. There was no difference here, he would argue.

"I didn't kill no innocent people. Let's put it that way."

While Jimmy was busy making cases, Jean was doing time. The day Jimmy signed his bare-bones agreement with Ahearn and DeFeo, Jean's life was suddenly ripped out from under her.

At first, FBI agents surrounded the Palm Springs condo. She was told not go outside or make phone calls without approval. And they told her she couldn't use the pool without their okay. This went on for several days before Jean decided "the hell with this" and walked out to the pool for her daily workout, trailed by an entourage of agents in three-piece suits and sunglasses.

After a few days she got a call from Terry Walters, a U.S. Marshal, who instructed her to pack a bag with enough clothing for a few days and meet him at the Bonaventure Hotel in Los Angeles.

"I don't want to go anywhere," she told Walters. "No one around here knows who I am, I mean about Jimmy. Why can't I stay here?"

Walters was unyielding. "Let me put it to you this way," he said. "About a year ago a young couple in Las Vegas wanted to wait an extra day, they wanted a little more time to think about going into the program. They were killed that night."

Jean packed her bag: bathing suits, a few light dresses, silk blouses, a pair of gabardine slacks, and a trench coat, sweater, and her mink for the evenings.

A week later, after signing away her life to the Marshals Service in Los Angeles, Jean and her little bag of possessions were plunked down in Boise, Idaho, where it was the dead of winter. Her mother, who had been living with her in Palm Springs, came along. They were escorted by a marshal to a motel where he left them. The extent of her protection from that moment on was the local marshal's home and office phone numbers and his occasional visits.

On one of their few outings Jean and her mother went to a bookstore where they pored through every book they could find on the Witness Security Program. They were distressed by the unanimous conclusion: Given the opportunity, none of those who had been on the program would do it again.

It could have been Idaho's deep freeze or the negative appraisal of WITSEC. In any case, her mother didn't last the month.

"Now sweety, you take good care of yourself," Jean remembers her mother saying as the woman boarded a plane bound for LAX. "Eat all the good vitamin foods you can. And if they send you someplace warm let me know"; with that she flew off into an overcast morning.

Jean didn't fare much better. Her idea of winter, her notion of cold, was when the mercury dipped down into the low fifties. She tried to adjust. She even considered buying "one of those ridiculously shapeless, puffy down coats." But on the $15 a day the program provided for expenses she couldn't afford it.

And Jimmy was of little help to her. He couldn't receive calls at MCC and he wasn't supposed to know where she was. So they passed messages through Dennis McDonald, who relayed such advice as "sell your jewelry and furs if you need money."

For a woman like Jean, selling the jewels and furs would be a measure of desperation, and she hadn't sunk to that depth yet.

She began complaining long and loud to the marshals that her health was failing in this climate. They must move her someplace warm. By March, her complaints were being heard, and she was moved to Seattle and placed in a Hilton hotel.

Seattle was "a nice little town," and Jean found her way around pretty quickly. The temperature was above freezing and the place seemed to have potential.

After a few days, Jean wandered into a Unitarian Church about a mile from her hotel. There was a prayer meeting underway. People seemed nice enough; they were welcoming and didn't ask too many questions for which she didn't have answers.

One man, his first name was Bob, seemed particularly nice, well-dressed, articulate; probably a professional of some sort. After the meeting, they stopped for coffee.

She introduced herself as "Jean, just Jean"—she didn't know her new name yet, or, for that matter, anything else about who she was supposed to be. She told him she had just arrived from Boise, and what a pleasure it was to be out of the cold. She talked about growing up in Southern California. She said she moved to Seattle because of, "Well, uh, my husband's work . . . he works for the government."

"We're living over at the Hilton until we get settled," she said.

As they walked toward his car, parked in a private garage, Bob suggested, "Hey, the night's young. Why don't we go over to the hotel, get your husband, and I'll show you around a little."

"Well, Jimmy's out of town and I'm a little worn out. But I'll take a ride over there, if you don't mind."

Bob helped Jean into his Buick Electra, tossing her trench coat in the backseat. He stood holding the door as she sat, and then bent toward her, pressing his left hand against her chest, his mouth against hers, while groping under her dress.

"You shit," she screamed, pulling her face away and trying to get out from under his arm.

She reached for his face with her nails, but in her panic was unable to gain enough grip to do any damage. He pressed her flat on the front seat of the car as he lifted her dress to her thighs and ripped away her underwear. His hand was working at opening her blouse.

Jean began to scream. In a reflex action, he removed his hand from her chest to cover her mouth and Jean took advantage of the moment. She shifted her body upward to gain some leverage and swung her right leg up between his legs, catching him squarely in the groin. For an instant, he continued trying to pull at her clothes, and then his knees gave way and he collapsed, moaning on the cement floor.

Jean grabbed her coat and ran out of the garage, hailing a cab for the ride to the Hilton. She packed, went out to the airport, and wrote a worthless check for plane fare to San Francisco. While waiting for the late flight, she called McDonald to have him pick her up when she arrived.

"I'm through with that program," she told McDonald. "I'm going to take Jimmy's car and get away. I don't know where I'm going, but I'm not staying with those people anymore."

When Jimmy called McDonald the next morning he was surprised to find Jean there. After filling him in on what an awful time she'd been having, Jean got down to business.

"I'm taking your car and leaving. You know I've got to be desperate if I'm taking that pimpcar of yours. I don't know where I'll end up, so I'm going out this morning to put new tires—"

"Hey babe, I just put new radials on, Dunlaps, don't worry about it."

"Yeah, but your friend Skinny took your brand new radiums, or whatever you call them, and put his worn out tires on the car."

"He what!" Jimmy yelled. "That dirty motherfucker."

"And I'm going to need money, cash. Dennis said he'd lend me a few thousand."

"There's no need for that. Lookit, here's what you do. I had Bob Sigliano sell the condo last month and there should be a check for our share of the profits, in your name at that bank, I think it's the Crocker, in Palm Springs."

"How much?"

"I don't know for sure, but I guess we had about $6,500 in furniture and he sold it for 72, so our profits are like $12,000 or $14,000."

Jean left the next morning for Murietta Hot Springs, where friends were holding eleven suitcases containing her clothing and possessions from the Palm Springs condo.

When she got to the bank and found only $7,200 waiting for her she raised a little hell, but then decided to take the money and run— maybe Jimmy was mistaken, maybe they'd been ripped off or maybe Jimmy was lying and had arranged for Sigliano to stash some money where she couldn't get at it.

In any case, feeling as she did, like a convict on the lam, she decided not to make a scene. She took the cash, loaded the eleven suitcases into the Caddy, and drove off to search the length and breadth of the United States for a new home.

Later that afternoon, Jimmy called Ahearn.

"Hey Jimmy, I've been meaning to tell you. They finally broke that leak case in Cleveland."

"No kidding?" Fratianno said slowly. "What happened?"

"Turns out this made guy, Tony Libatore, had a friend whose girlfriend was a clerk at the Bureau. Libatore paid them something like $15,000 for the informant files."

"What's the name?"

"Let me see, it's here somewhere. Oh, yeah, Jeff Rabinowitz and Geraldine Linhart. Mean anything to you?"

"No. Never heard of them."

"Well, anyway, this woman, Linhart, copied the files and her boyfriend gave them to Libatore, who was handing the stuff over to Kenny Ciarcia, a made guy, who was keeping the stuff at his office at a car dealership. A few days back, Ciarcia's boss finds the stuff packed in a Fruit Loops cereal box behind Ciarcia's desk, and called Griffin.

"It seems Linhart's handwriting was all over the thing. When they called her in she admitted the whole story and they all had a good cry together. She was really well liked and trusted over there, but had gotten herself involved with this Rabinowitz who was just no good."

Jimmy broke in. "See, I told you guys it was a broad who was taking the stuff. Jesus, why did it take so long to find her? How many broads they got working in that office?"

"Yeah, Jim," Ahearn said. "You're always right."

"You know this Libatore, I made him in the Cleveland thing in 1976. Him and John Calandra."

"Why you?"

"Because Scalish never made no one and those guys didn't remember the ceremony. So I stopped off on my way to New York and did the thing for them," Fratianno said. "Small world. Listen, Jim, here's what I called about. You know Skinny? Well, I want to tell you something about this dirty motherfucker. Keep your eye on that place of his, Select Dry Cleaners, he told me when he bought it that one day he'd torch it to collect the insurance. He bought it back in October for a lot less than it's insured for."

"Whoa, Jimmy. I thought this was your friend. Why do you want to turn on him?" Ahearn asked.

"Hey man, don't go lookin' no gift horse in the mouth. You know what I mean? Besides, I'm workin' with you guys now, ain't I?" he said and laughed.

5

Life in the Theater

NICK AKERMAN was a self-assured, ambitious young man with little pretension and a straightforward style of no-apology honesty. Some regarded him as arrogant or even ruthless; all agreed he was at the very least aggressive.

In the 1970s, he still had a boyish appearance, the kind of slightly awkward, dark good looks that must have carried off well in grade school—earnest, with an upper lip that he would catch between his teeth when thinking hard or hurrying off to perform a task. And Akerman always seemed in a hurry to get something done.

So it was in Washington, D.C., in the spring of 1973, when Akerman, a recent graduate of Harvard Law School, decided to leave his job pushing papers up a mountain of big monopolies at the Federal Trade Commission. He went to see Jim Vorenberg, whose criminal law classes he had attended two years earlier. Vorenberg had come to town with Archibald Cox to assemble a staff for the Watergate Special Prosecutor's Office. Days later, Akerman was one of thirty-seven young lawyers on Cox's staff. He was assigned to the Plumbers Task Force, looking into the so-called White House Plumbers Unit as well as abuses of the CIA and federal agencies by the Nixon re-election committee.

One morning in August of 1973, Akerman joined in an interview of John DeLuca, a deputy mayor of San Francisco, who had come to Washington on behalf of Mayor Joseph Alioto. DeLuca claimed that Nixon's dirty tricksters, wanting to bar Alioto, a Democrat, from seeking the California governor's office in 1970, had leaked confidential Justice Department files to *Look* magazine. On the eve of Alioto's planned announcement for the governorship, *Look* published an article citing those files, which, among other things, claimed Alioto was a longtime associate of top mobster Jimmy Fratianno. The adverse publicity forced Alioto to withdraw from contention, and Ronald Reagan went on to his second term as governor.

DeLuca claimed Nixon aides had arranged for at least one FBI agent to cooperate in providing information for the article as well as the Bureau of Narcotics, Customs, IRS, Immigration and Naturalization, and the Justice Department.

Akerman, along with others reviewing Alioto's allegations, determined that Attorney General John Mitchell, head of Nixon's reelection committee, had held the view that if Alioto became governor "he would be our principal threat in 1972." And there was reason to suspect that higher-ups in the Justice Department had a hand in arranging the release of files alleging a relationship between Alioto and Fratianno.

An August 22, 1973, report of the matter, prepared by Akerman and members of the Special Prosecutor's staff, recommended further investigation. While Alioto's charges were never pursued to completion—there was an abundance of stronger cases to be made—they did raise two sticky issues: the prosecutors wanted to avoid the appearance of playing partisan politics, and no one wanted to impose the specter of La Cosa Nostra into an already volatile investigation.

Still, Fratianno's name stuck in Akerman's mind. Here was a man, Akerman thought, who had been convicted of nothing more than a series of petty crimes, was not at the time believed to be a crime boss, and yet his reputation was so inflammatory that by mere association he may have changed the course of political history.

Late in 1975, as the Watergate office began winding down, Akerman landed a job as an assistant U.S. Attorney for the Southern District of New York, widely regarded as the crown jewel of federal prosecutors' posts, with jurisdiction over Manhattan and its northern suburbs—home to many of the nation's largest corporations, Wall Street, and the leading Families of La Cosa Nostra.

From the time he arrived in April of 1976, Akerman displayed an arrogant sense of independence: failing the bureaucracy by not filing the appropriate memoranda, or bypassing his bureau chiefs in dealing with FBI and IRS investigators. Like many of those coming out of the Watergate office, Akerman had experienced a level of freedom unknown to most federal prosecutors, and it was hard for them to change their ways.

After nearly a year in New York and twenty convictions in narcotics, pollution, and mail fraud cases, Dan Beller, chief of the General Cases Squad, paid a visit to Akerman's corner office. Beller was in shirt-sleeves and held behind his back a case file marked "Premier Theatre, Westchester."

"Nick, you've had some pretty good cases, so far," Beller said, warming up to the subject at hand. "And you've done well with them."

Akerman was cautiously appreciative of the kind words.

"Well, what I have here is a dog," Beller said, extending the file across the desk. Akerman didn't reach for the file, but allowed it to settle squarely within his view atop the clutter of papers he'd been working on.

"You know, Nick, you have to take the good with the bad," Beller offered as he turned and left.

The theater case had been knocking around since 1973, and probably would have died of old age except that it was a hot item, surrounded by reports from half-assed informants claiming that Carlo Gambino and his heir, brother-in-law Paul Castellano, were involved in financing the 3,500-seat concert hall, and that they had installed one of their soldiers to run it, secretly siphoning money from its bars, restaurant, and ticket sales to pay off the mob debt.

On Christmas Eve 1976, the theater corporation had gone into U.S. Bankruptcy Court for financial reorganization, seeking to eliminate its creditors and find a buyer for the showplace. The rumor mill churned out new stories about mob factions vying for control. But there were never enough credible reports to justify a full investigation of the place.

Even if a young assistant U.S. Attorney had the tenacity, vision, and dumb luck to make a case—to find and prove some mob involvement at the theater—it would still likely be a futile effort, for a senior member of the staff would undoubtedly come along just in time for trial to grab the glory. And Akerman was very much aware of the glory.

Akerman did what most everyone else in the office had done; he gave the file a cursory look and stored it away.

That evening, Akerman joined several of his colleagues at Aldo's, a Tiffany-lamped restaurant that was an after-work hangout for the young prosecutors. He told his associates that he had become the latest recipient of the theater case. "I buried it as deep as I could in my files, but I still heard it barking whenever I walked by," he said, imitating a baying hound.

Not long after that evening remarkable things began happening.

Charles Ross Carino, a hapless soul serving a seven-year prison term for check kiting in Virginia, got slapped with another set of bad check charges in New Jersey, which could bring an additional fifty years in prison. And this was a trend that had Carino worried. He had made a small fortune investing the proceeds of bad checks he'd written in as many as sixteen states between 1963 and 1970, and it seemed they were beginning to catch up with him.

Then Carino got word that some made guys in New York, concerned that he couldn't keep silent, were arranging to have a shiv rammed into his chest. That was enough for Carino. He called his lawyer, his lawyer called the FBI, and they notified Akerman. Before Carino knew what hit him, he was trading up, snitching on his friends at the Premier Theatre in return for promises of a reduced sentence and a ride in the WITSEC program.

He said he had been a "secret partner" in the theater, created by his childhood friend Eliot Weisman, of Scarsdale, New York. He said the landfill and construction phase of the operation had run millions over budget, which led Weisman to the mob for hundreds of thousands of dollars to complete construction. And when there were problems selling enough stock to complete the prospectus' minimum requirements for raising cash in the stock market, more money was borrowed from the mob to buy stock under phony names and bribe officials at Warner Communications, Inc., who arranged for the entertainment conglomerate to buy the stock.

Akerman and several FBI agents spent an entire day with Carino and were convinced that they were getting a straight story. Carino was in deep trouble, and the yarn he was spinning was too detailed, too elaborate, to be anything but the truth—at least the truth as best as Charles Ross Carino could put it together. Besides, no one suspected Carino of being bright enough to dream up so intricate a plot on his own.

The mob involvement was not surprising, but Warner Communications? Akerman couldn't understand why one of the world's largest entertainment conglomerates would be involved in such a relatively petty scheme. And most importantly, how could they prove any of it?

As they spoke in Manhattan on that warm spring day in 1977 other pieces of the puzzle were falling into place.

They have been called the Alfa tapes, a strange collection of evidence from a strangely truncated probe. The investigation centered on Thomas Marson, a wealthy New York businessman who had retired to Rancho Mirage, California.

Marson was a short, stout man; loud and crude, intelligent and wily. A caricature of Marson would picture someone blustering obscenities; his body would be a medicine ball ready to burst at the seams with arms just long enough to bring a vodka bottle to his lips.

After serving five years of a fifteen-year sentence for counterfeiting in 1950, Marson made a legitimate fortune climbing through the basements of New York homes with a chemical treatment process for waterproofing leaky cellars. He built Vulcan Basement Waterproofing Company into one of the largest plumbing concerns in the New York City metro area.

In 1971, Marson left Yonkers, New York, a suburban stronghold for Brooklyn mob émigrés, and settled in a modern, three-bedroom home on the edge of Tamarisk Country Club in Rancho Mirage, about 6 miles south of Palm Springs, where he counted among his neighbors and acquaintances Frank Sinatra and Zeppo Marx.

Fratianno entered Marson's life in 1975 by way of Irving "Slick Jack" Shapiro, a mutual friend from Las Vegas. Slick had palled around with Marson in Detroit in the 1940s before moving to Las Vegas, where he became one of Fratianno's men, that strange sense of possession made guys have over others by dint of threat or friendship. Fratianno and Marson became fast friends. Marson liked being around wiseguys—he had learned from his associations with them back East that they could provide access to business deals that were otherwise unavailable. And Fratianno saw in Marson a chance for financing some big deals.

After a few months they were merging their lives, bringing together their friends and families. Fratianno brought along Rizzi, Bompensiero, and Brooklier for day-long bull sessions at the twelve-foot bar that dominated Marson's living room. Marson returned the favor, paying for Jimmy's flights to Palm Springs and introducing "Dr. Schwartz," his nickname for Jimmy, to Billy Marchiondo, the Albuquerque defense lawyer, and Greg DePalma, Marson's close friend from Yonkers.

DePalma was a gruff-talking vivacious character, with a granite complexion, icy blue eyes, and one of those shoddy rugs that gives baldness a bad image. But DePalma's foreboding appearance was overcome by a sardonic wit that made him the center of attention. At forty-six, he was working hard to please the Gambino Family and had hopes of soon becoming a made guy.

He was also one of the principal operators of the Premier Theatre, a wizard of backroom finance who worked tirelessly to keep the theater afloat. He had convinced Marson to raise $1.4 million to invest in the project in 1975, a cash infusion that was desperately needed to stave off creditors.

Concerned about his investment, Marson would speak to DePalma on the phone every day. Soon Fratianno was joining in the calls and was eventually brought to New York—gratis Marson—where "Dr. Schwartz" met the theater's owners and operators, who knew full well that Fratianno was no medical man.

The action around Marson's house became a loud and long affair that couldn't help but draw attention. FBI agents, tailing members of the Los Angeles mob, found themselves congregating outside the house. Jack Barron was among them.

Barron decided to leave it alone for nearly two years. But Bompensiero's murder in early 1977 was quickly followed by a decision to target Marson and find out what was going on in his house.

Alfa Chemical Company was the excuse. Word on the street was that Marson, Teamsters boss Jackie Presser, Las Vegas mobster Tony Spilotro, and Fratianno were partners in Alfa, a Las Vegas–based company manufacturing detergent and offering cleaning and janitorial services. The company was supposedly coercing Las Vegas hotels and casinos into buying Alfa's products and services; those unwilling to go along risked union troubles or having their Teamsters pension fund loans recalled. Marchiondo, who prepared Alfa's incorporation papers, was reportedly using his political influence with New Mexico's Governor Jerry Apodaca to win state contracts for the company.

FBI agents Barron, Jack Armstrong, and Melvin Flohr each came up with an informant alleging the criminal conspiracy. Flohr's affidavit was filed with the court on March 10, 1977, and a wiretap was authorized the same day.

The place was hot. FBI agents were listening in on a cross-country web of activity; it wasn't just Fratianno and his friends from California;

they had mobsters in New York, Chicago, and Cleveland on the line discussing extortion, loan-sharking, land frauds, bribery of public officials, bankruptcy frauds:

• There was talk of a $35,000 loan that Fratianno was trying to collect for Marson and DePalma.
• An eye doctor from Cleveland was working with Marson and Fratianno to create a prepaid eye care plan for the International Culinary Workers Union, from which they would reap kickbacks to the tune of about $100,000.
• A San Diego city councilman had been targeted for a bribe on a zoning change, which if approved would bring Marson an additional $18 million from a Chula Vista, California, housing development.

And there was always the pretense: Alfa was active and growing. There was a series of phone conversations that indicated Marson had used union connections to win service contracts for Alfa at the Tropicana, MGM Grand, Dunes, Aladdin, and the Jockey Club in Las Vegas. In a March 26, 1977, conversation, Slick Jack Shapiro, Alfa's Las Vegas president, reported that he had wined and dined Governor Apodaca and a New Mexico state contract would soon be theirs.

The FBI hadn't learned anything about Bomp's death, but they had struck a mother lode; they had wired themselves into a vein of criminal activity that could keep them busy for years.

The FBI expanded the investigation. They created an undercover company, Tamex; agents posing as detergent salesmen went into New Mexico in hopes of finding the governor's bagman. And they took their wiretaps into Alfa's headquarters in Las Vegas, and up the coast to Fratianno's favorite pay phone in San Francisco.

And then, suddenly, in late April or early May 1977, everything came to a grinding halt. Alfa's Las Vegas headquarters and Fratianno's pay phone went silent. The FBI's undercover agents found not a hint of bid rigging in New Mexico. Alfa closed down. It failed to meet obligations in Las Vegas and withdrew its bids in New Mexico. It seemed to have been swallowed up by the earth.

In July 1977, a new company, Star Glo, Inc., manufacturers of charcoal briquettes, would open its doors at the Las Vegas location once used by Alfa. Shapiro was its president and Marchiondo's firm its attorneys. Its phone numbers were reportedly the same as those used by Alfa.

Somewhere, somehow, word had leaked out. Alfa and the probe

that had seemed so promising were dead. But it wasn't a complete loss.

Days after Carino's New York confession that spring, Jack Barron decided to let the FBI in New York in on the Alfa wiretaps. He called Tommy Vinton, supervisor of the FBI's organized crime squad in New Rochelle, New York, and told him, "I've got some wiretaps that I think will interest you."

On May 5, using the Alfa tapes as evidence, agents in New York were up and running with their own court-authorized wires on the theater's offices and DePalma's home phone. It was just in time for Sinatra's performance there late in May.

Marson either never got the word that Alfa was a target, or no one ever figured out that Marson's phones had been bugged. He and DePalma kept right on talking.

Before it was all over, late in July of 1977, there were 12,000 conversations intercepted; the vast majority were people calling for tickets, but many were glimpses into the criminal conspiracy.

Akerman may have rated among the most aggressive federal prosecutors in New York, but no one could accuse him of having nerves of steel. His hands were cold and mildly trembling as he waited at MCC's conference room in San Diego on that Monday morning, St. Patrick's Day, in March of 1978.

He had already heard more than he ever wanted to know about Fratianno, the murderer. And he suspected reports of a $100,000 contract on Fratianno's head could be sufficient inducement to buy a prison guard or U.S. Marshal.

He and the two agents leading the theater probe—Brendan Fisk and Robert Tolan—had been pressing for an interview with Fratianno since January, when they had received a teletype from Lore saying Fratianno was cooperating and probably could assist in their case. But Akerman was wondering if maybe he should've waited back in New York, where he was still presenting evidence in the theater case to a federal grand jury.

During the last ten months, aided by the New York wiretaps and Carino, they had built an impressive case. Using Carino's grand jury statements as a bludgeon, they had turned disbarred securities lawyer Norman Brodsky, who claimed to be a "secret partner." And Brodsky's efforts—wearing a body recorder to secretly win confessions from other conspirators—had snared Bruce Kosman, who offered details of an elaborate $105,000 payoff and kickback scheme involving the theater and Warner executives.

The wiretaps showed DePalma slipping money out of the theater and sending it to Marson and others. By itself, that was no crime. But because the theater was in bankruptcy court for reorganization, failing to declare the revenues and disbursements *was* a crime.

Akerman had targeted more than a dozen men on a case of securities, mail, and bankruptcy frauds; obstruction of justice; and RICO.

Fratianno, escorted by Lore, walked up to where Akerman was sitting and stared, appearing a little uncertain about something.

"Excuse me, sir, that's my seat," Fratianno said.

"Jimmy, this is Nick Akerman, the assistant U.S. Attorney from New York I told you about," Lore said.

"Good to meet ya," Fratianno said, nodding, then settling into the chair Akerman had silently vacated.

Lore completed the introductions of Fisk and Tolan, and then faded into a corner with a legal-size notepad and the newspaper.

Akerman began by explaining that in return for Fratianno's cooperation, he would inform any sentencing judge or parole board of his assistance. Fratianno wasn't moved; he'd heard that speech before. Akerman then introduced the topic. He explained in the most general terms their interest in the theater. He told Fratianno about the wiretaps, and that they knew he had been hanging around with Marson.

The questioning focused on incidents, not names, trying to draw on Fratianno's independent recollections to create an outline of his knowledge. Most of the questions began with the phrase, "Tell us about . . ." and then an area of the case they knew he had knowledge of.

What they got initially was a lot of "Hmmm" and "What do you want to know about it?" Fratianno was sizing up this new crew. It was unusual for a prosecutor to come along for the ride, but he liked having the top guy there.

The one-sided discussion always seemed to come back to Marson.

"Yeah, this guy was scared to death," he said finally, focusing a stare into Akerman's eyes.

"Who was that?" Akerman started.

"Marson. He was always crying to me about his money, afraid they was going to screw him out of his 1.4 million."

"So what happened? Tell us what, if anything, you did about it," Akerman said.

"Well, nothing really. He offered me . . . he told me if I could make sure his money was secure, you know, we'd eventually invest it in a land deal he had in San Diego or with a contractor I got in L.A. and split the profits. Forget about it; I could have made millions."

Jimmy waited for the next question. He wanted to be coaxed.

"Tell us what happened," Tolan urged, already knowing, from the wiretaps he had supervised day and night throughout the past summer, what had gone on.

"Well, I just got it protected. Spent a lot of fuckin' time chasing back and forth to New York, to make sure this guy was fully surfaced. Now I know the score with this motherfucking theater, boy, and so does that Eliot guy, the president of the place," he said with a knowledgeable snort and nod.

"What's that mean? Eliot who?" asked Fisk, a young well-groomed agent with tortoiseshell glasses and smart suits, the very image of the "new FBI."

"I don't remember his last name. Rosenthal, Weisman, Goldman; something Jewish. Well, anyway, he's the front, the fall guy, and he knows it. This DePalma, he belongs to Gambino, and he's been stealing that fuckin' place blind paying back all these shylocks. Fuck, this Eliot got himself so deep in debt to these people that he just handed them the keys. DePalma's been running that place while this Eliot just booked the acts. Richie Fusco, he's with the Colombo Family, he runs the box office. Anyway, those three and Marson are the partners in the thing.

"Then Sal came in, you know about Sal Cannatella, don't you?"

"Go on," Fisk said, nodding. "Let's hear your version of it."

"Well, Cannatella is president of this investment house, up in Buffalo I think, and he put like a million dollars into the place."

"When was that?"

"Fuck, I don't know. You guys can find that out, can't you?" Fratianno asked.

"Sure we can," said Tolan, a gentle bear of a man, whose coplike appearance was softened by a near-whisper voice. "But that's why we're here, you know, to make all these pieces fit together."

Jimmy froze up.

"Look, is there anything you can think of to put this in time sequence, I mean, any events going on in New York when you were there, maybe a ballgame or fight or something you attended?" asked Fisk.

That was the key to opening Jimmy's memory. He outlined his trips to New York, each in connection with Marson and the theater, dated to an event linked to Sinatra. He had first come to New York in February 1976 for the Friar's Club Man of the Year dinner honoring Sinatra at the Waldorf-Astoria, during which Marson introduced Jimmy to the theater's operators. In April and September of 1976, he returned for Sinatra's concert engagements at the theater. He was in town for the last time during Sinatra's final Premier Theatre engagement, a show with Dean Martin, in May 1977.

Then he remembered:

"It was in the fall, after that second Sinatra thing, in September seventy-six, that Marson called. He begged me to come back to New York, to check on this Cannatella. Cannatella put up his money just before that show and then started acting like he'd taken over the place. Well, it turns out that this Sal is with the Funzi Family."

"What's that, what Family?" Akerman asked, suddenly at a loss.

"Frank Tieri, everyone calls him Funzi. He's the boss, the Old Man of the Genovese Family. Fat Tony Salerno is his underboss."

"Hold on there. We've been going on the belief that the theater was controlled by the Gambino Family," Tolan said with some disappointment.

"Are you kidding? That fuckin' place is everybody's. Sure, Greg belonged to Paulie Castellano, he must have put a jillion dollars into the thing. But forget about it, no one had an exclusive, let's put it that way.

"Anyway, this Marson calls me in San Francisco and has me come into New York to talk to Cannatella. Well, that's when I find out this guy's connected—he tells me to go see this Fat Dom [Alongi] who's one of Funzi's *capos.*

"After a day or so I get a sit-down with this Fat Dom and I tell him that Marson's with me, that he's going to help me make some money for the Los Angeles Family. Well, Fat Dom tells me Cannatella is some financial genuis, that he's going to fix all their problems, and I should get Marson and the rest of the partners to go along, put Cannatella in charge."

Fratianno then recalled a meeting at the theater offices the next day. He said Cannatella and all the partners—Marson, Weisman,

DePalma, and Fusco—attended the session and with little haggling agreed to put Cannatella in charge. Everyone would retain their respective jobs and the theater would be put into bankruptcy court, where legitimate creditors could get ten cents on the dollar while the other lenders would be fully repaid from money skimmed off the theater's profits.

That evening, Jimmy said, he met with Louis "Louie Dome" Pacella, a short, dark man in his mid-fifties whose face seemed locked in a permanent snarl. He was by profession a restaurateur, owner of Sepret Tables, a romantic little Continental bistro and saloon in the East 20s, the inside of which was nearly as dark as Pacella's face, but just bright enough to make out the black-and-white celebrity photos lining the oak-paneled walls.

Pacella had two claims to fame. The first was his position as a soldier in Tieri's crime Family, a financier of narcotics deals in East Harlem; the second was as a close friend of Sinatra's. He had arranged for Sinatra's appearances at the theater in return for a cut of the action; as a member of Tieri's Family, he had an interest in seeing Cannatella take charge.

Pacella didn't like Fratianno. Perhaps because he didn't want Sinatra's reputation sullied by association with so renowned a killer, or maybe because Fratianno never pronounced Pacella's nickname properly.

"So I met Louie Dones at his restaurant and told him about this sit-down with Fat Dom and that Cannatella was in charge and he said 'if Fat Dom says Cannatella's okay you can count on it.'"

Jimmy's last visit to the theater was for Sinatra's final performance there in May 1977. Marson was again worried that his investment might be wiped out in the Chapter XI bankruptcy process. This time Fratianno said he went to the top.

"I went to see this made guy I know and he set up a meeting for me with the Old Man, at a luncheonette somewhere downtown. I told Tieri my concern over Marson's money and he said he'd make sure Cannatella did the right thing."

"Hold it right there," Akerman said. "I want you to hear something."

It was a wiretapped conversation recorded on May 19, 1977, the afternoon that Jimmy met at Bobby's Restaurant in Manhattan with Mike Rizzi and Tommy Ricciardi, the triggermen in Bomp's murder:

UNKNOWN MALE: Bobby's.

DEPALMA: Uh, Jimmy please.

UNKNOWN MALE: Jimmy, just a moment, Jimmy, Jimmy. Hold on please.

DEPALMA: Okay.

FRATIANNO: Hello.

DEPALMA: Doctor. Some twelve o'clock you were going to call.

FRATIANNO: I did. The line was busy, busy, busy.

DEPALMA: Well, that must have been.

FRATIANNO: And then you weren't there.

DEPALMA: That Fat. Well, didn't you get a message from the kid?

FRATIANNO: No.

DEPALMA: I left all the information.

FRATIANNO: No.

DEPALMA: Well, you got six tickets on five twenty-seven, late. [May 27 for the late show of Sinatra and Dean Martin]

FRATIANNO: When?

DEPALMA: Five twenty-seven, late.

FRATIANNO: When's that?

DEPALMA: Next Friday.

FRATIANNO: Not, when? You mean next week?

DEPALMA: Yeah.

FRATIANNO: Ah, Mike's leaving Sunday.

DEPALMA: You need them before then?

FRATIANNO: Well sure, I told you this week.

DEPALMA: No, you didn't. You said for Mike's mother.

FRATIANNO: Mike's mother, his wife, ah, my other guy's wife. . . . I don't give a fuck. Now I got to meet the Old Man tomorrow, see. He couldn't show today.

DEPALMA: Ugh.

FRATIANNO: I didn't have an appointment today. I thought he was going to be someplace. I got it tomorrow. I'm going to tell the Old Man.

DEPALMA: Ugh.

FRATIANNO: About, you know, make sure these guys, you follow me?

DEPALMA: Yeah.

FRATIANNO: I'm going to tell him, you know. I'm going to run it down to him to make sure that, of course Fat Dom sent word, you know?

DEPALMA: Yeah.

FRATIANNO: Did you know that?

DEPALMA: Yup.

FRATIANNO: He sent word to tell Tommy that, don't worry about the money.

DEPALMA: Ugh.

FRATIANNO: And, ah, what the fuck, I mean, hey Greg, ah, like Tommy says, he told me. He says, if I ever get the money and we need three, four hundred or two, three.

DEPALMA: Available.

FRATIANNO: We could, it's available. Which is good. We'll all make a buck with it.

DEPALMA: I know that.

FRATIANNO: You know what I mean, Greg? You're in with it. You know that.

DEPALMA: I know that, Jimmy. I never worry about you.

FRATIANNO: Well, fuck, it's just the idea.

DEPALMA: I'm sure, I'm sure you know me by now. I don't look at pennies.

FRATIANNO: But this guy cries all the time. He just keeps crying and crying. Everytime I see him.

Jimmy was chuckling throughout the tape. "You guys got it all right there. I was going to see Tieri, the Old Man, the next day to make sure Fat Dom told him about Marson's money."

"Who's the guy who 'cries all the time'?" Akerman asked.

"Like I said before, that's Marson."

"And what did you mean when you told DePalma, 'You're in with it.' "

"Nothin' really. Just that any Marson's money we got out of the theater we'd invest in these schemes and DePalma would get a cut."

"And you say Eliot had no role in any of this?" Fisk asked.

"Fuck no. Believe me, Brendan, this guy was just like, what do ya call it? A pawn. Poor bastard. You know Jews can't do no time. I'm surprised this prick hasn't turned," Jimmy said.

"He almost did," Akerman volunteered. "We arrested him last September for making a false statement on a mortgage application, squeezed him a little and he started talking. He told us about the $120,000 they'd skimmed during the last Sinatra series."

"What happened? He get cold feet?" Jimmy asked.

"Yup. As soon as we asked him to start wearing a body recorder, he ran to his lawyer and dropped out of sight."

"I'll tell you right now, if he gets any prison time, he'll try to square some kind of deal with you. Believe me, Jews can't do no time. Hey, how about $100—a hundred bucks says he turns," Jimmy said, laughing and shaking his head.

Jimmy had arranged with Lore for lunch to be brought in that afternoon on the government tab: deep-fried artichoke hearts and sausage heros all around.

"Not as good as the Golden Bowl," Tolan said with a wry grin, knowing he'd catch Jimmy's attention.

"Hey, you from Cleveland?" Fratianno said with some delight.

"No, but I lived there a few years. It was my first assignment when I joined the Bureau in the sixties, so I got to know some of the places, like the Bowl."

The two men went on at length comparing eateries.

Tolan was trying to be polite, eating without complaint. But what he was yearning for was corn beef and cabbage and a couple of beers; even corn beef on rye with a diet Pepsi would have satisfied his craving. After all, it was St. Paddy's Day and this son of an Irish New York City cop was feeling a kind of withdrawal, locked up as he was in San Diego in a room with an Italian mobster eating a sausage hero.

Akerman listened and made mental notes. He was impressed with Jimmy's smooth delivery, his apparent memory for detail, and understanding of power relationships, such as Pacella's importance in bringing a hot act like Sinatra to the struggling concert hall. He could make a good witness. His one glaring deficiency was his inability to recall dates.

As they ate Akerman pored through Jimmy's address book, looking for names and phone numbers that might be helpful. Under the L's he found Bob Lane, listed with a New York City area code number.

"Uh, Jimmy, tell me about this Bob Lane in New York. Is he a friend of yours or what?"

"Lane? Oh, yeah. No man, that's not a guy, it's this babe, Linda Lanna," Jimmy said, chuckling. "Actually, I was introduced to her by Mike O'Brien, Jimmy Hoffa's stepson. I listed her that way in the book there in case Jean starts snooping around. But what does she have to do with any of this; she doesn't even know where Westchester is."

"Now hold on a minute here, Jimmy. Does she live in the village?" Akerman said, staring at the number in the address book, a sudden fearful recognition of that phone number overtaking him.

"Yeah, in one of them little row houses downtown."

"She's kinda dark, shoulder-length hair, about five-foot-five—"

"And real pretty blue eyes, and built nice, big chest," Fratianno interrupted. "Don't tell me you know this broad?"

"Know her? I was dating her for a few weeks last year."

"You're fuckin' kiddin' me," Fratianno said, setting down his sandwich and looking at Akerman through new eyes.

"Isn't that a stitch," Akerman said, laughing to mask his discomfort over the coincidence. "She was on a jury in a narcotics case I had. The same day the case ended she called me up and asked me out."

"Yeah, that's the same broad all right. Full o' guts."

They kidded for a while about their mutual friend, with Akerman, not the kind to kiss and tell, evading Jimmy's inquiries of carnal encounter.

Akerman's discomfort over the situation would later cause him to have the FBI make a background check on her. It turned out the woman Jimmy had known was Lanna's roommate. But for Jimmy the mutual acquaintance was important, it gave him a little traction, a connection with Akerman, someone with whom he shared some kind of history in this lonely period.

After lunch, Jimmy offered cigars to everyone. Tolan declined, lighting a Marlboro.

Akerman gestured to Tolan and they stepped outside the room. Akerman asked him to spend some time alone with Fratianno to see how far he could be pushed, to determine if his stories held up under grilling. Akerman would make an excuse and he and Fisk would leave them alone for about an hour.

During that session, Tolan hammered at Fratianno to determine the depths of his recollection and honesty, using information obtained from wiretaps:

Question: "Was there some name Marson and DePalma used in referring to the skim money?"

Answer: "Grocery money."

Question: "Do you know if DePalma is a made guy?"

Answer: "Yeah, he told me about it right after he was made, right after that last Sinatra concert."

Question: "Did Sinatra's people get any money under the table from the concerts?"

Answer: "Fuck yeah. Mickey Rudin [Sinatra's lawyer-manager] and Jilly [Rizzo, Sinatra's friend and bodyguard] got a cut from the scalped tickets, T-shirts, and programs. And Greg told me he had to go out to Vegas to give Sinatra something like $50,000 under the table before the second concert series. Can you feature that, a guy like this getting something under the table?"

When Akerman returned with Fisk, Tolan gave them a thumbs up sign.

Over the balance of the week Jimmy dedicated himself to recollection of the Premier Theatre, the scores of people he had met there, and the machinations of high-finance crime. During breaks he would re-count his going into the program, the contract on his life, and about those who failed him in his time of desperation. He counted among that long list of betrayals DePalma's lack of support and his belief that Castellano and Tieri had turned a deaf ear.

"No, I wouldn't say I'm looking for revenge," he told Akerman one afternoon. "But I'll tell you one motherfucker I'd love to testify against is this Aiuppa. Not just because he helped Brooklier try to clip me, but for Johnny Roselli.

"Johnny was somethin' else, man," he said, a smile taking hold at the corner of his mouth, aglow in the warm memory of a once-in-a-lifetime friendship.

The two men had met just after Fratianno arrived on the West Coast in 1946. They became fast friends and Roselli sponsored Jimmy for membership in the Los Angeles Family. Roselli had made his bones in Chicago and was inducted into La Cosa Nostra by Al Capone before going West to oversee the Family's interests. He later transferred his La Cosa Nostra membership to the L.A. Family.

"I'm telling you this guy was dap. After his parole he had to stay away from the wise guys, so he hung out with movie stars and these broads were all crazy about him, forget about it. But keeping away from the Family gave him less juice until in the late fifties he just transferred back to Chicago. [Sam] Giancana was the boss in Chicago, and he knew how to use Johnny. He sent him to Vegas and in just a few years, Johnny got the Chicago Family the Fremont, the Stardust, the Hacienda. What a guy, huh?"

Jimmy restated his opinion that as Chicago boss, Aiuppa bore at least indirect responsibility for Roselli's murder: "But I'll tell ya what happened. When this Aiuppa became boss in Chicago, he got jealous of Johnny. I mean, it's the 1970s and Johnny's retired in Florida, he wasn't hurtin' no one. And this prick ordered him clipped. They chopped off his legs, Nick, and stuffed him in a barrel and threw it in the Gulf. It was Santo [Traficante, boss of Tampa] who set him up; an FBI told me that Johnny and Santo were supposed to play golf together that day.

"So just after they found Johnny's body, about two years ago, I'm in Chicago, and this Aiuppa says to me, 'How about this friend of yours, this Johnny, Johnny, what's his name? Roselli. What do you think about that?' And he's staring right at me. Well, I know his fuckin' game; if I say somethin' bad I'm not walkin' out of that room alive. So I just said, 'Well, I guess it's one of them things, you know, none of my business.'

"But Nick, time's gonna come, boy; I'm gonna get even with that prick. One day I'm gonna sit in that witness chair and look this guy in the eye and tell the whole world about this dirty prick. And you know what, Nick, I won't even have to lie; I know enough to bury this guy for good."

As Akerman bid Fratianno farewell, he remembered something, a personal curiosity, he just had to ask about. "Say, Jimmy, this may sound strange, it's nothing official, but do you know Mayor Alioto?"

"Are you kidding me? I've known the guy since the early sixties. I was trying to make some money with this guy, all legit stuff, through my trucking business but nothing ever came of it. But I'll tell ya, after that *Look* article come out, this guy was so scared to have anything to do with me that he lied his ass off.

"I already told Ahearn about all this; what's your interest?"

"Nothing important," Akerman said. "Just something that came up a few years ago."

Tolan and Fisk stayed behind an extra day to flesh out details on some other New York matters Jimmy had offered up. He told them about $25,000 paid by an Australian shipping magnate to Benny "Eggs" Mangano, who was later acquitted of any wrongdoing, to assure labor peace on New York docks. And he described a meeting in New York at which Russell Bufalino, boss of the Pittston, Pennsylvania, Family had asked Fratianno to help locate Jack Napoli, who'd been placed in witness protection in the San Francisco area while waiting to testify against Bufalino at an upcoming trial.

He also filled them in on the Alfa case: The FBI's informants had it all wrong. Presser had nothing to do with it and Fratianno's only involvement had been as a friend of Slick Jack Shapiro's.

By the time the last of the New Yorkers departed, Jimmy realized that his cooperation agreement with the government had expanded; he now had two major cases. Each was as widely different as the cities in which they would come to trial, and each accurately reflected the level of La Cosa Nostra activity in those towns.

The Los Angeles case was what one might expect from an organized crime trial: a small group of men, distrusting of one another, hustling for a buck, extorting pornographers and bookmakers by threats of violence, and killing one of their own to keep from being detected. It was the seamiest side of criminal activity.

While in New York, the focus was the infiltration of a legitimate business by two organized crime Families, which led to the corruption of officials at the world's largest entertainment conglomerate.

The only common thread, the only thing shared by the street thugs of the West and the sophisticated mob bankers of the East, was Fratianno, whose greed had brought him to their company and whose thirst for survival and vengeance delivered him to government service.

6

The Road to El Paso

On JUNE 8, 1978, Jim Henderson took an early morning flight out of Chicago bound for San Francisco. At noon he was to meet at the local strike force office with Ahearn, Lore, McDonald, and Akerman. Later that day he would meet with McPherson, the U.S. Marshal in charge of Fratianno's detail, and the FBI agents interested in Fratianno.

This was going to be Henderson's debut replacing DeFeo as the Los Angeles strike force chief. He wanted it to be a meeting everyone would remember. He intended to come off as an uncompromising, iron-fisted prosecutor, unilaterally setting out what he viewed as a fair, but unwavering, agenda.

On a Sunday morning two weeks earlier, Henderson had received a call at his southside Chicago home from McDonald. Henderson, the top assistant prosecutor in the Chicago strike force office, had been appointed to head the Los Angeles office only a few days earlier.

The San Francisco lawyer was in a rage on the phone that Sunday. He had a litany of complaints about the government's handling of Fratianno. He said there was a never-ending stream of agents questioning Jimmy without any assurances that he wouldn't be prosecuted on those matters. He said the written agreement signed by Fratianno and DeFeo in January provided no guarantees of what would happen to Fratianno after he completed his prison term.

And, McDonald said, he wanted John Gibbons, an assistant strike force attorney, to stay away from Jimmy. A few days earlier, Gibbons, under orders from the acting strike force chief, Tom Kotoski, had attempted to test the depths of Fratianno's veracity. The effort backfired.

Gibbons had confronted Jimmy, accusing him of holding back information, telling him if he didn't start coming across he could kiss his deal goodbye and expect to spend what remained of his life in prison. Instead of responding in a servile manner, Jimmy told Gibbons to "stuff your deal up your ass," walked out of the conference room, and called McDonald.

McDonald's reading of the confrontation had been that the government was leaving itself an escape hatch in case it ever wanted to prosecute Jimmy, charging he hadn't been entirely honest.

In summary, McDonald told Henderson, Jimmy was being exposed to an uncertain future, and come Monday morning he was going to start action to take Jimmy back to Cleveland, reverse his guilty plea there, and fight any charges against him. Henderson prevailed upon McDonald to wait until they could meet face-to-face the next day in Los Angeles.

Henderson sat, somewhat uncomfortably, in his new corner office in Los Angeles that afternoon in May and again listened to McDonald's complaints and demands. He made no commitments, but bought some time. He told McDonald he didn't even know where the men's room was in this new office and wasn't about to start making promises he couldn't keep. Henderson said he needed a little time to review the situation, so they scheduled another meeting for June 8, at which he would let McDonald and everyone else involved know just where he stood; then, if McDonald wanted to back out, he could.

In preparation for that next meeting, Henderson examined the indictments handed up in February against Brooklier and company, read the FBI reports, and met with his recently inherited staff. He reached an unsettling conclusion: The case was a shambles, a rush job, based largely on Fratianno's grand jury testimony and lacking sufficient corroboration to go into court. He didn't see any way he could be ready to go to trial by the September trial date.

The second thing he did was to meet with Jimmy in San Diego. A meeting of such uneventful proportions that neither man would later clearly recall it having occurred.

But that could have been predicted. Under the best of circumstances Jimmy was cautious with new people, but after his confrontation with Gibbons, he was stiff as an I-beam and as distrusting as a banker. He had asked Lore and Ahearn about "my new DA," but neither could offer any insights—Henderson was an unknown quantity out West.

Jimmy's first impression of Henderson was distrust. Henderson's staccato, exacting fashion of speech, the slightly jutting jaw, deep-set dark eyes, and slicked-back dark hair left a stark impression of arrogance; and while it wasn't an entirely inaccurate impression, it was simplistic.

At thirty-two years of age, James Dale Henderson was already a man who had learned not to take anything for granted and to act with supremely deliberate caution; investing hours of work, but little emotion. Something he had learned playing baseball.

He had never intended on law as a career; law school was merely something to do between college and life. What he really wanted from life was baseball; to be one of the boys of summer.

In 1968, with one semester of law school under his belt, Henderson signed with the Kansas City Royals' farm team as a catcher and was shipped to Plessiville, Quebec, 150 miles from Montreal, in the Continental League. It was the realization of an ambition that had guided his life for as long as he could remember.

But by the end of that season, no one had to deliver the bad news. When he went up against other players, equally trained and just as anxious as he was for a shot at the big leagues, Henderson realized his talent was flawed, not by any personal failing, but by a broken ankle he had suffered playing ball in college. The ankle had never set properly, and now his speed around the bases wasn't up to the competition.

After the '68 season ended, Henderson joined the newly formed Global Baseball League and played in San Juan, Puerto Rico, and Caracas, Venezuela, for another year. He didn't really believe he would ever have a chance at the majors, but he wanted to hold on to the dream, to play out the fantasy, for just a little longer.

In 1970, he returned to his native Phoenix, Arizona, completed law school, and found a job with the Justice Department, where he worked his way up, a cautious step at a time, bucking a system rife with the Northeastern power elite from Harvard, Yale, and Columbia law schools.

By the time he was assigned to take over the Los Angeles office— one of the nation's most prestigious prosecutors' posts—Henderson had established himself as one of the government's bright young men, somewhat of a trouble-shooter at staff organization, with an extensive knowledge of wiretap law; and a man of great personal detachment.

Had Henderson been the type of personality to inject himself intimately into his work, or perhaps if he could have known the long-term relationship he and Fratianno were embarking upon, he might have opened up about his baseball history at their first meeting. It would have made all the difference, for Fratianno, a sports fanatic and an avid softball player during his early years in prison, always looked for a personal connection on which to open a new relationship.

As it worked out, their meeting was short, guarded, and businesslike, except for some passing comments about the new baseball season. Henderson made it clear that no one was out to get Fratianno and that his deal—that the government wouldn't use any of his testimony against him—was not in jeopardy.

Henderson made no promises, but said he would do everything in his power to see that Jimmy and his family were properly provided for as long as he was testifying.

Both men seemed content.

All that was left was for Henderson to take control, to be sure that none of the competing forces in the Justice Department—the FBI or U.S. Attorney's office—could upstage Henderson's authority over and responsibility for Fratianno.

As Henderson sat aboard the United Airlines flight on June 8, alternately studying Fratianno's debriefing reports and reading the sports sections of various big-city newspapers, he was getting himself psyched-up to make this meeting the last in which Fratianno and McDonald would try to jerk the government around.

Henderson was the last to arrive for the meeting. He said he was delayed at the airport, but it suited his purpose to be late, a reminder to the others that this was his show. Indeed, more than a dozen men—including Ahearn, Lore, Akerman, and McDonald and prosecutors from Los Angeles and San Francisco—sat in place, unable to start without him.

Akerman arrived flushed with the excitement of having just received national media attention. The Premier Theatre indictments had come out two days earlier charging Weisman, DePalma, Fusco, and Marson as secret partners in the corporation, fronts for organized crime. The grand jury had also charged six others, including Warner executive Leonard Horwitz, with taking part in the stock swindles used to create the concert hall or the bankruptcy frauds that bled it dry. Fratianno was named as an unindicted co-conspirator in the bankruptcy frauds aspects of the case and was being cast to play the part of co-star in the trial—one of two lead witnesses the government had cultivated by immunization or promises of reduced sentences.

The significance of those recent indictments wasn't lost on Henderson; Fratianno was now committed in cases on both coasts, but it was going to be on Henderson's terms.

The meeting took less than two hours, about ninety minutes of which was dominated by Henderson. He explained that so long as Fratianno cooperated fully with the government, he was personally committed to seeing him released from prison within twenty months. He said he would do everything in his power to see that Fratianno and his family's needs would be taken care of by WITSEC as long as he was providing testimony; that the Los Angeles case would take precedence over all others because it had been the one Fratianno was pleading out to and because of the time restraints he faced; and finally, that Henderson was taking charge of Fratianno, personally, which meant there would be no more interviews, no more FBI reports, not so much as a telephone call made to Fratianno without first getting Henderson's personal approval.

He added that he wasn't certain how all of this was going to be accomplished, that the Federal Parole Board and WITSEC had their own ways of doing things. But he was certain that with the resources of all those present they could pull it off. It required the personal commitments of everyone in the room to make it work.

Those were Henderson's terms. The speech was primarily for the benefit of McDonald. He knew McDonald would support him, and he was offering every assurance the lawyer had demanded. In return, McDonald would effectively put Henderson in charge. If anyone else balked at the deal, he knew McDonald would walk away from the table and take Fratianno with him. Henderson had effectively forged an alliance with McDonald in which none of the others could interfere.

Whatever else might occur from that time forward, the June 8 meeting marked Fratianno's final deal; a deal cut on the personal vows of those present without the usual bureaucratic machinations of governmental signatures in triplicate. There was no stenographer, no record at all of the meeting.

It was in effect a Star Chamber proceeding—not by virtue of any cruelty, but by the arbitrary and unilateral commitments made in secret by government officials to influence the course of justice for the benefit of a single man.

That afternoon McDonald called Jimmy. He told him of the commitments made around that table to have him out of jail the following summer and the promises of protection and funding for the foreseeable future.

"But Dennis, that program don't pay enough money for someone to live," he said. "You know what I get when I leave here? Everytime, this Bud McPherson hands me three five-dollar bills. Fifteen dollars a day! All you can eat on that is a marshal's steak—you know what that is? A McDonald's burger. How am I going to live?"

"Well, I've got an idea," McDonald said. "How many cases do they have you in now?"

"Three's all, I think. There's the thing in L.A., New York, and I think they're going to want me in that case against Rudy Tham, that thing where he was using Teamsters money to pay my hotel rooms and stuff."

"Is that all? I mean, aren't there going to be a bunch more of these cases coming up from things you've told the FBI?"

"I guess. Could be. How the fuck am I supposed to know? What are you getting at, Dennis?"

"How about writing a book; you know, your memoirs of life in the Mafia."

"Come on, Dennis. I've never even read a book, never read one in my entire life. How'm I going to write one?"

"No, Jim. No one really writes their own memoirs. We get some well-known author to do it. All you have to do is tell him your story and he'll do the writing."

Wheels started clicking in Fratianno's head.

"What do you think it would be worth? Couple grand or what?"

"I'd bet more like a hundred grand and—"

"How does that get divided? I mean, I don't want no agents or nothing. And all this guy is going to do is the writing, so what does he get, like ten, fifteen percent or what?"

Jimmy was hooked; it was quick money at a minimum of work.

"I have no idea exactly how this would work. But I'd guess the writer gets like half. And I'm going to get something for my trouble. You know I've been all over the country for you and spent a lot of time . . ."

"Oh, fuck, Dennis. With all the publicity you get from being with me you're complainin'?"

"Hey pal, I do negligence law. I'm not a criminal lawyer, so I haven't seen one cent from any publicity. In fact, I'm sure some clients have dropped me because I've been representing you. So I'm going to have to get something if I put this book together for you."

"Oh, Dennis," Fratianno whined. "All right. Just get it going, okay? I don't want to wait too long on this thing."

Jimmy's mind worked like a publicity agent's: "You know, we should try to get this book out while I'm still testifying."

A couple of days later Henderson got lucky.

He was in Washington, D.C., for a meeting of the nation's strike force chiefs. They were there to discuss strategy, review new cases that might overlap jurisdictions, hear about critical new Justice Department policies and court decisions, and generally hobnob with their fellow prosecutors.

In the middle of a round-table discussion, Henderson was asked to take a phone call. It was his office back in Los Angeles, an apologetic assistant calling to tell him that the indictments against Brooklier and company had been dismissed.

Days after Fratianno had appeared before the grand jury, *Time* magazine had published a detailed story about his testimony. The court determined that the grand jury leak had tainted the case and decided to toss out the indictments, but reserved the government's right to bring a new indictment.

Henderson, not usually given to loud demonstrative behavior, gave out a kind of cowboy "Yahoo" at the news. An almost unbearable weight had been lifted from his shoulders. He could go back into the grand jury when he was ready, having properly prepared the indictment.

At lunch that afternoon with several of the prosecutors Henderson shared his good news. It was still going to be a tough case to pull together, but now, at least, he would be able to do the proper preparation.

"I can't believe how stupid these defense lawyers were. I mean, they knew the court would let us reindict. I wouldn't have had a prayer of winning convictions the way that first indictment was drawn up."

Phil Fox—Hamilton P. Fox III, to be precise—set down his fork, removed his wire-rimmed eyeglasses, and, using the edge of the tablecloth, cleaned the lenses.

"Why, what was the problem?" Fox asked.

"To be honest, I'm not entirely certain," Henderson began. "I know there wasn't sufficient corroboration of Fratianno's statements to hold up in court. Plus they charged obstruction of justice on Bomp's murder, and I'm sure if we can prove the murder we can bring a stronger charge."

"It's too late to change the charge now," Fox said, noting the prohibition against upping the ante in a new indictment. "What they probably should have done was charged a civil rights violation, as the murder of a federal informant—that's a ten-year exposure."

Fox, informally known as the *consiglieri*, was the deputy chief of the Justice Department's organized crime section, a job created for him to review and evaluate strike force cases, endeavoring to find more innovative directions of investigation and prosecution.

The two men kicked ideas back and forth throughout the meal. Henderson wanted to personally prosecute the case, not leave it for one of his assistants to handle, but feared the demands of running his new office and the trial would be overwhelming. By the time they were drinking coffee it was apparent that Fox had more than a passing interest in the case.

The government had sufficient evidence of the pornography shakedowns from both the PORNEX undercover operation and pornography dealers who had been strong-armed by the mobsters and "convinced" by the government to cooperate. But there was serious trouble with proving the Bompensiero murder, which rested almost exclusively on Fratianno's testimony.

This was what piqued Fox's interest. He had been sitting behind a desk at Justice for more than a year and was seeing his considerable skills as a trial lawyer atrophy. He was becoming an administrator, which he viewed as a job for a man older than his thirty-two years.

Fox had a fairly broad perspective on which to base this conclusion. He had grown up in Salisbury, Maryland, where his father was the county prosecutor; he had clerked at the U.S. Supreme Court after graduation from Yale Law School, and had served in the Watergate Special Prosecutor's Office with Akerman.

In the two and half years before coming to the *consiglieri* post, Fox had been a federal prosecutor for the District of Columbia, handling a large volume of street crime cases—rapes and murders—because any crime committed in the District falls under federal jurisdiction. In one nine-month period, Fox prosecuted sixty jury trials.

Of all his experiences, prosecuting those street crimes had been the most compelling. And after a year of reviewing cases and instructing others in how to make a criminal charge stick, he was in desperate need of his fix; a hands-on, trial-induced jolt of adrenaline.

Before Henderson returned to Los Angeles, it was agreed that Fox would assist him in the case, handling the Bompensiero side of it. Two weeks later, Fox traveled to San Diego to look over the murder scene and speak to the investigators. He wanted a three-dimensional view of the case: an understanding of what happened and how it happened, a feeling for the events charged that you can't get from reading reports.

He also met Fratianno.

They spent three days together on that first visit. Fox pressed hard for what Fratianno knew, trying to cull fact from supposition to control Fratianno's tendency toward hyperbole. He came away with a page and a half of notes—coded with a key name, date, or phrase to avoid comprehension by defense attorneys—and a "sense" that Fratianno was going to make a great witness if he could be kept on the stand long enough to overcome the jury's initial repulsion at who they were listening to.

Fox's patrician, sharp features and metal-rimmed spectacles give him the appearance of a young idealistic intellectual who would be more comfortable in a corporate law library researching Northrop's potential product liability in the event of a nuclear winter than sitting in a prison talking about murder and extortion. But he was enthralled at being back on the trail of a good murder case, and wasn't for a moment repelled by Fratianno's presence.

The last time he had been disgusted by a criminal was when he interviewed an eighteen-year-old gang leader who had turned state's evidence against his fellow street hoods. Just before trial, in a personal moment, Fox had asked the boy to explain the thrill of cutting up and raping several terrified sixteen-year-old girls. The boy shrugged and offered more in his silence than he could ever have told Fox in words; there's no true accounting for the desires that drive people.

As summer approached, Jimmy was busy.

Akerman was calling regularly in preparation for trial, relaying questions to Jimmy by way of Lore.

Henderson, trying to reduce Jimmy's tedium and frustration in San Diego, was finding excuses to bring him up to Los Angeles for one- or two-day stints at the strike force offices.

High on the list of excuses were the never-ending meetings with

FBI agents from around the nation who were seeking Fratianno's assistance in investigations.

McDonald searched for and finally found an author that met with his approval. He called on Ovid Demaris, a veteran writer on organized crime, the author of the *Green Felt Jungle* and *Captive City*.

The meeting with Demaris occurred in a San Francisco motel. Demaris came with 200 questions, culled from his own detailed knowledge of La Cosa Nostra's activities, and proceeded to put Fratianno through a grilling session that made the FBI interviews pale by comparison.

Demaris was a tough-minded, unyielding interviewer who wasn't going to allow Fratianno the luxury of rambling through his usual warm-up stories. He wasn't going to coax and cajole; either Fratianno was going to be an entirely willing subject or he didn't want any part of him.

Fratianno didn't like Demaris's style, but he respected him, if not for his style at least for his assurances that there was a great deal of money to be made if the interviews and writing went well.

Demaris left that first interview as elated as an anthropologist who had just been guided to the perfect skeletal remains of the missing link. He was convinced that Fratianno possessed the most remarkable body of knowledge about the secret treacheries of La Cosa Nostra anyone could conceivably have amassed in a lifetime. And he was in awe of Fratianno's detailed recall of those events and the personalities involved. But he wasn't going to be blinded by Fratianno's potential. He understood who he was dealing with. Before he left Jimmy on that occasion, Demaris set down some working guidelines, the foremost being that he would walk away from the project if he ever once caught Fratianno in a lie. The other provisos gave Demaris complete editorial control of the work and an even split of the profits.

Demaris's caution was wise. Fratianno wasn't the kind of person to be trusted implicitly.

And yet there was a remarkable metamorphosis taking place. Fratianno was finding that speaking the truth about secrets he had guarded for a lifetime was providing him with just about everything he wanted. It had freed him from a life of crime, in which he had lost faith; it won his freedom from courtrooms and lengthy jail sentences; it had brought promises of financial support for the foreseeable future; it had won him the loyalty of these bright young men, agents, and prosecutors; it was beginning to give him some celebrity status, and, perhaps best of all, this book could give him legitimate financial rewards.

It was as Jean might instruct him: The truth will set you free.

In the final week of June, Ron Hadinger, accompanied by the Cleveland strike force attorney Ken Bravo and Thomas Kimmell, came to Jimmy, like a self-fulfilling prophecy.

Over the last four months the state case against the Cleveland mob had been slowly played out in front of a jury. State prosecutor Carmen Marino and his partner Edward Walsh delivered hundreds of pieces of evidence and called more than a hundred witnesses, including Ferritto, the government's star witness, who came across as a cold-blooded murderer.

The defense was able to cast doubt on most of Ferritto's story. Except for the Spoths, the two eyewitnesses who had seen Ferritto and Carabbia at the scene, there was little or no corroboration of his testimony.

Ferritto was also discredited by his having lied to the FBI. When he began cooperating, Ferritto told them it was Butchy Cisternino who helped him set the bomb that killed Greene. But just days before the trial began, the FBI found another informant who assured them it was Ronald Carabbia who had worked with Ferritto in detonating the bomb.

Hadinger met with Ferritto at the MCC in New York City, where Ferritto admitted the lie. He explained that he blamed Cisternino for his arrest. It was Cisternino who had obtained the cars—the blue Plymouth and the Nova, the Trojan horse car—that linked him to the murder. And besides, he said, Carabbia was an old friend he wanted to protect.

When the jury came back, only Cisternino and Carabbia were convicted—and later sentenced to life terms. The Cleveland mob's top players walked free.

Kimmell and Hadinger recounted the state trial to Jimmy. They told him they were preparing to go after the leaders of the Cleveland mob in a new federal RICO case, charging them with the Greene murder conspiracy and the bribing of an FBI clerk to leak confidential files.

But, they said, without Fratianno their case didn't stand a chance; Fratianno was the only government witness capable of linking Licavoli and the rest of the mob's leaders to the leak. Ultimately, they fell just short of pleading for his cooperation.

Jimmy had been fighting this battle against going home to Cleveland for almost a year—since he had first met with Ahearn the previous August. He had made it a singularly nonnegotiable item in his set of demands. And until that time, no one except Hadinger had insisted that his testimony was crucial.

But this was a different Jimmy Fratianno than the one Hadinger had met with months earlier; this was a far more controlled and alert character than the caged animal he had interviewed in Milwaukee in December. This Jimmy Fratianno was making arguments about lack of corroboration of his testimony and the conflicts between his account and Ferritto's.

They assured him that he wouldn't have to testify about the Greene murder or his relationship with Ferritto. All they wanted was his knowledge of the leak, his meeting with Licavoli at Dope DelSanter's funeral, and his informing Ahearn about the leak.

And then he began to negotiate.

He would testify if: his sister's family in Cleveland received protection; he was guaranteed no more than probation when sentenced in the Cleveland case; and he was removed from prison for the duration of his term and held at Elgin Air Force Base.

They said they'd see what could be done but made no promises. A good faith effort was all Jimmy was looking for it seemed, for he immediately began cooperating.

El Paso is hot, dusty, and lousy with tourists crossing the Rio Grande in Winnebagos during July. Jimmy came in on a commercial flight from San Diego, missing the city's tourist trade but getting a full dose of its heat and grit. He was already getting used to this travel routine: two marshals on board, others waiting on the tarmac in those big unmarked American cars. Nothing else on four wheels is as easily identifiable by virtue of being chromeless, scratchless, clean, and utterly devoid of markings as those big four-door "unmarked" police vehicles.

The cars took a slow ride to La Tuna, 15 miles north along Interstate 10, through the city and parallel to the Rio Grande to just about the furthest western point in Texas.

Fratianno was silent in anticipation of his new digs. He wore a blue business suit and carried a cigar. No handcuffs. A marshal carried his small, red-leather suitcase. He looked more like a United States Senator on an inspection tour than an inmate.

He had been promised the Valachi suite. He had been told it was a small apartment where he could do his own cooking and watch his own TV. There would be no other inmates, but a guard would be with him at all times. He had hoped for a terrace where he could get some fresh air. But when he felt the intensity of the desert heat, he began wishing for central air-conditioning.

After passing the checkpoints to enter the small, medium-security prison—authorities prefer calling them correctional facilities—the cars drove through a compound of stark adobe buildings to a small, two-story structure marked "Hospital."

Fratianno doesn't ask questions of obvious, common curiosity, so he expressed no wonder at their stopping there. He walked in silence, a hand slung deep in a trousers pocket, through a heavy steel gate, past the front desk and another gate, up a flight of stairs, and down a long hospital corridor, the entire time craning his neck to look at the surroundings, peering through the small barred windows of the hospital rooms.

At the end of the corridor was another iron gate and two TV cameras, one trained down the corridor, the other aimed to get a good view of whoever stood at the gate. Beyond it were two doorways. His was the first door on the left.

"You motherfuckers have got to be kidding me!" Jimmy said on first sight of his "suite."

The "Valachi suite" was a euphemism. It was nothing more than two small rooms, prison cells, and a bathroom, connected to a 15-by-12-foot private dayroom with a large window overlooking the prison yard. There was a couch so uncomfortable that on his first day there Jimmy dragged out a mattress from the unused cell to sit on the floor. There was a kitchen table and a couple of hardwood chairs, but no cooking facilities. The entire affair was done in drab institutional prison green.

Large black flies and Lone Star cockroaches—of such dimensions that they've been compared to hummingbirds—were his only companions, other than the guards who stood round-the-clock duty in the private dayroom. And the guards were about as talkative as the cockroaches.

Another man might have found ways to occupy his time in such a setting: reading books, writing, painting, or finding some project, perhaps jigsaw puzzles, model ships, or building a replica of the Parthenon from toothpicks.

But for Fratianno, without people to talk to, regale with his tales or work a con on, life is a living hell. Other inmates were off-limits to him. He couldn't even go out for exercise too frequently. And on those occasions when he did get some exercise—about a half-hour, three or four times a week—he would be taken to the prison yard in plain view of other inmates, including several Jimmy knew as members or associates of La Cosa Nostra. Jimmy assumed that the mob knew where he was held within weeks after his arrival.

His only luxuries were the telephone and the television, each of which Jimmy kept in near-constant use.

With the TV blaring any sort of mindless trash he could find, he would get on the horn to Jean, agents, prosecutors, and for three and four hours at a time with Demaris, the only person in the world who had nothing better to do than listen to Jimmy's tales.

Jean was his only regular visitor. The marshals had moved her to a condominium complex in the Rio Grande Valley, just outside El Paso, days after Jimmy arrived at La Tuna.

Her visits were a source of both comfort and frustration. They would talk about what they were going to do once Jimmy finished his prison sentence, how they could begin settling down to what she called "a normal life." But having her so close, with a prison guard only a few feet away, was a form of cruelty.

"This is the toughest fuckin' time I've ever done," he told Henderson at least twice a week by phone. "And I'll tell you all about this fuckin' place: the last three guys who lived here before me, well, the guy before me, a chief of police or something, committed suicide in here, Valachi died in here, and the guy before him went crazy in here and tried to commit suicide. Hey Jim, I'll be glad to get out of here alive."

Concerned for Fratianno's emotional well-being, Henderson and Fox arranged to spend a week with him, to debrief him in depth on the Los Angeles case. They could have waited a while longer, but Fratianno really needed the companionship. Their visit marked the first time Fox and Henderson would hear Jimmy's whole story.

The sessions were rigorous. They spent hours going over many of the same questions the FBI agents had discussed with him in January and February. But this time they were pushing for every detail. Unlike the earlier debriefings, where the agents just listened, this was a relentless grilling, driving down broad avenues and narrow blind alleys, searching for signposts that would corroborate Fratianno's accounts of the roads he and the Los Angeles mob had traveled together. The slightest, seemingly most inconsequential piece of information could give veracity to his claims: someone who had seen him with Brooklier or Dragna, a waitress who might have overheard a portion of their conversation at a restaurant, a dated receipt to show he was in town when he said he was. It would be very circumstantial, but that's better than nothing at all.

When they became tired of the Los Angeles case, they would begin going over how La Cosa Nostra operated, the rules and allegiances. And after that they would go over his murders and other crimes so they'd know the very worst the defense might use to discredit his testimony. And then they'd start all over again.

At the end of each day, Henderson and Fox drove back to their motel exhausted. They had reached a level of mental absorption that left them incapable of thinking about anything but work. Over a late dinner and a few drinks they'd compare notes and prepare for the next day's interview, which began before breakfast.

Jimmy was delighted to see them so early in the morning. It meant fresh eggs, spicy hash browns, Canadian ham, and toast for breakfast. Otherwise he got powdered eggs or cold cereal.

"What happened to the cooking I was supposed to be able to do in here? There ain't no stove or refrigerator. You know, I spoke to this warden and told him what I was promised and he said there was no way I was getting to cook in here."

"We'll try to get it straightened out when we get out of here, Jimmy," Henderson said.

"I'll tell you what I'll do," Fox offered. "When I get back to Washington next week I'll go see Norm Carlson, he's the head of the bureau of prisons and a very reasonable guy. I'm sure he'll understand that we need to keep someone like you happy."

"While you're at it tell him about that couch and the chairs," Fratianno said, seated on his floor mattress while Henderson and Fox sat along the floor, propped up against the wall.

Ultimately, there were no revelations from the sessions; just a lot of detailed information that gave color and depth to the bland written reports investigators had filed. But they did come away with an understanding beyond the mere facts of the cases and crimes. Jimmy was capable of providing a feeling for why things had happened as they did, explaining motivations in a rich personal and historical perspective.

"These are like a bunch of overgrown kids playing Mafia," Fox told Henderson as they packed to leave El Paso. "I expected to hear about vast amounts of cash, labor racketeering, that type of thing, but most of these guys can't buy lunch."

"I tell you, what I was really fascinated by was Fratianno. I mean, this guy wouldn't hurt a soul on his own. But the boss tells him to whack someone and he doesn't give it a second thought."

"I don't know," Fox said. "I think the rules of his reality are different; you sign on to play a game and one of the rules is that you can get dead. And only a very special kind of guy can enforce that rule, so that makes Jimmy a very special kind of guy in the context of his reality."

"Well, whatever made him special in his last incarnation is sure going to make him special for us," Henderson said. "You know, it's not unrealistic to think that we'll never get this kind of witness again."

The men departed El Paso International Airport: Henderson headed West; Fox back East.

The first thing Fox did when he got back to his office in Washington was to arrange for Fratianno to get a microwave oven and a small refrigerator.

7

The Premier Performance

FRATIANNO arrived in New York on October 1, 1978, weeks before the Premier Theatre trial was to start, for final meetings with the prosecution team and a chance to escape the confines of his prison suite.

He was held under heavy guard at Fort Hamilton, an army base in Brooklyn at the foot of the Verrazano-Narrows Bridge, overlooking New York harbor.

Bud McPherson, the marshal from Los Angeles, was running the show. They had taken over an abandoned warehouse that had several rooms which doubled as bedrooms and a makeshift kitchen. They expected to live there for the next several months.

In 1978, the Marshals Service was making do with whatever tools it could scrape together. Heavy army blankets, mattresses, and panels from old packing crates were used as blackout curtains on the warehouse windows; a collection of tin cans was strung together and hung at the doors to act as intrusion alarms. They were "going to the mattresses" with all the sophistication of mobsters holing-up during a street war.

Whenever a breeze would blow off the Lower Bay, up the seawalls, and through the warehouse, one of the "intrusion alarms" would rattle the marshals to attention, sending them searching for an assassin. Jimmy would pick up a loaded pump-action shotgun and crouch in a corner, his back against the wall.

After the search was abandoned, Jimmy would rail at his keepers for leaving him alone. When they stood guard outside his door, he screamed that they should be inside. When they spoke on their radios, he complained that someone might intercept the communication and figure out where they were.

Jimmy didn't like New York. He didn't feel safe there. He would never admit it, but he was scared of New York. New York was the home base of La Cosa Nostra. The Five Families in New York were the final arbiters of all La Cosa Nostra disputes nationwide. Their dominance over many of the city's industries—the docks, trucking, textile manufacturing, meat packing, construction—made them the wealthiest and most powerful crime leaders in the nation.

There were 2,500 made guys in New York, a small army of serious workers and money-makers. And for every made member there were perhaps another ten men willing "to do the right thing" if they spotted someone like Fratianno.

New York still believed in the Family rules of conduct and discipline. If you clipped a guy like Fratianno in New York, you would be justly rewarded—not necessarily with cash, but with jobs, prestige, and influence. Nowhere else in the United States could the rewards for carrying out such an execution be greater.

And Jimmy understood the significance of his testimony in New York. This wasn't going to be like Los Angeles, where he was expected to help put Brooklier and his gang in prison. That was no big deal. Prison was the cost of doing business in this thing. In New York he was threatening their enterprises and exposing the millions of dollars they had invested. The root purpose of La Cosa Nostra, as Jimmy defined it, was to make money. His testimony, therefore, was aimed right at the heart of the organization.

The only thing standing between Fratianno and near-constant New York–based hysteria was Bud McPherson, who had a very special knowledge of the city, the wise guys, and Fratianno. McPherson, forty-four at the time, was a former New York City cop who, after ten years' service, retired on a disability pension. He moved to Los Angeles in the late 1960s, bouncing from job to job—chief of security at a Warner Bros. studio for a while and then as a trucker—before finding the Marshals Service.

He had grown up about 2 miles from Fort Hamilton, in Bay Ridge, Brooklyn—a predominantly Italian neighborhood—where he gained a basic knowledge about mobs. He knew the older boys who dropped out of high school, disappeared from the old neighborhood, and returned a year or so later dressed in fine silk suits, Italian shoes, and driving fancy cars. A cousin would explain: "He's with good people."

As far as Jimmy was concerned, he couldn't have asked for a better protector than McPherson. Bud knew how mobsters think; the two men could converse easily. And most important, McPherson understood how to provide Fratianno with that extra ounce of care and protection that would get him to court relaxed and safe.

It was the little things that made McPherson special, like the food kitty he organized. Every day, Jimmy's $15 government stipend would be put in the kitty with the marshals' contributions. McPherson would then visit the local Italian markets, returning with raw materials that Jimmy would transform into gourmet delights. Or, on days when there were no agents coming to visit the oracle of mob knowledge, no Demaris interviews set, no cooking to be done, and no football on TV, McPherson would load his team into cars and take Jimmy out for "a haircut"—a short tour of Brooklyn.

Jimmy sat expressionless in the backseat for most of the sightseeing, lighting up only when a mini-skirt strode by. The only part that excited him was when McPherson pointed down a street near Fort Hamilton, explaining that Funzi Tieri lived just a block away. Despite Jimmy's pleas, McPherson wouldn't drive by the house. He wanted Jimmy to have a little distraction and relaxation, not a flirt with danger.

On Akerman's next visit, Jimmy told him about Tieri living so close by.

"That old son of a bitch probably has every made guy in town looking for me and I'm hiding out in his backyard," he said with a deep belly laugh.

Akerman was amused but had trouble laughing. This espionage routine—constantly having to look over his shoulder to see if he was being followed, not being able to tell anyone where he was going or at what time he'd be back—was unnerving. Still, he had a job to do, and that was to make Jimmy's testimony sparkle. It was up to Akerman to hone Fratianno's testimony to pinpoint accuracy and train him as a skilled witness. To accomplish this they conducted days of mock trial drills, asking questions as if Jimmy were on the witness stand.

The only proviso was that Jimmy couldn't mention La Cosa Nostra by name. Akerman had decided to avoid invoking the mob at trial, believing the so-called white-collar criminal defendants in the case would complain of its prejudice and successfully argue for separate trials.

Aside from that, these sessions were instruction in style, not substance: how to go about answering a question, not what answer to give; coaching him on how to tell his story without telling him which facts he should tell. To some extent, Akerman played Professor Henry Higgins to Fratianno's Eliza Doolittle.

"Okay then, Mr. Fratianno, did there come a time when Mr. Marson told you of his position at the Westchester Premier Theatre?" Akerman asked, pacing the large, dark room they used for these sessions.

"Yeah, he told me that he had $1.4 million in the place and . . ." Jimmy stopped when he saw Akerman shaking his head in disapproval and jotting something down. "What?" he asked.

"The question was 'Did there come a time when Mr. Marson told you about his role in the theater.' I didn't ask what he told you. Just did he tell you. Okay?"

"All right. My answer would be, 'Yes.' Or, 'Yes, sir, he did.' "

"Fine. Now, what did he tell you?"

Jimmy stopped for a moment to think. He was seated bolt upright in his chair. He was still in bedclothes, but had adjusted the lapels and straightened the hem of his bathrobe to drape neatly. He always stiffened during these sessions.

"He told me that he was a partner in the theater along with—"

Akerman broke in, again writing something as he spoke. "I didn't ask anything about anyone else. All I asked was about his position in the theater. I know you're going to tell the whole story, and I'll get around to letting you tell it, but remember, just give your most specific answer. So again. What did he tell you about his position in the theater?"

"He told me he was a partner."

"Did he tell you who any of the other partners were in the theater at that time?"

"Yes, sir. He mentioned some names."

"Good. Did you recognize any of those names?"

"No, sir."

"Was there any name in particular that Mr. Marson asked you about?"

"Yeah, he asked me about Greg DePalma because he knew Greg was with the Gambino Family and I, uh . . . I, uh . . . Oh, fuck. Ask me again."

Akerman went through the question again and Jimmy replied with a simple "Yes, sir."

"And who was that person that Mr. Marson asked you about?"

"Greg DePalma."

"Did there come a time when you spoke to Mr. DePalma?"

"Yes, sir. At Tommy Marson's house. I mean, just, yes."

Akerman smiled and made a notation.

"When was the first time you spoke to Mr. DePalma?"

"At Tommy Marson's house, the first time I was at his house we spoke on the phone."

"Okay. Did there come a time when you actually met Mr. DePalma?"

"Yes, sir, it was, uh. . . . Yes, sir."

Akerman made another note. "When was that?"

"Do you mean the date? I'm not sure, sir, but I know it was sometime in early 1976," Jimmy said, his head cocked to one side, his eyebrows raised in a self-satisfied look requesting confirmation that he was catching on.

"That was really good. If you're not certain of a date or anything feel free to say so. Nobody remembers precise dates of things that happened years ago. Now remember, there may also be times that you know there's a document that would refresh your recollection and you can ask for it. For example, if something happened when you were on vacation six years ago, you may have sent a postcard and the postcard might be used to refresh your recollection. But whatever you do, never guess or estimate anything. Always feel free to say 'I don't recall.' Don't say, 'I don't know,' because if someone later refreshes your recollection with a document or something, you may find that you did know, but just didn't recall.

"All right, next question. Was there an occasion, some special event at which you met Mr. DePalma?"

"Yes, sir."

"What was that event?"

"The Man of the Year dinner for Frank Sinatra at the Waldorf-Astoria."

"Good. I want to jump around a little today to some key areas, all right? I mean, we're not going to plow through from beginning to end. So assume I've asked you all about Marson introducing you to DePalma, Weisman, and Fusco as his partners. Now, you come into New York the second time. You're there for the Sinatra show in April 1976.

"Here's the question: During that concert series, did you learn what Mr. DePalma's job was at the theater?"

"Yes, sir. That he ran the concessions."

Akerman made a note.

"Okay, now Jimmy, you answered that too fast. You shot back without pausing that he ran the concessions. Do you know he ran the concessions?"

"Nick, I know that for sure!"

"The point is, how do you know that? You've seen things and heard things that make you believe he ran the concessions. Tell me what you saw or heard, not what you believe. Okay?"

"I see what you mean. So, uh . . . ask it again."

"All right. Can you tell us what was Mr. DePalma's role in the theater?"

"Well, sir. Mr. Marson told me he ran the concessions and I seen him handling the money from them concessions."

"Good. Now, if you recall, what were those concessions?"

"They had things all over the theater. A restaurant and bars, a hot dog stand, and champagne carts. That's all I remember, but I know there was others."

"Good. Now, did Mr. Marson ever tell you how many seats were in the theater?"

"Uh . . . well, yeah."

"When would that have been and what did he tell you?"

"Sir, isn't that two questions? Could you please ask one at a time," Jimmy said with pride.

"Great. That's the way to do it. Now when would that have been that he told you about the seats?"

"During that April seventy-six Sinatra concert, sir. I can't say for sure exactly when."

"What did he tell you about the seats?"

"Well, he told me there was 3,500 permanent seats and that during that concert they were using somethin' like a couple hundred folding chairs additional."

"Good. Did Marson tell you anything about the sale of tickets for regular seats or these folding chairs?"

"Yes, sir."

"And what did he tell you?"

"Well, he told me they scalped tickets for some of the chairs, like double the face value."

"Did Mr. Marson tell you what would be done with the proceeds on the sale of scalped tickets, the folding chairs, and concessions?"

"Yes, sir."

"What did he tell you?"

"He said that the money would be used to pay these shylocks, and whatever was left over would be split between them four partners: Marson, Fusco, DePalma, and Weisman. Oh, yeah, also that Louie Dones, Mickey Rudin, and Jilly Rizzo would get a cut."

Akerman was making notes again. "Okay, Jimmy. Look, all you know is that the theater owed these men money. You can say how you know that, I'll ask you about the rate of interest and all of that, but don't characterize them as loan sharks or anything of that kind. Okay?"

"You mean, like times I heard DePalma telling Marson how much they owed, their obligations to Nino Gaggi and Mike Fusco?"

"Yes, wonderful. Now, do you know who Mickey Rudin and Jilly Rizzo are?"

"Yes, sir."

"Who are they?"

"Jilly Rizzo is like Sinatra's bodyguard and Rudin is his manager or lawyer."

"Did Mr. Marson tell you why Mr. Rizzo got a cut?"

"Yeah, because of the Sinatra T-shirts; he provided them and got a piece of the profits."

The questioning went on through the morning. After several days of this, Akerman would script his entire direct examination, determining Jimmy's response to any question.

After several hours, Jimmy stepped away to get lunch started.

In the kitchen, he rousted two marshals who had been playing cards. He barked out his orders, treating the marshals like scullery maids. Inside of a few minutes everyone was working. A long loaf of Italian bread was being sliced and plugged with garlic and butter; a pot of sauce from the refrigerator was warming on the stove; a tray of lasagna was heating in the oven; precooked pieces of Italian sweet sausage and fried chicken were waiting on a side board to be reheated in the sauce.

Akerman stood by admiring the impending feast and nibbling any loose ends he could find. He asked about the sauce and Jimmy agreed to give him the recipe before the end of the day.

"We got some time before we eat," Jimmy said, settling back into the makeshift witness stand. "Let's get back to work."

"Okay, now I'll play defense lawyer for a while and see how you do," Akerman said.

"You have a deal with the government, don't you, Mr. Fratianno?"

Jimmy stopped and thought for a moment. "I don't know what you mean by a deal, sir."

Nick nodded approvingly. "Okay then. Mr. Fratianno, you have a deal that you won't be prosecuted for any murders you committed, isn't that true?"

"No, sir. I have an agreement that I'll testify truthfully."

"But Mr. Fratianno, isn't it a fact that the government is letting you off on several murders in return for your testimony?"

"No, sir, that is not a fact. I'm in prison right now, sir."

"Come now, Mr. Fratianno, isn't it a fact that you're spending a whole lot less time in prison because of the deal you made with government?"

"I really couldn't tell you, sir."

"Very good, Jimmy."

It was clear that Jimmy needed little coaching in dealing with hostile questions—he was naturally combative.

"Tell me, Mr. Fratianno, you would like to stay out of jail, wouldn't you?"

Fratianno got stuck on that question and paused.

"Just answer it truthfully," Akerman said. "If you lie, especially on a question like that, no one will believe anything else you say. Just always tell the truth."

"Well, I'd just say something like, 'Yes, sir, but I don't have to lie here, if I lie here my deal's busted and they'll prosecute me on everything I've told them.'"

"Okay. Now they're going to want to know about these preparation sessions. They may want to know if there are any records that they can use. They'd be entitled to see any notes of these sessions, so they might ask, 'Mr. Fratianno, when Mr. Akerman met with you to review your testimony did he take any notes of what was said?'"

"I guess I'd have to tell them, 'Yeah, Mr. Akerman took lots of notes on them sessions.'"

"How do you know that, Jimmy?"

"Nick, I've seen you doing it."

"You're sure? You're sure I've been taking notes about our interviews?"

"Hey man, I've been watching. Everytime I say something wrong you make a little fuckin' note there on that yellow pad of yours."

"Is this the pad?" Akerman said, holding up the legal pad with his scrawl on it.

As Jimmy nodded, Akerman handed it to him.

"Read it out loud," he said.

Jimmy read aloud: "Pick up two cartons milk . . . get dry cleaning . . . call Lisa . . . I'm getting hungry."

"Hey, what's this shit?"

"Jimmy, I've been setting you up to make a point. Sure I've been writing things down during these interviews, but you've had no idea what I was writing; you never once saw what was written on that paper, so you can't answer the question of whether I took any notes about these sessions. Don't assume or guess anything. Only testify to what you know."

Jimmy was smiling with a new awareness while he continued looking at the legal pad filled with pages of notes, much of it nonsense. It was like a magic act; Jimmy was stunned. Akerman's point hit home.

"Okay, I see what you're driving at. But man, you have bad handwriting. You should have been a fuckin'doctor," he said as they headed toward the kitchen.

Akerman spent five days at Fort Hamilton before jury selection began October 18, and then for a week spent evenings hidden in the basement of the U.S. Attorney's office with Fratianno before putting him on the witness stand in early December.

In the interim, Jimmy flew back to Los Angeles, and on November 6, 1978, he entered his guilty pleas to federal obstruction of justice charges in the murders of Frank Bompensiero and Danny Greene.

The U.S. Courthouse for the Southern District of New York is an imposing, granite structure, with an almost-block-wide stairway sweeping up from the street to a formal, columned threshold. Brass trimmed revolving doorways mark the entrance to its wide marble corridors. Oaken doorways along the corridor lead to courtrooms and labyrinths of offices and record rooms.

The courthouse rises more than thirty stories from the street and is capped by a brillant, gold-leaf pyramid, which on sunny days provides a glimmering, radiant market along the city skyline demarking Foley Square, the city's small government district, which is crowded at every side by the city's extreme diversity.

Just to the south, separated from the courthouse by a cobblestone courtyard, is New York City's Municipal Building, a forty-story behemoth of WPA architecture, built atop three-story-high vaulted arches and passageways. A monument to modern bureaucracy.

Across the street is City Hall and the old Boss Tweed Courthouse, a small squat building, similar in design to the White House, resplendent in internal detail, for which the former corrupt city fathers robbed their constituents blind.

A few short blocks to the north and east is the Bowery, littered with the spoiled and often rancid remains of human potential.

A block to the north begins Chinatown and three blocks farther up is Canal Street, defining the southern border of Little Italy. Each community a tangle of narrow streets and crowded immigrants' dreams; each with its own language, subdivided by dialects and customs; a horizontal tower of babel whose residents look upon the evening tourists with gazes of such distrust as to make one think they'd fallen upon some secret cabal.

Start again at the courthouse and turn an equal distance to the south and, within the shadow of the Brooklyn Bridge, lies Wall Street and the financial district, also navigable only by narrow twisting streets, where secret meetings and cabals are assuredly taking place, plotting with equal distrust of strangers.

Beneath this ten-block stretch rumbles the steady rhythm of the city's massive, grimy subway.

It was at the center of these extremes of American society, in the U.S. District Courthouse, that the Premier Theatre trial opened in one of the oak-paneled, 30-foot-ceilinged formal courtrooms.

The trial began an unusual mid-October Indian summer day, during which the courtroom's tall narrow windows were opened to allow air and the city's noises to enter. It would end thirteen weeks later, when Manhattan was gripped by a particularly freezing winter, during which the courtroom's aging pipes would clank, rattle, and hiss, drowning out testimony.

The defendants gathered at a 35-foot-long L-shaped table—nine defendants with at least one lawyer each, squeezed in shoulder-to-shoulder, twenty-one people in all. Their physical proximity was not a statement of collective purpose. There was no unified defense strategy except for a gentlemen's agreement to avoid ever placing the blame on a fellow defendant. Other than that, it was every man for himself.

Prominent in his absence was Marson, whose lawyer had successfully argued that his failing health should prohibit his enduring a lengthy trial in the Northeastern cold, so far from his Palm Springs home.

Akerman sat at a smaller table, between the judge's bench and the defense table. Seated with him amid a sea of documents and tape cassettes were Special Agent Robert Tolan, Assistant U.S. Attorney Scott Campbell, and Joan Alexander, a legal research coordinator.

U.S. District Judge Robert W. Sweet was presiding. A former deputy mayor under John Lindsay, he had recently been appointed to the bench. This would be his first major trial and neither side knew what to make of him.

The only certainty was that Sweet's handsome patrician appearance—slim and angular with salt and pepper mustache and hair—lent an air of dignity. His infinite patience, sense of whimsy, and attention to detail would become apparent later.

Sweet's pretrial decisions had been largely routine. He had found no problems with the government's wiretaps. And he had rejected the defendants' arguments for separate trials—they were all linked to the conspiracy, either in the theater's creation, operation, or demise, which formed the basis for the "continuing criminal enterprise" charge under the RICO law.

He had reserved decision on the use at trial of a photograph—the one Jean Fratianno had turned over to Jack Barron—showing Frank Sinatra embracing DePalma and Marson and flanked by Carlo Gambino, Paul Castellano, Fratianno and others in Sinatra's dressing room at the theater.

There was only one pretrial issue in which Sweet took the prosecution to task. He chastised the government for its clumsy attempt to coerce Weisman's cooperation a year earlier by arresting him on a flimsy bank fraud charge. Sweet characterized it as an "illegal arrest." He barred the use of statements Weisman had made to Akerman and the FBI on the day of that arrest; statements confirming wiretap evidence that money was being siphoned from the theater's profits to pay loan sharks.

Weisman, then forty, raised in the affluence of Scarsdale, New York, and a graduate of the Wharton School of Business, was the government's key target. Not because he was such a heinous criminal, but because he had become the front for organized crime, the fall guy, for the organized crime interests, secret backers, and corporate intrigue that had created and bankrupted the theater corporation. He was the one person who knew it all and could open all the doors the government wanted open.

Weisman would have gladly cooperated, but he believed himself caught between two evils: while the government threatened to take his freedom, the mob might take his life. And when Weisman chose to preserve his life and stand up to the charges—most of which he believed himself innocent of—it only fueled Akerman's determination.

Perhaps the only defendant Akerman wanted as much as Weisman was DePalma, the theater's leading mob figure.

Next on Akerman's list, if such a pecking order could be properly constructed, would probably have been Leonard Horwitz, the Warner executive charged as the go-between for bribes and cash kickbacks between the theater and Warner.

And not at all lastly, Akerman wanted Louis "Louie Dome" Pacella, the Sinatra connection.

It was not that those men had committed such bad acts; this was not a matter of short-term justice. The real significance of the case, what Akerman and the Justice Department were looking for, was long-term results, hoping that convictions in this case would serve as bludgeons to win the cooperation of these defendants in cases against the leaders of the Gambino and Tieri mob Families, executives of Warner Communications, and Sinatra.

What was being prosecuted was a concept: criminal conspiracies in the entertainment industry, the world of live theater and living legends. And Fratianno was the only one able to provide insight to the core of the criminal conspiracy. It wasn't so much what Fratianno knew, as who he was; merely his involvement with the theater spoke volumes.

The media arrived before the trial began. Weeks before a single juror was selected, the *New York Times,* which usually buried mob dramas in its cavernous back pages, found cause to move this one into prominent play. And the *Wall Street Journal,* that bastion of lower Manhattan money-making enclaves, was offering in-depth coverage.

The media recognized the significance of the case: The indictment promised to demonstrate at trial La Cosa Nostra's infiltration of a legitimate corporation and how that corruption had tainted some of the best-known names on Wall Street and in Hollywood.

After three days of jury selection, the stage was set for the rise and fall of the Premier Theatre. But only by listening carefully to each side, and applying a healthy dose of cynicism, could a spectator or juror discern what had actually happened there.

Akerman was the first to rise, empty handed, to the podium.

He wore a new blue suit and appeared much younger, more nervous, and not quite as confident as the older, experienced defense lawyers. For them, this was just a job. Win or lose they would collect their hefty fees, about $150,000 each on average, and hopefully realize some pride and enjoyment in a job well done. For Akerman, all that really mattered was winning. And he wore his good luck charm on his wrist: a Mickey Mouse watch.

Akerman began, his voice in a steady, strong cadence:

"One day in 1971, three men gathered together in Scarsdale, New York, and conceived the idea of the Westchester Premier Theatre, which was ultimately built in Tarrytown, New York, approximately one hour's drive from this courthouse.

"The purpose of that theater, the ostensible purpose, the supposed purpose, was to bring live entertainment to Westchester County. But for these three men that theater had a different purpose, because from that day forward, for approximately seven years, these three men systematically and methodically, through clever schemes and simple schemes, through bribery, corruption, and fraud, looted and stole hundreds of thousands of dollars from innocent citizens of this community in total defiance of the law."

He paused for a moment, looking about the courtroom to locate the defendants. And then, with his voice booming, he pointed to each one with a jabbing, accusatory thrust of his hand and he rattled off their names. First the three core defendants: Gregory DePalma, Eliot Weisman, and Richard Fusco. Then "their cohorts in crime for seven years": Murad Nersesian (AKA Mike Fusco or Mikey Coco); Leonard Horwitz (AKA The Fox); Lawrence Goodman; Salvatore Cannatella; Louis Pacella (AKA Louie Dome); and Anthony Gaggi (AKA Nino).

And, to be certain that the jurors knew who was who, as he pointed out each man Akerman noted some distinguishing characteristic, the color of his suit, necktie, or hair.

"As I have stated, this is a very simple case about two straight-forward simple themes: greed and money."

Akerman broke his rapid-fire delivery. Starting again, slowly, he explained the specific charges as they applied to each defendant, using a color-coded chart, a different color for each charge: Weisman had every color in Akerman's rainbow; DePalma and Fusco were bathed in most of the hues; the other defendants had several colors each.

There were three separate criminal conspiracies: stock frauds employed in creating the theater corporation; bankruptcy frauds, which involved looting of theater revenues not reported to the bankruptcy court; and obstruction of justice, charges that several defendants sought to mislead the grand jury.

Akerman used the chart and the charges to explain the history of the theater, beginning with Weisman becoming president of the corporation in 1973, with DePalma and Fusco as his secret partners.

He described how they sought to raise $2 million in a public stock offering, but omitted DePalma's and Fusco's status as partners in the stock prospectus and "did not state that Carlo Gambino had loaned the theater money and that the theater had been loaned money by John Capra, a reputed narcotics peddler."

He included in a list of schemes employed to complete the floundering stock sales: the Gambino and Capra loans, used to purchase stock under the names of unsuspecting brokerage clients; offers to purchasers of a free share for every two bought outright; and cash bribes paid by Weisman, through Horwitz, to two Warner executives as inducement for them to approve Warner's purchase of 40,000 shares of stock.

After the theater opened in March 1975, he said, Weisman, DePalma, and Fusco looted the profits to "line their own pockets" and pay off their undisclosed debts, their actions driving the theater corporation into bankruptcy court in December 1976 and, ultimately, forcing it to be declared bankrupt in April 1978.

The evidence would take various forms, he said, including testimony from former theater employees, FBI agents, and "a very special kind of witness, what we call an accomplice witness, four who actually participated in the crimes with these defendants."

Akerman had assumed many voices in this monologue: excited storyteller, moral accuser, trustworthy explainer of the law. Now there was a tone of calm sincerity, laced with just a touch of humility, as he explained about the bad people who were assisting the government in this prosecution, their criminal histories and their deals for leniency—to defuse the inevitable assaults from the defense.

He described in some detail the cavalcade of less-than-sterling personalities who would give life to the theater case: Charles Carino, the bad check artist; Norman Brodsky, the stock swindler; and Bruce Kosman, an aide in the Warner kickback scheme.

And then there was Fratianno, "who to these particular defendants was known as Dr. Schwartz."

"You will hear from Fratianno how he was a trusted and close friend of the defendant Marson, and how as a result of his friendship with Tom Marson [he] became very friendly with Weisman, DePalma, and Fusco."

Weisman, who had listened impassively until that moment, let out an audible "Ha" at the suggestion of his "friendship" with Fratianno.

"Mr. Fratianno will give you the inside story as to how the defendants skimmed and looted hundreds of thousands of dollars out of the Westchester Premier Theatre.

"You will also hear, however, that Mr. Fratianno has a prior criminal record, and that he has entered into an agreement with the Justice Department, in Los Angeles, California, where Mr. Fratianno has agreed to plead guilty to two murders."

"Mr. Fratianno has been promised that in return for his guilty pleas to these particular murders that the maximum exposure which he is to receive in jail will be five years."

And then came the most important part of Akerman's introduction to the four accomplice witnesses—the disclaimer:

"Now remember one thing: Nobody is saying that you should decide whether or not these people are good, because if there is one fact that is undisputed in this case, it is that these four accomplice witnesses are bad. Indeed, one of them is a murderer.

"The only question which you must decide is whether or not these four accomplices are telling the truth. I'm going to ask you to listen very carefully to what these witnesses say and to scrutinize their testimony with the utmost care. Make a mental checklist, continue to ask yourself, 'What else tells me that these people are telling the truth?'

"In that regard, some of the most significant evidence that you are going to hear are some of these defendants' own voices memorialized on tape-recorded conversations in which they actually discuss the crimes for which they are charged."

And then the monologue wound down with an explanation of the RICO statute, the jurors' civic duty, and a bit of old-fashioned American flag-waving before he rested his voice, sitting back to await the inevitable volley of defense outrage and indignation.

Indeed, after the jury was sent out for lunch, they lined up. As impressive—and expensive—a collection of defense counsel as has ever been assembled in an American courtroom took to their feet with cries of "reprehensible" and "prejudicial." Some of the arguments were sound; most were specious.

Each in turn, they took their best shots, all except Norman Ostrow, Weisman's lawyer, a Park Avenue, white-collar criminal lawyer, who said nothing. Ostrow wasn't the type to waste his arguments in bouts of personal indignation. On those occasions when Ostrow rose to make an argument, the judge, prosecutors, and jury knew it was going to be something worthy of consideration—or at least amusing—not mere rhetoric.

After lunch, Robert Ellis, DePalma's lawyer, led the pack. As he approached the jury box, they had to have taken note of his slightly wrinkled and disheveled stature. He stands about six feet but carries himself in a manner that makes him appear larger and beefier.

Pacing in front of the jurors, he began with a discourse on "those witnesses" in such a naturally resonant baritone voice that he couldn't help but capture their attention.

"Who are those witnesses? Who told Mr. Akerman the facts that you heard this morning? One was a fellow by the name of James Fratianno—and if there is a sin against mankind that this fellow hasn't committed yet, it's only because it hasn't been invented.

"Let me hasten to make sure everybody understands; I am not claiming Mr. Akerman has done anything wrong. But a man guilty of multiple murders, who knows his maximum exposure is five years if his cooperation is correct, does not interpret that deal to require him to get on the stand and say that these people are innocent.

"You may sit here two months, you may sit here three months; you will not see a document saying that Mr. DePalma is a partner, you will not see a share of stock, you will not see any evidence of that fact, except from the mouths of the witnesses who want to use Mr. DePalma's liberty as currency to buy their way out of jail."

Ellis proceeded through a description of each of the prosecution witnesses and then a history of DePalma's role in the creation of the theater: its inception during golfing sessions at Lake Isle Country club in Westchester, and the purchase of land, which later turned out to be a swamp.

DePalma, along with Fusco, took charge of the landfill operation in 1973, during which they discovered they were filling a nearly bottomless pit, requiring seven times more fill than had been predicted. Loads of garbage, debris from demolished buildings, even the façade and innards of Yankee Stadium, then under renovation, went in and sank to the bottom of the merciless hole.

The process continued for more than a year, before 100,000 yards of fresh soil was brought in to cover the uncertain terrain and a glamorous, modern round theater was built.

"By the time the theater construction was completed, before the doors opened, and this is as critical as can be, construction difficulties and legal problems resulted in that place being $3.5 million in debt. Before they had a chance to make their mistakes in operating the place, before the doors were opened, they were $3.5 million in debt, and that's above the mortgages that had to be paid off.

"Now they started booking acts. The so-called professionals that had the job of booking acts paid people like Diana Ross $225,000 for a week's performance—a quick way to bankruptcy. Other acts were paid at a comparable rate. An awful lot of money for a 3,500-seat facility.

"The place could not make money. It could not break even unless it operated at close to ninety percent capacity on a Tuesday night in January with snow on the roads." He grasped the rail in front of the jurors box for added effect. "The place was doomed from the day it opened. But that's not a crime; being wrong in business is not a crime."

Ostrow was next.

He adjusted the hem of his Paul Stewart suit jacket, straightened his tie, and brushed back his coiffed, curly, graying hair as he approached the jury. He began with his eyes cast downward in contemplation of his speech. He spoke softly, a touch of sardonic humor in his slow deliberate style.

"Eliot Weisman got all the colors," he said, pointing to Akerman's chart in the corner. "Yup, every color he could be lumbered with, he got. Well, this is a show business case," he said with a shrug, and a shake of his head, "but this isn't Barbra Streisand's 'My Coloring Book.' His guilt has to be proven.

"While we're on the subject, I don't care about who's wearing the blue suit in this courtroom or who has white hair or whether old blue eyes is back." Ostrow turned from the jury with a disgusted sweep of his hand in Akerman's direction. Then he turned back to them and leaned forward. In almost confidential tones, he said, "You know, I was concerned as I sat there that I might have an infirmity; I hid my tie for a moment, that I might be pointed to as the man with the red tie.

"It occurred to me as I sat there that the only face that might be acceptable to this prosecutor is a Nick Akerman mask. But that's not what this case is all about."

Unlike Ellis, or those who would follow him, Ostrow was getting personal with the jury, letting them know he was taking this case, and Akerman's conduct, personally. It was a role that Ostrow had to play, for his client was the only one with every color and ostensibly the one responsible for all the theater's receipts and records. Only Ostrow would be on the line with every witness, every document, every one of the 117 charges.

"You see, Mr. Akerman wasn't there in 1973 and 1974 and 1975 and 1976 and 1977. Although he was eavesdropping in 1977 and 1978, he really only knows what has been told to him by witnesses in this case; nothing more and nothing less."

Ostrow described Weisman—his education, background as a stockbroker, his wife and two children—and spoke of the theater as "Eliot's impossible dream, which soon turned into a nightmare."

In a short statement, Ostrow reviewed many of the same areas Ellis had touched upon, but focused on the lack of documentation of the stock frauds charge and said that by the time the theater was going into bankruptcy court, "I believe the evidence will show that although Weisman continued to book acts, he was no longer involved in the operation of the theater.

"Others took the checkbooks and ran the theater. Did he really know what was going on after that? Does he really deserve all the colors? We'll see."

The other seven defense lawyers followed in order.

Martin Adelman, Fusco's lawyer, spoke of the lack of proof that Fusco was anything more than an employee of the theater.

Murray Richman, who enjoys playing the comical nebbish—a sharp contrast to his precise, needle-sharp mind—represented Nersesian. He argued that this was a case of conspiracy and "conspiracy, like beauty, is in the eye of the beholder.

"I ask you not to lump everything together. There is safety in numbers, numbers in the indictment, numbers of people around this table. Don't get lost in the shuffle."

Next up was Jonathan Lubell, a noted First Amendment lawyer, a slight, scholarly looking man who was representing Horwitz. He was the only one to stand at the lectern with notes. He argued that the jurors should listen carefully, that they would find no evidence that Horwitz was involved in bribing Warner officials. And, he argued, the only plot to obstruct the grand jury probe was one concocted by Brodsky to win immunity.

Richard Asche, representing Larry Goodman, insisted that there would be virtually no proof of Goodman selling theater stock to anyone but members of his family.

Marvin Segal held everyone's attention—and not just because he wore gray flannel in contrast to the sea of blue pinstripes. Segal, a defense attorney in the Watergate trial of former U.S. Attorney General John Mitchell, was loud, blustering, and indignantly red-faced in his defense of Cannatella.

He told the jury that the government had omitted a few details in its opening statement: "Unimportant things. Maybe $1.6 million— you were never told that that was the amount of money Mr. Cannatella invested in this enterprise. Yet he is charged with bankruptcy fraud. He is charged essentially with defrauding himself."

Hugh Johnson & Co., a firm worth $8 million, in which Cannatella held an 85 percent interest, had performed a scrupulous accounting investigation of the theater, records of which would be presented later, before investing the $1.6 million; enough to take control of the theater, and enough to bankrupt Hugh Johnson when the theater went under.

Pounding his fist on the rail of the jury box, Segal scoffed at the indictment that charged Cannatella took $30,000 in skim money: "Put a million dollars in to take 30,000?"

And then, in defense of Pacella, there was Barry Ivan Slotnick, tall, lean, and bearded, counsel to some of the best-known crime figures in New York, and who, years later, would represent Bernie Goetz in his subway shooting charge.

"Let me start with Frank Sinatra," he said, leaning against one corner of the lectern. "You will find that Frank Sinatra and Louis Pacella are very, very, very close and dear friends. In fact, the evidence will show to you that they were brothers; not because they shared the same mother and father, but because they shared love, admiration, and friendship for many, many years."

In a long-winded explanation, Slotnick said that Pacella, as a favor to the theater operators, had approached his dear friend and asked him to play the theater. He soon found himself involved in making arrangements for Sinatra's appearance and eventually appears on the wiretaps discussing those arrangements.

"Frank and Dean came. The theater grossed $1.4 million. The entertainers got paid for the show, the expenses, about $800,000; $460,000 was put into the bank account of the Westchester Premier Theatre. It wiped out a four-month loss.

"Nick Akerman said Louis Pacella was part of a scheme to the detriment of the theater's creditors. That's what he's charged my client with. Ladies and gentlemen, if not for Louis Pacella, that theater would have perished many months before it did. If not for Louis Pacella, the creditors wouldn't have had a fund of $460,000.

"An indictment? They should give my client a testimonial dinner."

The clean-up batter, down at the end of the long L-shaped table, was John Mitchell, a husky, blond man in his thirties with an unsettling sense of self-assurance for someone so young. But perhaps he had earned the attitude—he was a member of the law firm of James LaRosa, one of the city's preeminent criminal law firms, which was representing Anthony Gaggi.

Mitchell pointed out that the substantive charge against Gaggi was receiving $700 under the table from the theater; he neglected to mention other alleged payments totaling $10,000.

"I would like to characterize this case as the government's deal with the devil. And the devil, ladies and gentlemen, is James Fratianno.

"Do you remember Charlie Manson? Charles Manson. He was a mass murderer in California. Do you remember the horrible things that Charles Manson did? Ladies and gentlemen, the evidence from that witness stand will prove unequivocally that Charles Manson is nothing compared to James Fratianno.

"The government mentioned the fact that James Fratianno committed two murders. We'll see how many murders he has committed. The deal is that James Fratianno, who's committed virtually every crime there is and who happens to be an admitted murderer, is going to plead guilty to those murders and maybe get five years. If the government comes forward and tells how swell he was from the witness stand, he may get nothing.

"What do you think Mr. Fratianno will say?

"As you may or may not know, the United States Supreme Court has ruled that people can be electrocuted for killing one another. As I said, we are talking about two murders. What do you think someone will do to get away from the electric chair? What do you think he will say?

"Let's continue analyzing this noble bargain that the government has struck with Mr. Fratianno: 'Come in and testify and you get off for murder, murders.'

"It's not something that the government does lightly. They have to justify to us, to you ladies and gentlemen, to the people in the audience, to me, to the citizens of this country, they have to justify using their powers to let somebody who is a murderer get off. So what do they do? They construct the biggest possible case they can. Anybody who was anywhere near the Westchester Premier Theatre is a defendant in this case. Why? Because they have to tell their superiors: 'Oh, no, we got a big case here, we got ten defendants.'

"When the case is over you will find out Anthony Gaggi didn't get $700, or, if he did, it wasn't part of the bankruptcy fraud. Even if it was, you let a murder go? A mass murderer? Someone who I will prove to you is more heinous than Charlie Manson; you let him go to bring Nino Gaggi in and make him sit for two months to defend himself about $700?

"Well, that's a noble deal."

Carino was a disaster. He was a forty-three-year-old burn-out. He sat slumped in the witness stand, appearing to be either deranged or perhaps the victim of a daily Valium overdose. Except when asked to identify the defendants he wouldn't cast a glance in their direction. He answered questions like an automaton—"Yes." "No." "Huh?"

He wore the same thing through seven days of testimony: a three-piece blue suit, severely starched white shirt, striped necktie, and new black shoes, the soles of which had no more scuff marks on them on the last day of his testimony than they did the first.

Outside the courtroom, DePalma and Fusco, constant sidekicks in polyester sports jackets, took it all in stride.

"It looks like there's something wrong with him, like they got him drugged or something," DePalma offered to Weisman.

Weisman, chain-smoking Marlboros, broke his incessant pacing—a swaggering duck-walk—long enough to offer his standard conclusion to almost any conversation: "What the fuck's the difference. I'm the one getting fucked here."

Inside the courtroom, the defense was using the power of sheer numbers like a team of unsynchronized jack-in-the-boxes, popping from their seats in a steady stream of objections or cries for mistrials, effectively obliterating large portions of testimony.

Akerman and Campbell were seriously outgunned. Their relative lack of trial experience was being challenged constantly.

This wasn't the "simple case" Akerman had promised. This was a complicated matter of stock transfers and accounting reports, at least that was what Ostrow was turning it into, drawing the jury's attention away from the simple stories and focusing them on an endless flurry of stock reports, ledger sheets, checks, and other documents Weisman had provided.

Gradually, with leading questions, Carino's story came out—and was later shredded by the defense, first for its substance and later by attacks on Carino's credibility. But despite the defense's efforts, there were a few things Carino stood firm on: he had been made a secret partner; he had seen John Capra deliver $50,000 as a secret investment in the theater; he had sat with Weisman and Horwitz as they finalized a $50,000 payoff to Jay Emmett, a member of Warner's three-man office of the president, as inducement to have the entertainment conglomerate buy theater stock; and he had seen a shoebox containing $75,000 or $100,000 that Weisman said came from Nersesian.

Next up was Norman Brodsky, a thirty-five-year-old, bearded and balding, self-assured wheeler-dealer who walked into court every day wearing a $600 suit, silk tie, and freshly cut rose in his lapel.

Brodsky seemed unflappable in his descriptions of the stock manipulations he had engineered to complete the theater's stock offering. He spoke of receiving an attaché case with $220,000 in cash from Weisman and friends, which he "laundered," transferring it into bank checks, some of which he kept and some he used to buy theater stock in the names of unwitting friends, relatives, and clients.

He also described the deals with Warner executives Emmett and Solomon Weiss, the corporation's assistant treasurer. He said they had authorized Warner's purchase of $250,000 in theater stock, for which they were paid $70,000 in bribes.

The final element of his testimony dealt with the obstruction of justice charges, what the defense called entrapment. Those were the tape recordings he instigated, in which he was heard repeatedly cajoling and harassing Horwitz and Weisman to help him concoct a grand jury alibi. He threatened that without their help he would walk into the grand jury and tell all. Horwitz eventually caved in, helping him outline a story, which Weisman approved.

On one of the tapes Weisman told Brodsky that Mickey Rudin and Warner's lawyers had been conferring on the case: "Mickey, ah, said that however we arrived at what we did here is ingenious. What can they prove?"

The best the defense could do with Brodsky was make him out a thief, a cheat, and a liar who had ripped off his friends, business partners, and even his mother in the past. He readily admitted that snaring Horwitz and Weisman was essential to his immunity.

But he also confirmed the dire financial straits the theater had operated under. He described Weisman as being under such emotional stress trying to keep the theater afloat that he developed a recurrent twitch in his arm that made him incapable of holding a pencil for weeks at a time.

Bruce Kosman, a rather nondescript forty-year-old lawyer, claimed to be the go-between for more kickbacks between Warner and the theater, using the camouflage of "consulting fees." He was taken apart on the stand. By the time the defense was through with him he was literally shaking, and prefacing every answer with: "I could stand to be corrected, but I believe . . ."

The courtroom filled to capacity—at least 300 spectators pressed into the gallery of sturdy, ageless oak pews—and then was cleared.

Weisman had to go to another floor of the building to find room enough to pace.

DePalma and Fusco stood together, marveling at the crowd.

The spectators had come from across the country. The slickly groomed TV reporters and slightly shabby print journalists; prosecutors and agents; defense lawyers and private investigators; low-level mobsters, elderly court buffs, and the curious courthouse personnel.

A local radio station was playing Sinatra's rendition of "That's Life" as background to their hourly reports on the trial. The *New York Daily News*, strikebound since August, had recently returned to the stands, leading with a story about the Sinatra-Gambino photo, under the headline: PROBE SINATRA LINK TO GAMBINO.

McDonald was there and so were Ahearn and Demaris.

Tony Brooklier, the lawyer-son of the L.A. mob boss, huddled with the defense lawyers to offer some last-minute background wisdom on Fratianno's plea bargain and past crimes.

McPherson deployed six discreetly armed marshals to patrol the corridors and the courtroom. When a team of marshals had completed searching for bombs and weapons, everyone was allowed back into the courtroom—after passing, one at a time, through a metal detector.

Only then was Jimmy called to the stand.

He wore his powder blue Brione suit and a wide, pastel-striped necktie. He appeared thin and nervous as he took the oath for the first time. He wished he could have a cigar to hold—not to light, just a little security to hold on to.

McPherson stood behind him.

The light pouring through the courtroom's tall windows was the closest thing to outdoors he had seen since he'd been locked up ten days earlier in the cellar of the New York MCC, adjacent to the courthouse. He had spent the next ten days living in an empty courthouse office as he completed his testimony.

His basic introduction—where he grew up, his nicknames, his past crimes, and his agreement with the government to "testify truthfully"—came in staccato replies.

His eyes darted around the courtroom, yet he initially avoided eye contact with the defendants.

Weisman was in a state of disbelief. He could deal with Carino, Brodsky, and Kosman testifying against him, but a notorious hit man?

DePalma was staring right at him. Up until then, DePalma had shown little interest in the testimony. But now he was engrossed, he was leaning forward in his chair, a constant smile chiseled on his face.

Fusco, a genius at juggling ledger sheets, was following his lawyer's instruction of keeping a slack-jawed, drowsy look on his face, doing his best to appear too stupid to have anything to do with sophisticated crimes like stock and bankruptcy frauds.

Fratianno's answers were crisp, precise, and honest. He recounted his trips to Marson's home, where he learned about "the grocery money," and his first trip to New York for the Sinatra Man of the Year dinner, where he was introduced to Weisman, DePalma, and Fusco as Marson's partners.

It was about then that Fratianno caught sight of DePalma's sneering grin. Without flinching, they locked eyes for several moments as Fratianno continued to answer Akerman's questions.

He smiled: "You think I'm a motherfucker," Jimmy thought to himself. "Well, you were part of it. I asked you to help me out when Brooklier came after me. You didn't do a thing. So now you're fucked."

The defense did their usual routine, jumping to objections, breaking the flow of his testimony, but they weren't going to distract him.

Fratianno described his trip to the theater for the first Sinatra series, in April 1976, where he learned that DePalma ran the concessions, Fusco had the box office, and Weisman was booking acts.

Q. Did there come a time during the week when you were at the West-chester Premier Theatre in April 1976 that you had a discussion with Eliot Weisman?

A. Yes, sir.

Q. Where did that discussion take place?

A. At the restaurant.

Q. Would you please describe to the jury exactly what happened and what was said.

A. Well, I was sitting at one of the tables and Eliot was kind of mad and he come over to me, he said that "I don't know what I'm doing here, I've got nothing to say." He said, "I am more or less the fall guy. If anybody goes to jail, it will be me."

He described Marson's introducing him to "Louie Dones," who he was told was the one who got Sinatra to play the theater.

He told of Marson's descriptions of how they were scamming the joint: taking money from the sale of tickets on folding chairs and unregistered seats, scalping tickets, and skimming money from the concession to pay "their obligations."

He also said he was present when Pacella complained he had been short-changed, receiving only $50,000 as his share of the skim on the Sinatra show.

There was lengthy questioning about a scheme Jimmy had hatched. Inspired by the Premier Theatre's skim operation he had envisioned an opportunity to make some money for himself. He had heard that Sinatra had always wanted to be a member of the Knights of Malta, a Catholic layman's honor society, and Jimmy knew the organization's U.S. representative.

Backstage, in his dressing room, Jimmy proposed to Sinatra that he would arrange for him to be inducted, and in return Sinatra would do a Knights of Malta benefit concert. He didn't involve Sinatra in his plans with Marson, DePalma, and Pacella to skim a cut from the benefit.

Sinatra went for it in a big way, instructing him to arrange the concert date with Rudin. Jimmy put up the $5,000 investiture fee and months later, back in Rancho Mirage, Sinatra and Jilly Rizzo walked the half-mile from his compound to Marson's home for the grand ceremony.

Jimmy said he spent months speaking to DePalma, Pacella, and Rudin, but they never pulled it together and then he was arrested and entered his new vocation.

At the early afternoon break, Jimmy was taken to a secured room behind the courtroom and he grabbed for a cigar.

Akerman and Campbell came in to find Jimmy, his tie loosened and feet up on a desk, puffing away and drinking coffee from a Styrofoam cup. It was an entirely different image than the polite supplicant he had played on the stand.

"Did you see the looks on those bastards' faces," he said with laughter. "Those lawyers ain't never seen someone like me before."

Indeed they hadn't. There was something coming across, a powerful, charismatic attraction that kept the audience leaning forward en masse to catch every word. It was more than his notoriety. There was a special presence on the witness stand; a captivating, dominant, one-in-a-million personality.

And Jimmy was keenly aware of the attention he was being paid. He was feeling more confident as he realized the leading edge of celebrity.

In the corridor, Weisman was pacing with Horwitz, a tall, athletic-looking man in his fifties with a head of snow-white hair. Horwitz spoke only in whispers and scorned the company of all his fellow defendants except Weisman.

Jimmy had nothing to say about Horwitz and little of significance about Weisman. The only thing troubling Weisman was the Sinatra-Gambino photo, scheduled as evidence supporting Fratianno's claims that he was part of the theater crowd's inner circle.

"Thank God I had the good sense to stay away from the theater that night, Lenny," Weisman said.

"What do you mean?" Horwitz asked.

"Greg told me, you know, that Big Carlo was coming for that Sinatra show and I just packed my briefcase and got the fuck out of there, okay? Well, when I got in there the next day and saw those photos, okay, Sinatra with all those wise guys, well, I called Rudin and told him about it. I told him it was no good, that this picture was going to end up in the *Inquirer* or some shit.

"So you know what happens? Mickey talks to Frank and calls me back. He says. 'Frank doesn't care.' Fuck 'em, you know? Frank says, 'What's a picture? If I go to Rome, I get my picture with the pope. In New York, I get a picture with Carlo Gambino. What's a picture? I get my picture taken with anybody.' That's his attitude.

"All I know is I'm glad I stayed home that night, or it would have been my face in that picture with all of them."

Cannatella was off in a corner with a reporter, seated on a bench. They were off-the-record, deeper than deep-background. Cannatella knew that what was coming next wasn't going to look good. The scrappy-looking little man was ashen with distress. He had already suffered a severe angina attack and had been laid up in the hospital for several days since the trial began. He appeared to be on the verge of another.

Cannatella's entire role in this thing made no sense at all, the reporter was saying. He was an exceptionally bright and articulate man in his forties who, without formal higher education, had pulled himself up from the old mob neighborhoods in Brooklyn to a position of success. The FBI had dug long and hard for an angle on him and found none: He was a self-made man of enormous ability, with no known links to organized crime before the theater.

"Look, I'm not going to tell you any lies. Nor am I going to tell you the entire story," Cannatella said, his eyes showing his exhaustion, his breath coming in short, shallow gasps. "But I can prove, without any question, that I was taking legitimate control there. The theater had the potential of being a successful venture with the right management, but it was burdened; there were tremendous outside influences. You know what I'm saying? So legitimate control meant nothing unless you had a way of also containing the other influences."

"So you went back to the old neighborhood and picked up a few friends, a little muscle, to protect your investment. Is that the idea?" the reporter asked.

Cannatella smiled as he got up, heading to the water fountain to take a pill. "Like I said, I'm not going to tell you the whole story. But remember one thing, when you think about this theater, and you hear all the innuendo about organized crime, just remember: One thing these guys never were, was organized."

Back on the stand, the balance of Fratianno's story dealt with his trips to New York to protect Marson's money—a tale of mob arbitration told in a most circumspect manner.

Segal, Cannatella's lawyer, was not taking it well. As he listened to Fratianno, Segal began nervously tapping his index finger along the edge of the defense table. When he rose to make an objection, it was like the shrill whistle of a steam kettle going off. By the time Fratianno came around to his first meeting with Cannatella, Segal's nervous rhythm had reached a furious pace and his finger was raw and bleeding.

Q. Would you please tell the jury what Mr. Marson told you.

A. Well, he told me that a couple of fellows came in the theater with Sal Cannatella, fellow by the name of Kid Blast and Jimmy—

MR. SEGAL: Your honor, at this time I would object and I would propose a motion [for a mistrial].

THE COURT: All right.

Q. Do you know Kid Blast's real name?

MR. SEGAL: Objection and a similiar motion.

THE COURT: All right. Overruled.

A. I think it is Gallo. I was told it was Gallo.

MR. SEGAL: I object to that and ask that it be stricken.

THE COURT: Denied.

Q. Tommy Marson told me his name was Gallo—it was Joey Gallo's brother.

Fratianno described his meeting with Cannatella and subsequent meetings with Fat Dom and "the Old Man," Funzi Tieri, where he received assurances that Marson's money would be protected by Cannatella.

Q. After you met with Funzi Tieri . . . did you have a discussion with Mr. Pacella?

A. Yes, sir.

Q. Would you please tell the jury what you said to Mr. Pacella and what he said to you.

A. I told him I talked to the Old Man in regards to Tommy's money and . . . he said that he would make sure that Tommy wouldn't lose his money.

Q. Who said that?

A. I told Louis Pacella that and then Louis says, "Well, you don't have to worry about Chapter Eleven. If the Old Man told you that, forget about it."

Q. Forget about what?

A. Don't have to worry.

Q. Did Mr. Pacella say anything else?

A. All he says, "Chapter Eleven don't mean nothing, don't worry about it."

And then Akerman sat down.

The only defendants really damaged by Fratianno had been Pacella, DePalma, and Cannatella. But everyone had been effectively smeared by the unspoken association with organized crime.

Jimmy hadn't mentioned organized crime by name, but the jurors would have to have been deaf and blind not to have figured out what was going on, what with monickers like Gambino, Gallo, Kid Blast, the Old Man, and Fat Dom.

And if Fratianno's testimony was to be believed, it was clear that the conspirators felt they had a higher authority to answer to than the U.S. Bankruptcy Court: one Funzi Tieri.

Ellis began in a slow, deliberate, unhostile fashion. He figured on making short work of Fratianno. The man was an admitted killer; how hard could it be to make him out a liar?

Q. The story you told the government came from you, isn't that correct?
A. That's correct.
Q. And you told it because you made a certain arrangement with the government, isn't that correct?
A. What do you mean by "arrangement"?
Q. With respect to certain crimes that you had told them that you'd committed?
A. That's correct.
Q. And there were a number of those crimes?
A. Quite a few.
Q. Quite a few. And some of them were extremely serious, were they not?
A. I would say they are, yes, sir.
Q. Did you ever sit down and sort of figure out in your own mind what could have happened to you as a result of all those crimes you admitted you committed?
A. What do you mean, "could have happened"?
Q. Well, for one thing, you could have been put to death, could you not?
A. That's correct.
Q. And if it meant not being put to death, wouldn't you tell a lie?
A. I don't understand your question, sir?
Q. Well, you're a pretty savvy guy, aren't you?
A. You mean I would lie to save myself to go—
Q. To save yourself from execution.
A. That's correct.
Q. Nine murders?
A. That's quite a few.

Fratianno was dripping with bold honesty, willingly admitting his bad acts, teasing the jurors and spectators with just how much farther he could go if unbridled.

Q. How much time do you think you could get if you string out nine murders, Mr. Fratianno?
A. I don't know.
Q. You really don't? You think you might have spent the rest of your days in jail if you max'd out on those nine murders?
A. I don't know.

Q. What do you think? Was it a distinct possibillity?
A. I really don't know.

He was getting under Ellis's skin with his accurately nonresponsive answers.

Q. You think they would have given you the Legion of Merit and sent you on your way?
A. No, sir.
Q. But as it turns out, you made a deal, right?
A. That's correct.
Q. And for that deal you can't get more than five years, right?
A. That's right.
Q. You wouldn't have a deal for five years maximum if you didn't have a story to tell in this courtroom today, correct?
A. I had a deal before I came to this courtroom, sir.
Q. Yes, sir?
A. Way before I came here. Even before I knew I was going to testify in this case.
Q. Was that deal for five years?
A. That's correct.
Q. And Mr. Akerman had no part in that deal?
A. No, he did not. I made a deal right after I got picked up . . . about a year ago.

Ellis changed direction and turned instead to the Greene and Bompensiero murders, which Fratianno readily admitted involvement in. But Ellis wouldn't leave well-enough alone and pushed for details, learning that Fratianno had only played a minor role in those slayings.

Q. Tell me, Mr. Fratianno, which murders did you actually commit?
A. Do you want the names?
Q. Give me the names.
A. Frank Borgia, [Tony] Trombino, [Tony] Brancato, Frank Niccoli . . .
Q. Who else?
A. And Russian Louie.
Q. Now, in the case of these people, you are the one who actually shot, bombed, or strangled them or whatever the case may be, is that correct?
A. Yes, sir.
Q. Mr. Fratianno, have you ever been punished for any of these crimes?
A. No, sir.
Q. Did you ever kill a guy for not paying a debt?
A. No, sir.
Q. Never happened? You mentioned Niccoli, didn't you?

A. That's correct.

Q. You had a disagreement with Mr. Niccoli, didn't you?

A. I don't know what you mean by "disagreement."

Q. A difference of opinion.

A. No, sir.

Q. On the last day of his life he came to your house in California, didn't he?

A. I was ordered to kill him, sir.

The defense lawyers were on their feet all talking at once.

"Your honor, would you instruct the jury that orders to take people's lives come from God?" Ostrow requested.

Sweet cut it off without responding to any of the defense requests. Ellis had pushed Fratianno as far as he could and was getting just what he should have anticipated.

A little later the lawyers assembled with Sweet in the robing room to sort out just how far they could go in questioning Fratianno on the murders without "opening the door" to a line of questioning from the prosecution about the witness's role in La Cosa Nostra. They were on shaky ground and deeply concerned.

Akerman was arguing that "the door" was already ajar:

"The problem is that the jury has been left with the impression that the reason Mr. Fratianno entered into his deal with the government is to get those murders behind him.

"The truth of the matter is that the government had no evidence of the Bompensiero murder, some in the Cleveland case, and virtually nothing on any of the other slayings until Mr. Fratianno told them about those crimes. The reason he entered into his agreement with the government was that there was a contract on his life.

"Once the defense starts inquiring into the details of the murders, the government, I believe, is entitled to bring out that Mr. Fratianno was acting at the direction of the Family boss in California; that these were Mafia murders."

Akerman had the defense cornered. Either they had to pull their punches on demonstrating what a bad person Fratianno was or take the full load of who he was.

The defense was outraged by the position into which they were being placed. But Sweet held largely to the government's view: The defense couldn't inquire beyond the most cursory level about the murders—and if they did, they did so at their own risk.

When they finished their tête-à-tête, the lawyers, judge, clerks, and stenographers returned to their places; the jury was called; and lastly Jimmy took up his position again, looking a little smug, winking to a juror who had winked at him as he took his seat.

Ellis's questioning didn't last long:

Q. Isn't it a fact, Mr. Fratianno, that you first became a so-called informer in or about 1970?
A. I talked to the FBI in 1970, but I didn't become an informer in 1970.
Q. When did you become an informer for the first time?
A. Well, in my opinion, I actually became an informer when there was a contract put out on me. I never—

The questioning was halted by a new round of objections. The courtroom was emptied and the lawyers trundled off again to continue their private debate.

Fratianno was subverting their cross-examination, and he knew it, taking every opportunity to let the jury know exactly who he was. It was decided to have Akerman instruct Fratianno to limit his responses.

When Ellis returned to the questioning, he focused on other crimes, such as pornography, gambling, and extortion:

Q. Did you participate in an extortion of one Benny Binion?
A. I wouldn't call it extortion. I got some money from him.
Q. Is that because he wished to give you a present?

Jimmy didn't like Ellis's snide questioning. He knew he could give Ellis an answer he wouldn't like, but he didn't want to ignore Akerman's instructions. He decided to give Ellis the option:

A. Would you like to know why, sir?
Q. Not why. That would be Mr. Binion's state of mind. Did you get something for him by force or threat of force?
A. I got some money from him for committing a murder.

Ellis completed his inquiry with an aborted attempt to show that Marson was a braggart and a drunk whose information to Fratianno might have been subject to doubt. But Fratianno kept it from going too far:

Q. Did you often see him drunk?
A. Anytime I ever saw him he always knew what he was talking about, regardless of how much he drank.

And then, at the very tail end of his examination:

Q. Incidentally, you had several meetings with Mr. Akerman before your testimony.

A. Yes, sir.
Q. How many?
A. A dozen or more.
Q. And he interviewed you?
A. That's correct.
Q. And he wrote down what you told him?
A. Went over my testimony, right.
Q. Did you see him take notes?
A. I don't know what he was writing. He was making some notes.
Q. You don't think he was writing poetry while you were talking to him, do you?
A. He might have.

Ostrow kept his questions with Fratianno to a minimum. He was conducting a white-collar crime case and wanted to distance himself from this killer. He made his disgust with Fratianno clear from the start:

Q. Is it true, Mr. Fratianno, that you have begun serving a term of imprisonment and can possibly be released from that term of confinement within the next eight months?
A. Possibly.

Ostrow nodded and then looked with mock concern at Fratianno:

Q. By the way, do you know who I am?
A. No, sir.
Q. That's good.

The crowd laughed. Most of them felt the same way. Although there was something appealing about Fratianno, something refreshing in his willingness to admit exactly who he was without hesitation, he still wasn't anyone you'd want to ever see again.

Ostrow wasn't too interested in discrediting Fratianno's testimony, especially the part about Weisman being the fall guy, with little or nothing to say about the theater's operation. He did, however, make sure the jury understood there was no discernible link between Weisman and Fat Dom or Funzi Tieri.

Q. Did Mr. Weisman instruct you to go to that meeting?
A. No, sir.
Q. In fact, you had not even discussed it with him before the meeting, had you?
A. No, sir.

Q. Did Mr. Weisman, in connection with those two meetings, ever authorize you to speak for the Westchester Premier Theatre?

A. No, sir.

Fusco's lawyer, Adelman, was in a similar position, reviewing his lack of concrete knowledge of what Fusco had done at the theater. The lawyers for Goodman, Horwitz, and Gaggi didn't even want to question Fratianno. But Segal, Cannatella's contentious counsel, was chomping at the bit for a shot at Fratianno. His theory was simple: He was going to show that Marson had brought Fratianno into the theater as muscle, to protect his unsecured loan against the legitimate takeover by Cannatella's Hugh Johnson & Co.

It was an interesting approach, and one requiring a surgeon's skill to avoid "opening the door." But Segal, unlike the rest of the attorneys, didn't seem particularly concerned: his best defense was to show that Cannatella was working to eliminate the organized crime influences at the theater.

His biggest problem was that Jimmy was getting stronger with every passing hour on the stand, and the jury was becoming increasingly fascinated and drawn to him. Akerman's questions had only established the barest bones of Jimmy's story; the lengthy questioning by the defense was putting flesh on the skeleton and making him live. The longer he stayed up there the more he became a person, with depth and background.

Segal hammered away about Jimmy's relationship with Marson, demonstrating how Marson had showered him with kindness—free trips to New York, introductions to Sinatra, and days at his luxurious Rancho Mirage home—in return for his helping to get Marson's money out of the theater.

A. I wouldn't say I was helping him get his money out. I could try to assist in protecting his money. I don't know how you figure I was trying to get his money out.

Q. Well, Marson wanted his money out, didn't he?

A. Yes, he did.

Q. And you wanted what Marson wanted, didn't you?

A. I was hoping that he would get his money out.

Q. Because if he got his money out you would get a piece of his new action, isn't that correct?

A. If he got his money out.

Segal was indignant and confrontational. He treated Jimmy as he would have the jury perceive him: as someone not deserving any consideration.

Q. Did Mr. Marson have any promissory note from the theater showing that he had loaned that money?

A. Not that I know of, sir.

Q. Did Mr. Marson ask you to become his contract; his shares and his condition for getting his money back?

A. Did Marson ask me what?

Q. Did he ask you to get it back even though he had no paper, no proof of having lent the theater any money at any time?

A. He has never asked me that, sir.

Q. Before you went to prison [and began cooperating], you enjoyed a certain reputation in the community, did you not?

A. That's correct, yes.

Q. And that reputation in the community was one in which you were held in high regard, is that right?

A. A Family man.

Q. A Family man?

A. That's correct.

Segal's voice had a sneering edge to it, which Fratianno wasn't enjoying. He did his best to resist, but Segal was clearly asking for trouble:

Q. And was this a family man with children and a home and everything else?

A. No, it was a Family man with an organization.

Several more questions of little significance went by before Ellis stood up, politely objecting to the line of questioning and said he would "have an application" to make later. The others sat frozen expressionless in their seats.

After the jury had left, the defense asked for a mistrial and Akerman demanded that the door was open to questioning about La Cosa Nostra.

Segal was enraged. "We're sitting here with the government putting in things like Fat Dom, Funzi, Kid Blast, and if we dare to step on any toes we're opening the door.

"We cannot tread around this, your honor. Just because we approach this man who is validly what he seems to be, do we open the door? The government is saying we can't cross-examine. Anytime we touch a nerve, we open the door."

Rather than take either side, Sweet chose to strike a balance and ignored them both. The jury now had a pretty clear notion of who Jimmy was, but the government wasn't going to get a chance to expand on it. Segal had made his points about why Jimmy was palling around with Marson, but there would be no mistrial.

Slotnick, Pacella's lawyer, had last licks on Jimmy, or perhaps it was the other way around. Jimmy was feeling comfortable and in full command by this point. Slotnick would score some important points, but Jimmy would get his as well.

He picked up where Segal had left off about Jimmy's financial arrangement with Marson:

Q. In terms of your interest, would you have received a percentage of that deal?
A. Well, if he got the money. But it never came about, so we never . . . we never discussed it. It was what you call a fantasy.
Q. Like most other things you discussed with Mr. Marson, it turned out to be a fantasy?
A. That's correct.
Q. Tom Marson sat with you in his Rancho Mirage [home] and told you all about millions and you were interested, is that correct?
A. At one time, yes, sir.
Q. And then you realized that he was a big fantasizer, full of baloney?
A. I realize that now, not then.
Q. And Tom Marson put the con on you?
A. I suppose he did.
Q. Mr. Fratianno, you really don't even know whether half of what he told you was the truth and half of what he told you was fiction, is that correct?

Akerman objected and Slotnick withdrew the question before Jimmy could answer, but he had made his point.

Most of the rest of the time they argued, mostly about the Knights of Malta benefit, which Slotnick claimed was another "fantasy." Slotnick spent as much time defending Sinatra's reputation as Pacella's.

He suggested that the date and place for the never-held benefit kept changing because Marson, DePalma, Pacella, and certainly Sinatra and his loyal crew wanted nothing to do with Fratianno.

Q. Remember Marson telling you somewhere in July 1977 that Mr. Pacella told him that you were not to be involved with Mr. Sinatra, and that you were not to come to his restaurant because you were a creep?
A. I don't recall that, sir.
Q. Do you remember Mr. Marson telling you that Mr. Pacella said he didn't even want to see you eating at his restaurant?
A. I don't recall that either, sir.

Q. Remember getting a message from Mr. Pacella that you were nothing but a two-bit hoodlum, and to stay away from Frank Sinatra?

A. No, sir.

Q. Do you remember Mr. Marson telling you that he was told if you came near a Sinatra show or Frank Sinatra, Jilly Rizzo would bounce you out on your—do you remember that?

Q. He never told me that, sir.

As the discussion became heated, Slotnick came closer and closer to Jimmy until they were nearly within arm's reach of each other, and Akerman asked Slotnick to move away.

"Do I make you nervous?" Slotnick asked as he stepped back.

"No," came the reply. "Do I make you nervous?"

When the jury and Fratianno stopped laughing, Slotnick replied: "Yes."

Slotnick had realized Jimmy's weakest point was dates—a common problem for most witnesses—and pressed him.

Trying to set the date that Fratianno came to New York for the second Sinatra show, he asked: "Is there anything I can do to freshen your recollection?"

Fueling the animosity between them, Fratianno shot back, "Stand on your head," and drew more enthusiasm from the jurors.

That pretty much completed it, except one last round of questioning in which Ostrow became the only defense attorney to make a real dent in Fratianno's armor. Ostrow produced a wiretapped phone call, between Fratianno and DePalma, showing Jimmy had left New York days earlier than he had claimed in testimony, thus demonstrating that he couldn't have been around to see the final skim from the last Sinatra concert divvied up, as he had claimed.

Jimmy was asked later to identify some photos and they were admitted into evidence, including the shot of Sinatra and the merry mobsters. A copy of the photo leaked out to the press, and if a picture might commonly be valued at a 1,000 words, this one gave birth to several million.

And with that ended the in-depth press coverage. As soon as Jimmy was off the stand, the crowds abated and the press largely forgot about the trial.

The last of the prosecution's evidence came in the form of the wiretaps. It was devastating. A full day of tape recordings that left every one of the defendants visibly shaken. All the sharp cross-examination that had gone before meant nothing in the face of the defendants' recorded conversations corroborating the stories Fratianno and others had told.

First came the simple discussion of association, the defendants on the phone asking about one another's families.

Then there was Marson, demanding his "grocery money" from the "extra seat money"—"Fuck the theater."

There was DePalma and Fusco talking about how many tickets they were holding back to scalp for the Bay City Rollers or a Sinatra show.

Weisman called to say he was making a delivery on a portion of the skim money.

And then, the pièce de résistance. DePalma, on May 30, 1977, the final day of the final Sinatra show, had just seen Tommy Marson off at the airport. Weisman called to ask about the T-shirt and program concessions, from which Mickey Rudin got a commission, and then the funds skimmed elsewhere:

WEISMAN: Tom go?
DEPALMA: Yeah.
WEISMAN: What does it look like?
DEPALMA: Oh, it ain't bad at all. You know, I gave him [Marson] ten, you know.
WEISMAN: Who, Tom?
DEPALMA: Yeah. Quarter to Sal.
WEISMAN: Yeah.
DEPALMA: Fifty to Louie.
WEISMAN: Yeah, what do we get?
DEPALMA: Ten to the box office.
WEISMAN: Yeah.
DEPALMA: You'll see what we got left.
WEISMAN: Well, give me an idea.
DEPALMA: I don't even know what we got left.
WEISMAN: Oh, come on, you . . .
DEPALMA: I swear to God. I did not work on it. I made Richie take care of all them guys last night.
WEISMAN: You mean you got no idea what the story is?
DEPALMA: Well, without the other things, you know, we're going to, you know the other things. I really really would like to see you in person.
WEISMAN: I understand, all right forget about it.
DEPALMA: Really Eliot.
WEISMAN: Right, you're a hundred percent right.

DePalma had suspected for several months that his phone might be bugged. He had complained to Weisman on several occasions that they shouldn't talk freely on the phone. But the conversation continued nonetheless.

DEPALMA: Sal was weeping, too, you know, last night.
WEISMAN: Oh, yeah? What about?
DEPALMA: With his.
WEISMAN: Why? He thought it was going to be more?
DEPALMA: Yeah. They ending up with more than us. I'll tell you that fuckin' right now.
WEISMAN: How could that be?
DEPALMA: Well, you figure it out. Sal gonna end up with thirty. Louie fifty. That's what, eighty?
WEISMAN: Yeah.
DEPALMA: Tom ten; ninety.
WEISMAN: Yeah.
DEPALMA: Ten to the box office.
WEISMAN: Yeah, so.
DEPALMA: Ten Nino. Bean ten. I got to get rid of this . . . you hear that clicking shit. Would you see me tomorrow?

The wiretaps, however, cut two ways. Combined with the theater's accounting records and the testimony of experts and the accomplice witnesses, the wiretaps certainly showed the defendants engaged in crimes, but they also showed what Ellis had spoken of in his opening statement: These were inept businessmen, barely able to keep the theater afloat, having to steal from themselves to pay off secret loans and make some personal income.

When the prosecution rested its case, Gaggi was sent home by Sweet for lack of evidence.

The jury began its deliberations in January 1979. They were asked to consider ninety-seven separate verdicts, 617 pieces of evidence, and testimony from forty-seven witnesses.

After fifty-five hours of deliberation over seven days, the jury came back—hopelessly deadlocked.

Allen Shafer, a frail man in his thirties, was the lone hold-out juror, refusing to convict on any count in the indictment. "How can you let Fratianno walk free and put a man like Weisman in jail?" he had argued. The other jurors replied that Fratianno had been a credible witness, and that was their only concern.

The jurors, who were never less than 9-to-3 for across-the-board convictions, agreed to a compromise, offering to convict every defendant on just one charge each. But Shafer wouldn't budge.

The jury was dismissed and streamed out of the courthouse as Akerman stood by, nearly in tears. Several stopped to apologize for not bringing him convictions.

The FBI opened an investigation of Shafer, suspecting that he'd been bought, but found no proof whatsoever to support their suspicion.

A few months later, as a retrial was about to get underway, the trial's top mob figures—Pacella, DePalma, Fusco, and Marson—those whom Fratianno's testimony focused on, pleaded out.

The government severed Larry Goodman from the retrial and eventually dropped the charges. It cost Goodman more than $100,000 in legal fees and he nearly lost his career as a broker. Nobody apologized.

Weisman, Cannatella, Horwitz, and Nersesian stood trial, on what became a trimmed down white-collar case, without Fratianno's testimony. Nersesian was the only one acquitted.

At sentencing, everyone got one to three years, except, that is, for DePalma, who got four and a half, and Weisman, who drew a six-and-a-half year term. A few months later, Weisman was cooperating and hoping for a reduced sentence. With Weisman's grand jury testimony, Akerman indicted Horwitz and Jay Emmett, president of Warner Bros. And when Emmett pleaded guilty with a cooperation agreement, Akerman was able to indict Solomon Weiss, the Warner treasurer.

Akerman was convinced that a string of indictments, convictions, and heavy sentences would bring him the informant-witnesses he needed to take the Warner case to the top: He wanted the Warner chairman Steven J. Ross. From what he had been told by Weisman, Emmett, and others, Akerman was convinced that the cash bribes paid to the Warner executives weren't for the enrichment of Emmett or Weisman, but were poured into a corporate cash slush fund that Ross controlled.

But the Warner trail ended with Solomon Weiss being convicted and sentenced to community service rather than jail. Ross was never formally charged with any wrongdoing. Three years later, the U.S. Attorney's office issued an unusual statement, announcing the end of the Warner investigation.

Weisman's testimony had been instrumental in getting the Warner case as far as it went. He refused to testify to anything about Sinatra and company, insisting he knew of no skulduggery. He had been placed on Rudin's payroll before the first trial began—an arrangement that government officials privately had characterized as hush money.

The government, however, was satisfied with what it saw as Weisman's partial cooperation. His sentence was cut to about eighteen months, which he served in the New York City MCC, while using Akerman's outer office to book acts for Rudin clients like Liza Minnelli and Sinatra.

But Jimmy testified that DePalma had paid Sinatra $50,000 or $60,000, in person, in Las Vegas, to get him to play the theater in 1977. He claimed to have been party to several conversations with DePalma about the payoff.

On the strength of Jimmy's claims and some less reliable informant reports, Akerman dragged DePalma and Pacella into a grand jury in April 1980. Neither would testify about Sinatra. Pacella wouldn't even acknowledge if he knew "an individual by the name of Frank Sinatra." They were each cited for contempt and did an additional year in prison.

The government—Akerman and his superiors—felt there was enough to indict Sinatra. But it would have been a petty tax evasion charge that would have fallen apart in court. They decided to drop it.

Ultimately, seven of the original ten defendants went off to prison. Carino joined WITSEC and got a suspended sentence on the check kiting charges; Brodsky moved to New Jersey and made a fortune in the courier service business; nothing of note happened to Kosman.

As for the theater, the 3,500-seat, Las Vegas–style arena: The Lincoln First Savings Bank, holder of the mortgage, took it over after failing to find a buyer at auction. They cast about for someone to operate it under a lease arrangement. A few people tried, including Dick Clark, but no one could make it work. They needed big name acts to draw customers to a suburban showplace and those acts demanded more than the relatively small hall could afford to pay. "The place could not make money unless it operated at close to ninety percent capacity on a Tuesday night in January with snow on the roads. . . ."

In 1982, the theater's contents, including the folding chairs, were auctioned, a wrecking ball came in, and "Eliot's impossible dream" was finally demolished.

8

Busting Out
of El Paso,
1979

JEAN'S MIND was blinking on and off like a bulb on a faulty circuit. There were moments of brilliance, followed by inconsistent flashes of illumination; then darkness, until something would jar her and start the process again.

She had always had trouble keeping her mind focused on a subject. She had a tendency to ramble inexplicably from one time frame to another. But remarkably, when reminded of her original direction, she would find a link between the uncertain tale and the subject at hand. She knew where she was going all along. It was the listeners, those who anticipated a certain direction or response, who were confused, not her.

Clearly reassuring was that somewhere in those adrenaline jags was the very essence of honesty; it was like a child's sincerity, fragile and sometimes disoriented, but pure illumination.

Jacques Beugelmans tried his very best to deal with it, but saw it was a lost cause. Beugelmans was her lawyer. He was attempting to do with Jean what Akerman had done so successfully with Jimmy—train her to the witness stand.

At the very same time Jimmy was preparing for his debut in New York—telling his tale about Marson, the Rancho Mirage scene, the theater, and Sinatra—Jean was preparing to tell her tale about the same Rancho Mirage social set in a state court in Indio, California, about a half hour from Tamarisk Country Club.

Just days apart, Jean and Jimmy would both make it to the witness stand, though on opposite sides of the country.

Hers was a simple assault and battery case: She was suing a former beau for a beating she said she had received in April 1973, when Jimmy was in prison, before they were married.

It amazed everyone in Rancho Mirage that anyone would have the audacity to beat up on Jimmy Fratianno's main squeeze. But the defendant was Zeppo Marx—the last survivor of the Marx Brothers, a living legend in his own right. He apparently took Jean at face value. And he didn't seem overly impressed by the reports of her boyfriend.

Before arriving in Indio, Beugelmans spent hours on the phone with Jean, getting her side of the story, and later with Jimmy, who, inspired by a cash settlement and vengeance, was only too willing to help Beugelmans with this particular Marx brother's not-so-comical reputation in Las Vegas and Palm Springs. Zeppo was known as a "degenerate gambler," he had been thrown out of Tamarisk after a cheating scandal, and had a reputation as a curmudgeon, womanizer, and as a man with a violent temper, or so Jimmy said.

This was rough terrain for Beugelmans, then twenty-seven, facing his first solo fight in the courts. He had been working for Richard Chier, a lawyer with a large criminal law practice in Los Angeles, for more than a year.

He drew the assignment after others in the law firm had pretty much written it off as unwinnable—what with the defendant being an American legend and the plaintiff now the wife of a notorious mobster, in addition to what Marx's lawyer would try to portray as a sordid past, complete with too many men and too much alcohol.

So Beugelmans was tossed the case as a good chance to get some practice. If he won everyone would be offering up praise; if he lost no one would hold it against him.

Beugelmans drove his seven-year-old VW Bug from Los Angeles to Indio several days before the trial, where he met his client face-to-face for the first time in the Riverside County Sheriff's lock-up, surrounded by shotgun-toting marshals.

Security was such that Jean was prohibited from going to the bathroom unless there was a female officer available to escort her. And since there were no female marshals on her detail, she sometimes had to wait hours.

With her guards looking on, Beugelmans directed the tedious process of asking the questions as if she were on the witness stand, trying to evoke crisp, salient replies. He explained the process over and over again before realizing there was no point—he might as well just let her rip:

"I met Zeppo at the wedding of a friend of mine, Bo Wheat, a really wonderful person, she married that golfer, Ken Venturi," Jean said with a touch of the Southern accent she had cultivated in El Paso, where she been relocated while waiting for Jimmy to complete his jail term.

"Anyway, at the wedding all the girls were just going crazy for Sinatra, and—did I tell you Sinatra paid for the entire wedding reception? It really was very sweet of him. But I never was attracted to him, you know. And, well, I just never took to him the way all my girlfriends around Palm Springs did. Once I went to see him perform with a girlfriend and she was just wild for him and afterward I asked her if she would like to meet him and we went backstage and she just was so delighted—it was like the most important thing that ever happened to her. I mean these girls can talk about that man endlessly. It always bored me to tears. I'd heard all that stuff about him hanging out with mobsters and it just turned me off. But look who I ended up marrying? You never know what you're going to do, huh?"

Beugelmans listened. His patience, something he prided himself on, was wearing very thin.

"Jean, how did you meet Mr. Marx?" he asked in his best triallike manner.

"Well, didn't I just tell you that? It was at Bo's wedding."

"When was that?" he asked.

"Well, let me see. Yes, it was at the reception. I was standing with my girlfriend Diane and she was dragging me over with her to see Sinatra when Zeppo came over and Sinatra introduced us. He and Frank were friends, you know. I thought Zeppo was really quite handsome and distinguished-looking. Yech. Looks can certainly be deceiving, can't they? You know he was older than Jimmy.

"So he found out where I lived—I was living with my father at the time. Can you imagine, a thirty-two-year-old woman still living with her daddy? It probably had something to do with being married so young the first time—ohh, I really hate thinking about my first husband. You know I do believe Zeppo is older than my father."

She corrected her course with a laugh. "I'm drifting, aren't I? Well, Jacques, you just tell me if I'm not doing this right."

Beugelmans took a deep breath, and before he could exhale and ask again when the wedding was, Jean was off and running.

"Well, at first I didn't want to go out with him because I thought he might be mean—just a vibration, a feeling, you know. Well, he wouldn't take 'no' for an answer. He started sending me flowers and candy and things, and after a while I began going out with him," she said, her voice slowing to normal pace and dropping low.

"Okay. That's *how* you began dating him. What I need to know is *when* did you start dating him?"

"Yes," she said quietly, escaping into her own thoughts. "You know I was still drinking quite a bit then. And I guess he was still recovering from Barbara."

"Who is Barbara?" Beugelmans asked, again assuming his court-room demeanor.

"Barbara Marx. Sinatra's wife. Jacques, you know that," Jean said, snapping out of her mental drift and sounding annoyed.

"How long did you date Mr. Marx?"

"Oh, I guess it must have been six or eight months."

"When was that," Beugelmans persisted.

"Soon after Bo's wedding. Oh, do you mean a month or something like that? I really couldn't say. No, wait a minute. It had to be . . . No, I really can't be certain."

"Did there come a time when you moved in with Mr. Marx?"

"No. That's what the fight was about. We were at Tamarisk. I was pretty drunk. I always drank stingers at Tamarisk. Anyway, he'd been after me to move in with him for several weeks and I just didn't want to. I guess I—no, I'm quite certain, I still loved Jimmy. Anyway, we started arguing at the clubhouse and I staggered out, and we argued and pushed and shoved all the way up to his driveway, where I tried to get into my car and he got absolutely crazy and began hitting me and grabbing my hair and pounding my head against the car door. He pulled clumps of hair out of my head. Oh, he's dreadful."

Beugelmans and Jean had two days to work together before the trial opened. There were moments during their preparation when Beugelmans would lose all composure and begin yelling, trying to focus Jean on the questions at hand. Jean would respond by crying or screaming obscenities.

"You're not too damned bright, are you?" Beugelmans screamed at her in their final minutes together before trial.

Jean just wept.

The jury was chosen and the case set to start. Beugelmans was silently bemoaning his fate as he approached a coffee machine in the court-house lounge.

"You're the lawyer in that Marx case, Bugle-something, aren't you?" an elderly men asked, tapping toward him with a blind man's walking cane.

"Name's Buegelmans and, yes, I'm the sucker. Can I do something for you?"

"Nothin'," the blind man said, extending a hand in friendship. "They call me The Seer. I just wanted to greet you and thank God you're here."

"Well, thanks, I think," Beugelmans said, shaking hands with The Seer.

"I work here in the courthouse and picked up the nickname be-cause I predict the outcome of the trials. I can't read the newspapers, or learn anything except what I hear being said. They tell me I'm pretty good at it."

Beugelman smiled. "Okay, I'll bite. What are my chances?"

The Seer hitched his cane on his forearm and held Beugelman's right hand sandwiched between his two, swayed slightly from side to side, and said with a thick guttural laugh, "Son, this case is in the bag."

Two marshals, conspiciously armed with shotguns, stood by—one at her side, another at the door—as Jean testified. The jury was told to disregard their presence, that they had nothing whatever to do with the case.

She told her story as only Jean could. She cried and laughed, became confused by some questions and went on at length in the wrong direction on others.

When she was attacked as a liar on cross-examination she became angry and screamed, her arms and hair flying wildly. When asked about the lurid aspects of her life—the wild, all-night parties and the men she had been with—she replied with complete honesty, emitting an almost tangible quality of contrition.

Her country-girl good looks, spiced with her enticing sensuality, were an arresting presence that filled the courtroom. She was well-spoken, with a broad vocabulary, evidencing intelligence. Her good posture added something. Her strong voice, too. And she was charming the pants right off Judge Warren Slaughter.

She played to the judge and jury the way Marilyn Monroe had played to a camera. There was something captivating in her emotional outbursts and apparent vulnerablity.

She was also very shrewd in her vindication, but that was only Beugelmans's perception.

"I apologize for what I said the other day," Beugelmans whispered to Jean as she completed two days of testimony. "You're absolutely brilliant."

Marx, on the other hand, was haughty. He denied having any more than a few dates with Jean. He argued that the fight she described was merely a playful pushing and shoving bout—not nearly enough to cause the loss of hair as well as neck, back, and spinal injuries she had reported to doctors days after the fight. He said the fight followed his refusal to marry her.

Marx, seventy-two at the time of the assault, claimed he was too old and infirm to have inflicted those injuries, and he denied ever showering her with gifts.

Beugelmans came back with photos of Jean and Zeppo, partying with Sinatra or John Gavin at celebrity hangouts over a six-month period. He also presented a photo of the "infirm" gentleman holding aloft a mighty powerful-looking swordfish he had caught on a Caribbean fishing expedition weeks before the beating. And he had Jean produce from her wallet the Standard Oil Credit Card Marx had given her during their courtship.

Marx said she had stolen the card and that it was his efforts to retrieve it, as Jean prepared to leave his home, that triggered the shoving match.

The press was eating it up. It was pure Hollywood: aging millionaire screen star sued for beating up on beautiful blonde bombshell, who later married one of the nation's most notorious mobsters. But the media are always gluttons—they anxiously awaited courtroom appearances by Fratianno or Sinatra.

Marx's lawyers repeatedly hinted at the reputation of Jean's husband, and made veiled threats that they might open the door to a full-blown discussion of her mob associations and subpoena Jimmy.

But Beugelmans held them in check, leaving two subpoenas in clear view on his table: one for Sinatra and the other for Barbara Marx Sinatra.

It was a Mexican standoff.

The jury listened for nine days and deliberated for ninety minutes—awarding Jean $20,690.

"I don't know why you folks didn't ask for more," a juror told Beugelmans after the trial.

He would have. But the young lawyer hadn't understood an important social aspect of Palm Springs and Rancho Mirage. The vast majority of those living in the area—and certainly of those who sit on juries—are working people who spend their lives as serfs in the shadows of fiefdoms created by the Sinatras, Marxes, and Walter Annenbergs. There was greater resentment than reverence for the landed aristocracy in this California desert town, Beuglemans learned at post-trial interviews with the jurors.

Zeppo Marx, at least a majority of the jurors felt, was part of that aristocracy. And according to a few of the jurors, despite Judge Slaughter's instruction to ignore the marshals, they were convinced Marx was linked to organized crime and must have made some threats on Jean's life.

Jean and Jimmy didn't see each other again until early in 1979, when they both got back to El Paso.

They were both flushed with excitement for what had happened to them in recent weeks and months. The notoriety of Jimmy's testimony in the Premier Theatre case had not only won him national press attention, but had increased his value for the government. He wasn't only a knowledgeable witness, he was a remarkably good witness. And Jean earned high marks from Jimmy for scoring a quick $20,000.

Jimmy was traveling to Los Angeles for debriefing and grand jury sessions and staying as long as he could. He spent almost as much time in Henderson's office or on Los Angeles military bases as he did in La Tuna in 1979.

On the road, he was treated as royalty. At one time he stayed for several weeks in a vacant general's quarters at El Toro Marine Base—as fine a home as he had ever known. He generally had the run of the military bases for walking around and exercise. And he had the constant companionship of marshals or FBI agents who gathered around at mealtime to listen to Jimmy's tales, much as children listening to their grandfather's war stories.

On one trip, he convinced McPherson that he needed additional exercise.

"So what do you want to do, Jimmy? Get a pick-up football game going?" McPherson asked.

"Naw," Jimmy said, reclining in a overstuffed easy chair. He thought for several minutes and then said with a warm laugh, "I got it, Bud, let's go ice skating."

McPherson laughed along with him.

"No, really," Jimmy said. "There's an indoor place just off Route Five."

McPherson was dumbfounded. But after he was convinced Jimmy was serious, he thought it through, pulled his team together, and off they went.

Six men arrived at the rink. McPherson stationed two at the entrance while he looked on from the perimeter of the nearly empty rink. Two others unwillingly joined Jimmy on the ice.

McPherson felt, as did Jimmy, that although Los Angeles was a designated "danger zone," it was actually fairly safe. Unlike New York, the Los Angeles mob lacked the manpower and sophistication to track Jimmy. And if by some circumstance a member or associate of La Cosa Nostra happened to be out ice skating on a weekday afternoon, he would still have to muster a hit team—by which time Jimmy and his guards would be gone.

The greatest danger confronted at the rink that afternoon—and on several subsequent visits—was the injuries sustained by falling marshals, as Jimmy scooted effortlessly across the ice, his teeth clenched firmly on a cigar.

At Henderson's office, Fratianno spent hours in FBI interviews, assisting the progress of the case.

Fox and Henderson had decided to use the dismissal of the first indictment—charging Brooklier's mob with Bompensiero's murder and the Forex sting shakedowns—to their advantage, building a stronger case before bringing a new indictment.

The two prosecutors, along with Agent Melvin Flohr, set to work to find some support for Fratianno's uncorroborated grand jury testimony about the murder conspiracy.

They tracked down scores of FBI and police surveillance reports that described meetings at which, Fratianno said, the murder plot was hatched and refined. While those reports rarely offered insight to what was discussed, they provided some independent verification that the meetings occurred.

Next, the prosecutors expanded the case to reflect Fratianno's descriptions of the Family's systematic efforts to enforce its long-ignored territorial prerogative over pornography. As supporting evidence, Flohr did a little arm twisting to win testimony from several of the mob's shakedown targets.

Charges from the Forex sting operation—body-wired conversations and undercover agents' testimony—needed no additional proof.

And lastly, Flohr dredged up a few conversations from the Alfa tapes in which Fratianno and Brooklier discuss the shakedowns.

On February 20, 1979, with an expanded case, Henderson reindicted Brooklier's mob. But Jimmy would continue to ferry between Los Angeles and El Paso to flesh out details that would give support to his testimony.

In El Paso, Jean had developed a friendship with a local school administrator, Annette Pauling, a down-home Texan, whom she had met at the local Unity Church. The two women quickly became inseparable, running around town on shopping sprees and sitting up late into the night telling tall tales. When Jean went off to California for the Zeppo trial, she told Annette that she was going to visit family, and left her a key to her garden apartment so she could come by to water the plants. Jean returned late on a Friday. She got halfway unpacked before falling into bed.

The next morning she heard a key in the lock and rushed downstairs to find Annette sitting at the kitchen table thumbing though her collection of Zeppo-trial press clippings.

"You mean you're one of those people in that protection program, Jeanie? And your husband is this Weasel character. My word. And all this time I thought you were just some little old divorcee taking it on the lam."

"Annette, I really don't want anyone knowing about this," Jean said, gradually awakening.

"Honey, your secret is safe with me. But just one question: Where the hell is the cavalry? I mean, you don't look too damned protected here. I've been walking in and out of this place here for the last two weeks without being stopped or anything. I could have been putting a bomb in here or something."

"Protection? They don't give me protection," Jean said angrily, heading for the Mr. Coffee. "All they do is keep me hidden away here and give me a monthly allowance, about $800, until Jimmy and I can move somewhere."

"How are you supposed to live on that kind of money?"

"I don't. Jimmy's lawyer sends me another $800 or so every month to make ends meet. And as for protection, you can't imagine what I've gone through with these people," Jean said, hitching one hand to her hip as she leaned against a kitchen counter. "I mean, the simplest things. Like the time I moved in here. You know, every time they move someone on this program, they take all their furniture and ship it across the country to a warehouse in Virginia or somewhere. They let it sit there for a few weeks and then they get another company to come pick it all up and move it to the new location.

"So, after all that, when these movers are unloading my stuff here I ask this one guy if he can help me hang a mirror and you know what he says? He says, 'Look ma'am. Our boss told us not to talk to you because you're involved with some murders or the Mafia or something.' Well, I was just furious and I did a little asking around and found out that the marshal who rented this place for me told the building superintendent that I was under protection. Can you believe that?"

They talked some more about Jean's life with "The Weasel," as Annette insisted on calling him, before agreeing that they wouldn't discuss it again.

But the next afternoon, Annette showed up with a small pearl-handled revolver.

"I know we're not supposed to talk about this anymore," she began. "But honey, if this is the best the government is doing to protect you, I think you should learn how to use this thing."

Jean abhorred guns, but Annette possessed a contagious sense of panic that could spark fear in Dirty Harry. She convinced Jean to spend a few weekend afternoons in the Hueco Mountains, taking target practice on tin cans and bottles. Several hundred rounds spent at their makeshift, rustic target range proved Jean an able shot—and each recoil drove home her fears.

Despite her new friendship and new source of protection—or maybe as a result of them—Jean didn't last too long in El Paso.

Early in March, stories hit the local newspapers indentifying a man gunned down a mile from her apartment as being in the Witness

Security Program. After refusing to step out of her apartment for a few days, Jean became ill and one evening silently escaped to her mother's home in Barstow, California.

When the marshals caught up with her, she told them she had pneumonia and needed her mother's healing ministrations. It was agreed she could stay with her mother for a few weeks.

At the beginning of April, Jean tiptoed back into El Paso. But within twenty-four hours of her arrival, she learned that one of Jimmy's former mob friends from Albuquerque was keeping his mistress in the same apartment complex. Jean went to see Jimmy that afternoon, told him her plans, called the movers, and took off again, back to Barstow and then to stay with friends in coastal Oregon.

Jimmy's last instructions to Jean had been for her to call Phil Fox as soon as she was settled somewhere.

By virtue of his high rank in the Justice Department and his having joined Henderson in a verbal pact to support and protect Fratianno, Phil Fox was becoming Fratianno's advocate in Washington. He had the kind of status and personal reputation that got people to open doors to him. And once inside, he had the intelligence and sincerity to bring people around to his way of thinking.

Jean called Fox from a phone booth along Route 101 in Seaside, Oregon, where she was sheltered from a steady spring rain. "Their whole idea is to yank you out of your home, change your identity, toss you into a new town, and put you to work—all with little or no protection," she said. "They treat me like a criminal and I've never committed a crime."

Fox told her he had expected her call and had already spoken to Howard Safir, head of the Marshals Service, who told him that she would be thrown off the program for breaching security. The only way she would get her stipend was if she lived by their rules.

With Fox's intervention, Jean was reinstated to the program in late May and moved to Milwaukee, under the protection of U.S. Marshal Mike Zapp.

But that only led to more headaches.

This time it was Jimmy on the phone: "Phil, they put Jean in a town with a Family! What's wrong with these motherfuckers? That's a small town where a woman like Jean is gonna draw attention. And she tells me they want her to get an apartment and a job there so

It was Cleveland that got Jimmy into trouble in the first place. Ray Ferritto *(above)*, the hired gun who fingered Jimmy in the Cleveland gang war, seen here after his arrest in 1977; Tony "Dope" DelSanter *(below right)*, Jimmy's best friend in Cleveland and the Family underboss, whose funeral in August 1977 started Jimmy on the long road to becoming a witness; James "Jack White" Licavoli *(below left)*, Cleveland boss whom Jimmy avoided testifying against at all costs—yet eventually assisted in convicting.

Frank "Bomp" Bompensiero (ca. 1950), the San Diego mob leader and government informant whose murder brought down the Los Angeles Family of La Cosa Nostra. *(AP/Worldwide Photos)*

Dominic Phillip Brooklier, boss of the Los Angeles crime family, leaving the courthouse on opening day of the 1980 trial in which he faced charges of racketeering in connection with Bompensiero's murder. *(AP/Worldwide Photos)*

Mike Rizzitello—at one time Fratianno's most trusted soldier, who later turned against him—waits outside federal courthouse in Los Angeles on opening day of racketeering trial. *(AP/Worldwide Photos)*

Louis Tom Dragna, acting boss of the Los Angeles Family whom Fratianno describes as his co-equal, arrives for opening day of the Los Angeles mob trial in 1980. *(AP/Worldwide Photos)*

Left to right: Attorney General Edwin Meese III, former FBI Director Clarence Kelly, Clarence and Lucille Newton. Clarence Newton spent his final years with the FBI as a field agent chasing Fratianno—later becoming one of Jimmy's closest friends.

Jim Henderson, chief prosecutor and head of the U.S. Organized Crime Strike Force in Los Angeles, sealed the secret deal which won Fratianno's cooperation.

Phil Fox, casually known as the Justice Department's "consiglieri" on organized crime, became Jimmy's closest contact in Washington, D.C. *(Eileen Colton)*

Jim Ahearn, while assistant agent in charge of the FBI's San Francisco office, carefully balanced deceit and friendship to draw Fratianno away from La Cosa Nostra and into the ranks of the government witnesses.

Backstage at the Premier Theatre in September 1976—the photo that cemented public opinion of Sinatra's friendship with mob figures and came out at trial as proof of Jimmy's association with the mob-backed concert hall. Appearing are: *(standing, left to right)* Paul "Big Paul" Castellano, later to become boss of the Gambino Family; Greg DePalma; Sinatra; Tom Marson; Carlo Gambino, the prototype boss; Jimmy Fratianno (photo altered for his protection); Salvatore Spatola; *(seated, left to right)* Joseph Gambino; and Richie Fusco.

The Premier crew: Rousted in June 1978 pre-dawn arrests were ten men charged with financing the Premier Theatre through mob banking and stock frauds and later diverting theater profits to enrich themselves. *Left to right:* Greg DePalma, Gambino Family soldier, who ran the theater; Louis "Dome" Pacella, Genovese soldier and restaurateur, who brought Sinatra to the theater; and Eliot Weisman, theater founder and president, who became the mob's front man.

Nathaniel "Nick" Akerman, assistant U.S. Attorney in New York, was the first man to train Jimmy as a government witness. Akerman used Jimmy's testimony in the Premier Theatre case as the foundation for a series of landmark organized crime cases against crime bosses in New York and Pennsylvania—as well as targeting Sinatra and Warner Communications. *(Robert Deutsch)*

Frank "Funzi" Tieri, boss of New York's Genovese Family, the quintessential godfather model, under arrest in New York on RICO charges— engineered by Akerman on Jimmy's testimony. *(Robert Deutsch)*

Joseph Aiuppa, boss of the Chicago Family, called to Congressional inquiry (ca. 1962). Jimmy believes Aiuppa, as head of the Chicago Family, bears responsibility for the murder of Jimmy's best friend Johnny Roselli. Getting Aiuppa became a near obsession for Jimmy as a witness. He got his chance to testify against Aiuppa in 1985, in a trial resulting in convictions of Aiuppa and other Midwest mob bosses who controlled the Las Vegas casino industry. *(UPI/Bettmann Newsphotos)*

Carmine "Junior" Persico (ca. 1963), boss of the Colombo Family, was convicted along with the entire leadership of his Family in a 1986 trial. Other witnesses described the Family's crimes—Jimmy testified about the structure of the Family and his knowing "Junior" as the boss. (UPI/Bettmann Newsphotos)

Donald "Bud" McPherson, chief of the U.S. Marshals Service in Los Angeles, became Jimmy's constant companion and champion when Jimmy was hiding out or in protective custody.

Noted Albuquerque criminal lawyer Billy Marchiondo *(at left)* on the witness stand during his libel suit against the *Albuquerque Journal*, while his lawyer, F. Lee Bailey, conducts the questioning. *(Eugene Burton)*

she'll be all settled when I get out of jail. People there know me; I can't live in a place like that."

Fox went back to Safir and won assurances that when the time came, Jean and Jimmy would be moved to another location, but until then she would remain in Milwaukee.

In keeping with the Henderson-McDonald pact in San Francisco, Jimmy went before the federal parole board at Terminal Island in Los Angeles in July, eighteen months after he'd been arrested.

"Look, you guys might know everything there is to know about getting a guy into prison, but I know all there is about getting out," he told Fox on the phone after his parole board appearance. "These people on the local board here have no say in what goes on. If someone there in Washington wants to bust my chops, I won't get out in the twenty months you guys promised."

"Don't worry yourself over it, Jimmy. You've been keeping your promises and we'll keep ours."

Jimmy remained in Los Angeles for three weeks after his parole hearing. Upon returning to La Tuna he found a letter waiting for him. His parole had been approved by the regional board—and then rejected by the national board in Washington, which ordered him to do his full five-year term.

He was on the phone to Fox before he had unpacked his bag. By the end of the day Fox had scheduled appearances before the panel for himself, McDonald, and Ahearn. The national board had rejected Jimmy's parole based on a probation report that claimed Fratianno had killed Bompensiero and been a participant in killing Danny Greene.

In their August appearance before the board, no one mentioned the promises made in the San Francisco pact. McDonald described the negotiation of Fratianno's plea bargain: Fratianno's decision to plead guilty to charges on which he could have won acquittal in court and his desire to cooperate.

Ahearn explained Fratianno's cooperation in the Cleveland leak case, the Bompensiero murder, the Premier Theatre, and several other cases.

And then it was Fox's turn. He repreated the essence of what his associates had said, adding that in his opinion as a federal prosecutor, Fratianno could not have been convicted for either of the murders, and without his aid they wouldn't have solved the Bompensiero case.

"This is a unique person who has given us a unique opportunity to get inside the traditional barriers surrounding La Cosa Nostra. If we can't show some leniency for someone who's done what he's done we're never going to have this opportunity again." He went on to lay out the cases Jimmy had made and was expected to assist in.

He concluded with: "The goals of incarceration are to punish people, to rehabilitate them, to put them away so they can't hurt anyone for a while, and to serve as an example to others.

"Certainly he should be punished, but he's already spent nineteen months in jail, faces a lifetime in hiding, and is entitled to some leniency for all that he's done. By keeping him imprisoned, we aren't going to rehabilitate him to the extent of teaching him a new trade. He isn't going to hurt anyone now because he's too old and is likely to be under the near-constant supervision of the Marshals Service. And it would be a good example for others to know that Jimmy Fratianno aided the government and that the government appreciates that assistance."

The parole board agreed.

On September 15, 1979, Jimmy unceremoniously packed his bags for his final journey out of La Tuna. He headed to Los Angeles for two weeks, to make his final preparation for trial, set to begin in October, and get instructions to McPherson about his new life.

His name would be Marino, Jimmy Marino, a retired import-export furniture salesman who grew up in Cleveland and moved to Los Angeles after World War II. He had received a medical deferment from military duty for the collapsed lung he had suffered as a child. He would eventually receive a passport, social security papers, driver's license, and high school records. He would receive $90 a day, untaxed income, to cover all of his expenses as long as he continued testifying; an additional daily allowance would be paid when he was on the road for trials.

McPherson told him to read all of the agreement forms carefully, to take his time and ask about anything he didn't understand. Jimmy signed the stack of papers and initialed each page with hardly a glance.

Days later he was on a plane bound for Boise, Idaho, with two marshals. They escorted him to a residential motel, rented him a car, and then left him on his own.

Jimmy spent two days strolling the streets of Boise in his Sunday best, sizing up the town. There was already a chill in the early October air. The people seemed down to earth, he thought. They looked like they worked for a living, unlike the stylized dandies of the West Coast. He liked that.

Jimmy didn't need the West Coast or big-city action. By this time in his life, he had made repeated dramatic changes in locales; he had spent nearly twenty years in prisons and about the same amount of time in Cleveland, with the balance of his years evenly divided between Los Angeles, Sacramento, and San Francisco. So starting life over again in a new town wasn't as traumatic as it was for most of those in WITSEC.

On his first night in town he went cruising—he'd been in custody for close to two years and wasn't going to lose any time. Besides, Jean wasn't going to join him for a couple of days yet.

He found the lounge at a Holiday Inn to be a particularly hospitable place. Jimmy wasn't a big drinker, but he could bide his time at a bar waiting for some action as well as any man. He didn't have to wait long.

Pauline was a divorcee in her late thirties who stopped in at the Holiday Inn lounge after work most evenings before heading home. She worked at a nearby car dealership as a salesperson. Her stock in trade were Chevys—her sales pitch had a lot to do with demonstrating her long legs and tight chassis.

"Hi there. Can I buy you a drink?" Jimmy volunteered as soon as she slid onto a bar stool.

She pushed a wealth of auburn hair back from her face, set her dark brown eyes to work on sizing Jimmy up, and then nodded and smiled approval.

Before she could order, the bartender was setting down an old-fashioned.

There was some talk—was Jimmy staying at the hotel; what brought him to Boise; why would anyone move from Los Angeles to here? Another drink. Some more talk. And then off to the front desk.

Pauline called in sick to work the next day. Jimmy had found his first new friend.

Jean arrived on Friday under escort of Mike Zapp. Jimmy convinced Zapp to remain at the airport, rather than following them to their motel.

Zapp had been a constant nuisance. Every time Jimmy had called to speak to Jean in Milwaukee, he had to go through Zapp. And nearly every time, Zapp would have a million and one questions for Jimmy. Zapp said he was familiar with organized crime operators in Milwaukee and Chicago and was pumping Jimmy for information about who he knew. Jimmy found it all rather odd. The questions weren't the kind the FBI always asked relating to mob operations, but more like a who's who. Jimmy didn't trust Zapp.

Jean and Jimmy didn't leave their motel room that first day. During the next week, they visited real estate agents and looked at two homes they could rent or buy. Jimmy had about $25,000 from Times Books, which had bought the rights to his memoirs. Jean knew nothing about the money—he had never told her anything about his business and finances and wasn't going to change now.

On Sunday, Jimmy got up early and went out to a nearby pay phone to call McDonald. He didn't trust the motel phones. He was standing at the phone booth, searching through his pockets for his government-issue credit card number, when he noticed a beat-up Plymouth parked across the street, the engine running. The driver, about thirty-five-years old, well-dressed, dark, and Italian-looking, stared in Jimmy's direction for a few seconds. Jimmy began making his call as he watched the car pull away. McDonald's line was busy.

As he waited to make the call again, he noticed the Plymouth turning into the alleyway behind the motel and back to the street, where the driver stopped, stared at Jimmy through a pair of binoculars, and drove away, only to come around for a third look.

"This motherfucker," Jimmy muttered to himself as he hung up the phone and headed to the street to get the car's license plate number. When the driver spotted Jimmy in the middle of the street, he slammed his brakes, threw the car into reverse, and parked by a median divider.

When the driver remained in the car, Jimmy turned and bolted back into the motel. He waited in the lobby a few minutes watching the car through the lobby's plate-glass windows.

Jimmy went up to the room and told Jean he had to clear out for a while, but he would see her later.

"Where are you going?" Jean demanded.

"It's just business, babe. Wait here, I'll be back as soon as I can."

"Jimmy, it's Sunday. What business do you have on a Sunday?"

"Don't ask me so many fuckin' questions," he said, slamming the door behind him.

When he looked out the front of the motel, the Plymouth was

gone. He called for a cab to meet him in the alley behind the motel and went to the airport, where he called Ahearn, who wasn't home, and then the local FBI.

"What I want to do is lay a trap for these motherfuckers. See, I'll go back to the motel and you send a few agents over . . ."

"Look, fella. I don't even know for certain that you are who you say you are. If you got a problem you're supposed to call the Marshals Service, not the FBI," said an agent.

Jimmy hung up without another word and called the local marshal, who told him to go to another motel where he was to wait.

"Hey, you ain't tellin' me where to go," Jimmy hollered into the phone. "I'm going to another motel, but not one you send me to. I'll call you first thing in the morning and tell you where to meet me. Meanwhile, you get in touch with Bud McPherson and tell him I've got trouble."

The next morning McPherson was at the marshals' office when Jimmy called. They went back to Jean, finished packing her up, and flew her out—this time to Charlotte, North Carolina—with two marshals.

Jimmy flew back to Los Angeles with McPherson, where he spoke to Safir.

"Lookit Howard, someone in this program, one of your marshals, gave me up."

Safir didn't buy that.

"Who in the fuck gave me up: my lawyer didn't know, Henderson didn't know, Fox didn't know, nobody, Ahearn didn't know. I never told nobody where I was at, they didn't want to know."

"Well, if they were after you why didn't he kill you when he saw you?" Safir asked.

"Howard, look, they don't work that way, they don't carry a gun when they're looking for someone. Believe me, I've done this kind of work. That's all one of these guys needs is to be caught with a gun, right? See, what they do is they got to go to a town with three, four guys and look for you. And when they know where you are at, they set it up with a getaway car. You don't just kill a guy when you see him."

Safir said he'd investigate what Jimmy said, including running down the license plate number he had taken from the Plymouth. But meanwhile, Safir said, he wanted Jimmy to fly to North Carolina with Jean.

"Hey man, I'm not going to stay where you tell me anymore. Too many people know where I'm at with this program. I don't want nobody but you and Bud to know where I stay."

"I think that can probably be worked out, but where would you like to go?"

Jimmy thought for a moment. "The only safe place for a guy like me is out of the country—like Australia or South Africa, maybe."

"And once you're that far away, how do we know if you're ever coming back, or if you're in trouble how can we get to you as fast as we did this time?"

"Look, you motherfucker, I'm a man of my word. I say I'm coming back to testify and I'll come back. And another thing: If it weren't for you and all your marshals no one would have known where I was. Don't worry, I can take care of myself."

They ended the conversation with Safir promising that no one except he, Bud, and one local marshal would know where he was living and that he would consider Jimmy's other requests and get back to him in a week or two. Meanwhile, he'd have to join Jean in North Carolina for a few weeks, maybe through Thanksgiving.

Jimmy called Fox to tell him his latest troubles, but Fox had important news of his own.

Fox told Jimmy that there was going to be another delay in the trial date and the case probably wouldn't get underway until the following year. And, he said, he was making plans to leave the Justice Department at the beginning of the New Year to go into private practice. However, he had already been assured that he would be retained by the government as a special attorney to prosecute the Brooklier case—a fairly common practice.

"So now you can be my lawyer," Jimmy said.

The Great Smoky Mountains and Charlotte, North Carolina, created a homey setting. The air was clear and the weather temperate. Jean found the people friendly enough, and she enjoyed the fine Southern atmosphere of the tree-lined streets and the clean, modern, downtown business district in Charlotte. And it seemed to her that there were more churches per capita in Charlotte than just about any city she'd ever been in.

They were living a small-town existence about 60 miles outside Charlotte, almost equidistant between the city and the mountains, in one of the mill towns scattered about the area, where names like Burlington Industries carry the same clout as Chase in Manhattan or MGM in L.A.

While Jean nested and fretted about curtains or carpeting in their rented lakeside apartment, Jimmy paced, fumed, or sat silent for hours at a time staring into the TV. At least it was early in the football season and Jimmy had some distraction Saturdays through Mondays. The four remaining days of each week he would spend on the phone to McDonald, Akerman, Henderson, Fox, Demaris, and Safir. He would also take long drives through the countryside.

But he was becoming increasingly annoyed with the program. He was also having difficulty adjusting to a stable family setting with Jean—feelings he identified as frustration with the program. The more she did to set down roots in the community—becoming involved in church activities and buying for the house—the more Jimmy complained about his safety.

Thanksgiving and the arrival of Jean's family—her mother, brother, and sister-in-law—was the final straw. All it meant to Jimmy was that now even more people knew where he was living.

A week after Thanksgiving, as soon as Jean's mother had left town, Jimmy packed his bags and announced that he was leaving for a while.

Jean stood in utter amazement. She didn't understand what was wrong with him. As they drove out to the airport she asked how he intended to live, where he was going to go, how she would be taken care of.

"Jimmy, you can't keep running around. Your life's in danger without protection."

"Hey, babe, the only way my life's in danger is if I stay with this program. I know how to take care of myself better than they do.

"The way I got it figured, as long as I'm testifying you and I will have to live separately. You'll be okay; they won't try to hurt you."

"But Jimmy—"

"Don't worry about any of it, babe," he told her. "You just do as the marshals say and remain in the program—that will help pay some of the bills. I'll send you money and I'll arrange to see you every so often. But it's better that you don't know where I'm at for a while, until I get things worked out."

They had a long kiss goodbye at the airport departure ramp. After Jimmy walked into the terminal Jean parked the car and secretly went in after him, watching him check his baggage and board a flight for San Francisco.

"Hey Jim, how you been?" Jimmy said, his voice resounding with confidence.

Ahearn had answered the phone in the family room of his East Bay home.

"Jimmy, how are you? Why are you calling me at home? Is there something wrong?"

"No. I'm just fine. Why does there have to be something wrong?"

"Because that's the only time you've ever called me at home," Ahearn said, knowing he had to go through this little song and dance routine before learning what was bothering Fratianno.

"Jim, I'm in San Francisco and I need to see you as soon as possible."

Ahearn was silent for a moment, his surprise at Jimmy's call turning to shock. "What are you doing here? I thought they had you stashed back East somewhere."

"They did. But these motherfuckers are no good—"

"Are the marshals with you?"

"Fuck no. I told you. These guys are no good; they're going to get me killed. I dumped them."

"You can't take chances like that. Where are you?" Ahearn said, a clear sense of panic growing in his voice.

"I'm okay, Jim, I'm with my, uh, niece here and, you know, well, she got me at the airport. Why don't we just meet somewhere."

An hour later Ahearn drove to a diner in Berkeley where Jimmy was waiting.

"Look, Jim, for enough money I think any of these marshals would sell me out in a hot fuckin' minute. Not McPherson or Safir, but the rest of them just ain't no fuckin' good. I don't trust them."

Ahearn saw what was coming next and was already thinking dollar and cents, security, and interagency rivalries.

"So? What are you going to do—move back to Moss Beach, or do you want me to fly you to South Africa?"

"How did you know about South Africa?"

"What? Are you fuckin' crazy," Ahearn scolded. "I was only kidding."

"Oh, because that's where I told Safir I wanted to go. No, I don't expect you to send me there. But I want you to arrange to guard me."

"How am I supposed to do that? The FBI doesn't have that kind of program."

"What fuckin' program? You know this protection program isn't any big fuckin' deal. All they do is give you some phony ID and drop you in some jerkwater, little-shit town and you're on your own. I got the phony ID and I can pay for an apartment for a while. All you'd have to do is get me some money for food and stuff and arrange for me to know a few agents who I could check in with every so often. Believe me, Jim, it's no big fuckin' deal."

Jimmy almost made it sound plausible.

"Well, where would you live? It would have to be a place where no one knows you."

"I got an idea. I know this place in Walnut Creek. It's an apartment complex with a lot of security. A few years back Rus Bufalino, you know, the boss in Pennsylvania, asked me and Rizzi to clip this guy who was going to testify against Rus. All we knew was that he was living in Walnut Creek. When I went looking for the guy I found these apartments, nice-looking and built like a bank, and I figured it was the kind of place that I'd live if I wanted to hide out. You know I tried to get in there for a week to find out who lived there and I couldn't even get my car into the driveway—that's how good this motherfucker is."

"I tell you what I'll do, Jimmy. I'll think about it and call Washington to see what they say. But I'm not making any promises."

"Oh, Jim. These guys in Washington won't go for it. You can't get a thing like this approved officially. And I'll tell you something. If they cause any trouble with this I'm not sticking with this program. You tell them for me, I ain't sticking my neck out no more unless they start treating me like a man—not some biker-scumbag-trash like most of them in that program."

Two days later, with approval from Washington, Ahearn moved Jimmy into a furnished, one-bedroom apartment at the Walnut Creek complex. Agents Bruce Gebhart and Donny Smith were in charge of the baby-sitting detail, and each of them stopped by for at least an hour every day. Gebhart and Smith were also avid golfers and would get out to a local course with Jimmy at least once a week.

This was a quiet period for Jimmy. He saw few prosecutors or agents about cases. He spent most days in the apartment on the phone or watching television, sometimes getting out with his agent-companions or cooking elaborate meals with Ahearn on weekends.

He did occasionally meet outsiders—in the building or while traveling with the agents—and he told them he was a part-time pilot for Pan Am, a cover story that served him well for the next few years.

Safir's investigation of the Boise incident turned up nothing. The license plate number Jimmy had picked up from the Plymouth was registered to a local man who was without suspicion. A few years later, however, Zapp left the Marshals Service under a cloud—something about missing funds—fueling Jimmy's belief that most marshals couldn't be trusted. WITSEC has always denied Jimmy's claim that Zapp turned him in.

While in the FBI's custody in Walnut Creek, Ahearn verified at least a half-dozen reports of hit teams searching for Jimmy, but they were always looking in the wrong parts of the country.

Regardless of where the hit men were operating, fear for Jimmy's life remained high, and Ahearn remained uncomfortable having him in his custody. Ahearn's only reassurance was that Jimmy recognized his precarious position and willingly enforced his isolation.

His only real escape came during overnight visits to see his brother, Warren Fratianno, who lived a few hours away in Grass Valley, on the edge of the Sierra-Nevadas. But even these visits with family and the companionship of his crew of agents didn't fill a void that Jimmy suffered. He yearned for the companionship provided by a friend of long-standing, someone with whom he shared personal history.

His escape from a lifetime of treachery had not only jeopardized his life, it had also drained him of personal attachments.

9

The Leak

CLARENCE NEWTON was from the old FBI school.

He looked like a cross between Broderick Crawford's tough cop and Ed Asner's thinking-man's blue-collar characters. His drink was Jack Daniel's; his smokes were Marlboros. He always wore the heavy soled, shiny black shoe of the cop on the beat and the crew cut of a cadet just beginning military academy.

His hands and forearms were massive, solid enough to bludgeon a man to death. He carried about 230 pounds packed tightly around a 5-foot, 9-inch frame.

There undoubtedly were those who would mistake Newt's slow, soft, and delibarate manner of speech as dull-wittedness. A folly for an adversary; the man had a mind like a steel trap.

He was one of those rare individuals not ashamed to speak openly about anything he'd done in his life. It wasn't that he was without shame, he just saw no point in trying to evade the truth. He openly declared, in an age when it was no longer fashionable, "I'm a Hoover man."

And while he was a tough cop, he also posssesed a gentle spirit. He had brought bank robbers and con men to church and gotten down on his knees with them to pray.

In his career with the FBI, Newt had bounced from one end of the nation to the other. He had had ambitions of moving up to a position of command in the Bureau, which required that an agent invest half his career in small and large towns he might otherwise have wanted nothing to do with.

He was working as an instructor at the FBI's training school at Quantico, Virginia, when his aspirations for command faded. In September 1955, when his wife fell victim to terminal cancer, Newt decided to return home to Los Angeles with her and their two children. She died a short time later, and Newt chose to remain in California, where his family could assist him in raising his children.

He remarried several years later and found his niche in Sacramento, where he remained until his retirement in 1972, spending much of his time keeping tabs on a nest of bad guys, including gangster-turned-trucking executive Jimmy Fratianno.

The Bureau was convinced that Fratianno Trucking Company, which Jimmy and his first wife, Jewel, had begun after his release from prison in 1960, was crooked. In only a few years Fratianno had gone from a one-truck independent hauler to a major operator in federal highway projects, employing dozens of drivers. But the FBI never found a shred of evidence to sustain their suspicions.

Newt's job was to do everything imaginable to drive a wedge between Jimmy and his women or his business associates, hoping one of them would give him the road map he was looking for.

On days when he wasn't busy, Newt would march into the trucking garage and pass the time talking with Jewel, who would plead with him to leave Jimmy alone, that they were trying to make a new, legitimate start.

Newt persisted in harassing Fratianno, showing up at the garage during business meetings and hollering, "Anyone want to talk to the FBI?"

Jimmy's daughter, Joan, was married and living in Sacramento. Her husband, Tommy Thomas, was cooperating with Newt, providing everything he could, which wasn't much.

He was also speaking with Jean, who Jimmy kept stashed in an apartment in Sacramento. Newt had won her confidence, befriending her during one of her breakups with Jimmy. Now she was telling Newt whenever she and Jimmy were leaving town together. In fact, she had given him keys to her apartment, which he used to collect photos and documents he thought could be of use to him.

On one occasion, in 1964, when Jean and Jimmy were out of town, Newt went over to the apartment, picked up some papers, and called Jewel to meet him for lunch at the Captain's Table, a restaurant in South Sacramento.

Jimmy and Jewel had been feuding for months at that point. Jewel didn't know that while she was working twelve-hour days running the trucking office, Jimmy was playing around in Tahoe and other fashionable resorts with Jean.

Newt arrived at the luncheon appointment feeling most uncomfortable. He was terribly frustrated by his lack of progress in turning someone around in the Fratianno organization. And he was prepared to make one last distasteful pitch.

As they ordered, Jewel continued to protect Jimmy, saying, "Sure, he can be a real son of a bitch, but he loves me and he's given me his word that this operation is entirely on the up-and-up. Besides, I control all the books, and I'd know if something was wrong."

"Jewel, I'm surprised at you," Newt said, girding himself for a tactic he despised. "That man's not the kind of guy you can depend on for anything."

"You can't tell me anything about him that I don't already know; I'm satisfied," she said, cutting Newt off.

"Well, Jewel, you shouldn't be so sure about that. You know, that husband of yours is giving you a royal screwing," he said, running his voice in steady, soft tones. "While you've been working yourself to death he's been having a good time with a little girlfriend he has stashed on Robertson Boulevard."

Jewel leaned across the table and practically spat, "That's a bunch of bullshit. I've known that man for thirty-seven years and there's no way he'd treat me that way."

Newt hesitated, and then reached into his pocket, saying, "I tried to warn you. What does this look like?" He held out a photo of Jimmy with his arm around Jean that had been taken at Harrah's Tahoe.

Jewel reached out to seize the photo and then froze without touching it. She stared for a minute before getting up and leaving the table without a word.

Days later, Jewel, in a drunken funk, picked a fight in front of houseguests including Frank LaPorte, a Chicago mob *capo*—and Jimmy threatened to hit her. A week later she filed for divorce.

Jimmy took a house down by the Sacramento River and Jean moved in.

In 1966, a new administration had swept into office in Sacramento, a new governor with a million-vote margin of victory, generated in part by a law-and-order campaign that counted among its war cries the demand that gangsters, namely Jimmy Fratianno, should be forced out of business.

Newt was designated as FBI liaison with Ronald Reagan's new administration. He was in regular contact with Edwin L. Meese III, the governor's top aide who then held the title of legal adviser, and Arthur VanCourt, security chief. It became apparent in their discussions that the new administration was disturbed that there wasn't a full FBI division office in Sacramento, only a small "resident agency" office operating under the direction of the San Francisco office.

A new federal judicial district had been established in Sacramento and the San Joaquin Valley a year earlier, but the San Francisco and Los Angeles FBI offices had fought to protect their turf, delaying Hoover's creating the new Sacramento office.

VanCourt suggested that Newt write a letter to Hoover, which would be put over the governor's signature, urging him to act on the new division headquarters.

Newt drafted the letter, in which he thanked "The Director" for having sent Reagan congratulations on his election. He said he had always been a great admirer of Hoover's, and, by the way, he was looking forward to working closely with the new Bureau office in Sacramento.

Hoover was always a sucker for flattery. In a matter of weeks, Sacramento went from an eight-man operation to a fifty-agent division headquarters, and soon encompassed two-thirds of the state.

Newt continued as the liaison with Reagan's adminstration, meeting regularly with Meese, who was running the governor's office and was always fishing for insider information from Newt.

Soon after Reagan won a second term, Newt was passing by and stopped to speak to Meese's secretary, Florence Randolph.

As someone opened the door to Meese's office to leave, Meese saw Newt outside.

"Hey, Newt, come on in. What've you been up to?" Meese said, standing to shake hands.

"Well, I've been scratching around for work. You know, I'm up for retirement and I'm looking for a way out of this chicken shit organization," Newt said, taking a seat in Meese's office.

"I didn't know you had your time in?"

"Oh, yeah, I have twenty-five and could have left at twenty."

"So what have you been looking at?"

"I've been talking to Flying Tiger, they have an opening as chief of security in L.A., and they've flown me down there twice now, but I really don't want to go back there. I hate that place."

The two men talked about how lovely Los Angeles had been before the boom years following World War II. Finally Meese said, "Would you be interested in coming over here with us?"

"Well, jeez, I don't know. I really hadn't thought about it. But I sure would like to stay around here—you know my daughter's in college here at Sacramento State. What do you have in mind?"

"Look, I have a meeting to go to, but let's check with Florence and see when I have some time open. Just don't make any decisions before we talk."

When he returned days later, Meese had it all figured out. They would create a new position, special assistant to the governor, head of the governor's Operation Evaluation Unit, an inspector general of sorts, who would answer directly to Meese and Reagan. Flying Tiger was offering $35,000 plus expenses. Meese offered $21,500 and a state car.

He took the government job.

One of the unstated incentives was Newt's understanding from Meese that "if the Governor ever made a run for the Big Casino"—as Reagan's inner circle referred to the White House—there was likely to be a top spot for Newton at the Bureau. Newt still possessed a lingering spark of ambition for Bureau command.

He worked for Reagan and Meese for three years, examining the operations of major state institutions, such as the prison system, offering his findings directly to the two men who ran the state.

But the run for "the Big Casino" wouldn't come until 1980. There would be a five-year hiatus from public service for Reagan's inner circle, during which Newt struck out on his own. Combining a hefty federal pension with his new state retirement rights, Newt opened a private investigation office in Sacramento, where he tried to keep his work load to a minimum, taking on just a few special clients.

One of those was Denny Walsh, the *Sacramento Bee*'s investigative reporter, a Pultizer Prize–winning journalist whose files on organized crime in California, Newt believed, rivaled those of the FBI.

Newt and Walsh had become fast friends after meeting at the San Franciso home of Michael Hamill Greene, a private investigator and mutual friend. The next time Walsh was sued for libel—a common hazard of doing business as an investigative reporter—Walsh hired Newt as his investigator, marking the beginning of a strong relationship.

Late in 1979, the *Bee*'s owners, Walsh, and others were sued by attorney Vincent "Louie" Todisco for $28 million after Walsh wrote an article describing the lawyer as a "known associate and sometimes business partner of organized crime figures."

Walsh had relied on newspaper clippings, state crime reports, and sources to make that statement. Newt was called in to see if more support of the allegation could be established.

His first thoughts were of Jimmy Fratianno, who had testified that he was in business with Todisco, selling machine guns, in the late 1960s. His first problem was getting to Fratianno. And if he got to him, what was the chance of getting him to cooperate?

Newt flew down to Los Angeles to meet with Jack Barron, head of the Bureau's organized crime unit in that city, during the first week of February 1980.

The two men had known each other for most of their careers in law enforcement, but were never particularly close. Their approaches were worlds apart—Barron was a fast-talking hustler while Newt was more methodical—but they shared a mutual respect.

To Newt's surprise, Barron said he couldn't help him reach Fratianno. Fratianno hated Barron like poison. And even though Fratianno was now the main witness in several cases Barron was directing, he stayed away from the former mob boss to avoid spooking him.

"Jim Ahearn, the ASAC in San Francisco, is your best bet," Barron suggested. "Fratianno does whatever Ahearn tells him to. I understand Fratianno feels he owes his life to him."

"Yeah, I know that, but Ahearn doesn't return my calls. Any ideas on how I get in to him?" Newt asked. "I only met the guy once, casually, while I was with Reagan."

"I couldn't say. Oh, but hold on a minute. You know Ralph Hill over in Milwaukee? He and Ahearn are real close, maybe he could get you in."

"Now there's an idea. Bill Roemer is working with me on this case. He and Hill were on the C-One squad in Chicago, chasing after Giancana. So, now that we've settled my problems, maybe, what kind of trouble you been getting into lately—got a piece of this Abscam thing?" Newt asked, always interested in the latest Bureau scuttlebutt.

Abscam had hit the newspapers a couple of days earlier, on February 3, and new revelations about congressmen snared by the FBI's sting operation kept surfacing with every morning paper.

Barron slid his chair closer. "Newt, I have an undercover thing that's going to make Abscam look like a kindergarten party. It's called

Brilab, for bribery-labor. I've got two agents working undercover who are in with Carlos Marcello."

"What do you mean 'in with'?" Newt asked.

Barron's voice dropped to a conspiratorial whisper, but was charged with energy. "I mean, so far in, so close into the New Orleans boss, that he's arranged for my guys to make payoffs to a shitload of politicians who are just about to deliver these undercover guys all of the insurance business for the state of Louisiana and a bunch of big cities in Texas. I'm talking so close that he thinks my guys are arranging to buy off the judge in the Brooklier case. So damned close, Newt, that I got Marcello and Sciortino asking my guys to arrange for a Mexican hit man to kill Fratianno."

"Shit, Jack. That's incredible. How did you get in?"

"We had this convicted insurance swindler, guy named Joe Hauser, who turned for us. He started telling us he could get us Marcello and I told him he was full of shit. Well, I'll be fucked if this clown doesn't get on the phone the next day, call Marcello while I'm standing there, and get a big 'Hey, Joe, how you been?'

"So, one thing and another, and next thing you know, they're doin' all this work together and one day the old man calls to say he needs to get to this judge, the one in the Brooklier case, and he'll guarantee a payoff of up to $250,000 on twenty-four hours' notice. And Newt, we have the entire thing on a body wire."

"How soon before you pull the plug?"

"I think we'll surface the thing in a couple of weeks. I just sent a teletype last week to the offices involved telling them it would surface next week, but I need a little more time. I'll tell you, though, if I don't surface pretty soon the fucking federal government is going to be the insurance carrier for the entire state of Louisiana," he said, bursting into laughter.

"What about this judge, is he—"

"Harry Pregerson. No, he's straight as an arrow and hotter than all get-out. Last fall, just after Marcello first approached our guys, saying he wanted to get to the judge to help out this friend in Los Angeles we, Jim Henderson and Phil Fox, the strike force lawyers, and I, went to see Pregerson and told him all about it.

"Well, the case was ready to go to trial in October. Pregerson bitched and moaned. He was furious at me because I lifted his personnel file and gave it to my undercover guy so he could make like he knew this judge. And he was furious at Sciortino for thinking he could be bought.

"Anyway, Pregerson agreed to buy us a little time. He okay'd a continuance on some personal bullshit excuse without telling the defense anything. Now he says he'll recuse himself when we're ready to surface."

Newt hadn't gotten all that he came after, but he still was feeling a warm glow of satisfaction after seeing Barron. He always felt good when he heard about the Bureau chalking one up for the good guys and this sounded like it would be a good score.

When he arrived home in Sacramento the next day there was a message for him to call Walsh.

"Newt, there's something I have to tell you and I don't know what to do about it," Walsh said. "I got a call from Michael [Michael Hamill Greene] and he wanted to get this word to you, that a reporter from the *San Diego Union* had stopped by his office before catching a plane back to San Diego; he had just had lunch with Jim Ahearn and he told Michael that the L.A. FBI office has something going that's going to be bigger than Abscam. They call it Brilab. Michael couldn't reach you so he called me and asked me to try to get through to you."

"Okay, Denny. I'll take care of it," Newt said, understanding the significance of the call, but volunteering nothing of what he already knew.

Frequently, reporters and federal investigators maintain a symbiotic relationship; a protective trading arrangement filled with surreptitious conduits of information. The trading takes many forms, but there is always the understanding that sources are protected at all costs. Some trade information outright for their individual profit. Others have a social relationship, where they speak openly and rely on the other party's good judgment to wait for the time to be ripe before using the information. In other instances, agents frustrated by technicalities barring a case from court might leak a story to a reporter, or a reporter might tip an investigator to information that the news organization is unable to use.

In all cases, it's a fragile system of trust.

In this incident with Walsh, the implication was that publication of the story might endanger the FBI's undercover operation and the Bureau should know that the word was out on the street.

Newt hung up with Denny and called Barron at home.

"Barron, let me tell you what I just heard," and proceeded to tell him the story—avoiding the part about Ahearn.

"Shit, I owe you one. My guys are with Carlos Marcello right now, and this could get their heads blown off. I'm going to have to surface this thing right away."

On February 7, Pregerson announced he was recusing himself from the Brooklier case. It would be more than a year before Sciortino, Marcello, and a third man would be indicted in the attempt to bribe Pregerson. On February 8, a spate of newspaper stories detailing Brilab surfaced in Los Angeles, San Diego, New Orleans, and Houston.

Disclosures regarding Abscam and Brilab were followed by reports in the *Wall Street Journal* about Pendorf, another FBI undercover operation. All three appeared in the press between February 2 and February 9, a week that shook the Justice Department's trust in its employees.

The Justice Department reacted swiftly, ordering an internal investigation, led by Richard Blumenthal, U.S. Attorney for Connecticut, to learn the sources of the leaks and ordering appropriate discipline.

The internal probe, regarded by many as an inquisition, came just as the FBI was recovering from years of bad press resulting from the Watergate era. Any detente that had developed between the media and the Justice Department was seriously eroded by the probe as federal employees distanced themselves from the media.

During the next year, thirty-three FBI agents conducted 1,253 interviews and sought lie detector tests of agents and lawyers in seventy-seven cities resulting in disciplinary action against seven agents and prosecutors.

Barron, who acknowledged having tipped the *Los Angeles Times* to the story after learning that the *San Diego Union* knew about it, was censured after the internal probe and retired from the Bureau in December 1980 after twenty-six years as an agent.

Nick Lore in San Diego was one of those asked to take a lie detector test and passed without any disciplinary action being taken.

Henderson was interviewed at length and bitterly answered the questions put to him, finding it one of the most humiliating experiences he had ever faced in public service.

When agents approached Phil Fox, by that time in private practice, he was outraged. He refused to talk to them. Fox was offended by what he viewed as Blumenthal's pandering to the press, which included a feature interview he gave to the *Washington Post* and his announcement that he wouldn't seek to interview reporters during the probe. Fox felt the entire process was becoming a political springboard for Blumenthal.

Days later, when Blumenthal called, Fox told him, "I'd be delighted to testify, but not in an internal probe, rather, in a grand jury, on the record, under subpoena, and under oath. I will not be interviewed by you. I have no faith in your integrity and ability to carry out the investigation."

Efforts to interview Fox ended with that conversation.

Weeks later, Fox called Henderson. He said he had just been told by Attorney General Benjamin Civilletti that because he had refused to cooperate in the internal probe, the Justice Department wouldn't bring him back as a special attorney to work on the Brooklier case

Newt was also approached for an interview. "Look," he said, "I think the world of the Bureau and, yeah, I told Barron that there's been a leak, because if I were in the same position as those agents, I wouldn't want to have my ass hung out to dry. But look, I'm not telling you any more than that. I'm no longer with the government and what I know or do is of no concern to the Bureau unless I've committed a crime or have knowledge of a crime and I don't believe either of those areas apply."

The agents left, asking Newt to get back to them if he changed his mind.

That evening Newt got a call from Walsh. He told him about the agents who'd come to see him. He also told Walsh that Roemer had arranged, through Hill, for a meeting with Ahearn, but that no time had been set.

"Well, when you see Ahearn, tell him this: I got a call from a damned good source who says Fratianno's brother Warren is living in Grass Valley and Jimmy is living there with him. Now, if this source has that information, someone from that outfit is going to have it pretty soon."

The next morning Newt called Ahearn's office and left word about Warren Fratianno and Grass Valley. They set a meeting at Charley Brown's, a restaurant in the East Bay, for dinner that night.

After some shop talk, Ahearn got down to business. "So what's this about Warren Fratianno living, uh, where was it, in Grass Valley?"

"Yeah, that's what I heard and also that you have Jimmy Fratianno stashed up there."

"Well, where did you get this?"

"Shit, Jim, I'm not going to tell you that. But if it's true, you've got problems, because I'll tell you this much, my information is third-hand, from someone outside the Bureau, which means the word's out on your guy."

Ahearn sipped his beer and stared blankly at Newt for a moment. Jimmy wasn't living in Grass Valley, but he was in touch with Warren frequently enough for it to endanger his life. "Well, maybe in that case, I do have problems."

After a few more drinks, and a lot of silence broken only by more shop talk, Ahearn asked the obvious question. "If this was all you wanted me for, you could have done it on the phone. What've you got on your mind, Newt?"

"Jim, I'd like to talk to Fratianno. I got a case that I think he could break wide open for me. Now I know you'd be skirting the rules a little but—"

"Oh, come on, I can't do that. Skirting the rules? I'd get fired if I jeopardize this guy. We're talking about the best witness we've ever turned, and I can't risk it."

Firmly, but softly, Newt played his ace. "Well, Jim, you know I was interviewed by a couple of inspectors on this Brilab thing and, uh, I didn't tell them a damn thing and they want me to get back to them. And, well, I know the name of a reporter down in San Diego who had lunch with a certain agent in San Francisco just before the story hit the *San Diego Union.*"

Ahearn focused his thoughts for a moment.

"Well, you know that doesn't necessarily mean anything," Ahearn said. "Maybe the agent didn't tell this reporter anything, or maybe he just listened to the reporter's story and told him where he had the story wrong."

"Yeah, well, that's pretty much the way I figure it—maybe."

"Well," Ahearn began slowly. "When would you want to see Jimmy? Maybe I can arrange something."

"How about right now?"

Ahearn left the table to make a phone call.

It was well after midnight by the time they pulled up to an apartment complex in Concord, the home of an agent, where Jimmy had been brought for the meeting. The building was surrounded by unmarked Bureau cars.

Jimmy walked out of the guest bedroom and the two of them sat in the living room across from each other. There were two agents sitting in the dining room, one outside, and another at the door.

Jimmy at first scowled.

Newt told him he looked well, and then immediately saw the distrust in Jimmy's eyes.

"No, really, Jimmy, you look as well as, well, what's it been, fifteen years?"

"Yeah, something like that. You know these guys keep me pretty busy answering questions, so it keeps me young, you know what I mean?" he said, chuckling.

"Yeah, sure, Jim. I got a few questions of my own."

"So?"

"Well, I'm a private investigator now and I'm working for this newspaper, the *Bee,* which is being sued by a guy I think you had some business with years back. Vincent Todisco?"

"You mean that attorney in Fresno?"

"That's the one."

"Sure, I knew him. We had two or three business deals working in the sixties—never came to much, let's put it that way."

"Well, Jimmy, here's what I need to know. We need to find out what those deals were and how close you were to Todisco."

"Like I said, I knew him."

"Can you give me some names of the businesses and what role you each played."

"Shit, Newton, that goes back a ways."

"Hey Jimmy, call me Newt. And just a rough outline will do for now."

Jimmy was going through his usual slow start with a new inquisitor. But with a little more cajoling he opened up—offering his views, which ultimately would be used for deposition in the Todisco libel case, but never resulted in criminal charges against any of those whom Jimmy named.

"Seven-Eleven Tours was the first thing. You see, we were running this tour bus outfit that took people from San Francisco, San Jose, and Sacramento to Tahoe and Reno. Now this Todisco owned a piece of Barney's in Tahoe, and the way it worked was that the casinos would pay us a dollar a head for everyone we brought in. Well, at Barney's Todisco had arranged this so that he could get a secret kickback from us—we'd give him twenty-five cents, I think it was, for every dollar."

"Did you deal with him on that?"

"No, it was one of the partners, the guy who got me involved,

Bob Tegay. But he showed me a statement every month of what we'd made, the split, and what Todisco got from us.

"So that was one of the deals. There was also—"

"Wait a second, Jimmy. When was that?" Newt asked, taking notes of the conversation.

"It was a couple of years after Jewel and I broke up," he said, meaning nothing in particular by it but leaving Newt with a burning sense of guilt, which squelched his questions for a while.

"I guess I started with them guys in sixty-seven and lasted for about a year. You see, the majority owner at Barney's, this Richard Chartrand, he got clipped and Todisco went up there and cleaned out the safe. The club got sold and Seven-Eleven went bust. Anyway, they started up again under a new name, but I just dropped out of it.

"So the second deal was this detergent company. Fellow by the name of Greg Caruso, good friend of mine. He introduced me to this fellow, Mazzie, Richard Mazzie, M-A-Z-Z-I-E. He's a chemist and wants to start a detergent company and he tells me that he, Todisco, and Todisco's law partner, Capriola or something, are partners, and they'll cut me in for twenty-five percent if I get them contracts in San Francisco. Well, I introduced them around to some people, but that never went anywhere.

"The last one was this machine-gun deal. Now this motherfucker could have been a real good money-maker. This fellow Carl Blohm, he was a friend of Mazzie's, he's got access to a machine that can make a modified Thompson machine gun with silencers built into them.

"I checked with Bomp and we figured we could sell a load of these things to Mexicans, and we tell Blohm to send as many as he can make. So I went up to Fresno and met Blohm and he's there with this Capriola and he starts to introduce us and we tell him we know each other already. Anyway, Blohm tells me Capriola and Todisco are his partners. I told them to get me as many of those guns as they can. But the thing fell apart when the government grabbed the machine for making them."

Newt and Jimmy went over the stories for about an hour, fleshing out details and trying to determine just how much first-hand knowledge he had about Todisco.

After things had warmed up a little, Newt couldn't resist a little jab.

"I thought you were entirely on the up-and-up in those days, Jimmy?"

"Hey, motherfucker, that trucking company was completely legitimate. Look, you were one of the best in those days and you busted my ass every week and never found nothing. Right?"

"No, I never did," Newt said gently. "But while we're on the subject, Jimmy, one thing I could never figure: Why were there eighteen phone lines running into that trucking company of yours?"

"What do you mean?"

"Well, my guess was that you were making book."

"Newt," Jimmy squealed, leaping from his chair. "I'm telling you that place was legit, one hundred percent."

He walked to the kitchen, motioning for Newt to join him at the refrigerator where they pulled out fixings for ham sandwiches.

"I maybe had a few things going on the side, but I never fucked around with that trucking company, forget about it," Jimmy said. "It was the one completely honest thing I ever done in my entire life and I was grossing a million a year," Jimmy said, wagging a mustard-smeared butter knife at Newt. "So what happens? The fucking government pinches me on that bogus charge—making a false statement on the federal hourly wage form. I just did the same thing all the contractors were doing on that project: paying drivers by the load rather than by the hour. We even checked with the drivers and they said they preferred to be paid that way.

"But they nailed me because your friend Reagan wanted to get me. So they close down my business, fine me ten thousand, and put me in jail for three years. For what?"

"Well, Jim," Newt said in a voice soft enough to soothe a baby to sleep, but evidencing just a note of sarcasm. "You have to understand, that was the only way they could get you. And they were going to get you any way they could."

For a moment Jimmy stared at Newt, uncertain of how to take the comment.

"Shit," Jimmy said, breaking into a belly laugh. "You know I never really minded your busting my chops; that was your job. And if you caught me, well, okay, I'm fucked. But Newt, you never should have bothered Jewel. She was a good woman and she couldn't handle the aggravation."

"Yeah, Jimmy. You're right about that and I felt bad about it."

Jimmy set his plate down at a kitchen counter and sat on a high stool.

"You know she's dying, Newt," he said almost reverently.

"No, I didn't."

He looked away and his voice deepened. "Yeah, she went to see my sister in Cleveland a few weeks back and while she was there she collapsed. When they got her to the hospital they found out her body was just loaded with cancer. She's in Vegas now, but she's coming back to Sacramento where my daughter will see to her when it's time."

"Jimmy, I'm really sorry," Newt said, surprised at how close Jimmy still felt to Jewel.

Jimmy shrugged. "What are you going to do. It's one of them things."

Newt was realizing something else at that moment: a closeness to Jimmy that he never would have imagined possible. Up until then he'd been on a case. There had been no personal feelings about seeing the elder-gangster-turned-witness. But now he realized that here was someone with whom he had a history, whose life had been a part of his life, whose wives and family he had known well, even if the two of them had rarely spoken in the old days. Now things were different. They may have been adversaries then, but now they were both independent operators, both working for the good guys.

The conversation drifted to Jimmy's daughter—her divorce and his grandchildren—who he hadn't seen in two years but spoke to every week no matter where he was.

They talked about Jean and her switching from booze to religion.

Before their get-together was over they had three bets going: two on the outcome of the NBA title and one on whether Reagan could beat Carter. Jimmy would eventually win all three.

At dawn, as Newt prepared to leave, Jimmy told him that he would be willing to testify if they wanted him, but they'd have to set a price with McDonald. He also suggested that he knew a real good lawyer, Phil Fox, who they should consider using in the case.

Newt arrived home just ahead of the morning rush hour.

10

Trial Run

DURING THE SPRING OF 1980, Jimmy traveled the breadth of the United States, testifying against some old friends and adversaries. These were not the cases that brought him to government service; they were spin-offs, made independent of Fratianno. Yet each in its own way was as important as the major cases he faced.

The first one began as a simple union embezzlement trial but gained national interest with the potential for Jimmy to expose first-hand mob control of the largest labor union in the U.S.

Jimmy and Rudy Tham, founder of Teamsters Local 856, had been drawn together by mutual need, which evolved into friendship. The former Butchertown Sausage Maker, as Tham was known when he won a 1941 welterweight amateur title, had grown tough and beefy as he fought his way up the Teamsters' hierarchy. But in the early 1970s, his union prestige began slipping; he was no longer being promoted to new titles.

In 1974, upon meeting, Tham told Fratianno of his problems, and Jimmy agreed to work his magic—traveling to Cleveland, Chicago, and Los Angeles—threatening some who stood in Tham's way and appealing to Jackie Presser to provide his blessing for Tham. In return, Tham promised his friend control of Local 856's dental and eye care programs, from which Jimmy figured he could pick up $10,000 a month in phony medical claims and kickbacks. All this took years to accomplish, during which their friendship blossomed.

Tham invested $12,000 to help Jimmy open a San Francisco boutique—Clothes Out—where Jimmy sold hijacked goods. In 1976 and again in 1977, they traveled to New York for Sinatra's Premier Theatre concerts. In 1977, they traveled to Lake Tahoe together, again to see Sinatra perform. On each occasion, Tham put the tab on the union. Jimmy introduced Tham to Billy Marchiondo. The Albuquerque lawyer offered Tham a West Coast distributorship for Star Glo Briquettes, the product that had replaced Alfa Chemical Company.

By the late 1970s, Tham's Teamsters problems were straightened out, and he was again among the most powerful union bosses on the West Coast. But Jimmy never got the dental and eye care programs.

Throughout this time, the FBI had been on Tham. But it wasn't until 1980, after a thirty-three-month probe, that he was brought to trial for embezzling union funds. It was Jimmy who made the difference; only he could contradict Tham's claims that all his union-paid expenses were legitimate. In total, the indictment charged Tham with making $2,791 in bogus charges. A cheap indictment, but enough to justify hitting Tham for five years in prison, a $50,000 fine, and barring him from union office if convicted.

The government had no trouble with the case, but Jimmy did. Unlike the others Jimmy was asked to testify against, Tham was not a gangster, he had never signed on to play the game. The best rationale Jimmy could come up with was that Tham had never delivered the union medical plan—and he had been stupid enough to get caught with his hand in the till. And besides, Jimmy was now a government buttonman, he had to testify to any crimes he knew about.

Taking the witness stand in April 1980, Jimmy was relaxed amid layers of security provided by the FBI and U.S. Marshals. Neither agency was entirely sure who had custody at that point.

When asked his profession he laughed and asked more than stated, "Gambler?"

John Emerson, the strike force attorney, spent an hour taking Jimmy through a sanitized version of his life, including vouchers, showing that the government had spent $61,753.52 on Jimmy and Jean over the past twenty-seven months.

Jimmy identified hotel statements, which corresponded to Local 856 checks, and explained the various trips he and Tham had taken. He explained several wiretapped conversations in which he and Tham discussed expenses paid for by the union. He also identified hotel bills Tham charged to the union for Rizzitello and Marchiondo without explaining to the court who either man was.

Emerson neatly avoided prejudicial questions of Jimmy's connec-

tions to organized crime. A rather bland discourse, it was left to
Tham's lawyer, Richard Rosenfield, to muddy the sterile waters.

Rosenfield dredged up every lurid account of Fratianno's La Cosa
Nostra associations he could find, including the five murders he had
a direct hand in. As he completed his cross-examination, the lawyer
appeared confident that he had discredited Fratianno as a figure of
such low character that the jury would reject his story.

The strategy was a failure of historic proportions.

With the door opened, Emerson came back and finished the job
Rosenfield had begun, establishing a motive for Fratianno's and Tham's
friendship and a lesson in the long-standing association between La
Cosa Nostra and the Teamsters.

It was the first time there had ever been such a public airing of
the relationship of the two organizations—and the first time Jimmy
would publicly explain his role in La Cosa Nostra.

To Jimmy's way of thinking, the Teamsters was a wholly-owned
subsidiary of La Cosa Nostra. After all, he explained, it was La Cosa
Nostra that controlled the selection of the Teamsters leaders.

For as long as Jimmy could remember, the bosses of the Families
would meet to decide who would run the union, passing the word
along to their La Cosa Nostra brethren, who had long ago muscled
their way to the top of union locals. The union local leaders would
then arrive at Teamsters conventions to cast their vote, in a "democratic" election, for whomever the bosses had ordered.

With that as background, Jimmy explained how he had "straightened out" Tham's problems with the International.

The union's leaders were concerned by Jimmy Hoffa's efforts at
a comeback in the early 1970s and were slashing the authority of
officials, like Tham, who were viewed as Hoffa men.

Jimmy had traveled to Cleveland in 1974, arranging, through
Dope DelSanter, for meetings at which he assured Presser, then an
International vice president, that he could control Tham.

He also went to see Chicago crime boss Joey Aiuppa to win his
blessing for Tham's reinstatement and for Jimmy to run the Local
856 benefits program.

After Hoffa's "disappearance" in July 1975, his supporters suffered
Hoffa's legacy: perpetual loss of union prestige. But with Jimmy's
intervention and Presser's blessing, Tham gained a new lease on life.

Tham took the stand to deny the entire story. He said he had
been unaware of Fratianno's mob connections, and that he had only

wined and dined him in hopes of securing a better health benefits package for Local 856.

In an encore appearance, Fratianno described visits to Tham's home, in which the union executive showed Jimmy books that described him as a mob executioner; he told of introducing Tham to Jack Licavoli, Leo Moceri, and DelSanter; and he described a party they attended, along with many of the bosses of New York's Five Families, at the Rainbow Room atop Rockefeller Center.

The jury deliberated for five days, returning guilty verdicts on fifteen of eighteen counts in the indictment, finding he embezzled $2,005.

While he battled the conviction, and the resulting six-month prison term and $50,000 fine, Tham added another title to his list of Teamsters credits, being elected by more than a 2-to-1 margin as president of Teamsters Joint Council 7, representing some 100,000 workers in Northern California.

The election made him the second most powerful Teamsters leader in California, a post he held for two years, until March of 1982, when his appeal attempts were exhausted and he went off to prison.

On April 16, Ahearn chartered a private jet from Oakland to Los Angeles, the start of a ten-week road trip during which Jimmy remained in FBI custody.

The first order of business in Los Angeles was reindicting the Brooklier case. After Pregerson removed himself from the case, the new judge, Terry Hatter, Jr., dismissed the indictment on a technicality, finding that there had not been enough jurors present when they voted the indictment.

But before going into the grand jury again, Henderson had a lot of work to do with Jimmy. The original plan had been for Fox to handle Jimmy's testimony, but that job now fell to Henderson.

Jimmy's stay at the strike force offices also provided Bruce Kelton some time to get acquainted with him. Kelton, a thirty-three-year-old former Manhattan homicide prosecutor who had joined the L.A. strike force team in late 1977, had been thrown into the case to take up Henderson's former role.

At first Kelton didn't like the idea. He felt trying a case with Henderson, the strike force chief, would relegate him to the role of a glorified go-fer. He felt his time would be better spent developing the Brilab case, which he had directed along with Barron. There were already Brilab indictments pending in Los Angeles, New Orleans, and three in Houston, which were demanding his attention.

But as time passed, Kelton came to realize that it was a two-man case. He took the porno-extortion side of the case while Henderson focused on the Bompensiero murder and Jimmy's testimony. It was an even division of labor.

While in Los Angeles, Jimmy met for several days with investigators from the Los Angeles District Attorney's Office who were interested in the murders Jimmy had committed or had knowledge of.

Jimmy didn't have full immunity from prosecution on those murders, although he thought he did. The only limitation, under the terms of his deal with the government, was for "use immunity"— they couldn't use any of his testimony or statements against him as long as he testified truthfully. He could still be prosecuted if he committed perjury, which would nullify his deal, or if authorities developed evidence of crimes entirely independent of his disclosures.

But as a practical matter, no one expected the district attorney would bother indicting Jimmy in any of the cases. They just wanted to close the books on the murders.

Jimmy spent late April and early May in southern Florida. The original purpose of the trip had been to testify at the RICO trial of Gambino Family *capo* Tony "TP" Plate, a ruthless Hallandale, Florida, loan shark, and Anielo "Mr. Neil" DellaCroce, the Gambino underboss in New York. He'd been prepped for the case about a year earlier, when Fred Schwartz, the strike force chief from Miami, had come to see Jimmy in La Tuna.

Fratianno's role was relatively minor. He was to tell the jury how Plate had muscled his way into California in the 1970s, bankrolling Hollywood bookmaker Sparky Monica. In 1975, as the recently appointed acting boss in Los Angeles, Jimmy demanded a sit-down at a New York bistro with Gambino boss Paul Castellano and underboss DellaCroce, at which they agreed Plate was out of bounds. DellaCroce was dispatched to give Plate the word.

The real meat of the case against Plate and DellaCroce was a series of extortions Plate made against hoods and businessmen in Hallandale, and his arranging through DellaCroce for the 1974 murder of a small-time Yonkers, New York, loan shark, Charles "Charles Bear" Calise, who had assisted the FBI in a grand jury probe.

But the prosecution's case began falling apart soon after Plate and DellaCroce were indicted. Plate had not-so-mysteriously disappeared in August 1979 and was presumed dead. He was last seen with Hymie Levine, a gambling figure, driving off to a luncheon appointment. Neither man was ever found.

Without Plate in the case, it was difficult for prosecutors to establish DellaCroce's link to the extortion conspiracy with Plate.

To add to the prosecution's problems, Jimmy's arrival in Miami was delayed by tensions between his FBI escort in Los Angeles and U.S. Marshals in the Miami area, who insisted he not arrive more than a day in advance of testifying.

Unfortunately for Schwartz, his witnesses completed their testimony a day ahead of schedule. When Fratianno, the last scheduled witness, was not present, the trial judge refused to permit any delay and the prosecution was forced to rest its case without Fratianno's testimony.

Jimmy arrived that evening.

The jury came in hung. DellaCroce was never retried.

But Jimmy's trip to Florida wasn't a complete loss. He was called to testify in a sentencing hearing for Marshall Caifano—better known as Johnny Marshall—the mobster who had tried luring Jimmy to Chicago in 1977 for what Jimmy believed would have been his execution. Jimmy was going to enjoy this one.

Caifano already had been convicted in a West Palm Beach federal court on charges of theft and interstate transportation of $4 million in securities, and was facing up to fifteen years. But the prosecutor, Robert K. Lehner, hoped Jimmy's testimony would prove Caifano was an especially dangerous felon, as defined by the Dangerous Special Offenders Act, and get ten more years slapped on the sentence.

Essential to Jimmy's testimony was his ability to identify Caifano as a member of La Cosa Nostra by virtue of their having been introduced to each other as *amico nostra*.

The balance of his testimony focused on Caifano's unique status as one of a very few people still living who had played a part in one of Jimmy's five murders: the 1953 murder of Russian Louie Strauss.

Jack Dragna had ordered Jimmy and Caifano "to do the work" after casino operator Benny Binion offered the L.A. Family a piece of his action as payment for eliminating Strauss. The problem was that Jimmy had to get Strauss out of Las Vegas, where he lived, in order to kill him. Mob etiquette prohibited murders in Vegas at that time.

Jimmy's plan—a rather complex ruse—worked this way: Caifano introduced Jimmy to Strauss in the lobby of the Desert Inn. Jimmy then invited Strauss to join him in a scam. It was well known that Ray Ryan, in Palm Springs, owed Strauss several hundred thousand dollars. Jimmy suggested to Strauss that they travel together to Palm Springs, and Jimmy would go see Ryan alone and strong-arm him for the money he owed Strauss. As it worked out, Strauss added a further dimension to the scam, telling Jimmy he needed to raise some quick cash, about $12,000, to pay off a debt. Jimmy suggested that Caifano, who was standing with them, could arrange to borrow the $12,000 from a friend in California; they would stop on their way to Palm Springs, pick up the cash, and repay it after they had finished with Ryan. So that afternoon, Strauss happily drove with Jimmy to a friend's home in Upland, California, where he was strangled to death.

What Jimmy didn't testify to was that he had created a legend that day. The disappearance of Russian Louie was so clean, and so obviously the work of skilled professionals, that it yielded a new expression in that town of a million markers: "I'll pay up when Russian Louie comes back."

Jimmy completed his testimony with a discourse on how La Cosa Nostra works:

Q. What is the basis of the power of La Cosa Nostra?
A. Silence.

And he told how Caifano had telephoned in the fall of 1977 asking Jimmy to meet with the boss in Chicago and arrange for Caifano's introduction to Benny Binion:

A. He wanted me to ask him for permission to bring Johnny Marshall to Vegas. And I said, "You know Benny Binion better than I do. Why do I have to go back there. I knew the whole play. I'm in this thing thirty-two years, believe me." He must have thought I was an idiot.

Try as they would, the defense did little to rattle Fratianno's story on cross-examination. The primary direction taken by Joseph Varon, Caifano's lawyer, was to show that Fratianno was a paid, "professional witness" providing customized testimony for the government.

Q. Don't you go from state to state, area to area at the behest and at the request of the government to testify against certain people?

A. No, sir.

Any damage that was to be done to his credibility came the next day when Benny Binion appeared at the hearing to deny Fratianno's tale.

Two weeks later the judge handed Caifano a twenty-year prison term.

Jimmy's next stop was in the woods of Connecticut, where he moved in with a bachelor FBI agent, cooking and meeting with Akerman on weekends to prepare for a case against Funzi Tieri. It was the Premier Theatre story all over again, only this time it was all about mob interests vying for control of the place.

This would be the first case of its kind in the U.S. courts.

The way Akerman was structuring the indictment, he would have to prove the existence of La Cosa Nostra, and that Tieri was the boss of a La Cosa Nostra family and the senior member of the Commission that oversaw the nationwide crime syndicate.

In previous indictments, including those in Los Angeles and Cleveland, the crime Family was identified as a hub of criminal activity, but there was only the need to show that crimes were committed around that organization. In the Tieri case, however, the courts were being asked to confirm that La Cosa Nostra existed as a nationwide crime syndicate.

Jimmy made his grand jury appearance on May 16, 1980, hung around the New York City metropolitan area for a few weeks more, and then, in June, went off to Cleveland for his toughest court appearance.

Jimmy returned home in shame.

The courtroom was packed with folks from the old neighborhood. They came to see their fallen angel. These weren't necessarily mob relations packing the pews; these were people who believed in the old ways, the highest commandment being loyalty to one's people.

This was the third time around for some of the Cleveland mobsters. In the first two trials, both state cases, there were four convictions and four acquittals. Those convicted in the murder of Danny

Greene were sent off with life sentences. They were the lowest men in the mob hierarchy, those who worked most closely with Ray Ferritto.

Among those still walking free were Licavoli and Angelo Lonardo, who had replaced the late Dope DelSanter as the mob's underboss.

By the time Jimmy testified, the case was already a shambles.

There were two problems. The first came some months before trial: Ray Ferritto refused to testify.

Like Jimmy, Ferritto had received a maximum five-year sentence, sweetened by vague assurances that he would be out in under two. When the federal court in Cleveland refused to show any leniency, forcing him to do his full term, he refused to cooperate. Ferritto figured Jimmy was getting off easy for nine murders, why shouldn't he get the same leniency for one?

Under the terms of his plea bargain and his agreement with the government they couldn't prosecute him—he'd pled out, been sentenced, and was doing his full five years. And the prosecutors figured that forcing him to testify would guarantee turning the trial into a circus.

After his release from prison late in 1982, Ferritto returned to Erie, Pennsylvania. Years would pass without so much as a threat on his life. Authorities suspected Ferritto had struck a deal with the mob.

The second problem came just a couple of weeks before the trial opened. The U.S. Court of Appeals, Sixth Circuit, ruled an illegal enterpise, such as La Cosa Nostra, could not be the basis for a continuing criminal enterprise charge in a RICO indictment. (The decision would be overturned in 1982 by the U.S. Supreme Court's ruling in another case.) That decision led to dismisal of the RICO count and conspiracy charges against the Cleveland mob, leaving prosecutors with only two counts of bribery—based on monies paid to FBI clerk Geraldine Linhart.

Fratianno's testimony was limited to the FBI leak. He explained how Licavoli had told him about the leak and shown him the Bompensiero informant file in August 1977, during the DelSanter wake. He explained how he began cooperating with Ahearn and had traveled back to Cleveland trying to ferret out more information.

But there was no corroboration for anything Jimmy said. Not even any FBI reports, for Ahearn and Joe Griffin, at that time the acting SAC in Cleveland, had agreed that Jimmy was too good an informant to jeopardize by filing reports at that early stage of his development.

Ahearn took the stand to corroborate what Jimmy had said, but the jurors didn't believe any of it. They felt that information as important as that would have been memorialized somewhere, in some kind of report.

Again, the only people convicted were two of the lesser mob figures who had dealt directly with Linhart's boyfriend, Rabinowitz.

Jimmy's stint under the protective wing of the FBI came to an end that spring when he returned to San Francisco.

"There's no more money" was the reason given by Ahearn; which wasn't entirely untrue. The FBI lacked the resources to care for Jimmy, protect him, escort him around the country, and keep up with his demands, which increased in direct proportion to the government's growing needs for his testimony.

The last ten weeks had demonstrated how effective and valuable Fratianno could be in a broad range of cases; as a character witness against such mobsters as Caifano or as an expert witness in union racketeering cases. There was talk of using Jimmy in two cases in Florida, at least two more in New York, something in Las Vegas, possibly one in Chicago, and another in Kansas City.

With each additional case, Jimmy's demands grew to the point that, by mid-1980, he was asking the government to pay for him to live year-round in the Caribbean, a new wardrobe, new cars for him and Jean, and an unlimited expense account.

Besides Jimmy's expensive demands, Ahearn was sensing that rivalries in Washington were making the FBI's top brass back away from carrying Jimmy any further.

Ahearn had caught wind of WITSEC complaints of the Justice Department that they were being undermined by the FBI. They argued: If the government's most prominent witness didn't avail himself of WITSEC's services, the program could be jeopardized, and with several more trials pending in 1980, the U.S. Marshals would have to handle his protection and transportation on the road. So why not make it a clean transition of custodial authority?

Ahearn didn't need to be hit over the head. He and Henderson guaranteed Jimmy that they would intercede if his safety was ever placed at risk by the marshals. However, they refused to guarantee any of Jimmy's lofty demands for financing.

"Maybe when this is all over," Ahearn told him, "when you're done testifying, I can get you one lump sum informant payment. No promises. But just some incentive to get you through the hard times that you're surely going to face in the next year or so."

What Ahearn didn't tell Jimmy was that he was relieved to have him somewhere far away from San Francisco.

During the Tham trial in April, before Jimmy was shipped off to Los Angeles to begin his long road trip, word was received from a reliable souce that a contract had been placed on Jimmy's life by his old friend Irving "Slick Jack" Shapiro, the erstwhile president of Alfa Chemical and Star Glo. Norman Duncan, Star Glo's chemist, had turned government informant after learning who he was working for. He reported overhearing a conversation about the Fratianno contract. He told the FBI that there was a hired executioner stalking Fratianno in San Francisco.

But even with Ahearn and Henderson urging him to return to WITSEC, Jimmy resisted—he wanted to gain a little leverage.

He told Safir that he wasn't coming back over to the program unless they could put him someplace where he was convinced he'd be safe—some place he chose.

After much argument, Safir and Jimmy reached agreement on a location. On June 24, 1980, Jimmy signed back on with WITSEC, was handed over to Bud McPherson at a secure section of San Francisco airport, and flew off to the Virgin Islands.

11

Vendetta

JIMMY returned from the Virgin Islands just after Labor Day tanned and rested, eager for his final confrontation with the Los Angeles Family. During the three years since he had first spoken with Ahearn he had grown impatient, railing at each trial delay, anxious to know what Henderson had made of his information.

He wasn't alone in his longing.

The media was on the case with the kind of attention usually paid to a superpower summit confrontation. From San Diego, where Frank Bompensiero had reigned and was ultimately gunned down, to Los Angeles, the mob's base of operations, to Jimmy's hometown of San Francisco, every nuance and shifting in pretrial posture brought headlines.

And it wasn't just local news. The networks were primed and the nation's top newsmagazines were close at hand. The wire services began filing daily reports more than a week before trial.

NBC News, "60 Minutes," and "20/20" had lined up posttrial interviews with Fratianno. *Newsweek* edged out *Time* for an exclusive by paying $2,500. News crews from Australia, Canada, and Great Britain were preparing documentaries about La Cosa Nostra and Fratianno.

The Last Mafioso, Jimmy's biography, had been delivered to the publisher at 1,600 typed pages, was trimmed to about 900, and was ready to roll off the presses for release in early 1981.

The Premier Theatre case had been a media event, but this was

245

becoming a media extravaganza of such increasing force that it would carry Jimmy atop a wave of publicity well into the next year.

This trial marked the crest of that wave.

On the surface, public fascination with the case focused on anticipating Jimmy's revelations about La Cosa Nostra's extorting pornographers, the Bompensiero murder, and other conspiracies in Los Angeles, Las Vegas, San Diego, Cleveland, and New York.

Henderson was prepared to deliver on that portion of the case. Using the PORNEX sting operation as a foundation and Jimmy's testimony as a blueprint, Henderson had engineered the substance of the case. Together with Fox, Kelton, Barron, and special agent Melvin Flohr, Henderson had unearthed reams of evidence to bolster Fratianno's tales. They had scoured police and FBI records throughout the United States, seized documents, phone records, or surveillance reports, and applied some persuasion to secure the testimony of those who functioned in the mob's marketplaces.

But that was only the evidence of the case. The underlying drama of *U.S. v. Brooklier, et al.*, of which the media and public were very much aware, was that this, unlike any other case ever tried in the United States, was a real-life La Cosa Nostra vendetta being settled with full public disclosure.

Standing in the dock were the men whom Fratianno saw as defaming his honor, threatening his life, and driving him to abandon *Omertà* and the Family: Dominic Brooklier, mob underboss Sam Sciortino, the *consiglieri* Jack LoCicero, *caporegime* Mike Rizzitello, and former acting boss Louis Dragna. Tommy Ricciardi, the *soldati* whose gun Jimmy said silenced Bompensiero, had died during heart surgery a year earlier.

During sixteen days of pretrial hearings, the defense attempted to defuse the government's case:

They argued that the Family couldn't be defined in legal terms as a continuing criminal enterprise. But the federal courts in California rejected the approach.

They fought, also unsuccessfully, to have recordings of incriminating conversations from the PORNEX sting operation disqualified as evidence.

And they asked to have Fratianno undergo psychological testing, arguing that he had a long history of "pathological lying and recurring examples of antisocial and psychotic conduct." In support of this motion, the defense offered the opinion of Dr. Frederick J. Hacker, a

Viennese-born psychiatrist with a list of credentials long enough to freeze a psychotic in his tracks.

Based upon Fratianno's criminal record and personal history—but without an examination—Dr. Hacker surmised that: "James Fratianno may well be suffering from a mental condition and pathological personality disorder which may affect his willingness or ability to tell the truth, his powers of perception and memory, and his ability to distinguish between reality and fantasy."

The court rejected the argument. It would be left to the jury to decide if Fratianno was truthful.

Jimmy's only comprehensive psychological testing, still intact, was done in prison in 1970. Prison psychologists found he had an average IQ, of 96, and suffered

some degree of impairment in intellectual functioning, particularly in the area of abstract reasoning . . . due primarily to some amount of anxiety.

He is a person who has marked and varying moods, alternating from depression to elation. When elated . . . he is the kind of person who may look for shortcuts. He could, under these circumstances, utilize bad judgment to the point of contravening legal codes.

The defense did win one important round in pretrial. U.S. District Judge Terry Hatter, Jr., permitted them to use portions of the more than one hundred hours of conversations taped by Demaris during his interviews with Fratianno.

Several of those tapes, apparently at odds with what Fratianno had told the FBI, Henderson, or any of the grand juries, could be used at trial to undercut Fratianno's credibility and Henderson's carefully constructed case.

In preparing Jimmy for trial, Henderson discussed those inconsistencies, but did not make too much of an issue of them.

He had decided to avoid the kind of lockstep precision Akerman had sought in the Premier Theatre case. After all, Jimmy had, by this time, proven his ability as a cagey and combative prosecution witness; there was no need to pull any punches in Los Angeles, the door was fully open to just about anything Jimmy wanted to say.

Henderson wanted Jimmy to appear natural and unrehearsed, to come across in his truest form; the Damon Runyon embodiment of the mob.

"You can't do it, Jim," McPherson was saying, shaking his head in disgust. "Too many people figure you're around here now; Washington absolutely refuses to approve it, and besides, Akerman will be here tonight to start preparing you for the Tieri case. It's unsafe and unwise for you to be traveling around California right now."

"Hey Bud, tell Washington they can forget about my testifying in this case or any other case if I can't go up to Sacramento right now. Tell them—"

"Damn it, Jim, this is a total breach of security, it could—"

"You see what I'm doing," Jimmy screamed, as he stomped around the makeshift quarters in the strike force office, tossing his belongings into a red leather overnight bag. "Fuck this program. Fuck this whole deal."

His own words caught him up short. He stopped his frenetic movement, sat on his cot, and looked over at McPherson.

"What am I supposed to do, Bud?"

Jimmy was on the verge of crying—an unlikely condition for the most notorious mob figure in the U.S.

"I have to go up there. My wife is dying, Bud. She's not going to make it for more than a couple of more days. My daughter is hysterical. I haven't seen my grandkids in years. Bud, I really have to go up there."

McPherson sympathized, but he also understood why he had to keep him from leaving. Jimmy was the most carefully insulated witness the government had. And now, on the eve of Jimmy's biggest trial, anyone looking for him would surely be laying in wait outside that hospital in Sacramento in case he showed up. It was a security nightmare.

This was always the most difficult part of McPherson's job: convincing witnesses that they couldn't attend to pressing family matters, such as the illness or death of a loved one.

Yet somewhere in the midst of all this there was a nagging question in McPherson's mind: Why was Jimmy so impassioned over his ex-wife? And wasn't it odd how he always referred to Jewel as his wife?

Since that spring, when Jewel collapsed while visiting Jimmy's sister in Cleveland, three specialists, in both Los Angeles and Las Vegas, where she lived, had diagnosed her cancer and predicted it was unlikely she would live out the year. In August, she had moved to Sacramento where Jimmy and Jewel's daughter, Joan, lived with her children and grandchildren.

On September 9, Jewel was hospitalized and now, four days later, as Jimmy and Henderson made final preparations for the Brooklier case, Jimmy got a call from Joan saying Jewel was on the verge of death.

"I'll tell you what I can do, Jimmy," McPherson said, offering a compromise. "Give me one more day to try selling this to Washington—"

"Oh, Bud, they'll never go for it. Never."

"Hear me out, Jim. Give me another day. At least enough to make some security arrangements, and if Washington doesn't go along, well, maybe we'll take it on our own authority."

Jimmy agreed. McPherson felt it was essential for Jimmy to arrive in court with the weight of Jewel's death on his mind.

The next morning, a Saturday, well before dawn, an armored car pulled into the garage across the street from the strike force offices. Jimmy was secreted through a labyrinth of underground passages by marshals toting shotguns and Uzis. He was taken to the Van Nuys Airport and flown in a private plane to Sacramento. No fewer than a dozen marshals guarded him at the hospital, where he was met by his daughter, and then was permitted an hour with Jewel.

She was at that point of terminal cancer treatment where it was impossible to tell whether the pain or the morphine was having a greater effect.

They didn't speak. He just stood there holding her hand. He said a few things, but she didn't reply.

The only thing Jimmy would remember from the visit was that her hair was still as beautiful as ever, naturally platinum—he had feared chemotherapy would have denied her that.

He was back in Los Angeles for lunch.

Jewel died the following Friday.

A cautious, closed-door jury selection process began on the last day of September 1980. Among the questions asked of jurors was whether they believed La Cosa Nostra existed—an affirmative answer automatically disqualified them—and what impact, if any, the book and movie *The Godfather* had had on their views about crime.

On October 14, seven women and five men, seated as jurors, heard opening arguments from the prosecution and six defense lawyers, which were dominated by the usual collection of attacks on Fratianno.

Sciortino's lawyer, Donald Marks, was the most concise. Pacing, imploring, and shouting, Marks told the jurors:

"He's lied all his life. He'd lie to stay out of jail. He'd lie to stay out of the electric chair. Without Mr. Fratianno, my client as well as the others would not be here today. Mr. Fratianno makes the case for the government. They ride or fall with Mr. Fratianno."

After all of the care in jury selection, and attacks on the government's case, Henderson quickly grabbed the momentum, asserting control over the courtroom. He couldn't have invented a more compelling lead-off witness to rivet the jury's attention and spark its imagination than Harry "The Greek" Coloduros.

At nearly 300 solid pounds and just shy of 5 feet 11 inches, Coloduros's physical stature was imposing. He filled the witness box. His coarse voice and slow speech held every ear in the somber, windowless, wood-paneled courtroom. A shock of thick white hair made him a beacon for the one hundred plus spectators—lawyers, media, agents, and general public—to focus on.

He was perfectly fit for the role he had come to play—that of mob strongman, enforcer of debts, and demander of tribute. He began by unloading his excess baggage: He had been convicted in the 1960s of extortion; in 1962 of forgery; and in 1975, a year after he'd gone into witness protection, for possessing stolen firearms.

He had been an FBI informant for many years before being indicted in a 1974 RICO case, which provided the impetus for him to cooperate, offering testimony against Sciortino and Brooklier. That was the same case Brooklier and Sciortino had pleaded guilty to, going off to prison in 1975, leaving Fratianno and Dragna in command.

Coloduros explained that in 1978, Henderson, Fox, and Flohr had come to Texas to see him, and while he was no longer under any obligation to testify for the government, he had agreed to appear in this case.

The defendants' eyes remained glued, their faces scowling, as he testified nervously, shifting and fidgeting, trying to settle his girth in place.

Coloduros testified that he went to Brooklier and Sciortino in the spring of 1973 to make a proposition. He wanted the blessing of Brooklier, whom he understood to be the underboss to boss Nick Licata at the time.

They met at the Bell Bail Bonds in Van Nuys, which was operated by mob figure Peter Milano.

"I told them I'd like to start shaking down the porno boys and bookmakers. I told them I wanted to grab a guy named Sam Farkas, who was one of the biggest bookmakers in Beverly Hills, for $10,000 cash up front and $500 a week. They talked about how $5,000 up front and $300 a week would be better, and I would get fifty percent and they would get fifty percent.

"I was told not to make any waves. Mr. Sciortino was emphatic that anybody we grabbed, we should say we represented the people—the *right people*."

Coloduros followed Sciortino's advice. He and Gino Massaro, his partner, told Farkas that they represented *the right people*. They warned Farkas that if he didn't pay up he would probably be abducted some evening, have his eyes and tongue ripped out, and then, maybe, killed.

During a series of meetings with Sciortino and Brooklier, Coloduros said they divvied up some $25,000 or $35,000, "paid in strokes" by Farkas.

At one of those meetings he told Brooklier and Sciortino that he had heard there was a $25,000 contract on Bompensiero, and that he was interested in pursuing it. They told him they'd think about it.

At another meeting, Coloduros said, Peter "Milano said if anything was to happen to Mr. Nick [Licata], either Dominic [Brooklier] or Mr. Sciortino would be the head of the Family."

When it became the defense's turn, they ripped at his credibility, using FBI reports from 1973 and 1974 in which he had reported meetings at Milano's office but said nothing about Sciortino, Brooklier, or Farkas.

He readily admitted that he had lied to the FBI then, but insisted, "I've been truthful since 1974."

By the third day of trial, when Jimmy was scheduled to testify, the media, several dozen strong, were whipped into a near frenzy. Film crews had been camped out overnight to get some footage of him being snuck into the downtown federal courthouse. One crew had accosted a pair of janitors wheeling a garbage dumpster into the building, only to find it empty.

The truth was, Jimmy had been snuck into the courthouse days earlier, during the weekend, before opening statements, and was living in makeshift quarters in a judge's chambers.

Bud McPherson and two marshals escorted Jimmy through a rear corridor, toward a secured entrance to the courtroom. Henderson walked at his side, leaning toward him and speaking softly.

"Look, Jim. I think we're in great shape. I want you to remember, keep this in mind: No matter how bad you think it's going to look, no matter what the defense lawyers pull, just tell the truth."

Jimmy paused, bringing his armed escort to a halt, and stared at Henderson. He brushed some lint off his gray silk suit and straightened his wide blue necktie.

"How do I look, Jim?" he asked, seriously concerned about his appearance.

"Great," Henderson shot back. "But did you hear what I just said?"

"Hey man, my eyes may be fucked up with this cataract thing, but my hearing is twenty/twenty. Lookit, don't worry about nothin', buddy. I'm just gonna tell them the truth, the whole truth, and nothin' but the truth. Okay?"

Henderson nodded in relief.

"And they are fucked," Jimmy added, laughing, as Henderson walked through the door into the courtroom.

But his easy manner disguised his feelings.

Jimmy had spent a lifetime learning the subject at hand and had invested the last three years preparing for its delivery. He had had warm-up sessions in New York, Florida, and San Francisco to master technique. Now, standing in a court anteroom, his stomach was knotted, his throat dry, and his heart pounding so hard he could feel the blood pulsing in his hands.

A powerful hatred was churning through his body; a burning excitement had overtaken his mind.

Never before had a witness been any more prepared, better trained, or more anxious to take the witness stand.

Q. How old are you today, Mr. Fratianno?
A. Sixty-seven.
Q. And where were you born?
A. Italy . . . near Naples, Province Combasso.
Q. When did you come to the United States, Mr. Fratianno?
A. I was five months old, 1914.
Q. Are you a United States citizen, sir?
A. Yes, sir.
Q. Are you married?
A. Yes, sir.

Q. Do you have children?
A. Yes, sir.

That's as far as the defense would let Henderson go.

Anything more about Jimmy's personal life drew a chorus of objections. They weren't going to let Jimmy Fratianno "the person" live in the eyes of the jury, only Fratianno "the killer."

But that wasn't going to disturb Jimmy's delivery. He may have been raging with hatred, but his demeanor was the very essence of calm.

There was magic in the air. The spectators and jurors, almost involuntarily, were drawn in closer, leaning to the edge of their seats as Jimmy spun his tales of induction into La Cosa Nostra; the need for Italian lineage and "to do something significant for the Family" to gain membership; the rules of respect and devotion; the hierarchy of boss, underboss, *consigliere, caporegime,* and *soldati;* the names of cities with Families; and the means by which they enforce their will or have the Commission settle turf disputes.

Q. Once an individual joins La Cosa Nostra, how can he get out?
A. There is no way out, sir. They tell you when you join, you come in alive and go out dead.

Henderson shuffled through some notes at the podium, allowing the chill that line had sparked to linger for an extra moment.

He continued: *Omertà* was the rule of order, and death the penalty for violating it or in some other way failing the Family.

There was more happening here than just dramatic news copy. Henderson was laying a foundation, preparing to demonstrate that it was the rules of La Cosa Nostra that had motivated the crimes committed by Jimmy and the Los Angeles Family; that the boss and underboss, Brooklier and Sciortino, ultimately had control of all the Family's undertakings; and that certain death was the force by which members stayed motivated and loyal.

Jimmy rolled through the rest of his introduction in rapid-fire order, putting names and faces to the organizational skeleton he had described.

He identified each of the defendants as members of the Los Angeles Family, explaining how he, Brooklier, and Dragna were inducted on the same day in the late 1940s.

After Nick Licata died, he said, Brooklier became the boss and Sciortino was appointed underboss.

Frank Bompensiero, Dragna, and he had taken Rizzitello to Murietta Hot Springs in June of 1976 and performed his initiation in the backseat of a car.

He said that Bompensiero—who had earned several nicknames, including "Cigars," because of his perennial stogie—was the Family *consigliere*. Following Bomp's death, LoCicero was named *consigliere*, Rizzitello became a *capo*, and Ricciardi was initiated. He also identified photos of Bomp, Peter Milano, and Sal Pinelli, describing each as a made guy.

Jimmy spent the final hour of his introductory remarks on personal history: twenty years in prison; the crimes he had never been convicted of, including the murders; his plea bargains in the Greene and Bompensiero murder cases; his agreement with the government to testify truthfully; and a minute breakdown of the $70,000 he and Jean had received from WITSEC since 1978.

And then, after three years of rehearsals, Jimmy told of the decline of the Los Angeles Cosa Nostra.

It was the summer of 1973 when he rekindled an old friendship with Brooklier, seeing him for the first time in twenty years, at Frank's Restaurant on Sunset Boulevard.

Brooklier, then the underboss, was dining with Peter Milano, a *capo*. They were both concerned by a grand jury investigation of their shakedowns of bookmaker Sam Farkas.

FRATIANNO: I says, "Well, how did they call you to the grand jury?" He says, "I think somebody dropped a dime on us." I says, "Well, are you doing the work yourself?" He says, "No." He says, "We've got a crew." And he mentioned Harry the Greek, and a guy named Gino Massaro.

He skipped eighteen months, to early 1975, the next time he broke bread with the Los Angeles Family, at a restaurant in the Silverlake section of the city, where he learned Brooklier had become the boss and Sciortino was his underboss.

They were still troubled by the same grand jury. Vic Werber, a victim of Brooklier's shakedown operations and a friend of Fratianno's, was a potential witness for the prosecution. They asked Fratianno to visit Werber and tell him "to put all the blame on Harry the Greek."

In April 1975, unable to evade the grand jury's charges of extortion, Brooklier and Sciortino pleaded guilty. Days later, Dragna called Fratianno and asked him to come to Los Angeles for an important meeting.

FRATIANNO: He told me that he'd met with Dominic Brooklier and Sam Sciortino and they wanted Dragna to run the Family while they were in jail. And he [Dragna] told them that "the only way I would run it is if Jimmy Fratianno was with me." And they agreed to it.

So did Jimmy. Weeks later he joined Brooklier, Sciortino, and Milano at Vic Werber's office.

FRATIANNO: The first thing he [Brooklier] said was that Louie [Dragna] couldn't make the meeting.

We shook hands, and he says, "I'm glad you're back. We should have done this a long time ago."

I told him, I says, "Well," I says, "You know I'll do everything I can to make some money for the Family while you're gone."

Then I asked him, I says, "How come you let all this pornography get away from you?"

And he told me that Nick Licata thought it was *por carilla*—that's Italian meaning dirt. He didn't want to fool with it. And he says, "From now on we're going to fool with it."

The first thing he told me, he said, "I want you to go to Cleveland. I want you to talk to Leo Moceri and Tony DelSanter and tell them to grab Reuben Sturman."

He says, "Tell them that he can't operate in California unless we have a piece of it."

He says, "Also, I want you to grab a guy by the name of Teddy Gaswirth." Then he mentioned something about Bompensiero.

Q. What did he mention about Bompensiero?

A. He said, "Jimmy, I want you to take care of this guy. He's going around shooting his mouth off. Try to straighten him out while we're away in prison."

Q. Was there any conversation between you and Mr. Brooklier as to how the Sturman shakedown was to work?

A. Yes, sir.

Q. What was said and by whom?

A. Dominic told me that Sturman [would] run to [the] New York [Family] and New York would contact Los Angeles and we would split it three ways. He said, Cleveland a third, New York a third, and Los Angeles a third.

Q. Now, Mr. Fratianno, were you aware at that time who Reuben Sturman was?

A. I had heard of Reuben Sturman. I had heard he was the biggest pornographer in the United States.

Q. Where did he live?

A. Cleveland, Ohio.

Q. Who was running the Family after this?

Q. Louis Dragna and myself.

That single conversation defined a criminal conspiracy that would take two years to unfold: the "grabbing" or extortions of pornographers

Gaswirth and Sturman, and "taking care of" the Bompensiero murder.
The bulk of Fratianno's testimony would be a recitation of more than
a dozen meetings, most with Dragna, at which the conspiracy was
planned or executed.

Jimmy said he met with Dragna days later and they agreed to
place LoCicero in charge of the Gaswirth shakedown.

In May 1975, Jimmy went to Warren, Ohio, where he visited his
Cleveland Family friends, enlisting their aid to shake down Sturman.

Upon his return to California he went to see Brooklier at the
federal prison induction center at Terminal Island, in Los Angeles,
to report his progress and to reassure his old friend that a share of
anything the Family made would be given to his wife.

Later, he said, he reported only to Dragna: "He was the boss."

In Jimmy Fratianno's La Cosa Nostra, making money is the primary
purpose. If that is so, maintaining order and security hold a very close
second.

Bompensiero's lack of respect had made him a threat to that order
and a liability that had to be eliminated. The two newly anointed mob
leaders made Bomp's murder a top priority—plotting during im-
promptu street meetings, or in more formal sit-downs at offices, restaurants, or at home over coffee.

Their plans took shape over a period of weeks. First, Dragna made
Bomp the Family *consigliere*. "He told me . . . that way it will relax
Frank and it will give us a good chance to kill him."

They devised three scenarios: In Fratianno's, they would blow up
his car; Dragna's suggestion was to send Bomp with Sal Pinelli to the
Valley, "and maybe Sal would get a chance to kill him."

Each of the first two got a halfhearted try and failed.

Then there was the phone booth option: luring Bomp to a phone
booth in the dark of night to execute him:

Q. And whose idea was this?
A. Louie Dragna's, sir.
Q. Now, will you tell us what you did?
A. Well, I called Frank, and we would discuss a lot of things on his phone
   at home. I told him, I says, "Frank, this is no good, you know, me talking
   to you on the phone at home."
      I says, "Why don't you get the number of a pay phone where I could
   call you, and that way if I want to talk to you on something important,
   you go to the pay phone."

And, he says, "Well, I'll get you the number tomorrow."

Q. Did you ever give the number to anyone else?

A. I gave it to Louie Dragna and Mike Rizzitello.

Q. Did you take other steps toward the killing?

A. Just lure him. Not that I can think of, sir.

Months passed. Despite Fratianno's efforts none of his plans were coming together. LoCicero had approached Gaswirth, but got no money. A Cleveland mob figure, Glenn Pauley, had rattled Sturman's cage without results. And Bompensiero was still on his feet.

After a trip to Cleveland in July 1976, Fratianno said he reported to Dragna at Murietta Hot Springs. It seemed that Cleveland was so distracted with their gang war problems that the Sturman affair had been placed on a back burner, but they promised to get to it in a few months.

FRATIANNO: At one part of the conversation I asked Louie, I says, "Lookit," I says, "I've got to have some money. You know. I need some money. I got to get an in to something."

He says, "Well, what do you want?" I says, "Well, I want a piece of the porno." He says, "Don't worry about it. You'll get it."

The final element of Jimmy's testimony that day dealt with Bomp's call in late summer to get Fratianno and Dragna interested in shaking down Forex, the FBI's PORNEX front company.

Jimmy said he and Dragna chose not to go after it, but Rizzi, Ricciardi, and LoCicero couldn't resist it. That fall, after they were all served with grand jury subpoenas, Bomp's role as an FBI informant became suspect. Seated at the bar at Marson's house, Fratianno said he shared his suspicions with Brooklier and Sciortino, who had been recently released from prison.

FRATIANNO: So Sciortino spoke up and says, "The guy is a lying son-of-a-bitch. We ought to kill him." And Brooklier agreed with him, and he said, "Yes, we got to do something about him. He's an informant."

The next thing he knew of Bomp's execution, he said, was in February 1977 when Ricciardi called him to make the dry run. A week later, while eating dinner at Montefusco's, a San Francisco restaurant, he said he heard that Bompensiero had been killed.

Soon afterward, control of the Family was returned to Brooklier and Sciortino.

Brooklier set to work trying to raise money—calling Fratianno, ordering him to shake down Benny Binion, and dispatching Rizzi to

Las Vegas to strong-arm former Cleveland racketeer Moe Dalitz, founder of the Desert Inn and Stardust, for $1 million.

In May, Fratianno was called to a meeting with Brooklier and Sciortino in Palm Springs.

As they drove to meet Brooklier, Sciortino told Fratianno, "Well, you know we clipped Bomp and there's more to come."

At the meeting, Brooklier put Fratianno on notice:

FRATIANNO: He says, "Well, Jimmy," he says. "There ain't going to be no more bullshit going on in this Family." He says, "You know, when Bomp got clipped," he says, "I'm the guy that made the phone call." . . . and he put his thumbs down.

On that line, Judge Hatter recessed for the day, instructing the jury to avoid news reports of the trial.

Jimmy smiled to the jurors as they filed out of the courtroom. Several smiled back.

The next morning brought banner headlines. The *Los Angeles Times* played it as the day's top story on page one:

HIT MAN BARES MAFIA SECRETS
"YOU COME IN ALIVE AND YOU
GO OUT DEAD," COURT TOLD

The media found his revelations about La Cosa Nostra "chilling" and the testimony of murder "dramatic," sharply contrasting his "nonchalant" manner on the stand. The reports went on at length about Bompensiero's murder—some failing entirely to mention the extortions, which were the foundation of the case.

As the trial prepared to resume, the number of curious spectators outside the courtroom doubled. Most had to be turned away for lack of seating.

Jimmy arrived on the witness stand with fire in his gut.

From his perspective, the first day's testimony had covered only the preliminaries. The second day would be his chance to explain why he had abandoned the Family and *Omertà*—and complete his vendetta.

Eager to tell his story of betrayal, Jimmy charged through Henderson's remaining questions about the murder: the confession Ricciardi had made to him at Bobby's Restaurant in New York.

FRATIANNO: I brought Tommy on the side and I asked him, I said, "Tommy, why did you call me in San Francisco that day?"

He says, "Well, we was going to clip Bomp, but instead we made it a dry run." So he says, "You know, when I clipped Bomp he gave me a little struggle." He says, "But it was beautiful." He says, "There was no noise. It went along beautiful."

So I says, "Well, who was with you?"

And he told me who was with him.

The jury was left to wonder who assisted in the murder. Jimmy was prohibited from naming LoCicero as the second man, the wheel man, in the killing. It was only through Ricciardi that he knew of LoCicero's role, and since Ricciardi's death, any statements he had made to Fratianno incriminating others were prohibited.

Throughout his testimony, Jimmy had broken early from the starting gate, pressing ahead with his story against a chorus of defense objections. Judge Hatter was struggling to maintain control of his courtroom. As the topic came around to Jimmy's reasons for becoming a witness, it only got worse.

Q. All right. Now, Mr. Fratianno, when did you reach your decision to begin cooperating with the Justice Department and the FBI?

A. It came in December of 1977.

Q. All right. Will you tell us what factors there were in the decision, sir?

A. Well, my main factor, sir, was the contract that the Los Angeles Family had on my life.

The defense lawyers were on their feet. Henderson tried the question several ways, and each time was driven back. The defense argued that attempts on Fratianno's life could have been orchestrated by his colleagues in Chicago, Las Vegas, or Cleveland. Finally, it was agreed that he must first establish the events, and then could offer his belief.

Henderson tried again. But Jimmy was still breaking away, uncontrolled, on a long tale of mob intrigue, seemingly far from the issues at trial.

THE COURT: Just a minute—

THE WITNESS: This was sometime in March.

THE COURT: Just a minute, Mr. Fratianno. When I say "Just a minute" would you please stop.

THE WITNESS: I didn't hear you, sir. I'm sorry.

THE COURT: All right. I will try to speak a little louder; you try to listen a little bit louder.

THE WITNESS: Yes, sir.

THE COURT: All right. See if you can zero in on the date.

THE WITNESS: This took place after they took back the Family. I would say it was a few months after the death of Frank Bompensiero. Sam Sciortino and Dominick Longo went to see the Detroit Family. They saw two fellows there by the name of—

THE COURT: Just a minute. How do you have knowledge of this?

THE WITNESS: Well, I'll come to that. The Cleveland Family—

THE COURT: Mr. Fratianno, you are going to come to it right now, or otherwise we aren't going to have it at all. Tell us now.

Jimmy's intensity abated with the increasing volume of Hatter's voice. He had never been treated this way by a judge. He paused for a moment, staring at the judge like a child reprimanded for an unknown indiscretion. He calmed and proceeded through his tale in a systematic manner, his hands folded in his lap.

FRATIANNO: Tony DelSanter called me, and he says, "Jimmy, get back to Cleveland right away." Something important had come up.

I go back to Cleveland. He told me, he says, "What's going on?" I says, "I don't know." He said, "Sam Sciortino and Dominick Longo went to Detroit and talked to Jackie Tocco and Carlo Licata [of the Detroit Family]."

They got instructed from Sam Sciortino to come to Cleveland and tell him [DelSanter] that I'm going around the country misrepresenting myself.

I says, "Let me go back and I'll straighten it out."

Jimmy said he spoke with Brooklier days later, and Brooklier claimed that it was a misunderstanding.

FRATIANNO: So he told me, he says, "Well, we'll straighten it out."

I says, "Lookit, I'm going to Cleveland this Sunday." I says, "You give me a number where I can call you and I will have the boss of the Cleveland Family and Tony DelSanter there, and you tell them on the phone that everything is a misunderstanding."

So Dominic Brooklier gave me a private number. He says, "Call there at six o'clock our time," which would be three o'clock Ohio time.

I went back there on a Sunday. We called at three o'clock. No answer. I had the boss and the *consigliere* there. So Tony DelSanter told me, he says, "Jimmy, you got a problem. They're trying to do something to you because they're avoiding everybody."

Jimmy was pressed forward in his seat, his hands white-knuckled from clenching the armrests, as he described his return to Los Angeles and his repeated, failed attempts to contact Brooklier: Mike Rizzi's trip to Russell Bufalino in September and Bufalino's suggestion for him to have Chicago intercede on his behalf; the call from Johnny

Marshall "to lure" him to Chicago; chasing off Joey Hanson's T-Bird; and finally, the call from Mike Rizzi, trying to get him to a pay phone late one night.

Q. Mr. Fratianno, based on these events, did you form a belief concerning your life at that time?
A. Sir, I didn't form a belief. I knew, sir.
Q. And did you inform anyone with the government there was a contract out on your life?
A. Yes, I did. Mr. Ahearn, sir.
Q. Mr. Fratianno, will you tell us what additional factors caused you to make your decision to cooperate?
A. Well, after I got indicted in seventy-seven, in December, I thought all of these things. I know that if I fight these cases and I beat them, I am going to get killed. So, I figured, when I got indicted I figured, well, I might as well be a government witness.

Sciortino's lawyer, Donald Marks, and Tony Brooklier, Dominic's son, double-teamed the leading assault on Fratianno. Marks did the questioning. The younger Brooklier had some problems—perhaps both ethical and personal—confronting Jimmy; he had known Jimmy all his life, his younger brother was Jimmy's godson.

The two lawyers made a brash, loud, and combative pairing, lacking any sense of subtlety. They began by picking at nits, attempting to show that Fratianno's testimony about the Sturman and Gaswirth shakedowns were a jumble of lies. It was an exercise in confusion:

At which of their meetings—at the Silverlake restaurant or Vic Werber's office—had Brooklier and Sciortino first discussed the Sturman extortion with Fratianno?

Which of those meetings came first?

Were both Brooklier and Sciortino present at both meetings?

Were both shakedowns discussed at both meetings?

And if only one was discussed, which was discussed first, at which meeting, with who present?

Marks's frenetic verbal gymnastics had just about peaked when Jimmy negated the entire line of questioning, conceding: "I was always confused if Reuben Sturman came up at the first or second meeting."

Marks's script didn't permit for such a righteous admission. So he continued the questioning, inadvertently offering Jimmy more credibility by playing a Demaris interview tape in which Jimmy conceded he was "a little confused" about when the Sturman shakedown was first discussed.

Q. And that is the story with regard to the two meetings that you were confused about; is that correct?

A. I would like to explain that, sir.

THE COURT.   Go ahead.

A. When I was giving [Demaris] this story, whatever came into my head I would tell him, sir.

I didn't really get into this case, sir, till I met with Mr. Henderson and Mr. Fox.

When I discussed it more and more I remembered more and more. When I was telling Mr. Demaris all these things, [they] were true, but I might have been confused on the dates, sir.

Jimmy had learned from previous trials that judges rarely objected to his offering an explanation. And the defense, not wanting the jury to think they were hiding anything, would raise no opposition. The long-term effect was that Jimmy had the opportunity to repair the damage inflicted by nearly every defense question.

The balance of the day was spent reviewing Jimmy's prior inconsistent statements: the many aliases he had used; lies he told in depositions years earlier, before becoming a government witness; his failure, as an FBI informant in the early 1970s, to report tales he was now telling; and then the murders.

Jimmy had a plausible excuse for each, including the murders: "Sir, I was ordered to commit whatever murders that I committed."

It was a calculated effort, working up to the question of whether Jimmy was capable of telling the truth in this case.

They sparred for a while about the Cleveland case. Marks emphasized that Jimmy had pled guilty and was still awaiting sentencing; he argued that it was fear of the death penalty that had made him turn, and that he now had to produce some significant testimony for the government to secure his deal.

A. I was aware of that penalty, but I wasn't concerned about it myself, sir, because my part of it was very, very little.

Q. Well, you weren't concerned because your deal was if you cooperated to the satisfaction of the government that your aggravated murder charge would be reduced. Is that correct?

A. The best of my recollection, sir, I had to testify truthfully, completely, and to the best of my knowledge in any case that I knew anything of, sir.

Q. Now you have also testified in New York, sir, with regard to your deal with the government that the first time you don't *cooperate* the whole thing is out the window; isn't that correct?

A. The first time I don't *tell the truth* the deal is off. That's correct.

Marks produced a transcript of the Premier Theatre case, and read from a portion in which Jimmy agreed, when Norman Ostrow asked: "The first time you don't cooperate, your entire deal would be out the window?"

Marks was playing with words, hoping the jury would accept the view that Fratianno saw cooperation, not truth, as his primary objective.

The third day of Jimmy's testimony opened with Marks and Jimmy exchanging pleasantries.

Marks's demeanor was far different than the day before. He was, in those first few moments, after the jury had been seated and Jimmy entered the witness box, calm and seemingly deferential.

Jimmy was proud of his earlier performance and was initially lulled into the belief that Marks had run out of ammunition.

Marks began slowly, questioning Fratianno's version of the Sturman shakedown, recalling testimony about Glenn Pauley, the Cleveland operative who Fratianno said had approached Sturman.

"Now that's a lie, is it not? Mr. Moceri and Mr. DelSanter never told you that it was Glenn Pauley who approached Mr. Sturman, isn't that correct?" he asked calmly, in the wake of Fratianno's angry denials and requests to offer an explanation.

Fratianno would get his chance to explain, but first the jury would hear another Demaris tape and get transcripts of the conversation to assist their listening:

DEMARIS: What kind of shakedown did he get?

FRATIANNO: The guys in Cleveland did, I don't know who did it. In fact, the FBI asked me about it. I don't know who they sent. You know, I never asked. If they did tell me, I wouldn't tell them anyhow.

Fratianno immediately protested. "I think this part of the transcript—'I wouldn't *tell* them anyhow'—is incorrect. I don't think I said that. I think you better play, uh, no, no. I says, 'I wouldn't *know* them anyhow.' 'If they did tell me, I wouldn't *know* them anyhow.'"

Jimmy was just getting in deeper.

Hatter instructed the jury that the transcript was just an aid; it was up to them to determine what the tape actually said.

The tape was played for a second time. Fratianno was right, the sound was slightly garbled. But it still sounded very much like: "I wouldn't *tell* them anyhow."

Then there was Jimmy's explanation: "The deal I made in Cleveland was that I would not have to testify in Cleveland, and when I was talking to Mr. Demaris I didn't want anything in the book in regards to anybody living in Cleveland because my family is there. I was worried about my family. And that's the reason I never mentioned any names. I never mentioned Licavoli too much, anything significant. I never mentioned, due to the fact that my family lives in Cleveland. I'm from Cleveland."

Marks, now with growing intensity, asked, "Then you lied to Mr. Demaris when you told him, 'I don't know who did it'?"

Fratianno conceded he had lied.

"And you lied to Mr. Demaris when you told him, 'In fact, the FBI asked me about it. I don't know who they sent'?"

He again responded: "Yes, sir."

With further questioning, Fratianno conceded he had never mentioned Glenn Pauley to the FBI or to the three grand juries; only in his La Tuna meetings with Fox and Henderson had he mentioned Pauley.

And then, almost as an aside, Marks asked, "By the way, Mr. Fratianno, you testified for prosecutors in Cleveland, where you say your family lives, in the case of James Licavoli, whom you say you were protecting?"

Fratianno gave an affirmative answer, but protested, "This was a different thing altogether."

Marks had hit a raw nerve—Jimmy's friends in Cleveland—and used it to better advantage than anyone had before, forcing him to admit that he had lied to his biographer and, perhaps, admitted his willingness to lie to the FBI despite his pact to tell the truth.

Nothing else anyone could do would go any further toward demonstrating Jimmy's ability to twist the truth. However, while Marks may have engineered a large reservoir of doubt in the jurors' minds, there was still nothing to refute the substance of his testimony about the Los Angeles mob.

As the end of his questioning drew near, Marks's mood grew more aggressive. He addressed the Bompensiero murder, taking Fratianno through his recollections of the last time he had seen his old friend. It was the day before Bompensiero was killed. They met at the San Francisco Hilton. Bompensiero was accompanied by Chris Petti, Abe Chapman, and Jimmy Styles. Jimmy knew Styles as a worker for deposed mob boss Joe Bonanno.

Jimmy said he didn't recall what he and Bompensiero had discussed that evening.

Q. You can't remember the conversation that took place in your meeting with Jimmy Styles, Mr. Bonanno's man, and Frank Bompensiero that one day before your good friend, Mr. Bompensiero, was killed?

A. That's correct, sir.

Q. Now you do remember when Mr. Bompensiero was killed, do you not?

A. Yes, sir.

Q. Do you remember where you were when you heard the news?

A. Yes, sir. At Montefusco's Restaurant in San Francisco.

Q. Do you remember what you were eating?

A. Yes, sir, cioppino.

Q. But you don't remember the conversation one day before, the last time you saw Mr. Bompensiero?

A. I would like to explain that, sir.

Q. Is that true?

A. That is correct, sir.

THE COURT: All right. You may explain it.

THE WITNESS: The reason I know it was cioppino, because that's all we used to eat at Montefusco's. That's what we used to go there for. That's why I know it was cioppino.

Marks was fuming. He asked for a side bar at Hatter's bench.

He had carefully designed this line of questioning. He wanted the jury to believe Fratianno was hiding something about his last meeting with Bompensiero, but Fratianno's explanation had destroyed the illusion Marks had so carefully created.

At the side bar, Marks could barely contain himself to speak in the customary terms of respect afforded the judge. He demanded a mistrial, charging that his client "has been denied the effective cross-examination he's entitled to."

He continued: "I realize that the court has a responsibility, independent of the attorneys, to bring out the facts. But, your Honor, when you allow Mr. Fratianno to explain virtually everything that I have asked him you have emasculated my cross-examination." He said the judge was violating the rules of the "game."

"And when I say 'game' I don't mean it that way. I mean these are deadly serious proceedings."

By the time Marks completed his monologue, Hatter appeared to be the one fuming. He didn't like the suggestion that this was all a game in which each side took turns twisting reality to create an illusion, rather than eliciting facts from a witness. He bristled at Marks's instructing him on how to conduct a trial. He denied the motion for mistrial.

Marks returned to his cross-examination pumped with venom.

Q. Sir, you really hate Mr. Sciortino, don't you?

A. Well, I have no love for him. He tried to kill me.

Q. Sir, you set up the murder of Mr. Bompensiero, did you not?

A. I got him to go to the phone, sir, if that's what you mean—

Q. Sir—

A. . . . by setting him up. I started it, sir.

Q. Sir, you set up the murder of Mr. Bompensiero, did you not?

A. I set him up going to the telephone, sir. So if you call that setting it up, yes, sir, I got him to go to the telephone first.

Q. Sir, you told Mr. Demaris that you set it up, did you not?

A. I set him up going to the phone. That's correct.

THE COURT: Will you please answer the question, Mr. Fratianno?

THE WITNESS: Well, sir, it's a broad question.

THE COURT: No, it's a very simple question. Did you tell Mr. Demaris that you set it up?

THE WITNESS: That I originally set it up. That's correct.

Q. In fact, sir, when you were arrested on December 5, 1977, the FBI found in your car a little twenty-two automatic, did they not?

A. That's not true, sir. It's a twenty-five, sir. It's a twenty-five automatic.

Q. You know the weapon that was used to kill Mr. Bompensiero, do you not?

A. Just what I was told.

Q. You were told a twenty-two, weren't you.

A. A twenty-two. It wasn't an automatic.

Q. And you committed, you committed the murder of Mr. Bompensiero, didn't you?

A. Are you . . . are you kidding?

THE COURT: Would you answer the question.

THE WITNESS: That is a lie, sir.

Q. Mr. Joseph Bonanno, Sr., is a friend of yours, is he not?

A. I don't even know him, sir; never met him in my life.

Q. And you know his sons, do you not?

A. No, I don't, sir.

Q. Joe Bonanno, Sr.?

A. No, sir.

Q. Joe Bonanno, Jr.?

A. No, sir.

Q. Bill Bonanno?

A. No, sir.

Q. You told Mr. Demaris that when you went back to New York—and this is before the killing of Mr. Bompensiero—that Funzi Tieri told you that he had heard that you were going to Tucson to see Mr. Bonanno?

A. That's correct. That's what he told me that he had heard.

Q. You were angry at Mr. Bompensiero because [he] was telling people that you were seeing Mr. Bonanno; isn't that correct?

A. Well, I wouldn't say that I was happy. But I wasn't angry at him. I didn't know for sure if it was him telling it. I had an idea—that was my opinion.

Q. This telephone number that you say you used to call Mr. Bompensiero . . . is the same number that, in fact, Mr. Bonanno had to call; isn't that correct?

A. I don't know that, sir.

Q. And, in fact, the day before Mr. Bompensiero was killed, at that meeting in San Francisco with Mr. Bompensiero and Jimmy Styles, you told Mr. Bompensiero in the presence of Mr. Styles and Mr. Petti that you were going to call Mr. Bompensiero the next night, didn't you?

A. No, I did not, sir.

Q. And, in fact, you did call Mr. Bompensiero the next night; isn't that correct?

A. That is not correct, sir.

Q. And you got him to the phone booth so that, in fact, you and Mr. Bonanno and his sons could execute Mr. Bompensiero as he walked from the telephone booth?

A. That is a lie, sir.

Jimmy sat in red-faced bewilderment as Marks readied another recording from the Demaris-Fratianno interviews:

DEMARIS: You know you have a good way of lying, too. You are an expert at it.

FRATIANNO: What do you mean?

DEMARIS: Lying.

FRATIANNO: Oh, lying, yeah.

DEMARIS: Yeah.

FRATIANNO: I did a lot of lying in my life.

DEMARIS: Do you know the truth from lying?

FRATIANNO: Oh, yeah.

DEMARIS: Okay. As long as you do.

If he hadn't already made his point, Marks introduced one last item of Jimmy's own words.

Q. And sir, one month after your plea agreement, did you not state as follows in your testimony under oath in New York:

Q. Well, you're a pretty savvy guy, aren't you?

A. You mean would I lie to save myself . . .?

Q. To save yourself from execution, yes, sir.

A. That's correct.

And without so much as another question, Marks sat down; he wasn't going to allow Jimmy the opportunity to offer any further explanations.

Most of the damage that was going to occur had been inflicted by Marks. Yet the others took their shots, picking up loose ends.

Alvin Michaelson, Brooklier's lawyer, brought a courtly sarcasm to the proceedings.

He opened by suggesting: "Isn't it a fact that you got your nickname, 'The Weasel,' because . . . you have a habit of committing criminal acts and attempting to weasel out of them by blaming it on others?"

Jimmy flatly denied it.

But Michaelson came back with examples of crimes Fratianno had committed but found others to incriminate, such as his testimony implicating Marshall Caifano in the murder of Russian Louie.

He returned to the issue of Jimmy's relationship with the Bonanno family, asking the same question time and again in different forms, until Jimmy exploded.

"You've asked me that twenty times. I never met anybody in that family, none of the Bonannos. I don't know what they look like."

Playing off Jimmy's anger, Michaelson asked if this was the way he had erupted after determining that Bompensiero had set him up in the Forex sting operation.

"I didn't get angry with him, no. Nobody got angry with him because they were going to kill him. You don't get angry with a guy when you're going to kill him," Jimmy said.

Howard Weitzman brought an orderly, crisp defense on behalf of Dragna. His approach was simple: There was no La Cosa Nostra in Los Angeles and Louie Dragna was no boss, acting or otherwise.

He and Fratianno sparred for a while before Weitzman got around to playing his favorite tapes.

DEMARIS: Yeah, but you are not running the outfit then.

FRATIANNO: Wait a minute. What do you mean, I'm not running the outfit? There's nothing to run, Ovid.

DEMARIS: There is no guys, there is nobody?

FRATIANNO: Nah, what the fuck, ah, there was just myself and Louie. That's it. There was another four or five guys, but they're doing their own thing. They're making a living.

DEMARIS: You guys didn't make any money in that time?

FRATIANNO: Not big money, but we had a lot of things cooking. There is no rackets in L.A., Ovid. You see, L.A. isn't like New York. You ain't got no . . . they didn't organize nothing, they never did, you know.

Fratianno was disgusted by Weitzman's toying with words, suggesting the L.A. Family of La Cosa Nostra really didn't exist, merely because they had no successful rackets.

"Look, I didn't mean there wasn't a Family," he instructed, speaking to the jury, not Weitzman. "What I meant was they never did nothing to make money for the soldiers.

"It's just like the Angels," he said, referring to the local cellar-dwelling baseball team of the late 1970s. "Could I say they ain't got a team because they're in last place?"

Weitzman backed off as the courtroom erupted in waves of laughter.

In the final series of questions posed by the defense, Weitzman's skillfully honed inquiry raised doubts about Fratianno's most essential frailties: the motivation for his testimony and the government's ability to check his veracity.

Q. Did you want Mr. Bompensiero killed?
A. Myself? Personally? No, sir.
Q. Let me ask you this, Mr. Fratianno: Is it your testimony here today that every time you killed somebody you didn't want to do it, but you had to do it?
A. That's correct, sir.
Q. So basically you have done all of these acts without your own volition; because somebody else told you to do it?
A. No, sir. I was ordered to do it. That is the penalty you get for going into this organization, sir. You do what the boss tells you. If you don't you get killed.
Q. And now you are working for the government, aren't you?
A. I'm working for nobody, sir. I'm testifying.
Q. Well, are you getting paid for your testimony?
A. No, I am not, sir. They are paying me for my food and my subsistence.
Q. In exchange for some of the monies, or all of the monies given you by the government, you have agreed to testify; isn't that correct?
A. No, sir. Not in exchange for money, sir.
Q. What do you think would happen to you if the government thought you were not truthful?
A. I don't know, sir. You tell me.
Q. You testified earlier that if you didn't testify truthfully, that you would have to face various charges that have been in kind of a holding pattern over you.

A. That is if I don't testify truthfully. But if I testify truthfully—

Q. Who knows besides you whether your testimony is truthful or not truthful?

A. Well, I don't know.

Q. Basically, they have to accept your word for what you said took place. Isn't that correct?

A. I would assume that, sir.

The trial continued for two more weeks after Jimmy left the stand, strutting, and was secreted out of the courthouse.

With Jimmy's story fresh in the jurors' minds, Henderson and Kelton brought on their supporting cast.

Teddy Gaswirth and Reuben Sturman took the stand, admitting they were pornographers with large interests in Los Angeles. Neither man was any more candid than he had to be.

Gaswirth described Ricciardi and LoCicero approaching him at his Los Angeles office in August 1976 and telling him he would have to pay $20,000 if he wanted to continue doing business. On the Friday when he was to make the first installment in his payoff, Gaswirth said he went into hiding, evading his pursuers.

Sturman said he had been approached by Glenn Pauley in front of the Cleveland YMCA and again on a city street in September 1975. Pauley also demanded $20,000, he said. But rather than paying off or running to his contacts in the New York Families for protection, Sturman went to the FBI.

Ahearn described Fratianno's gradual change from mobster to informant to government witness. He said that the 302 reports written in the early months of 1978 were only an outline of what Fratianno had said; explaining why, as the defense had pointed out, the early reports frequently omitted key bits of information Fratianno had testified to in court.

Police ballistics experts described the gun used to kill Bompensiero as a silencer-equipped .22.

The San Diego medical examiner said Bompensiero had put up a struggle.

Agents of the FBI and Los Angeles Police Department lined up to describe their surveillances: the meetings of Brooklier, Sciortino, and Milano at Bell Bail Bonds, which Coloduros described; LoCicero and Ricciardi at Gaswirth's office the Friday they were supposed to get their payoff; Sal Pinelli taking Bompensiero to the San Fernando Valley; many of the meetings between Dragna and Fratianno in Los

Angeles, where Fratianno said they discussed Bompensiero's murder; a meeting at Murietta Hot Springs, during which curious agents looked on as the mobsters drove into the desert to perform Rizzitello's initiation; and, of course, there were the meetings at Marson's home.

In all, there were more than twenty surveillance witnesses who testified about meetings or events Fratianno had described. There were also phone records, including one showing a call made on Ricciardi's credit card from a Seven-Eleven near the Bompensiero pay phone in San Diego to Fratianno in San Francisco a week before the murder.

Without question, the most important of all the surveillances was one conducted by Agent Jack Larson on March 7, 1976, at the Murietta Hotel Coffee Shop where, he said, he sat close by and listened in as Jimmy told Dragna, "Well, I want a piece of the porno," and Dragna told him, "Don't worry about it. You'll get it."

That conversation, when reported to Jack Barron in Los Angeles, gave birth to Forex and set in motion a series of events that ultimately led to Bompensiero's murder, Fratianno's becoming a government witness, and the trial of the Los Angeles Family.

Agent Jack Armstrong, Bompensiero's FBI contact, told the jury that the San Diego mobster never knew that Forex was an FBI front. Armstrong said that all he had told Bomp was that the Bureau was interested in Forex; that it was a new company and it was making $100,000 or $200,000 annually selling pornography in South America; and anything Bomp could tell him about the company would be greatly appreciated.

Armstrong said he knew Bompensiero could be counted on to take the bait and run to Fratianno.

The Forex tapes were devastating. Agents Larson and J. C. Fishbeck, playing the roles of pornographers, recorded every threat, every payoff, and several gratuitous comments LoCicero or Ricciardi had made describing their organization.

In one of their earliest meetings, Ricciardi and LoCicero explained the facts of life to Larsen:

RICCIARDI: Anything illegal done in California goes mostly through us because we represent the people in California here. You understand that?

LOCICERO: We want a piece of the action . . . and if you don't come across, you might as well pack and move, because we, uh, we're gonna stop you [from doing] business. . . . So you better make up your mind, you know. We . . . we're not here to talk about it, we're not here to negotiate it. Maybe we'll negotiate it to the percentage that we want. You know, because I promise you that inside of seventy-two hours you're out of business.

They began by demanding $20,000, and then brought in Rizzitello, who agreed to $5,000 down and $1,000 a week. Eventually, a total of $7,500 was paid.

The last payment was made at the MGM Grand hotel in Las Vegas, where the undercover agents told Ricciardi they had been approached by the police, who had shown them photos of Rizzitello and Fratianno and explained who they were.

At that meeting Fishbeck said he wanted to meet Fratianno to arrange a loan, but Ricciardi explained he would have to wait:

RICCIARDI: That's like the president of the bank. You go see the teller and [from] the teller you go see the assistant, then you go to the vice president, and then you see the president. See, and you [have] come to the teller.

LARSON: When we look at it, Mike and Jimmy are gonna have to clear it, and we're gonna have to depend on you to do a good selling job.

RICCIARDI: You see, we don't use people's names, we don't say anything.

LARSON: I'm sorry.

RICCIARDI: I'm not going to mention any names, just if you're talking to me, that's good enough.

LARSON: The point is that you're gonna have to clear it through him.

RICCIARDI: Yes.

As the last tapes played out, LoCicero, an overweight, elderly man, rested his forehead against the palm of his hand, his eyes closed.

The government's last witness was a surprise. Jack Barron, who viewed mob informants as the single most important tool of law enforcement, told a tale of the big one that got away.

Louie Dragna had briefly joined the ranks of Bompensiero and Fratianno as an informant. The incentive had been the October 1976 Forex grand jury subpoena.

Barron said it was at Dragna's request that he and Agent John Nance met with Dragna at Barron's West Covina home. After assurances that there was nothing illegal about merely being a member of La Cosa Nostra, Dragna opened up, offering a who's who of the L.A. Family.

"I asked Mr. Dragna if he was the acting boss of the Los Angeles La Cosa Nostra and he replied that he was. I asked Mr. Dragna if Fratianno was the temporary underboss of the Los Angeles Family of La Cosa Nostra, and he replied that he was."

Barron told Dragna that if he cooperated with the FBI, they could get him out from under the grand jury investigation. But soon after that meeting, Barron said, Dragna dropped from sight.

The defense brought only one witness. Eugene Ehmann, assistant director of the Arizona Drug Control District, arrived under sub-poena.

He and his staff of eagle-eyed trash pickers, disguised as sanitation men, had been sifting through garbage taken from the Tucson home of Joe Bonanno, Sr., from 1975 to 1979. Most of what they had turned up was meaningless. But the lawmen had spent days on end reassembling and cataloging little shreds of paper, notes, letters, and bills, in search of telltale hints of criminal conspiracies.

Ehmann came to court with two pieces of paper, reassembled from trash collected at Bonanno's home on February 15, 1977, five days after Bompensiero's slaying. Both notes were in Bonanno's handwriting, and were written in broken Italian and English:

> Call Turi, *PM*
> *Tell Turi—Thursday night*
> Con Semiautomatica
> Scanzalora (corta) 22
> Che non fa tanto *rumore*

Turi was the nickname Bonanno used for one of his sons, Salvatore.

The note said, in English, "Tell Turi—Thursday night, with a semiautomatic, gun (short) 22, that doesn't make much noise."

The second note, a scrap from a blue index file card, said only: "Casetto—9261." In English, "Phone booth—9261."

The number at Bompensiero's phone booth was 273-9261.

Ehmann said twenty-three other references to the 9261 phone number had been recovered from Bonanno's garbage since 1975.

Henderson conceded that Bompensiero had been in touch with Bonanno—and been informing on the deposed mobster—for many years. He then tried to recoup his losses. He had Ehmann identify three newspaper articles from the *Arizona Daily Star* and the *Arizona Republic*, both circulated in Tucson, which, on February 11 and 12, carried the details of Bompensiero's murder days before the notes were retrieved.

However, Ehmann said, there was no evidence that Bonanno had received copies of those articles. And none of the articles contained the phone number.

Weitzman and the defense had subpoenaed Bonanno, but his failing health had put him in the hospital and, his lawyer said, even if he were well enough to come to court, he would assert his Fifth Amendment privilege and refuse to testify.

Summation is a time at trial for opposing sides to shout, cajole, and indignantly jab fists at the air. It's a time of impassioned pleas for justice and exaggerated statements of righteousness.

It is a time to speak of plain truths, giving logical order to the facts that have been presented while an adversary casts those same facts in an entirely different order, defining an opposite reality.

It is a time for forceful persuasion and gentle deception in the molding of facts, omissions, and gut instincts.

It is the final assessment and debate in what is touted as a search for truth.

It is when the courtroom becomes a test tube of justice, heated to a flash point that will hopefully distill some essence of truth, despite the fragile nature of the jurors' human reason.

What most often emerges from this process is rarely the truth, but rather justice, the fundamental by-product that seems to find its way through the ravaged remains of truth.

It would take two days to complete the summations.

Because the prosecution has the greater burden—proving their case beyond a reasonable doubt—they get to argue twice, before and after the defense.

Kelton opened with a review of the law and how the various witnesses and evidence supported Fratianno's story. He took special care on the Bompensiero murder, recalling the medical examiner who confirmed that there had been a struggle; the phone record of Ricciardi's call the night of the dry run; and the surveillances of the Fratianno and Dragna meetings.

But most important, to justify and dignify the government's deal with Fratianno, he told the jurors they had to understand Fratianno's unique role in this trial:

How do you get inside the organization? How do you get past the people on the street, the front men, the men like Ricciardi and LoCicero who knock on doors and scare people? And how do you get up the ladder to the people that are beyond that?

There is only one way to do that, and that is with people like Mr.

Fratianno, people like Mr. Coloduros, because they are the only people in this world who are in a position to give us those facts.

It is a cold fact of life. There's no getting around it.

To put it bluntly, you don't find swans in a sewer.

Marks responded, as all the defense lawyers would, by attacking that notion, saying that people like Fratianno are conning the government to win their freedom.

Once more he questioned which meetings occurred in what order, who was present, and what was discussed. And he listed other apparent inconsistencies in Fratianno's testimony, saying, "He is lying. And a liar can't tell the same story twice."

He explained the surveillances:

"What Mr. Fratianno has done very cleverly, very cleverly, is to give the evidence that he needs to get off the hook with regard to the death penalty and all the other murders. He has fitted selectively certain new facts, new false facts, into the meetings that were, in fact, held. And that way he corroborates some facets of his falsehoods. Very clever. A very clever man."

The Bompensiero murder seemed the most vulnerable target.

It was a remarkable coincidence, Marks said, that Fratianno would have met with Bompensiero and Jimmy Styles, the Bonanno man, the day before the killing. And he raised an interesting argument about Fratianno's inability to recall what they had discussed:

Now, you could say, "Well, how do you remember things that happened two, three years ago?" Do you remember what happened on February 10, 1977? Of course not. But what jars one's memory is the fact that something happens immediately thereafter and the clock stops. And you say, "My gosh, Mr. Bompensiero has been killed. I just saw him last night. We were discussing this, we were doing that."

That is how you remember.

And I suggest to you that Mr. Fratianno does not want to tell us what was discussed that night because he had discussions that night with Jimmy Styles with regard to the killing of Mr. Bompensiero.

And I suggest that the meeting in San Francisco was for the purpose of setting up the killing of Mr. Bompensiero by way of Jimmy Styles, by way of Jimmy Fratianno, and by way of Joseph Bonanno, Sr.

And then there were the Bonanno notes:

If this were an innocent note why would Mr. Bonanno, Sr., rip [it] to shreds? And more importantly, maybe most importantly, if Mr. Bonanno, Sr., wrote this note after reading in the newspapers that Mr. Bompensiero was killed, why would he ever write the phone number? If Mr. Bompensiero had already died there would be no need to write his telephone number anymore.

Finally, look at the language of the note. It is so important.

When he says, "Call Turi and tell Turi," he talks about a "gun that doesn't make much noise." That is the future tense: Use "a gun that doesn't make much noise." He didn't say, "that didn't make much noise."

Howard Gillingham, Rizzitello's lawyer, attacked the FBI's sting operation as an insidious giant of law enforcement, feeding upon the greed of the weak-willed. And in an attempt to show that his client was not a member of the mob's inner sanctum, he attacked Fratianno's description of the Rizzitello initiation:

Bim. Bam. Abracadabra. No sword and pistol. No long table. No thirty or forty men standing around. No winery. No notice to Mike; just going to make him right there in the car.

This most serious occasion, if you believe Mr. Fratianno, induction into this society; the one you enter alive and leave dead; the one you mess with a member's wife and you die. The one where you must leave a dying wife if Family duty beckons.

And it comes down to a scene out of *American Graffiti*, Mike is made in the backseat of a car.

Gillingham was raising the same argument Marks had made: Fratianno was weaving new false facts to fit the surveillances.

Terry Amdur could not hide what everyone had heard: LoCicero's role in the Forex shakedown was unmistakable—"I told you, I'm a lawyer; I am not a magician." But with a little sleight of tongue he suggested that perhaps there had been no crime committed: Forex never existed; it was a fake; no one had really been extorted. And besides, LoCicero is a sick, old man: "Do you think the FBI agents paid the money to Mr. LoCicero because they were afraid of him? Hardly."

As to the Gaswirth shakedown, charged as part of the RICO conspiracy, Amdur denied there was any conspiracy: "Mr. LoCicero was freelancing, he was on his own."

Brooklier's lawyer, Michaelson, who had assumed a low profile throughout the case, avoided details, dealing almost exclusively in the realm of reasonable doubt, repeatedly instructing the jurors that should they believe the evidence could point toward either innocence or guilt, they must vote to acquit.

Weitzman was left with little to say, except to review ground already covered by the others. He persisted in arguments that it was

Bonanno and Fratianno, not Brooklier and the others, who were the primary targets of Bompensiero's informing to the FBI and therefore had the best reasons to want Bomp dead.

Henderson got the last word—the last chance to plead his case, Fratianno's case, to the jury.

Without histrionics, without even so much as raising his voice, Henderson delivered a simple, keenly reasoned summation. He had to allay any lingering doubts about the conspiracies committed by this ragtag band of hoodlums.

He began: "Ladies and gentlemen, this is the Mafia, this is La Cosa Nostra."

It is the Los Angeles Family of La Cosa Nostra, he said, which is charged, as the core of the conspiracies, with committing the acts of racketeering. And while each defendant was not involved in every criminal act, he said they all had a role as members of the organization.

For example: "With regard to Forex, we are not saying that was a completed extortion because, technically, you cannot extort from FBI agents. What we are saying is that they attempted to do so. They conspired to do so. It was done pursuant to a plan. And that is what this case is basically all about. It is about attempts and conspiracies."

He reminded the jurors of consistencies evidencing conspiracies: Coloduros's and Fratianno's testimony about a contract on Bompensiero's life; Barron's confirming Fratianno's testimony about the Family; Gaswirth, Sturman, and the FBI's Forex undercover agents, all testifying that the opening demand from the mobsters had been for $20,000; and the surveillances.

But it was the Bonanno notes, more than anything else, that presented hard evidence of a reasonable doubt about the government's case. Standing in front of a poster-size blow-up of the two notes—the one instructing "Call Turi" marked as Note A, and the phone booth number marked as Note B—he characterized them as "a red herring."

He questioned: If Bonanno was plotting a murder, why would the two notes be on different pieces of paper? Why would they turn up in the garbage five days and two garbage pickups after the murder rather than immediately after he had instructed Turi to carry out the execution? Note B appeared to be a piece of an index card, the kind used for address and phone files, so wouldn't it make sense for Bonanno to discard the number after learning of Bompensiero's death?

And while it was agreed that Bomp was informing on Bonanno, where is there "one scintilla of evidence that Mr. Bonanno knew that"?

"But what did come out was that the defendants in this case found out that Bompensiero was an informant, because they believed he set them up in Forex."

And then Henderson turned a defense strategy—their barring Fratianno from naming LoCicero as the wheelman in the killing—to his advantage:

> Now it seems to me that defense counsel have overlooked one major point, and that is that . . . there is not one thing in that note inconsistent with the involvement of any defendant in this case.
>
> In Bobby's Restaurant, [Fratianno] is told by Tommy Ricciardi how it went down, that he and another guy perpetrated the killing.
>
> How is that inconsistent? He and another guy? Who is the other guy? Is it Turi?
>
> Well, if you buy the defense argument, maybe it could have been. I don't think you should buy that argument, and I am telling you not to, because it is nonsense.
>
> Now defense counsel say, "One final point with the note. This is written in the future tense."
>
> If I tell you, "Frank Bompensiero *was* killed with a gun *that doesn't make much noise*" that doesn't make that note in the future tense.

Appropriately, in capping off his argument, Henderson acknowledged Fratianno's special role in the case. It was, again, a discourse on the insular society that can only be penetrated with the aid of bad people like Fratianno:

> It is not the kind of society that you and I grew up in. It is a different set of ethics, one that I don't understand and one that I don't expect you or most of the people in this courtroom to understand.
>
> But it is one that exists, it is one that he grew up in, it is one that he was involved in with these defendants. And it is one that you have to understand, to some extent, at least that it does exist, before you can really understand what this case is all about.
>
> Defense counsel have noted that Mr. Fratianno got a pretty sweet deal here. And, of course, he does.
>
> But again, you don't have to like it. I don't like it.
>
> But you can certainly understand it. It's an opportunity that without Mr. Fratianno's cooperation you don't have. Whether you agree with it or not, it is the only way to do things, and it is what was done here.
>
> And just because Mr. Fratianno didn't get everything he deserves there is absolutely no logic in using that as a reason for not dishing out what is

deserved to other people, who were involved with him in the commission of very serious crimes.

No one expected a decision overnight. It had been a three-week trial with a mountain of evidence. Yet even without a verdict, one thing was clear to all observers—and was noted repeatedly by columnists and in commentary. After all was said and done, the Los Angeles Mafia, or La Cosa Nostra, certainly existed, but it was unmistakably, as it came to be called, "the Mickey Mouse Mafia."

It seemed at any given time there were as many members running off to talk to the FBI as there were loyal members working their modest rackets.

At one point, both of the Family's acting bosses and its *consigliere* had been cozy with the FBI, turning on each other and the soldiers who were supposed to be providing insulation and doing the dirty work for their superiors.

And those doing the dirty work were incapable of even shaking down a pornographer. When they did find one they could collect from, it turned out to be the FBI.

This wasn't La Cosa Nostra of old, the one Jimmy remembered. These were common American crooks—and pretty bad ones at that.

Overcoming an eight-day deadlock, the jurors appeared in the court-room and read their verdicts to the defendants, who stood expressionless. All five were convicted on eleven counts, including the RICO charge, from the twenty-count indictment.

Basically, the jury convicted on every charge where there was an overwhelming preponderance of evidence—much of it circumstantial—to support Jimmy's testimony.

Jury Foreman William Wasil told the *Los Angeles Times:* "Everything we listened to from Fratianno we had to weigh. We viewed him with the greatest of care and doubt. In every instance [that] we used [his] testimony we had to have corroboration.

"The Bonanno note we looked at in both ways—as something done in the past [after reading the newspapers] or [as] an order. It could be read either way. So we took the way pointing to innocence."

Charges stemming from the Bompensiero slaying and Gaswirth extortion were the only areas of acquittal.

The defense, though not entirely satisfied, was pleased. They had beaten the murder rap, which was contained in an obstruction of justice charge, claiming Bompensiero was killed to silence his communication with the FBI.

Although the obstruction charge carried the lightest sentence in the indictment—five years—the defense understood it was the most serious crime alleged. They felt the acquittal assured them lighter sentences.

Nonetheless, Henderson deemed it a victory, crowing to reporters outside the courtroom that the convictions "destroyed the myth that the Mafia cannot be successfully prosecuted."

Indeed, it didn't prove much more than that.

On January 20, 1981, Judge Hatter followed the defense's reasoning.

"The Mafia here is second rate. It would also appear that the crimes are second rate. I just don't see the fruits of all this illegal activity," Hatter said in handing down minimal two-to-five-year sentences. They each had faced maximum terms of twenty to sixty years in prison.

"Obviously, the sentences were less severe than we felt they should have been," Henderson told reporters. "But I've been around too long to be upset by things like this."

The local media was outraged. No one questioned Hatter's integrity, but it was widely believed that the judge distrusted Jimmy's information and had decided to view the convictions on their simplest terms: a series of inept extortions strung together in a RICO conspiracy.

The defendants exhausted every conceivable appeal before surrendering to serve their prison time: LoCicero was sentenced to two years and Rizzitello got five years. Dragna, who drew two years, eventually was remanded to a halfway house rather than prison, enabling him to go to work every day and see his family. He also was fined $50,000.

On December 11, 1981, while still free on bail pending appeal, Sciortino was convicted in the Brilab case on charges of attempting to bribe Judge Pregerson. Having drawn a four-year sentence in the Los Angeles case, for Brilab he was sentenced to an additional five years and a $5,000 fine—the maximum.

Carlos Marcello, the New Orleans boss, was convicted in the Brilab case and was sentenced to ten years and a $25,000 fine.

Judge Pregerson was elevated to the Ninth Circuit, U.S. Court of Appeals.

On July 18, 1984, after serving eleven months of a five-year sentence from the Los Angeles case, Dominic Brooklier died in a prison medical center in Tucson.

12

Face-to-Face with the Godfather

THE MEDIA was chasing Jimmy's shadow; analyzing his Los Angeles testimony, searching for an exclusive piece of his story, when he slipped from town unnoticed.

He completed testifying on a Thursday. Late that Saturday, wrapped in a flak jacket, he was snuck out of the courthouse. His armed escort drove onto the tarmac at Los Angeles International where he and McPherson boarded the red-eye for LaGuardia in New York. They sat in the back of the jetliner, Fratianno in the window seat.

In New York, they disembarked before anyone else and were again met on the tarmac, this time by a three-car motorcade that delivered them to the marshals' office adjacent to the U.S. Courthouse in lower Manhattan.

Jimmy bitched about one thing or another all the way through Manhattan's rain-slicked streets. He even complained that sunrise came too early; they should have moved him in darkness. Jimmy still didn't like being anywhere near New York, and now, in mid-autumn, with the weather turning chilly, he disliked it even more.

Akerman had been waiting since 6 A.M. at his uptown apartment to hear that Fratianno had arrived safe and sound.

Jimmy was too tired to want to talk to anyone, but was sincerely impressed that someone in this godforsaken town cared enough to awake before dawn to check on his arrival.

Akerman was rather amazed himself. But he had been preparing for Fratianno's arrival for weeks; his adrenaline was pumping and his

281

nerves were slightly jarred. Jury selection was scheduled to start Monday in the case against Frank "Funzi" Tieri, and Jimmy was the lead-off witness. The Los Angeles and Tieri cases had fallen back-to-back, and this split-second timing offended Akerman's sense of orderliness.

"How did it go in L.A.? How was Henderson?" Akerman asked.

"Henderson?" Jimmy shot back. "I was the whole fuckin' case out there and I done great. I made monkeys out of these guys. Anytime they thought they had me cornered, I turned right around and stuffed it up their ass with an explanation."

Akerman had to laugh. He was always tickled by Jimmy's bravado and bluster.

They talked about his flight and all the publicity he had received.

"Nick, you know I arranged to do an interview with this guy from *Newsweek*, Ron LaCreek or something, as soon as I finish up here in New York. How much you think they're paying me?" Jimmy boasted.

"What do you mean 'you arranged'? That guy from *Newsweek* is Ron LaBrecque and I went to college with him. He was bugging me for weeks about you, so I turned him over to McDonald. You turkey."

Both men laughed.

"But what a deal, Nick. I mean, this guy's going to pay me $2,500 just to sit with him for a couple hours," he said, chuckling. "I got a few other things working, too, you know."

"Oh, yeah? What's that?"

"Well, I got these newspaper attorneys from New Mexico want me to testify for them against Billy Marchiondo. He's suing this newspaper in Albuquerque for a couple million because they ran his picture with a story about some gangsters. Now catch this, he says he never met me; knows nothing about me. Can you feature that?" [Marchiondo later conceded that he knew Fratianno, but insisted he knew him as Jimmy Fratello, a California businessman.]

"Fox told me something about it. You know, they're going to try to get depositions from DePalma, Marson, Louie Domes—the entire theater group."

"I forgot you and Fox know each other—from Watergate, right? They're never going to get those guys to say anything. Made guys can't say nothin'.

"Anyways, Fox got these newspaper attorneys together with McDonald and I'm asking 250-an-hour, as an expert witness. They're supposed to work out the details later this month when I go back to Washington."

"Hey Jimmy. I don't want to know where you're going to be, okay?"

"Yeah, you're right. So's anyway, I got that thing in Albuquerque and then Bob Guccione wants me to testify in the libel case La Costa has going against *Penthouse*. He's already guaranteed me 250-an-hour, which should bring me somethin' like $30,000, I figure."

"Jeez, Jimmy. You're gettin' rich on this protection deal: $128,000 up front on the book; magazine interviews; libel suits. Pretty soon you're going to have Jimmy Fratianno dolls. We're making you a celebrity."

"Hey Nick, don't go sayin' I'm gettin' rich here. I need every cent of that money. I've been sending my wife like $800 a month and these marshals are only paying me twenty a day to live on. You can't even get a steak for that kinda money. I still have to pay all my bills and pay for my cars and clothes and stuff. Shit, Nick, if I didn't have to do all this to stay alive, I'd walk away from this program right after I finished this Tieri case."

It was a story Akerman had been hearing with increasing frequency for two years; his eyes glazed over as Jimmy's voice grew shrill. Akerman waited for a while and then cut Jimmy off in mid-sentence.

"Look, Jimmy. I'm going to come by the marshals' office this afternoon to see you and go over your testimony. So get some rest. All right?"

"Why not come over later this morning? I'll be ready by then," he said, his exhaustion overcome by his desire to see a friendly face.

"No, Jim. I'm training for the New York Marathon next Sunday. I've got to get out and run. But I'll see you later."

"Okay, pal. Talk to you later."

On June 30, 1980, Tieri had been arrested as he left his home in Brooklyn and was brought to the FBI office in New Rochelle, New York, to be booked. He was helped up the concrete steps to the building by two agents who towered over the small, elderly man.

Tieri wore tinted, designer eyeglasses, a French-tailored powder-blue suit, a garish necktie, and blue suede shoes. On the forth finger of his left hand was a blue star sapphire, the size of a walnut, surrounded by diamonds in a gold setting. On his right wrist was an inch-wide gold ID bracelet on which "FUNZIE" was spelled out in diamond chips.

In his pockets, Tieri carried $1,000—not a dollar more or less—in crisp, unwrinkled currency and a solid gold social security card; no credit cards, no driver's license, nothing else.

And he had clutched in one hand a leather bag, about the size of a football, containing vials of medication from which he ate or injected hourly doses throughout the day.

As he moved up the concrete stairs, past photographers who had been tipped off that someone important was being brought in, he never bowed his head or covered his face; he just walked firmly, defiantly toward the whirring sound of Nikon motor drives, his thin lips drawn tight.

This was the face of supreme confidence; no cheap hood, deranged torpedo, or greed-driven corporate scam artist looking to deny reality. Only punks hide from the camera.

At seventy-six, Tieri was well-tanned, dapper, and alert; yet his slow movements, apparent weakness, and sagging flesh evidenced his age. In recent years, Tieri had undergone treatment for colon cancer, liver failure, diabetes, and cranial insufficiency resulting from circulatory problems, which had caused convulsions and blackouts. Since suffering a stroke in 1975, his heart had deteriorated to the point that bypass surgery was out of the question. He had a hearing aid in his right ear and was nearly blind in his left eye.

Still, despite his maladies, Tieri remained the Godfather in every conceivable respect.

"The Old Man" had amassed all the appropriate titles of mob nobility. He was boss of the Genovese crime Family and, since the death of Carlo Gambino three years earlier, the senior member of the Commission overseeing mob disputes nationwide. If there had been at that time a boss of bosses, a *capo di tutti capi*, it would have been Tieri.

Unlike the West Coast or Cleveland Families, Tieri's authority and prestige didn't flow from a few beefy characters enforcing their will on bookmakers, pornographers, or low-level racketeers. Rather, his authority was so well entrenched that no one working on the fringes of the law would contemplate operating without first securing his Family's blessing.

Tieri's command was so broad, it was widely agreed that, had he ever wanted to, he could have crippled commerce in New York City and on much of the East Coast. He virtually controlled trucking of vital goods—for example, food—through strategically placed *capos,* like Tony "Pro" Provenzano, in the Teamsters union. Another associate, Michael Clemente, ran the Port Authority of New York and New Jersey, overseeing stevedores who handled all cargo moving to and from the city by sea or air. Tieri was also the garbage czar: His Family owned or governed many of the largest private sanitation companies in the city and its suburbs. Matthew "Matty the Horse" Ianiello, Tieri's top money-maker, held interests in restaurants and bars and secretly directed the operations of many related service industries and unions.

And those were only a few of Tieri's holdings in legitimate commerce. He also held enormous interests in pornography and narcotics; he was said to have had, personally, a million dollars on the streets as loan-shark money, collecting two or three points a week vigorish; and his Family had seized nearly a majority share of the city's illegal gambling operations.

He had as many as 800 soldiers to do his bidding, and for every initiated member there were, perhaps, another ten hoping to become buttons.

Tieri was without question one of the most powerful men in the city—and the nation. Yet with all this wealth, he led a relatively modest, unassuming life. He and his wife, America, lived in a comfortable, three-story house in Brooklyn, where they had raised two daughters and twelve grandchildren, cultivated fig trees in the backyard, and trained grape vines to climb over their two-car garage. Tieri's presence in the Bay 28th Street neighborhood of Bath Beach, Brooklyn, guaranteed residents a crime-free existence—many of them never bothering to lock their doors at night, a unique urban existence.

Tieri's only other real estate holding was a summer retreat in the mountains around New Paltz, New York, a few hours north of the city. He had no cars registered in his name; no stock certificates or large bank accounts. His only stated sources of income was as owner of Endicott Sportswear Co., in Brooklyn, and Resource Sales, a lower Manhattan clothing close-out business. He declared income of about $40,000 a year.

And yet, in 1972, when agents searched his Brooklyn home, they found hidden windowsill compartments lined with a small fortune in diamonds. Tieri claimed to have no idea how they had gotten there— perhaps the former owner left them.

Like the folkloric godfather figure, Tieri was a devout Catholic and courtly gentleman who held doors, bowed, and kissed the hands of young women.

Yet his likeness to *The Godfather*'s fictional Don Vito Corleone went beyond the predictable similarities of Old World charm, criminal enterprise, and devout Catholicism.

Like the young Vito Corleone, who made his way to the United States from Sicily by way of France, Tieri was smuggled into the U.S. by way of Marseilles after leaving Castel Gandolfo, the papal summer retreat, in 1912, when he was eight.

Without ever seeking U.S. citizenship, Tieri grew up in the Italian ghettos of lower Manhattan and later moved across the East River to Brooklyn where he quietly went about building his business and even more quietly ascending through the mob hierarchy. He was indicted or arrested on numerous occasions for a variety of minor charges, but only once did he go to jail—briefly, in 1922, to Sing-Sing for assault.

And, like the raspy voice made famous in Marlon Brando's performance, Tieri had been unable to speak in any more than a gruff whisper since undergoing throat cancer surgery in the 1950s. He came to be known to some of his cohorts as "the man with the bad throat," a reference he found disrespectful and later prohibited.

Tieri began to realize his ambitions in 1972, when the Genovese Family boss, Thomas "Tommy Ryan" Eboli, was gunned down in Brooklyn.

Carlo Gambino, the senior member of the crime Commission—the only mob leader with greater holdings than Tieri and the only one powerful enough to have approved Eboli's murder—offered his blessing for Tieri, his close friend, to assume leadership of the Genovese Family.

By 1976, as Gambino's health began to deteriorate, Tieri assumed many of the powers and duties as senior member of the Commission overseeing the nation's mob Families. But Gambino's death triggered power struggles, both for control within the Gambino Family and for dominance over the Commission.

There would have been no question about lines of inheritance in the Gambino Family, except that Gambino had divided his empire into two separate parcels: Gambino underboss Aniel DellaCroce, whose power derived from a crew of killers, hustlers, and loan sharks, was in charge of the rackets; while Gambino's brother-in-law, Paul Castellano, who disdained mob violence, regarding himself as a legitimate businessman, controlled the Family's "legitimate" holdings in the trucking, meat packing, and garment industries.

The Gambino Family was primed for an internal power struggle, pitting Gambino's blood relatives, led by Castellano, against DellaCroce's crew of street thugs. The victor certainly would have been DellaCroce, then clearly the single-most-powerful mobster in the nation next to Tieri, but it would have been a pyrrhic victory in which large segments of the Family's wealth and power would have been reorganized to assure loyalty or lost in the struggle.

It was DellaCroce who stepped in with an olive branch, holding his thugs at bay, recognizing Castellano as the legitimate heir. DellaCroce understood when bloodshed was necessary and when it wasn't.

DellaCroce became the keystone in a precarious balance that kept the Gambino Family the most powerful mob empire in the United States.

Tieri had sat gleefully on the sidelines as the tensions settled. No matter what the resolution was, Tieri benefited. If there was a Family civil war, he would pick up the pieces lost by the Gambino Family— and with Castellano peacefully assuming power, it meant DellaCroce was denied a seat as a boss on the Commission and Tieri's role as senior member was all but secure.

The only remaining threat to Tieri's supreme authority was Carmine Galante, a renegade boss whose extensive narcotics operations had enabled him to take control of the Family once led by deposed boss Joe Bonanno. But in 1976, Galante was in prison on a narcotics charge, giving Tieri time to consolidate his authority as America's senior mobster.

In March 1979, Galante won parole. In July, he was killed by three shotgun-toting men who burst into the garden of the Joseph and Mary Italian restaurant in Brooklyn. The photos of Galante, sprawled face up on the ground, bathed in blood, a cigar firmly clenched in his teeth, became a national reminder of how the mob still settled disputes over power and wealth. Tieri faced no further rivals.

Hours after his arrest that day in late June 1980, Tieri sat silently in court, appearing tired and frail as his lawyer, Jay Goldberg, argued for little or no bail.

Goldberg, tall, lean, and quick-tongued, held a reputation as one of the city's best and brightest trial lawyers. He had learned his craft as a former assistant attorney general in the mob-busting staff of Attorney General Robert Kennedy. He had mastered a rapid-fire style of cross-examination that left most witnesses gasping for breath, and had an energetic, courtly manner with a jury.

In Tieri's behalf, Goldberg made no pleas for mercy; he never denied that Tieri was who the government said he was. He asked only that the court cast its eyes upon this weak and dying defendant to determine if there was any risk that he might flee to avoid trial.

When bail was set at a meager $75,000, Tieri looked to the very last row of pews in the packed courtroom and gestured with a nod to a man in blue pinstripes who was carrying a metallic attaché case containing $250,000 in certified checks.

Tieri was home before dinner.

The case against Tieri was a measure of Akerman's ability as an aggressive prosecutor.

Using the RICO law, Akerman had reached back thirteen years to fashion a case involving racketeering, tax evasion, and conspiracy to commit bankruptcy fraud—the latter stemming from Tieri's role in the Premier Theatre frauds.

Other than Fratianno's testimony, none of the charges were newly developed; rather, they were the remnants of two indictments Tieri had evaded by successfully claiming he was too infirm for trial. Fratianno's testimony about La Cosa Nostra was the essential ingredient for breathing life back into those cases, providing the matrix for the continuing criminal enterprise.

It was the first time a defendant was charged as the boss of a La Cosa Nostra Family. It was essential to prove not only that there was a La Cosa Nostra and that Tieri was a member, but that he was the boss and therefore responsible for crimes committed in the name of that organization.

The next phase of the case was in Akerman's view the toughest.

On nine previous occasions since the 1930s, Tieri had avoided trial because of ill health or on some other technicality. And in that time Tieri's health had only worsened.

In early September 1980, medical hearings to determine Tieri's ability to stand trial began in a second-floor courtroom overlooking a cobblestoned open-air market, where street vendors peddled sausage and pepper wedges, scungili, shrimp marinara, clams oreganato, espresso, cappuccino, and Italian pastries.

Judge Thomas Griese ordered the windows closed when an accordion player's rendition of "The Godfather Theme" distracted everyone's attention from the testimony of medical experts.

One after another, the doctors—experts in physical and psychological diagnosis—lined up on behalf of the prosecution and defense.

They all agreed that Tieri was so debilitated that he couldn't assist in his own defense or comprehend the charges, two standards used when judging a defendant's fitness for trial.

The only remaining question was whether a trial would endanger Tieri's health.

Appearing for the defense, Dr. Henry Dolger characterized Tieri's diabetes as "a time bomb lurking in Mr. Tieri's system." Dr. Seymour Gendelman predicted a trial would be "a significant and substantial risk" to Tieri's health because of circulatory problems.

The prosecution cardiologist, Dr. Meyer Texon, was the only one to disagree. He testified that the stress of a trial posed "no additional, significant risk. There are no life-threatening problems to this man, and it wouldn't make any difference if he stays home or goes to court."

That was when the tide began turning in Akerman's favor. To bolster Texon's view, Akerman presented two employees from Tieri's Endicott Sportswear Company.

Margot Atoria, a bookkeeper, didn't understand why she had been called. She knew Tieri was accused of being a mobster. She thought she was helping him when she described what a good, hard-working man he was; how he arrived at the office early every day, put in a full day, and had total command of every aspect of the business.

An accountant gave similar testimony.

And then Akerman rolled his videotapes. For two months before his indictment, FBI agents had tailed Tieri, recording his every movement. He was seen going to and from work, carrying packages and groceries, attending street-corner business meetings, going to church, packing up his family and friends for a trip to his country home, or visiting social clubs, bars, his paramour's apartment, and Club Napoli, a Brooklyn disco, in the same neighborhood where the recently released movie *Saturday Night Fever* had been filmed.

"The government isn't contending that Mr. Tieri is John Travolta, but there is no reason he shouldn't stand trial," Akerman argued.

Judge Griesa ordered Tieri to stand trial beginning October 20.

"It was Tieri's theater," Jimmy testified as Akerman's lead witness, offering his best analysis of the mob conspiracies at the Premier Theatre.

He described his relationship with Marson, and how through Marson he had met DePalma, Louie "Dome" Pacella, and the rest.

The major difference here, what had been lacking in the Premier Theatre trial, was that Jimmy could now explain his role as acting boss in Los Angeles, providing the perspective needed to understand how he could represent Marson, a California resident, in his problems with the New York mobs.

He reviewed the meetings with Fat Dom Alongi, a *capo* in Tieri's Family, in which he sought to protect Marson's money; his efforts on behalf of Fat Dom to place Cannatella in charge of the theater; and ultimately the sit-down with Tieri, "the Old Man," who guaranteed Marson would be "fully surfaced," protected from loss, during the theater's bankruptcy proceedings.

He acted as an expert witness, explaining in minute detail the customs and practices of La Cosa Nostra and then, turning to a map of the United States, identified twenty-four La Cosa Nostra Families in twenty cities: Los Angeles, San Jose, San Francisco, Denver, St. Louis, Dallas, New Orleans, Kansas City, Milwaukee, Chicago, Detroit, Cleveland, Steubenville (Ohio), Tampa, Philadelphia, Pittsburgh, Pittston, Buffalo, Providence (Rhode Island), and New York.

He explained about the Commission, the five New York bosses and one from Chicago, which he said oversaw the divvying up of turf and the resolving of disputes to stave off open warfare, as occurred in the 1930s. He said Tieri was the senior member of the Commission.

LaBrecque, the *Newsweek* correspondent, had followed Jimmy from the West Coast to the East in preparation for his interview. He hardly took notes during the Tieri case; the testimony was nearly a verbatim replay of Fratianno's appearance in L.A.

The significantly new element to his story was a meeting he and Mike Rizzi had attended with Tieri at a diner in lower Manhattan, near Little Italy, in September 1976.

The sit-down was called to further discuss Marson's investment in the theater. But when the two California mobsters arrived, they were ushered into a back room where Tieri was seated with his top lieutenants: *consigliere* Fat Tony Salerno, underboss Eli Zeccardi, and *capo* Vincent "Chin" Gigante.

A. He asked me if I knew a guy by the name of Ullo. I told him, no, I didn't know him. I asked Mike if he ever heard of the guy and Mike says he never heard of him. So we're just listening there and they're talking about some money.

Q. What was the substance of what was being said in that meeting about Ullo?

A. Well, this fellow owed money. He owed some money and they sent somebody out there after him.

Q. Did anyone tell you where Mr. Ullo was from or lived?

A. California, sir. He was in California. That's why they brought me in the back room to see if I knew him, or, you know.

Q. Could you describe to the jury what happened after that?

A. Well, Chin was talking about they sent this guy out there and . . . this fellow owed quite a bit of money. So Gigante says, "Well, I vote hit."

Q. What did he do then?

A. With his fingers down, Frank Tieri says, "Hit."

Q. What did he do?

A. Thumbs down. Tony Salerno did the same thing and so did Eli.

Throughout all of this, Tieri sat at the defense table slumped in a wheelchair, largely expressionless, looking up on a few rare occasions; otherwise his head remained hung forward, his eyes cast down at his lap.

He wore none of his customary jewelry. Three-piece business suits replaced his usually natty attire. He wore a heavily taped gauze pad over his left eye. A nurse sat at his side.

Only in the absence of the jury would Tieri step from his wheelchair, seeking out the prettiest of the TV reporters to pass the time during recesses and lunch breaks.

And only when Fratianno referred to him as "the Old Man," or discussed the Ullo sit-down did Tieri's stony, olive-skinned face break into a broad attentive grin.

Even in the jury's presence, despite his frail or disoriented appearance, Tieri's eyes glowed with crystal awareness. It would seem Tieri's body may have been failing, but his mind was keen.

It took less than a day for Fratianno to complete his testimony about how La Cosa Nostra works, Tieri's involvement in defrauding the U.S. Bankruptcy Court in the Premier Theatre case, and, finally, the Ullo murder plot.

It took Goldberg four days to complete his cross-examination of Fratianno.

Goldberg's posture from the opening of the trial was not to deny Tieri was a member or leader of La Cosa Nostra: "We are not trying the issue of whether Frank Tieri, an old man, is a choir boy. The issue is whether he is responsible for the acts" charged in the indictment.

The crimes charged, he argued, were "wholly fabricated" by the government's four primary witnesses, each one having struck a deal for lenient sentences and a place in WITSEC in return for their cooperation—a practice he characterized as "encouraging perjury by tempting immoral men."

Goldberg's delivery was the essence of strutting sarcasm. His questions came so quickly that Fratianno could barely answer one before the next was asked. And on numerous occasions, Goldberg would ask a question, turn on his heel, and ask that it be withdrawn, denying Fratianno an opportunity to answer:

"Isn't it true that you told the FBI, when you were arrested in December 1977, that you were only a soldier and never the acting boss?"

"Didn't you testify in a deposition in the early 1970s that you were not a member of the Mafia?"

"Didn't you face the electric chair or twenty-five years in prison for the murder of Danny Greene, to which you pleaded guilty?"

"Haven't you testified in the past that you'd lie to stay out of jail?"

"How much money have you been paid by the FBI?"

"Haven't you testified in the past that you wouldn't serve one more day in jail for all the money in the world?"

The answers to those kinds of questions was not important; what was important was driving home the question, and the resulting doubt that this witness was capable and willing to lie to save his neck.

Goldberg was just getting warmed up. He was in the midst of a frenetic examination about Fratianno's earnings in the years preceding his cooperating with the government when Jeff Hoffman, Goldberg's trial partner, jumped to his feet.

Tieri was reeling.

"Could we have a recess, your honor," Hoffman called out.

Tieri wheezed, gasped, and keeled forward.

Goldberg's long strides brought him to Tieri's side as two portly young women, Tieri's granddaughters, approached the collapsed figure in the wheelchair.

The jurors looked on with confusion stitched to their faces.

Griesa cleared the courtroom.

Tieri was wheeled into an anteroom where his nurse searched with some difficulty for his pulse—it was weak and rapid. His blood pressure was high—180 over 90. He had been complaining of severe headaches and light-headedness ever since Fratianno's discussion of the Ullo murder plot earlier that day.

An ambulance was called to the front of the courthouse and Tieri, robed in a black overcoat, was rushed down the hallway, one of his granddaughters at his side, tears rolling down her cheeks, her heels echoing through the marble corridor.

"It's really bad," she cried to John Russo, a body guard.

He was taken to Beekman Downtown Hospital where his condition was stabilized, and he was transferred that evening to Mount Sinai Hospital, where his own doctors could care for him.

"I knew this old bastard would pull something like this. It's the oldest ruse going," Jimmy told Akerman that evening.

"I don't know, Jimmy. I think this one was for real."

"Nick, this bastard's on so much medication, all he had to do was take too many of one kinda pill or two few of the other thing and, bingo, he's showin' all the signs of being real sick. This is one smart motherfucker, Nick."

"Well, whatever it is, he's too sick for trial right now. So we got a few days off."

The trial stood in recess for five days as Tieri recuperated.

"Hey Newt. What's doin'?"

Jimmy has an unmistakable voice, requiring no introduction. It rings with a sharp tone of malevolent authority.

"Jimmy, I'm just great. How the hell are you?"

"Good, good, Newt. I'm on this Tieri case in New York and we got a couple days' break."

"Yeah, I read something about it. The Old Man got sick or something, right?"

"Something like that. What's happening with the Todisco case? When am I going to get some money?"

"Well, Jimmy, we expect to get you going on that deposition sometime in the spring—like April or May. The newspaper got a hold of that lawyer you were talking about, Phil Fox, he'll be doing that deposition with you."

"Sure, Phil told me about it. You know, he's also handling this Marchiondo case. He's a real smart guy; I'm glad he's gettin' some work from me.

"Hey Newt, did you see where this prick Presser endorsed your pal Reagan for president? A hardass, conservative, antiunion guy like Reagan getting endorsed by the biggest union in the country. Can you believe that?"

"Listen Jimmy, I've been wanting to talk to you about that. You know all that stuff you keep telling me about Presser and Sinatra being friendly with people in the mobs . . ."

"Yeah, what about it?" Jimmy asked, suddenly more attentive.

"Well, after talking to you last week in L.A., I got a call from

Denny. He's got a source on the Nevada Gaming Commission who handles all the applications. It seems Sinatra is using Reagan as his top reference for a new gaming license."

"That doesn't surprise me. You know there was always rumors that Nancy Reagan had a big crush on Sinatra."

"Sure, it's no big secret that they're friends. What concerns me is that Carter's people may try smearing the governor with it, saying he's got all these connections to organized crime types; you know, first Presser, now Sinatra."

"I'll tell you something else, Newt, but you can't spread this around. Akerman has a grand jury tryin' to prove that Sinatra got 50,000 under the table from these guys at the theater. . . . So what are you going to do? I mean all I've ever heard about Reagan is that he's clean—"

"Hey, Jim, you think I don't know that? I've been trying to warn them. I called Meese the other day, but didn't get a call back. Then I tried calling Deaver, but I know that's a waste of time—all he cares about is pleasing Nancy, and she'll protect Sinatra. So I spoke to Lyn Nofziger and he was real surprised. Well, don't you know, about three hours later Meese calls me from the Waldorf-Astoria. Anyway, when I told him all about the Sinatra stuff he acted real surprised, like he knew nothing about him using Reagan on the gambling license application."

"Did you tell him about Presser, how this prick doesn't make a move without clearing it first with the Cleveland Family?"

"Sure I did, Jim. But from what I'm hearing, it seems they don't care about your opinion of Presser as long as he's never been indicted. You know the Teamsters endorsed Reagan a few weeks ago and that's a big boost for his campaign."

"I can't believe these guys. This guy's gonna get elected fuckin' president and he's got people like Sinatra and Presser around him," Jimmy said in disgust.

"Well, that's no big deal. Wasn't Kennedy pals with your friend Roselli?"

"I guess, Newt. Maybe I've been hangin' around too many FBIs and prosecutors too long. You know a couple FBIs have asked me about Presser, they're trying to get something on him. But they're never going to get this guy now—not if he's a friend of Reagan's. But does anyone else know about these calls you made, Newt?"

"Oh, sure. When I spoke to Meese I had Bill Roemer, Ralph Hill,

Bob Olson, and Bill Hill there in the room when he called back. And I don't know why, but I taped the conversation."

"Good. I wouldn't trust any of Reagan's guys."

"Tell me something, Jimmy. Is there any way to get a hold of you when I need to?"

"Yeah, what you're supposed to do is call the marshals' office in Virginia and they'll get a message to me. I talk to this guy there, Phil Tucker, like every day when I'm in protective custody. Otherwise he calls me where I'm living every couple of days to tell me when they've wired me money or if I have messages waiting or shit like that. But Tucker's leaving soon and I'm going to have this broad, Marilyn Mode, handling me. Can you believe they're going to have a broad handling a guy like me?"

"Hey Jimmy, maybe they figure a woman can keep you in line," Newt said, laughing.

"These people just don't understand how a guy like me thinks, Newt. You know what I'm sayin'? A guy who's been in this thing as long as I have doesn't have business with a broad."

Jimmy and Newt ended their conversation with a discussion of the football season—and the betting line on the presidential election, set for that Tuesday. They agreed the Cowboys and Reagan were favorites.

When the trial reconvened, Tieri appeared no worse than he had earlier. The jury was instructed to disregard what they'd seen, at least so far as it might affect their deliberations. They were also instructed that the trial would proceed on a shortened daily schedule.

Goldberg picked up where he had left off, with attacks on Fratianno's credibility—but really never had much impact.

Akerman and his co-prosecutor, Barbara Jones, presented three more prime witnesses: Herbert Gross, Ralph Picardo, and Joseph Cantalupo. Each of them was a former mob associate who testified about mob rackets he'd engaged in with Tieri. The least effective was Picardo, who had had too many scrapes with the law since joining WITSEC.

Goldberg presented several witnesses on Tieri's behalf, including a six-term state assemblyman, but none refuted the prosecution's evidence.

After five weeks of trial, on the eve of summations, Goldberg was buttonholed by a few kibitzers—reporters and court buffs—as he prepared to leave the courthouse.

"So, what are you going to do, Jay? It doesn't look too good," one of them said.

"You want to know what I'm going to do? I'll tell you what I'm going to do," Goldberg began, setting down his attaché and straightening his jacket and tie, as if preparing for summation. He broke into animated delivery:

"I'm going to grab Tieri by the throat and lift him out of his wheelchair. I'm going to slap him around and toss him on the ground. Then, while he's rolling on the ground—we have this all worked out—I'm going to kick him in the stomach, I'll kick him in the groin, I'll crush the heel of my shoe into his face. And then, I'll turn to the jury and say, 'Ladies and gentlemen of the jury, if this is the *capo di tutti capi,* would I be doing this?' "

Laughter from the assembled group echoed in the corridor as Goldberg smiled, his arms outstretched palms upward, inviting appreciation of his imminent victory.

"But Jay," said an elderly court buff, "you'd be killed for doing something like that."

"Ah, yes," he said, lifting his attaché case and walking down the corridor. "But I'll win the case."

In truth, Goldberg delivered a summation the likes of which is rarely seen; calling it impassioned would be an understatement. It was a performance of such eloquent fury that one could almost lose sight of anything the government had proven.

For nearly two and a half uninterrupted hours Goldberg strutted and stomped, his tall, lean, angular physique dominating every inch of the courtroom as he bent toward the jurors to deliver sarcasm, wagged a long finger at the prosecutors, or pounded his fist on a convenient solid object to emphasize his claims of "tainted testimony" presented by the government's witnesses.

"The critical issue in this case is not if there is a La Cosa Nostra, a Mafia. Maybe there is a Mafia, a La Cosa Nostra," he said with a shrug. "The question is: Does Frank Tieri have any responsibility for the criminal acts outlined in the indictment.

"You might rightly conclude that Frank Tieri is not somebody who you would have admiration for. But you shouldn't decide this case on whether you feel he is a candidate for a civic award."

That was the basic thrust of his delivery. He never once intimated that Tieri was anything but what the government said he was. However, he argued, the jury should also accept the witnesses for what the government concedes they are: gangsters making deals to save their necks.

If there had been any substantial evidence to disprove the government's case, Goldberg would have won on the strength of his summation. As it worked out, after less than one day of deliberations, the jury convicted Tieri on all but the tax evasion charge, which was based on Picardo saying Tieri received $25,000 as a payoff from Korvettes, a department store seeking labor peace with the Teamsters.

In a sentencing memo to Judge Griesa, Akerman claimed the government had substantial information that Tieri had ordered the murder of Philadelphia mob boss Angelo Bruno, in March of 1980, after Bruno opposed the mob's infiltrating Atlantic City's casino industry. Bruno's death sparked a power struggle in that city which continued for years.

In January 1981, Griesa handed down a ten-year prison term, but permitted Tieri to remain free pending appeal.

On April 5, 1981, Tieri died peacefully at Mount Sinai Hospital, casting Paul Castellano unwillingly into the role of senior member of the Commission.

13 *Frontier Justice*

TOM LANG awoke one morning in Fort Lauderdale, Florida, to find he was a millionaire newspaper publisher.

At twenty-three years of age, he was the youngest publisher of a major metropolitan daily in the United States. Hundreds of people were depending upon him for their livelihoods; tens of thousands more were relying upon him as a watchdog of state affairs and events. This was no Kafka-esque dream; it was a matter of sudden inheritance.

Lang had grown into manhood in the mid-1960s with a set of capped teeth as proof of his volatile temper and obstinate will.

He had a cold spark of defiant self-assurance and a voice that ran on in hushed tones, like a steadily burning fuse. He was short on expression, but long on feeling, which he kept hidden behind a shallow mask of stoicism.

His father, the stern, iron-willed publisher and majority owner of the *Albuquerque Journal*, New Mexico's largest newspaper, had understood his eldest son well; requiring that his boy spend every spare moment, outside of school, working at the newspaper plant. He started off cleaning latrines when he was twelve, and by the time he reached his late teens he had worked summers and after school in every aspect of newspaper production.

The boy, a native gringo, born and bred in Albuquerque, was indeed his father's son; he was energetic and hard working, rarely passing the day lazing about in the desert sun.

298

Father and son shared another distinguishing characteristic: They were both intensely private people. As a teenager, a period when most kids travel in large groups sharing secrets and trust almost indiscriminately, Lang was already a loner, counting among his confidants only one person, Augie Seis, an utterly devoted friend.

In most families of such wealth and prestige as Lang's, the children customarily find their way to an Ivy League graduate degree in business or law; perhaps, among the newspaper-owning families, they would remain in the news business, establishing themselves in the advertising side, or working toward a career as a reporter, columnist, or editor. They might even find adventure in seeking out the newest hi-tech frontiers of journalism, such as broadcasting, satellite communications, or computers.

C. Thompson Lang, Tom's father, hoped heavy exposure to the newspaper business would help mold some direction for his roughneck son. He didn't necessarily want Tom to follow him into newspapering, but he wanted him to understand that just because the family had wealth it didn't mean he would never have to earn his keep.

The formula worked. The boy found his area of fascination, his life's passion, right there in the newsplant. It was the presses—those behemoth power plants, whose heavy iron casings and silky-smooth silver cylinders cut, fold, press, and print, weaving abstract thoughts into words on a page, churning out daily reports from around the world at blinding speed.

But Lang's interest in the presses went beyond a fleeting fascination: He had a natural mechanical ability, which enabled him to quickly grasp the workings of those giant machines.

By the time Tom Lang was eighteen, and nearly fully grown into his lanky adult stature—6 feet 2½ inches, with a narrow 190-pound frame—he had, through hard work, achieved two goals: He had an advanced mastery of the *Journal*'s press room, and he had been accepted by everyone, from the newest guy on the loading dock to the *Journal*'s top editors, as "Tom."

Lang's apprenticeship in press operations was disrupted by his efforts at formal education. He spent three uneventful years at the University of New Mexico and then, early in 1970, went to the University of the Americas in Mexico City, where he lasted only a few months, ending his education in a brutal brawl with three local teenagers and a cop—over the honor of several American girls—which landed him in jail.

He returned to Albuquerque days later to work full time for his father, honing his special abilities in newspaper production.

Romantic notions aside, newspapers are in the business of selling a product. They are not, as some may believe, altruistic institutions. Inside a newspaper plant there are two distinctly separate, physically divided worlds: the reporters and editors on one side, and the advertising and production team on the other. When their talents are combined they create a product, and if they're any good at their craft they make money.

Lang chose the production side, the side of the bottom line, where quality is defined by advertising rates and the cost of rolling a paper off the presses, not by the content of the news columns. And he proved he was pretty good at making newspapers and making money.

After returning from Mexico, Lang was loaned to Scripps-Howard Newspapers to assist or direct several production projects, including installation of a new engraving plant in Hollywood, Florida.

Flying between New Mexico, Florida, New York, and California on business that year, he logged more than 200,000 miles on commercial jetliners. He decided that if this was the way he would be spending his work weeks, it was time that the Journal Publishing Company had its own corporate aircraft. So he began flying lessons. Months later, Lang met Ray Hodge, a pilot with a vision for creating tax shelters by investing in commuter airlines. The two men became fast friends and partners.

While in Florida, this desert native became fascinated by the ocean. In what little spare time there was, he began scuba diving, bought a 53-foot cabin cruiser, and soon turned his seaside hobby into a deep-sea salvage business.

He also decided that instead of going out on loan to teach others how to design, manufacture, install, and operate presses, he should launch his own company. And thus, with a $20,000 investment and the assistance of Sandford Walker, a friend he'd made while on the Scripps-Howard project, Masthead was born.

He wanted to be hands-on master of every project he envisioned. He wanted to be the *Journal's* primary pilot. He wanted to design and install the Masthead presses. He wanted to do all the feasibility dives for the salvage business.

In little more than a year after leaving Mexico, Lang had shaped a busy life, criss-crossing the U.S. with a variety of business ventures, learning new skills, and molding a staunchly independent style.

Then, on April 15, 1971, while in Fort Lauderdale with Walker, he got a call from his brother Bill, five years younger than Tom, that their father had died, suddenly. He would have to come home to run the newspaper.

He initially resisted, but ultimately accepted, the mantle of family responsibility.

The young man with the sleepy brown eyes, long dirty blond hair, and thin mustache decided if he had to go home, he would do it on his terms: he wouldn't surrender his outside interests; he would never expose himself to public notoriety; and he would avoid the limelight of New Mexican high society. He would continue to be just Tom. But he also insisted on having full authority and responsibility for the newspaper: he would be named president, chairman of the board, director, and chief executive officer of Journal Publishing Company as well as publisher of the *Journal*.

The *Albuquerque Journal* carried a small obit on C. Thompson Lang's death and never mentioned Thompson H. Lang's succession as head of the family-owned publishing business, valued at more than $100 million.

Don Bolles, the investigative reporter for the *Arizona Republic*, was killed by a car bomb in June 1976. His death sparked national outrage. It was assumed that he had gotten too close to something big.

Investigative Reporters and Editors, Inc., a nationwide organization of journalists, led by Pulitzer Prize–winning editor Bob Greene of *Newsday*, descended on Arizona to finish Bolles's work—if for no other reason than to prove that you can't kill a reporter and walk away clean.

Bill Hume, a reporter from the *Albuquerque Journal*, helped out with information on land fraud schemes in New Mexico and spent six days in January 1977 working at the project headquarters in the Adams Hotel in Phoenix.

After five months, the Phoenix Project, the IRE's team of forty reporters and editors, produced a twenty-six-part series of articles detailing organized crime's relationship with the Southwest. Much of the information was old, most of it was poorly written, and portions were based on less than substantial documentation.

The thrust of its findings was that there existed a network of connections linking Southwestern political and business figures, perhaps unwittingly, with known crime figures. They identified 200 persons in that region of the U.S. with La Cosa Nostra ties. They charged

U.S. Senator Barry Goldwater, his brother Robert, and Arizona GOP chairman Harry Rosenzweig with "condoning the presence of organized crime through friendships and alliances with mob figures." Specifically, they reported, the Goldwaters and Rosenzweig were linked to "a web of relationships in Arizona, Nevada, and California with important lieutenants of underworld financier Meyer Lansky."

The *Journal*, one of four Southwest newspapers sponsoring the investigation, was asked to run the entire series. The articles were more like rough drafts than completed articles; each one needed heavy editing by the newspapers.

Early in 1977, Lang and Hume flew to Phoenix, where they met with Greene. The IRE's 300-pound, gravel-voiced chief editor showed Lang the files and records, allowing him to pull at random and inspect the source documents on which the articles were based.

Lang wanted to believe Greene and the work his team had produced. Although he generally stood clear of imposing editorial philosophy, Lang believed newspapers had a singular responsibility to expose corruption—another quality he had shared with his father.

After hours of poring through the Phoenix Project files he and Hume flew out of Phoenix. Lang was excited. He let Hume pilot the Learjet while he puffed on his corncob pipe, talking incessantly in his soft, near-whisper of a voice. He was impressed with the files. He wanted to run the series. The only question was how to do it without exposing everyone involved to libel suits.

At home that evening, he called his friends: Augie Seis, Walker, and Hodge. He never mentioned the Phoenix Project. He went out to tinker with his growing fleet of cars, which at one time included a Rolls-Royce, Ferrari, Porsche, and Jeep.

After dinner, he stuffed his pipe and made a round of calls to the *Journal*'s board of directors, setting a board meeting for the next morning.

When the board members gathered at the *Journal*'s red-brick downtown offices, Lang sat at the head of the table in his customary open-collar sports shirt, his long legs propped up on the table, looking out on the collection of blue suits. As majority shareholder, Lang dissolved the board. He told them about the Phoenix Project and that he was assuming full responsibility for a unilateral decision to run the series. He then reinstated the board, asking anyone who disagreed with his decision to resign. No one took him up on the offer. The group was dismissed before he called Bob Brown, the *Journal*'s editor, to tell him of his assignment to rewrite the Phoenix Project articles so they were readable, accurate, and highlighted New Mexico's problems.

ORGANIZED CRIME SHOWING INTEREST IN NEW MEXICO read the headline, running across the bottom of page one on March 26, 1977.

There was no byline to the lengthy story—just a line saying "Another in a Series," and the "IRE's Phoenix Project" logo written in a 2-inch deep, by one-column wide, box. There was no need to explain to anyone in the Southwest what the Phoenix Project was—it had become as well known in the region as Watergate had been years earlier.

The story began:

The black hats no longer arrive at the American frontier on the afternoon stage. They come in shiny jets and stolen garbage trucks.

They come as scouts for modern-day organized crime, as fast-buck artists taking advantage of lax supervision by public officials, and as profit-taking speculators with visions of money to be made in the wide open spaces. . . .

The IRE investigation shows that gangland figures are still wending their way into New Mexico from East and West.

Some of those who have been in and out have established contacts with prominent figures close to the levers of power. Fast-buck artists have worked with and met with various attorneys, including some known to have political clout. . . .

On the jump page, where the story continued inside the paper, the reader's attention was grabbed by a photograph, 4 inches deep and two columns wide, of a broadly smiling Billy Marchiondo playing cards. The caption read: "William Marchiondo During 1976 Legislature, Attorney Well Known to State's Lawmakers."

The article didn't get around to explaining who Marchiondo was until the last element of the story, after about 2,000 words describing a series of mob-land transactions, mob-backed corporations and schemes, none of which involved Marchiondo.

IRE reporters, after visiting New Mexico, quoted law enforcement sources as saying that James Napoli, described in 1974 as the director of the largest gambling operation in New York City, flew into Albuquerque in 1972 and visited with William Marchiondo, Albuquerque defense lawyer, and former New Mexico attorney general Boston Witt. They noted that Marchiondo is a close friend of Gov. Jerry Apodaca, a fact which neither Marchiondo nor Apodaca have sought to hide. . . .

Asked about his friendship with Napoli, he [Marchiondo] said: "James

Napoli is a good friend of mine. Are you saying he is with organized crime? I know Jimmy Napoli very well, his wife, his children. To me he's a beautiful person."

He said he first met Napoli after Napoli's son Anthony was accused of armed robbery, and Napoli asked Marchiondo to represent him. . . .

From the time he defended his son, said the attorney, "He [James Napoli] and I have become very close friends. I do some work for him." . . .

Unfortunately, Napoli hasn't been painted over the years as the "beautiful person" described by Marchiondo. New York newspapers have described him as . . . "The Mr. Big" of the Cosa Nostra's East Coast gambling empire.

This wasn't the first time Marchiondo, a prominent criminal defense attorney with an outstanding record of acquittals, had been the target of a less than flattering *Journal* article. He had filed libel charges against the paper in 1974 for a paid political ad and an editorial column on then-gubernatorial candidate Apodaca, which mentioned Marchiondo as a political wheeler-dealer and close friend of the later-victorious Democratic candidate.

In his interview with IRE, Marchiondo said he was never associated with people that are connected with organized crime, denied he has any political power or clout in New Mexico, and reminded reporters that he has a lawsuit pending against the *Journal* for "claiming I was an influential person and I am not."

Marchiondo, then forty-nine, wasn't going to allow this latest guilt-by-association slur on his reputation go unchallenged. He was convinced that the IRE had been put up to doing the interview by Lang and the *Journal*—that he'd been set up. In what eventually amounted to a $17 million libel suit, Marchiondo charged Lang, the *Journal*, and editor Robert Brown with malicious and reckless disregard for the truth. He never charged any error in the facts of the story; he later conceded that the words in the story were accurate. Rather, he claimed his reputation had been damaged and his business suffered as a result of his photo being placed directly beneath the jump-page headline: ORGANIZED CRIME SHOWING INTEREST IN NEW MEXICO.

Lang had anticipated no less. He was convinced from the moment he saw the first drafts of the IRE story, which carried the Marchiondo interview, that the article was bound to land him in court. The IRE documents he had scrutinized most carefully in Phoenix were the police surveillance reports of Marchiondo with Napoli, and those describing Napoli's reputation as New York's top mob bookmaker.

He had also reviewed transcripts of the IRE's Marchiondo interview, conducted at the instruction of Greene by IRE reporters Myrta Pulliam and John Rawlinson. Lang was bothered by Marchiondo's view, expressed in those interviews, that he was, as a result of his earlier libel suits, being treated with deference by the press: "They . . . don't ask me any more questions. Whereas before they hounded me to death. . . . That's one of the benefits" of the lawsuit, he told Pulliam and Rawlinson.

Lang would be damned if he would ever compromise the paper's ability to speak freely. Nor would he back down from a good fight. There would be no "chilling effect"—the phenomenon of journalists not reporting a story for fear of lawsuits—at Tom Lang's newspaper.

Lang met with Eric Lanphere and Jim Dines of Johnson and Lanphere, the *Journal's* attorneys. Lanphere, a cautious man, warned Lang of the potential cost in time and money, as well as personal commitment. Such a suit, he said, would certainly expose Lang to public scrutiny; he'd be forced to surrender his penchant for anonymity in the community. There were ways, and there would be opportunities, to settle the suit out of court, Lanphere suggested.

But Lang would have none of it; if need be, the Journal Publishing Company would turn all of its resources toward investigating and exposing corruption in the Southwest. The hardest part of his decision was whether to abandon his reclusiveness—and even that was worth losing for this cause. He demanded that they win the case, or at the very least make sure that Marchiondo knew he had been in a good fight.

As Lang ran headlong into the libel battle, the Bolles murder was resolved. As it turned out, the case had almost nothing to do with La Cosa Nostra.

John Harvey Adamson had been picked up by police and entered into a plea bargain: admitting complicity in the Bolles murder and agreeing to testify against others in return for a twenty-year prison term.

Adamson testified that he had been hired along with Max Dunlap and James Robinson to murder not only Bolles, but also Bruce Babbitt, at that time the state's attorney general, and Alex Lizanetz, a local advertising executive. He said they had been hired for the murders by wealthy Phoenix liquor wholesaler Kemper Marley, Sr., who reportedly was linked to organized crime and who Bolles had denounced as a less-than-wholesome businessman.

Dunlap and Robinson were convicted, but later had their convictions overturned. When Adamson refused to testify at a retrial, he was prosecuted for the murder, convicted, and sentenced to death. Marley was never prosecuted.

By 1980, Lanphere and Dines were spending Lang's money—a large portion of it insurance funds—at a remarkable pace in defense of the libel suit.

The two attorneys, accomplished at corporate law, had never been involved in a libel case and had virtually no knowledge of organized crime. They were hiring outside counsel and private investigators, and traveling throughout the U.S. on research or for depositions.

Jack Barron, retired from the FBI, was hired for a brief time, as was Phil Fox, who directed some organized crime aspects of the case. John "Pete" Donohue, a rough-and-tumble ex-New York State police undercover detective, became the *Journal*'s chief investigator.

Donohue had retired from New York in 1976, amassing a unique knowledge of the Southwest in a short period of time, working first as a Nevada Gaming Board investigator, followed by stints as the chief investigator for both the New Mexico governor's Organized Crime Prevention Commission and the New Mexico attorney general's Organized Crime and Narcotics Strike Force. He quit all three jobs in disgust, convinced that the Southwest was suffering from institutionalized corruption. He took the *Journal* job only after receiving Lang's assurances that he would have a free hand.

With Donohue's knowledge of where to search, Lang mounted several legal battles, establishing a short-lived precedent, enabling the paper to gain access to wiretapped conversations in which Marchiondo spoke to Napoli, Fratianno, and others.

At the same time, Lang encouraged Hume to turn his attention to being a full-time investigative reporter, becoming the first reporter in the nation to reveal Alfa Chemical Company's links to organized crime—and its network of conspiracies in San Diego, Las Vegas, San Francisco, Los Angeles, Albuquerque, and New York. The Alfa case also gave Hume leads to connections between Marchiondo and Irving "Slick Jack" Shapiro, Anthony "Tony the Ant" Spilotro, Anthony "Tony Dope" DelSanter, Greg DePalma, and of course, common to each of them, Fratianno.

But Hume's success led to his being silenced. Fearing further libel action, Hume was assigned to work full time with Lanphere and Dines in preparing the case. A chilling effect had begun to take hold.

The growing reservoir of information collected for the libel suit needed a home. So Lang created "the Bunker," an unmarked store-front on a dead-end street, within walking distance of Lang's office. There, Donohue made his headquarters with several assistant investigators and deposited the files—wiretaps, videotapes, trial transcripts, FBI reports, affidavits, and depositions—in a 12-by-15-foot fireproof vault.

What Lang, the *Journal*, its lawyers and investigators were seeking was proof of mob incursions into the Southwest. In many instances these would be matters of guilt by association, generally regarded as repugnant forms of character assassination. However, what they intended to prove was that through those associations the mob gains a foothold in a community, eventually enabling them to corrupt legitimate businesses and government.

The *Journal's* IRE article had only suggested that Marchiondo "may have unwittingly fallen under some mobsters' spell"; it never accused him of criminal activity. But pushed to defend themselves, the paper now believed they had evidence that Marchiondo may have consciously played ball with these people.

Lang began to envision himself as the lone white hat on the wild west frontier, the guardian of Albuquerque, a burgeoning town, which was welcoming a dozen new settlers every day in the late 1970s and early 1980s. If the newspaper could not print the stories, if indeed a chilling effect was taking hold of his newspaper, Lang was determined to use the *Journal's* resources to expose in court the corruption they had found.

Lang took what he regarded as practical precautions—installing bullet-proof glass in his second-floor office, and a sophisticated alarm system at his home—and redoubled his efforts in the lawsuit.

Lang found his life had gradually become absorbed in defense of the lawsuit; it had become a cause of such intensity that it consumed him full time, distracting him from the newspaper and his other projects.

The salvage business had been jettisoned because it was too time intensive; Hodge had died in a plane crash, bringing an end to the tax shelter project; Seis had died suddenly in such a manner that Lang later couldn't even discuss it; and while Lang's Masthead press design and installation project continued, it had been crippled. Walker had called one day in 1980 from a pay phone at Chicago's O'Hare Airport to tell Lang that they faced heavy competition in bids to renovate the *Chicago Tribune's* presses. Moments after Lang hung up the phone, Walker died in the phone booth from heart failure.

Lanphere, a soft-spoken man, urged Lang to find some distraction from the libel suit, saying it was consuming him. He wondered if Lang had any friends, confidants he could turn to.

"They're all dead," Lang said without hesitation or expression. "My father, my friends—they're all dead. There's only me and my brother."

Lanphere, whose sensitivity could have made him a candidate for the ministry, urged Lang to find an outlet, a friend or confidant. Lang eventually found someone. He married Lanphere's stepdaughter, Kimberly.

In the marshals' windowless Potomac River hideout they silently sipped coffee from Styrofoam cups and waited as Jimmy, seemingly oblivious to his visitors, lectured Jean over the phone.

Lanphere was seated on an old, government-issue, oak swivel chair, which sent up piercing squeaks and creaks at the slightest shift in body weight, breaking into Jimmy's conversation.

Lanphere wanted to become invisible—and not solely to escape the embarrassing chair. This was a treacherous business, dealing with a La Cosa Nostra killer. He wanted to skip the formalities of introductions so they could get on with the interview he, Dines, Fox, Hume, and Lang had crossed the United States to conduct. Instead, he sat in near-motionless contemplation of how one behaves with a confessed murderer: Do you observe the customary social amenities? Do you—must you—shake hands?

But Jimmy was in his element, arguing with Jean and sizing up his company as he fingered an expensive cigar, which filled the small room with ribbons of smoke.

This was Jimmy's first foray in the world of civil suits. The government was good for protection—from the bad guys and prosecution. But these libel defendants—Lang, Newt's cases for the *Sacramento Bee*, and other newspapers and magazines—might be willing to pay him large sums for his recollections.

As Thanksgiving approached, Jimmy's life had reached a turning point. Completion of the Tieri trial a few weeks earlier had marked the end of his primary obligations to the government. And with the anticipated release of *The Last Mafioso* that spring, he had recently gone public, conducting interviews with *Newsweek*, "20/20," Mike Wallace of "60 Minutes," and now meetings on private cases.

While there was still some work to be done for the government, it was time for Jimmy to cut his final deal with WITSEC. During days of contentious meetings with Safir, Jimmy had increased his already lofty demands for funding and care, rejecting several sites for relocation as inadequate or because they were in areas controlled by La Cosa Nostra families, such as Northern Florida. It was eventually agreed that they could continue working on the deal while he wintered in the Caribbean with Jean.

Few things in life frightened Jimmy Fratianno, but he was scared to death of settling down with Jean. He told her it was for their safety that he kept away from her while testifying; he insisted that her inability to remain mum to friends and family about who he was and where he was endangered their lives. But the truth had more to do with his inability to settle in a traditional relationship; twenty years in prison can do that to a man, destroy his ability to live within any kind of confinement or without wild bursts of independence.

As the Albuquerque crew sat by, toying with their now-empty coffee cups, Jimmy told Jean she had to move again. And she was insisting that she wanted to settle in Denton, Texas, where Safir had moved her after North Carolina's dampness aggravated her asthma. Jean had reached the part in her argument where she invoked God in her demands for Jimmy to settle down and live "like a normal person" when he cut her off, insisting he had business waiting.

Jimmy set down the phone and, without a moment's hesitation, turned to charming his company. He had been studying the situation and understood the need to put everyone, especially Lanphere, at ease. He addressed himself almost exclusively to Lang and Lanphere, recalling his fondest memories of Albuquerque and inviting them to inspect a diamond he had set in a ring for Jean.

In short order, Lanphere found himself at ease in Jimmy's company, but insisted on calling him "Mr. Fratianno."

As Lanphere began his questioning, he hardly knew the depths of Jimmy's knowledge. From Hume's investigative reporting, and the New York, Los Angeles, and San Francisco trials in which Fratianno had testified, they knew Jimmy could connect Marchiondo to Shapiro, Marson, and Spilotro—the mob directors of Alfa and Star Glo.

The first order of business was to assure that Marchiondo knew who Jimmy was. In an earlier deposition, Marchiondo had insisted he had known Fratianno as "Jimmy Fratello," who he believed to be a California vineyard owner.

"The closest I ever came to owning a vineyard is that I planted a couple guys in a vineyard once," he said, laughing.

Realizing that Lanphere was not amused Jimmy straightened up, explaining that he had met Marchiondo at Marson's home, where he was introduced as "Jimmy Fratianno," and that Marson had made it clear that Jimmy "was calling the shots" in California—a reference to his post as acting boss in L.A. at the time.

He described occasions when Marchiondo had introduced him around in Albuquerque by his proper name and discussions they had about La Cosa Nostra figures, including Tieri's eventual successor, Fat Tony Salerno, whom Marchiondo claimed to have met. And, he said, Marchiondo had asked him once to "ask the people in New York" for money to finance a Las Vegas casino Marchiondo wanted to build.

Jimmy also described how he had introduced Jackie Presser to Marchiondo after Presser expressed an interest in finding someone with contacts in the Carter White House.

On one occasion, Jimmy said, he had visited Marchiondo's office when former U.S. Senator Joseph Montoya telephoned to ask about a judicial appointment: "And while I'm sitting there Billy picks up the phone and calls the governor, tellin' him to hold off on this appointment until they could get together and talk about it."

"Why would Marchiondo have any control over a judicial appointment?" Dines asked.

"Hey listen, Billy must've told me like a dozen times that he's the one got Jerry Apodaca elected governor and that Apodaca owed him a favor," Fratianno said.

Dines and Lanphere weren't taking Jimmy's tales at face value. They tried throwing him some curves, making up stories about evidence they had showing Marchiondo was involved in smuggling and land fraud schemes. It would have been easy for Jimmy to go along. But he denied any knowledge of it—insisting, in fact, that it was impossible: "Anything illegal this guy was involved in I would have known about; I think you got some bad information."

There was one story that left Lanphere in wide-eyed amazement:

"Marchiondo introduced me to this friend of his, Torres, Val Torres. So this guy had a beef over some business deal in San Francisco. Well, Marchiondo asked if I could help this guy out and I said 'sure.' "

"What do you mean by helping him out? What did they want?" Lanphere asked.

"They wanted me to break both this guy's legs. And I told Torres I had a guy who worked for me who'd take care of it—Skinny Velotta.

In fact, we talked about it on the phone a couple times; it's in one of them wiretaps you showed me before, the one where Marchiondo complains that it was taking me a long time to get this thing done for him; that's what he was getting at, without really saying it flat out."

After a pause, Dines picked up the conversation. "Did you or this friend of yours ever complete the task?"

"I don't know. I got pinched before we ever got around to it."

When it was all over, Lanphere was exhausted and Dines exhilarated by the extent of Jimmy's information.

While their notes were being typed—as an affidavit that Jimmy signed—Lanphere reviewed their agreement. Jimmy would be paid $250 an hour for his preparation and testimony—in recognition of his unique expertise—but only if the New Mexico courts qualified him as an expert witness.

"Sure. But you guys remember, when the time comes, you got to videotape my deposition. Fox tells me it could take years to get to trial, and by that time I'm gonna be livin' outta the country."

As they left—Lanphere avoiding shaking hands—Jimmy headed for St. Thomas while the others headed back to New Mexico.

A rapport had been established. Yet they were all perplexed by Jimmy's willingness, apparent eagerness, to testify against his erstwhile friend. They couldn't have understood Jimmy's overriding view that money is the root-purpose to life; it was what guided his involvement in La Cosa Nostra, and now his membership in that organization enabled him to speak with authority in return for protection and profit. In Jimmy's view, friendship aside, he had to survive, even if the truth sometimes hurt.

"But I really don't care what his motivation is at this point," Dines said as they flew out of Washington. "We finally have someone inside this thing to tell us the truth in this damned lawsuit. I'm convinced he's a straight shooter. . . . And could you believe the way he just sat there taking questions? I mean, he's tireless."

Lanphere listened and nodded, but was caught up in his own thoughts, until Lang pulled him up short.

"Eric, you okay? Is there a problem with Fratianno or his testimony?"

"I'm just kind of disturbed. I don't know, Tom," Lanphere said, slowly beginning to sort things out. "I guess what it comes down to is, we've spent the last ten hours with a man telling us lurid tales of how he snuffed out lives, extorted people, pornography—all of it—very candidly, without particular emotion."

"Yeah, so? You don't believe him or what?" Dines asked.

"No. I certainly believe him. I guess I'm bothered because I like him. He's really charismatic, kinda engaging, you know? And I'm fighting myself about it. I feel my reaction should be revulsion. I don't like myself for liking him."

On January 8, 1981, two marshals pulled up in a dark blue Chrysler outside the Bonaventure Hotel in Los Angeles to pick up Lanphere, Dines, Fox, and Hume. They'd been instructed to wait for the car. They were to be taken to an undisclosed location for the deposition.

They were frisked. Their attachés were searched thoroughly—for weapons, bugs, or transmitters—before being placed in the trunk of the car with the marshals' shotguns.

Throughout the next two days, as the *Journal* and Marchiondo's lawyer, F. Lee Bailey, conducted an exhaustive deposition of Jimmy, there was intense security and a constant show of armed force.

The lawyers were instructed ahead of time: There would be no leaving the location once the deposition began; they would change the location each day; if they went to the bathroom they would have to be escorted; guards armed with shotguns and automatic weapons would be stationed at the doorways.

None of the same precautions had been taken when the *Journal* staff met Jimmy, nor had there been anything quite so elaborate for his meetings with "60 Minutes," "20/20," or *Newsweek*. The clear implication was that the marshals regarded Marchiondo's presence as dangerous, and everyone was being treated with equal scrutiny.

The marshals had received word from the FBI at that point that Tony Spilotro, the Chicago Family's point man in Las Vegas, was carrying the contract on Jimmy's life. Weeks earlier, a microphone in the ceiling of Spilotro's jewelry shop, The Gold Rush, had picked up a conversation which was interpreted as a plot to use a sniper to kill Jimmy. And it was no secret that the U.S. Marshals and the FBI, along with Fratianno and the lawyers for the *Journal*, believed that Marchiondo was an associate of Spilotro and Shapiro.

The adversaries were taken to Henderson's strike force office for the deposition, where they gathered around a new library conference table. There was no judge present; the court would decide later what portions of the videotape could be presented at trial. Until then, the deposition would be a no-holds-barred affair, permitting the kind of verbal assaults on which Bailey had built his reputation.

There already had been years of pretrial action, but this was Bailey's first appearance for his friend Marchiondo. He wasted no time in challenging the simplest issues—where should the cameras be placed, could they be shut off for lunch, and what were McDonald's or Fox's roles—evoking the same attitude from Lanphere.

It was a posture Bailey was almost obligated to assume, for he carries the reputation as certainly the best-known and, indeed, one of the best lawyers in the United States. That reputation can cut two ways: like the old wild west gunslinger, it intimidates some, but also makes him a desirable target for others. So it seems almost his burden to come out shooting, aggressive at all times to keep his adversaries in check.

The bulk of the first day was devoted to Jimmy answering Lanphere's questions, fleshing out the material contained in his November affidavit.

He answered questions slowly, deliberately, and constantly through fourteen hours of testimony, during which he would puff on a cigar a few times or roll it in his fingers until it went out and he'd have to relight it.

Given any opportunity at all, he'd flirt with the stenographer, seated to his left, a tall, slender, striking woman in her late twenties with a mane of blonde hair cascading down to her waist. She smiled timidly, yet politely, when Jimmy asked if she wanted to meet him for a drink sometime.

Jimmy repeated his claim that Marchiondo knew exactly who he was. He said he had been to Albuquerque twice to visit Marchiondo and that Marchiondo had come to visit him in San Francisco on at least two occasions. He regarded them as friends.

Of La Cosa Nostra business interests, he said, "They use a lot of legitimate people—they use front men . . . to put something in their name. I'd say ninety-five percent of the time they never put anything in their names."

He described Alfa Chemical Company of Las Vegas as one such business. "When it was formed Irving Shapiro had twenty percent, Tony Spilotro had twenty percent, Al Barron [an acquaintance] had twenty percent, the chemist had twenty percent, and Frank Bompensiero and myself had twenty percent."

Later, he said, a second Alfa was created, this one in New Mexico.

"I don't know what name they put it under . . . at that time Tony Spilotro and Al Barron pulled out, and Billy Marchiondo was going to have a percentage of it," Fratianno said, grinning broadly at Marchiondo.

Q. Did you discuss this with Mr. Marchiondo?
A. Yes, sir. Well, he told me they were going to get some state contracts.
Q. Did he indicate to you how he was going to get state contracts?
A. He was going to get them through Jerry Apodaca, governor of New Mexico.

He said that Marchiondo had once told him that his dear friend Jimmy Napoli was "with Salerno," and that "Salerno was with Tieri."

He said that Marchiondo "told me they [Marchiondo and Napoli] own some property together and that they own a restaurant together in Palm Springs."

Demonstrating the extension of power through mob connections, Jimmy described his introduction of Presser to Marchiondo:

FRATIANNO: Jackie Presser wanted to get to somebody that had some clout with the Carter administration and I told him I had an attorney that was a friend of mine in New Mexico . . . and I talked to Billy Marchiondo about it and he says he'd like to be with the Teamsters, more or less represent them, and I got him together with Jackie Presser. And they talked on the phone and what happened, I don't know.

Q. What led you to state to Mr. Presser that Mr. Marchiondo had clout with the Carter administration?
A. Well, he told me they backed Carter in the presidential election and they [Carter's people] owed him a favor.
Q. What is Mr. Presser's relationship to La Cosa Nostra?
A. Well, he's very close with them, sir. With the Cleveland Family. He don't do anything unless the boss of the Cleveland Family gives the okay—James Licavoli. Jackie told me. He said, "I can't make a move unless he tells me." . . . Every time I wanted to see Jackie Presser I would see Jack White [Licavoli] or Tony Dope, the *consigliere* or the underboss, and they would make arrangements for me to meet him.

They run Jackie Presser, period. I know it and they know it.

Later he said Marchiondo became the principal promoter in Star Glo. He said Marchiondo told him he was going to Chicago to see Allen Dorfman, director of the Teamsters Central States Pension Fund, and Joey Lombardo, a *capo* in the Chicago Family, to raise $200,000 for the company.

And he described Marchiondo's offer to assist Benny Benjamin, a friend of Jimmy's, in incorporating a home siding business, which he told Marchiondo would be used as a front for bookmaking and loan-sharking.

There were a host of other questions about bit players, hoods and businessmen whom Jimmy had met through or introduced to Marchiondo; further reinforcing the general thrust of his testimony that Marchiondo was being used, intentionally or unwittingly, as the front man for the mob's incursion into New Mexico.

Lanphere had earlier established Jimmy's credentials as an expert witness: thirty-two years in La Cosa Nostra, one who had attained the rank of *capo* and acting boss, and the only person other than Valachi to defect from the Family. Now he was prepared to elicit Fratianno's views as an expert on organized crime.

"Before you ask any questions," Bailey broke in, "we object to the ludicrous notion that a professional killer can qualify as an expert witness in any court in the United States, or that there is such an expertise as expert criminal."

Lanphere noted the objection and proceeded without comment.

Q. As of March 26, 1977, was organized crime showing an interest in New Mexico?

A. Yes, sir . . . there has been people interested in New Mexico. The Chicago Family had a plastics company in New Mexico with Spilotro, Lombardo, and some others. I had an interest with Benny Benjamin.

Q. Who did you work through to demonstrate your interest in New Mexico?

A. Through Billy Marchiondo.

Q. Do you have an opinion: March 26, 1977, the *Albuquerque Journal* reported a headline, "Organized Crime Showing Interest in New Mexico."

A. It was true, sir. I was interested in it, Spilotro was interested in coming into New Mexico with Lombardo and Dorfman.

Q. Do you have an opinion if in March 1977 William Marchiondo had knowledge of an interest of any member of La Cosa Nostra in New Mexico?

A. Yes, sir. Well, he had knowledge that I was going to be interested in something and he also had knowledge of Alfa Chemical.

Q. Do you have an opinion if in March 1977 William Marchiondo could properly be described as associated with organized crime.

A. Yes. I would say he was associated with organized crime.

Q. Do you have an opinion if in March 1977 or prior thereto the relationship of William C. Marchiondo to organized crime was limited to that of an attorney representing a client?

A. Yes, I do. I would say it ain't a lawyer-client relationship, sir.

Q. Do you have an opinion as to what the relationship would be?

A. A partnership.

Q. Do you have an opinion, sir, whether the residents of the state of New Mexico have an interest in keeping murderers, extortionists, shylocks, gamblers, pornographers, and racketeers out of their state, whether they should want to keep La Cosa Nostra out of their state.

A. I would say they should want to keep them out.

The last question and answer sent Bailey into pronounced, almost exaggerated, fits of laughter, which came to an abrupt gagging halt on the next question.

Q. Do you have an opinion, Mr. Fratianno, if one of the practices of organized crime has been to file libel suits against newspapers or magazines who attempt to publicize the activities of organized crime?

A. Sir, they do file libel suits against newspapers and magazines—I filed a libel suit against *Penthouse* . . . I know a few people filed libel suits against newspapers in Las Vegas.

Q. Do you have an opinion, Mr. Fratianno, whether one of the normal and ordinary methods of operation of La Cosa Nostra is to try to obtain political influence in a community in which it becomes interested?

A. Yes. My opinion is that's the first thing they try to do is get somebody with some connection to law enforcement so they can operate.

Lanphere wrapped up his questions by reviewing Jimmy's accounts of how he had spent approximately ninety hours preparing for this deposition.

"You're hoping, Mr. Fratianno, to get paid twenty-five grand for this participation, right?" Bailey said in his opening assault, verbally leaping across the table at Jimmy, his voice dripping with sarcasm.

"Yes, sir," was about all Jimmy could muster before Bailey jumped in with another question.

"Have you ever legitimately earned that much money?"

"Yes, I have, sir."

Bailey asked if Jimmy knew that that was more money than was being paid to the *Journal* lawyers on an hourly fee basis; more than any expert witness has ever been paid in the history of U.S. courts. Jimmy couldn't answer, he wasn't given time; Bailey wasn't questioning the witness, he was scolding, attacking Jimmy's existence in those proceedings, apparently hoping some of his indignation would rub off when the jury saw the video.

Bailey's spitfire responses, trigger-fast mind, and bombastic voice modulations made a dramatic contrast to Lanphere's hypnotically gentle voice and slow delivery.

"Talk a little slower, sir," Jimmy said, holding up a hand in a stop gesture and smiling genteelly.

"You're having a little difficulty keeping up with me," Bailey said in a sneering, patronizing manner.

"Yes, I do, sir," Jimmy said, dropping his voice to an even softer volume.

"Do I understand that you read slowly and you comprehend slowly," Bailey said, referring to some earlier testimony in which Jimmy had complained of difficulty in reading a document.

"I have one eye because of cataracts, sir."

"And are you using your eye to follow my voice?" he asked.

"No, sir. I have a little trouble hearing, too."

Jimmy was absolutely unruffled.

Next Bailey attacked Jimmy's demeanor, suggesting he normally isn't as "affable" a personality as he appeared. When Jimmy said he didn't know the meaning of the word, Bailey took time once more to try getting under his skin.

"You think 'affable' is a lawyer's word?"

"It's a pretty big word, sir," Jimmy said with a smile.

Again, Jimmy was unruffled, but Bailey was beginning to appear unfairly critical. The tactic might work on some witnesses, but here it was falling flat. Bailey was making an error if he thought Jimmy Fratianno was the kind to show his temper quite so easily.

Bailey continued his badgering while turning his attention to hard facts: the murders.

Q. Now Mr. Fratianno, I'd like you to share with us some of your experiences in killing other people. Because, you understand, the type of person you are is now relevant to the jury which will decide this case, don't you?

A. Yes, I do, sir.

Q. You've been sitting here all day referring to counsel as 'sir' and being polite and affable—even if you don't understand that word—

A. I still don't know the meaning of the word.

Q. You know it means pleasant.

A. You just told me that, sir.

Q. You've been trying to demonstrate a pleasant personality?

A. I'm a pleasant person, sir.

Q. You are?

A. That's right, sir.

Q. You are? You only killed nine people and you're a pleasant person?
A. That doesn't mean I'm not a pleasant person.
Q. Oh, I see, you're a pleasant killer; is that it?
A. I say I'm a pleasant person—that has nothing to do with what I've done in the past.

Bailey's voice dropped suddenly from its agitated state to harder, less excited, more businesslike tones. "Okay, let's talk about murder. When was the first one?"

They rattled through the murders, though with some difficulty, as Jimmy was unable to place them in chronological order, which offered grist for Bailey's righteous indignation: "You can't remember?"

Bailey went on to make his point: Jimmy Fratianno was a killer, a bookmaker, an extortionist—he did his jobs, went home to his wife, ate a hearty dinner, and slept well.

But, Bailey challenged, were all those murders committed on orders? Hadn't he once threatened to kill a man who failed to pay a debt to him?

"When someone owes you money you're subject to say anything," Jimmy said in his defense.

Sure, he had threatened to kill the guy—Jimmy had put $5,000 into an oil exploration project in 1954 and when the explorers hit oil, they turned swindlers and refused to pay up. He called them on the phone and in midsentence realized there was something wrong with the conversation, the questions being asked didn't ring true—he had fallen into a trap, his call was being wiretapped.

"Were you scared?"

"Well, I wasn't scared. But I had a hunch the phone was tapped."

"Were you shaking in your boots . . . did you have to hold on to the phone booth for support?" Bailey asked, his voice again hostile.

"No, I didn't, sir. What are you talking about?"

"Did you ever tell anyone about the incident and tell them you were so scared that you had to hold on to the telephone for support?"

Jimmy was perplexed. He said repeatedly, "I don't recall that," and Bailey kept pressing with the question "Is that a false statement?"

Bailey ended the day with one more attack, asking if Jimmy thought he resembled a weasel.

The second day brought no change.

Bailey was shaping a line of questions to demonstrate that Fratianno was driven all his life by money and was willing to cheat, lie, or kill for financial gain. He asked about the fee Jimmy was promised if he qualified as an expert witness and suggested that he was banking on the judge agreeing he was an expert.

"I think I am an expert witness; I'm not taking too much of a chance," Jimmy said, filled with early morning energy and enthusiasm for a good fight. "And if he don't, I just shot a deuce, craps, you got that, sir. I shot craps."

"So you're here rolling the dice. Is that about fair?"

"That's correct, sir," Jimmy said, staring and chuckling at Bailey, his arms outstretched in a gesture of openness. "I gambled all my life, sir."

"And you're gambling now, during this testimony against Billy Marchiondo, [that] you're probably going to get 25,000 bucks. Right?"

"I'm just here telling the truth of what—"

Bailey broke in, scolding, "Oh, please don't give a lecture. Are you here today gambling that you'll get $25,000?"

"I'm here hoping the judge will say I'm an expert witness."

"And if you thought the judge would say you were not an expert witness you would not be here testifying?"

"That's correct, sir."

Bailey was unrelenting in his theme: lies for money.

He asked about *The Last Mafioso*—due for release in three weeks—how accurate is it? How many lies had he told Demaris in their taped conversations?

Q. Have you seen the book?
A. Yes, sir. But I've never read it.
Q. Do you know whether the book is accurate?
A. As far as my knowledge, it's accurate, sir. I don't say the book, but my tapes. He's got things in that book, other information he's gathered, sir. It's not only what I told him. . . . He has the authority to write it the way he wants.
Q. He has no obligation to write it the way you told it to him?
A. He has an obligation, sir. Anything significant, in regards to La Cosa Nostra. The only thing is that he more or less might dramatize it. Just like an attorney or yourself in front of a jury dramatize things. Okay?
Q. Okay.

The best-known lawyer in the United States and the best-known witness in the United States continued to dance around beneath the ever-watchful eyes of the *Journal*'s lawyers, a snickering Billy Marchiondo, and several heavily armed marshals.

Bailey badgered Jimmy about the book's lack of accuracy; the dramatization. And Jimmy argued right back. At this rate, both men would be exhausted by lunch.

Jimmy said he had wondered about the questions Bailey had asked the day before about the oil swindle and his "shaking in his boots." So he had called Demaris that evening to ask what he'd written in the book.

Bailey's voice suddenly dropped low as Jimmy became agitated.

Q. How did you know that came from Demaris?

A. Because he told me. I told you I asked him. I says, "Mr. Dem—" I says, "Ovid, what did you put in the book with regards to my calls to Terry?" And he told me.

Q. Yeah.

A. I says, "How come you did that?" I knew right then and there that you read the book and you're taking it out of the book.

Q. How did you know? You say you've never seen the book?

A. Oh, my God. Because he told me what you told me.

Q. How did you know to call Demaris in the first place?

A. Because I had a hunch that that's what you were doing.

Q. Oh.

A. You thought you were slick.

Jimmy was beside himself with joy, shifting in his seat and chuckling, feeling he had just outgunned Bailey.

Bailey's voice dropped softly as he inquired, amid Jimmy's laughter, "Mr. Fratianno, what gave you the clue that I was using the book as a source? Did your lawyer tell you?"

Jimmy stepped down hard on the last vowel of Bailey's question, switching suddenly from laughter to severity. Leaning forward across the conference table, he said with a chilling, brittle voice, "My intuition, sir. My intuition.

"I never checked with Mr. McDonald. My intuition told me that's what you were doing and I checked on you and you got caught. You got caught," he said, again feeling triumphant and starting to laugh.

Apparently rattled, Bailey sheepishly replied, mispronouncing Jimmy's name, "Mr. Fratiello, maybe it was you who got caught."

"No, I haven't, sir," Jimmy shot back.

"But you admit that story in the book is not the truth?"

"It's an exaggeration, sir," Jimmy said in disgust.

Jimmy was right; Bailey had been caught. *The Last Mafioso* was only that week trickling into bookstores. Bailey had obtained a copy of the galleys and hoped to string Jimmy along as long as he could, seeking inconsistencies of any kind to question Jimmy's veracity.

Reading from the galleys, which were now placed in front of him, Bailey continued. In response to most questions, Jimmy suggested that Bailey should subpoena Demaris or the tapes or both, "because I didn't write that book."

Q. You know a Joseph Alioto?
A. Yes, sir.
Q. Did you make this statement to Joseph Alioto: "Joe, you know, maybe I should have been a lawyer. I know how to handle myself in a courtroom. A lawyer told me one time that I was a spellbinder."
A. I'm going to give you the same answer. I don't recall everything that was said in that book. I might have said that.
Q. Do you consider yourself to be able to handle yourself well in a courtroom?
A. I don't know—no, I wouldn't say that, sir.

Jimmy conceded that he knew the San Francisco mayor for a number of years and that they had discussed joint business ventures, including Jimmy's purchasing stock in Alioto's bank and Alioto putting up the cash for Jimmy and a few others to buy into a Lake Tahoe casino, the Crystal Bay.

Q. Were you then a member of organized crime?
A. Yes, sir.
Q. Would you say then that Mr. Alioto was associated with organized crime?
A. I sure do, sir.
Q. In what way was he associated with organized crime?
A. Well, he done business with people involved in organized crime. Angelo Marino, he was a made guy, I know that for sure; Bompensiero and me had a deal [with Alioto] for selling lard to Mexico.
Q. Was there anything illegal about the deal?
A. No, sir?
Q. Did you disclose to Mr. Alioto that you were a member of organized crime?
A. No, sir.
Q. Did Mr. Bompensiero?
A. No, sir. He did not.
Q. Did you represent to Mr. Alioto that you were legitimate businessmen?
A. We never discussed it, sir.
Q. You say he was a part of organized crime?
A. If you're dealing with me, if you know it or not, you're dealing with a man that's involved in organized crime. And if you don't know it you should go to someplace to find out.
Q. Didn't you tell us yesterday, there's no place to go to find out if someone's a member of La Cosa Nostra?

A. Well, you read newspapers. You think Joe Alioto never read anything about me? Are you kidding?

Q. Don't you generally hold yourself out to be a legitimate businessman? When you deal with these folks we've been discussing you try to look like a businessman and talk like a businessman. You don't go around telling people, "I'm a mafioso?"

A. That's right, sir.

Q. That's the way you conducted yourself with Mayor Alioto, wasn't it?

A. That's right, sir.

Q. That's the way you conducted yourself with Mr. Marchiondo, isn't it?

A. That's correct.

Bailey's style for the balance of the day became less abrasive, more probing of specific allegations Jimmy had made. He tried to demonstrate that Marchiondo had never known Fratianno's true identity, suggesting he had been introduced to Marchiondo's friends and associates as James Fratello. Jimmy said he couldn't deny ever being introduced as "Fratello." He had no specific memory of how he'd been introduced in some cases, but in others, he insisted, he had been introduced as "Fratianno."

He also conceded that on each of his trips to Albuquerque he may have been checked into local hotels under the name Fratello, but he had no way of knowing, for Marchiondo and his friends had made his reservation and checked him in.

Jimmy insisted that Marchiondo had offered him "a piece" of whatever money he made for Star Glo; that he had interceded in Marchiondo's behalf in a land deal with Morris Shenker, owner of the Dunes in Las Vegas; they both had a piece of Alfa New Mexico; and, indeed, Jimmy insisted, he had been in Marchiondo's office to overhear the call from Senator Montoya and the call to Governor Apodaca.

On Jimmy's efforts to bring Marchiondo and Jackie Presser together, Bailey asked with mock wonder: "Is this the same Jackie Presser that President-elect Reagan appointed to his transition team?"

"That's correct, sir."

"So, what you're telling us, is the president-elect of the United States has appointed a person to an advisory position who's controlled by the mob?"

"Absolutely."

By the end of the day, both men were physically drained, yet intellectually alert; perhaps even sharper from the day's workout than they had been when they began. Bailey closed out by trying to reinforce his basic premise: There was no reason to believe Jimmy Fratianno had been reformed by the government, and that he remained as treacherous and immoral as he had been while an operative of La Cosa Nostra.

What the questions elicited was an unusual bit of soul searching, which Jimmy had never before, and would never again, engage in publicly:

Q. Have you now come to the point that you think lying is wrong?

A. If I was not a government witness and I was a citizen, I think I'd lie again.

Q. But you feel now morally it's wrong to lie to people and deceive them? Is that what your philosophy is now?

A. Oh, I don't think so, sir. I think everybody in this world lies, sir. I don't think there's a living human that doesn't lie. I think you lie at times.

Q. Do you have any bad feelings about lying these days?

A. Yes, I do, sir.

Q. Is this a new moral attitude you have?

A. It's not a new moral attitude, sir. It's an obligation I have to the government and to myself.

Q. Have you become a religious person in the last three years?

A. No, I'm not a religious person. I believe in religion, but I don't go to church.

Q. Would you say you were, before this turnabout in the custody of the government, a relatively bad person? As you now look back on your life?

A. I would say I was a bad person.

Q. A very bad person?

A. Yes.

Q. Now, do you feel at some point in the last couple of years you've turned into a good person?

A. I wouldn't say that either. I don't think I'll ever be good for the things that I've done, sir. I think that someday or another that there's a law of retribution that you'll pay for what you've done. I believe in that. Maybe in the Judgment Day.

The deposition ended after about fourteen hours. The combined cost for both sides ran in excess of $50,000 in legal fees, staff costs, travel expenses, and $20,000, which the New Mexico court would eventually award Jimmy in recognition of his being an expert witness.

Dines carried one full set—seven boxes—of videotapes with him back to New Mexico; a second set was left behind in the custody of the video company in case something happened to them or their airplane. Never for a moment, not even at airport security, did Dines permit the tapes to leave his hands.

Despite some glaring hole in his story, the *Journal* lawyers regarded Jimmy's deposition as the single strongest piece of evidence in support of their case.

Bailey faded from the scene as suddenly as he had appeared, not to show up again until trial. A local lawyer, Ernesto Romero, handled the balance of the pretrial work.

There were more depositions. New Mexican business executives, politicians, hoods, and *Journal* employees were called upon.

Apodaca denied Jimmy's allegations about Marchiondo arranging for Alfa to receive state contracts. He also denied ever discussing political or judicial appointments with Marchiondo. He did concede having met Irving Shapiro for a few drinks in Las Vegas—a meeting discussed at length by Shapiro in the Alfa wiretaps—but denied discussing Alfa.

A few of Marchiondo's friends contended that they had been introduced to Fratianno as Fratello.

DePalma, Pacella, and Napoli all refused to be deposed, claiming their Fifth Amendment privilege.

"I told you that trip was a waste of time," Jimmy told Dines on the phone. "Made guys aren't goin' to say nothin'."

Lanphere had wanted to ask Napoli if he had pressed Marchiondo to file the lawsuit against the *Journal*. The *Journal*'s entire theory was that this was a mob-inspired effort to muzzle the press.

Bailey's theory was that the paper had opposed Apodaca's gubernatorial campaign and had sought to discredit him through his good friend, Marchiondo. Whether or not that was the paper's intention, the articles and lawsuit effectively ended Apodaca's political ambitions. President Carter had planned to nominate Apodaca as the United States's first secretary of education, but dropped his name from contention at the last minute, soon after learning of the allegations.

Days before trial, Judge Richard Traub, who had jurisdiction over the case since its inception, held Hume in contempt, ordering him to serve a six-month jail term for refusing to disclose if Donohue, while a state investigator, had leaked confidential information to him.

"I'm not protecting anyone," Hume, nearly in tears, told Lang immediately after the sentence was handed down. "All I'm protecting is a newsman's rights to confidential sources."

Lang was sympathetic. He offered to pay Hume's bills in a legal battle. But, he insisted, it was up to Hume whether or not to disclose his relationship with Donohue.

Privately, Lang was furious over the contempt ruling, which became a vent for his deeper anger over Traub's requiring Lang to disclose his net worth to Marchiondo. That Sunday, the *Journal* carried a full-scale assault on Traub and Marchiondo in its news and editorial column. Lang wrote a page-one commentary attacking Traub's contempt ruling; inside the paper, a columnist expressed outrage at the judge's ruling. News stories quoted from federal investigative files obtained in the lawsuit, which linked Marchiondo to heroin and cocaine smuggling operations and identified him as a "front" for "Eastern" crime interests. The documents were based on unnamed sources and rife with speculation. No news organization could normally justify publishing those documents, except in this case, where they'd been filed in court.

In their next court appearance, Traub lashed out at Lang and the *Journal*, calling the articles about him and the trial "horrendously inaccurate." He stopped short of barring the *Journal* from covering the case. He granted Marchiondo's request to increase damages sought in the lawsuit from $3 million to $17 million.

It fell on Hume to defuse the hostilities. Considering that he had a new baby at home and had received Donohue's blessings, Hume appeared in court days later to answer the question: He had learned nothing from Donohue. He told Traub that he had previously refused to answer the question as a matter of principle, believing that he should never discuss anything of a confidential source nature.

On the eve of trial, in January 1983, Traub ruled that Marchiondo was not a public figure; requiring the *Journal* to prove the truth of its article, rather than merely showing that there was no "malicious intent" or "wreckless disregard for the truth" in its preparation of the March 1977 article.

Ultimately, the case rested on two factors: first, whether the layout and design of the March 26, 1977, article, and its photo of Marchiondo under the headline of ORGANIZED CRIME SHOWING INTEREST IN NEW MEXICO, followed good journalistic standards and practices; and second, whether there was substance to reports that Marchiondo was a conduit or front for criminal interests in New Mexico.

The trial got underway in the snowy little town of Las Cruces, New Mexico, on January 19, 1983. It had been moved from Albuquerque on the undeniable argument that there had been too much pretrial publicity in the state capital for an impartial jury to be seated there.

Bailey was present with Romero and a small support staff.

Lang played go-fer, flying the lawyers, investigators, and *Journal* support staff back and forth between Las Cruces and Albuquerque, as he had throughout the depositions. He also became the primary custodian of the Fratianno videotapes, editing them down to eight hours on the dictates of Judge Traub as the trial proceeded.

As Lang and Manuel "Buffalo" Chavez, a *Journal* press foreman, reviewed the tapes, electronically performing surgical cuts and splices, they were increasingly impressed with Jimmy's performance.

Lang's initial impression had been that Jimmy made a credible witness, but as he sat, for nearly thirty-six hours straight, editing the tapes in time for their showing to the jury, he was astounded by every nuance of Jimmy's sincerity.

"The jury has a choice of which of these guys to believe: Bailey or Fratianno," Lang told Chavez during a break in their work. "I'm convinced they'll buy Fratianno."

Bailey, a man of slight stature, was a whirling dervish of excitement in front of the jury. He would open each of his interrogations by virtually flying out of his seat, flicking back his suit jacket, unfolding his eye glasses with a snap of his wrist, whipping them to his face, and launching into his first question before reaching the podium.

Frequently, arriving at the podium after lunch breaks or midday recesses, he would find it had been cranked up to its full height, about level with his chin. There was mischief afoot here.

The case proceeded for seven weeks, during which the jury heard from fifty witnesses and reviewed more than 300 pieces of evidence.

The jury deliberated for three days before returning a 10-to-2 verdict clearing the *Journal* of any wrongdoing.

The trial had cost millions, but Lang didn't care: "It was small potatoes compared to what organized crime is costing the state."

In their closed-door deliberations, the jurors initially held in favor of Marchiondo. But after reviewing the law, they found the paper hadn't violated the libel codes.

"He ought to be more careful who his friends are," said one juror after the case.

It seems there was scant evidence, other than Fratianno's words, to show that Marchiondo had been used as a mob "front." Yet there was abundant evidence of his association with Napoli, Shapiro, and Fratianno as well as other notable crime figures—and, after all, that was all the IRE article had alleged, that he was an associate. Therefore it was justifiable to carry his photo as a New Mexico associate to crime interests from California, Las Vegas, and New York.

As they left the courtroom in Las Cruces, Bailey announced that Apodaca was committed to suing the paper for defamation of character as a result of the *Journal's* conduct during the suit. "The *Journal* has won the battle," Bailey told reporters. "But the war is long from over."

Marchiondo stood beside Bailey, his lawyer and friend, adding that he was upset at the verdict, but not unhappy that he had pursued the charges. He had set out to demonstrate that "the people at the other end of the pen" shouldn't be afraid to sue those of great wealth and power.

Bailey approached Lanphere to shake hands when it was all over. Lanphere turned and walked away.

Bailey was right. The *Journal's* conduct at trial, accusing not only Marchiondo, but others—lawmen and politicians—with having ties to organized crime, led to more lawsuits. But Lang didn't seem to mind: It was becoming his vehicle for frontier justice.

14

Celebrity Status

THE NAME on his passport was Jimmy Martin—the same last name Jean was using in Texas.

The name on his credit cards still read Lombardo—that was the one he and Jean had shared after La Tuna.

The identity tags on his luggage said Jimmy Russo—his favorite alias, the one he used when leaving messages for prosecutors and agents.

And some joker in McPherson's office had purchased Jimmy's airline ticket under the name "T. Kennedy," which caused quite a stir at LAX when word got out that this Kennedy was some kind of dignitary who was being allowed to board the plane early.

He sat alone in the back of the Pan Am 747 bound from Los Angeles to St. Thomas in the Virgin Islands by way of Miami. For the first time since his arrest in 1977, his only traveling companions were *Time* magazine and *Sports Illustrated*. There was no business on this trip—and no marshals holding his hand—just a period of rest and relaxation. After five months of back-to-back trials, meetings, and depositions, Jimmy looked forward to an equal period of seclusion, with only occasional meetings in Washington.

As the other passengers boarded the flight, he scanned the cabin for attractive young women to hit on. He had suffered constant male companionship and protection in motel rooms and courthouses for too many months, making the perfumed aromas of smiling young women the essence of freedom. He paid especially close attention to the legs and chests of the flight attendants as they passed, thinking of opening lines as he silently graded each: "she's built nice . . . she's too small . . . I'd pay good money for her."

He offered each his uniquely charming avuncular smile. Those who responded were fair game. He focused on one in particular, tall, muscular, and full-mouthed, with breasts that appeared strained inside her tight airline-issue blouse.

He thought about getting a moment alone with her once the plane was in the air. He was convinced that that was all he'd need, that was all he ever needed to bait a woman.

But as he sat belted-in, waiting for the airliner to take off, his thoughts turned to Jean and he realized, at least for now, visions of a rendezvous were an exercise in futility. Jean and her family were waiting for him at a safe house in St. Thomas—a beachfront hotel suite rented by WITSEC.

It was better just to sit quietly with his magazines, passing the time with his own thoughts without causing trouble.

It had taken the better part of three years, but Jimmy could finally relax. He had satisfied the last of his obligations to the government with the Tieri case; his exposure to prison had been wiped out after testifying in Cleveland and getting probation on the state charges he had pleaded guilty to in 1978.

But there was more testimony ahead: In Cleveland, Carmen Marino and federal prosecutors were preparing new cases against the mob; Akerman was ready to go to trial against Pittstown, Pennsylvania, mob boss Russel Bufalino; former Cleveland strike force chief Doug Roller had gotten his wish, becoming the strike force chief in Chicago, where he was working up a case against Teamsters president Roy Williams and Allen Dorfman, the Teamsters's financial conduit; federal grand juries in Las Vegas and Kansas City were looking into secret mob ownership of Vegas casino-hotels; and there was talk in Washington of a major assault on La Cosa Nostra in New York.

Jimmy could have refused. He could have said he had had enough, that he was done testifying and wanted to leave the program. He could have demanded that he and Jean be relocated to a permanent site where he'd get one more year of funding before being cut off. He could have begun a new life, free of marshals and courtrooms and crime. Instead, he had been calling officials offering his guidance to secure his continued role in WITSEC and government service.

From Los Angeles, after the Albuquerque deposition, he had called Safir. He explained that he had to continue testifying—"Howard, these lawyers keep getting me in deeper"—and that WITSEC should continue providing him with support. Safir had no argument with that.

"But here's the thing, Howard: I don't want to live in the United States," he told Safir. "I want to be relocated to another country. Somewhere like South Africa. It just isn't safe for me here."

"It's out of the question, Jimmy," Safir shot back.

"What are you talking about?" Jimmy demanded, his reasonable tone of voice turning suddenly bitter.

"It just can't be done that way. I mean, South Africa? That's on the other side of the world, Jimmy."

"All right then, how about Australia or Belize. Yeah, Belize isn't too far away, and I could live cheap down there."

"Look, Jimmy, it's okay for you to remain on funding as long as you're testifying, as long as you can't support yourself. Okay? But we can't give you . . . you can't get funding without living by our rules, and that means protection; and we can't provide protection outside the States."

"Howard," Jimmy yelled into the phone, "fuck you and your rules. I take care of myself. Most of the time I'm on my own anyway, like in a hotel or something. I tell you what, the next time a case comes up, you can testify. I don't need you to baby-sit me."

Jimmy slammed down the receiver.

It wasn't that Safir wanted to continue baby-sitting Jimmy. What Safir wanted was for Jimmy to relocate to a permanent site in the U.S. where he could be weaned from WITSEC money and protection. But Jimmy felt he had become too well known; if he were to remain in the U.S. to testify, he would have to move around constantly, separate from Jean, and WITSEC would have to pay for their individual lodging as well as a daily food stipend, at that time $20 a day each.

Jimmy wouldn't consider Safir's view. He assumed that Safir didn't trust him to return when he was needed to testify. But nothing could have been farther from the truth. Safir had seen the change in Jimmy: the transformation from a bad guy out to screw the system to a full-time informant out to use the system.

His deal with the government had become a sort of pension; retirement from the mob had its benefits. Jimmy had never been able to really make crime pay, at least never steadily or in a big way. He had made a lot more money in trucking than he ever did with the mob. And now he was making more steady income from the government—and his private deals in depositions, his book, and interviews—than he could have counted on in crime.

If his eager participation was ever in doubt, it had been recently reassured by Ahearn. Based on Jimmy's testimony and information—and his continuing complaints that he needed more money—Ahearn had circulated a letter, a petition of sorts, to each of the officials who had dealt with Jimmy in the past three years. In essence, it requested the Justice Department to make a lump sum payment to Jimmy for his cooperation, a kind of informant's fee. Justice had agreed to the idea and Ahearn was completing the paperwork for a $50,000 check to be deposited into Jimmy's account later that year.

Jimmy was counting on another $10,000 later that year when he testified in the Todisco case for the *Sacramento Bee*, and he was negotiating through Akerman for about the same amount from Thames Television, a British documentary crew making a seven-hour series on organized crime in the U.S. There was also a chance to make $30,000 or $40,000 testifying for Bob Guccione, the publisher of *Penthouse*, in a libel suit, and a similar amount from NBC for a suit brought by singer Wayne Newton.

He certainly needed as much as he could earn. He was burning a hole in his bank account as quickly as the cash was flowing in: $20,000 for Jean's clothes; $30,000 for cars; $60,000 for Jean to buy a condominium in Texas; perhaps another $50,000 on incidentals. Dennis McDonald had already floated him a couple of loans.

Thoughts of money and protection were rolling through Jimmy's mind on the flight to St. Thomas when he glanced over at the man seated across the aisle. The man's face was buried in a copy of *Newsweek*, which he held open with two hands. Staring back at Jimmy from the magazine's cover was Jimmy's photo.

"Motherfucker," Jimmy said under his breath as he virtually leaped up to go off in search of a new seat. "Some protection this program gives me," he muttered to himself.

Jean was waiting in St. Thomas with her mother and sister. Jean lasted about three weeks before heading back to her lakeside condominium in Denton, Texas. They spent most of their time fighting about money.

Her mother and sister stayed on for several months, gratis the government. It took another argument with Safir, but Jimmy, with the help of Henderson and Fox, convinced the Justice Department that his celebrity status had grown so large that someone might try to trace him through his in-laws, so they, too, were placed on WITSEC funding, protection, and medical support.

Just after *The Last Mafioso* came out, Jimmy left the island for business in Washington, D.C. Topping his agenda was an appearance before the so-called Pepper Committee—a crime committee chaired by Congressman Claude Pepper, the tough-minded, elderly Florida Democrat.

As many times as Jimmy had been to Washington since joining WITSEC, this was the first time he had seen anything beyond the marshals' offices. As they drove across Memorial Bridge, from Virginia to Washington, he strained his neck for a better view of the Lincoln Memorial. And he convinced them to stop for a moment in front of the Washington Monument as they rode along Constitution Avenue before dawn. His guards laughed off his request to stop at the White House. They kidded him about his "old buddy" Reagan, who had forced him out of the trucking business in California—they'd all heard Jimmy's stories a thousand times.

He was snuck into a congressional office building as the sun broke over the Capitol dome.

The congressional inquisitors didn't break any new ground, largely reviewing trial testimony. They asked about the structure and hierarchy of La Cosa Nostra, its operations in labor racketeering and business. The only thing that impressed Jimmy was Pepper's parting comment: "Mr. Fratianno, you certainly are an expert on organized crime."

Jimmy was swept from the hearing room and back to Virginia in a panel truck.

The next morning Jimmy convinced the marshals to take him out to get some dye to touch up his graying hair. While wandering the aisles of Memco, a discount department store, they stopped in the TV section, where Jimmy admired a 25-inch console with built-in stereo. Surrounding them were two walls of color televisions, 30 feet long and stacked five deep, all set to the same channel. Suddenly Jimmy's picture flashed on the screen as a newscaster explained who Jimmy was and what he had said to Pepper's committee and in his book about Frank Sinatra and Jackie Presser.

It was like being caught in a house of mirrors; wherever they turned, there was Jimmy, blown up larger than life on big screens or reduced to a 13-inch frame.

The marshals rushed Jimmy out to the parking lot.

He gave up shaving after that episode, hoping it would be a sufficient change in appearance to act as a disguise.

His next meeting that week was with investigators from the Nevada Gaming Control Board. They had seen his book and wanted to know what he could provide for their hearings on Sinatra's gaming license application.

Jimmy held his usual seat, a green leatherette swivel chair behind a desk that was covered in chipped and peeling walnut veneer, at the marshals' waterfront offices in Alexandria. The investigators sat silently like supplicants at the oracle, as Jimmy scolded.

"Are you kidding me?" he began. "You want me to go to Vegas to testify? Listen, you know as well as I that this entire thing's a sham. Nobody's gonna stop this guy from getting his license."

The investigators offered muted protests.

"Look at the set up," Jimmy was saying. "First, who appoints the gaming board? The governor, right? And how does the governor get into office in that state? Through the casinos which bankroll his campaign, right? And who controls the casinos? The mob, right? So how do you think this gaming board is going to have the balls to go up against the people who put them in their jobs? Give me a fuckin' break. The fix is in. The only thing I'd do by going out there is give Spilotro a nice clean shot at clipping me. Hey man, it's just like the way La Cosa Nostra runs the Teamsters: the mob has a lock on that town, let's put it that way."

While refusing to testify, Jimmy was willing to answer the investigators' questions about the now-famous Premier Theatre dressing room photo of Sinatra and his mob admirers. He explained Pacella's relationship to Sinatra, the theater, and the mob.

Two weeks later, the gaming board got an earful from old blue eyes as the Nevada hearing room filled to capacity with camera crews, reporters, and investigators from all over the country.

"Mr. Sinatra, do you know a Mr. Louis Pacella?" the board chairman asked.

"Yes, very well," Sinatra said, coughing to clear his throat.

"Would you describe him as a good friend?"

"Uh, that's right," he said, shifting in his seat.

Sinatra volunteered how Pacella had approached him to play the Premier Theatre and after discussions with Mickey Rudin and the theater's operators a contract was drawn.

The chairman continued, most uneasily, trying to ask more about Pacella: "Did, uh, is he the type of gentleman, uh, or . . . did he have a type of background that one might be aware of, uh—"

"I know what you're saying," Sinatra broke in, before the question was completed. "But I can't attest to that because I'd never been present if he had any form of activity. He had a restaurant in New York and I visited very often. I liked it. It was good food. And I became fond of him and that was the extent of the friendship."

Sinatra went on to say he was "well aware" that Pacella had been convicted in the Premier Theatre case.

Then he was asked about the photo.

"I was asked by one of the members of the theater . . . he told me that Mr. Gambina [*sic*] had arrived with his granddaughter, whose last name, by chance, happened to be Sinatra, and he said they would like to take a picture and I said 'fine.' They came in and I took a picture with the little girl and before I realized what happened there were approximately eight or nine men standing around me. That is the whole incident that took place."

"Did you have any acquaintance with Mr. Gambino prior to that; had you ever met him before?"

"No, I never did. Neither before nor after."

"Okay. Did you have any information about any of the people that were in that photograph with you?"

"Well, I know Mr. Marson, because he was one of the owners of the club. And, uh, I later found out, I was introduced to someone named Jimmy and I later found out that he was this fink, The Weasel," Sinatra said, emphasizing the word *fink*, and drawing sustained laughter from the crowd.

"Subsequently, did you have an opportunity after this picture received some degree of notoriety to learn what the background was of some of those people?"

"No. No. I didn't even know their names let alone their backgrounds," Sinatra offered. He wasn't being entirely forthcoming: He may not have known their names when the photo was taken, but he certainly came to know at least DePalma fairly well, dining out and golfing with him, according to wiretaps.

"I mean, subsequent to that, in the last little while."

"No. No. I haven't. Nobody asked me about it and I didn't discuss it with anybody."

"Well, certainly, all of the people in that picture, save and except yourself, it's quite a 'Who's Who and What's What' in the area of organized crime . . ."

And then, in what sounded very much like a prepared response, for which Sinatra had been awaiting an opening: "I wish we didn't have to discuss Mr. Fratianno because he's a confessed murderer, a perjurer, and I'd rather not discuss him involved with my own life."

"Well, Mr. Sinatra, unfortunately, I can appreciate what you're saying, but it's in the public record and Mr. Fratianno has received a great deal of acclaim as a very credible witness."

But with that moment of tension, the commission ended its inquiry into Sinatra's relationship to organized crime, and weeks later approved his license with only one board member opposed.

Jimmy got his opportunity to respond to Sinatra.

Martin Short, a documentary producer with Thames Television of London, had arranged an interview with Jimmy for a film on organized crime.

Short's researchers spent hours reviewing cases with Akerman and arranged an introduction to McDonald and then Fratianno. Despite warnings from WITSEC that a television appearance could endanger his security, Jimmy, with full beard by this time, became one of the featured commentators through seven hours of mob history.

The grand opening to the documentary was a tight camera shot of Jimmy against a darkened background, describing the killing of Russian Louie Strauss and the mobsters who had gathered to watch the execution.

"Most people would prefer not to be around to see someone strangled," Short's disembodied voice said as the camera held steadily on Jimmy.

"Not members of the Family," Jimmy replied. "They're all killers themselves."

"Then it's rather like being to a cabaret, a performance?"

"Yeah, just like a performance," Jimmy said, chuckling. "Like a magician. You know, something disappears."

"But in this case they never come back," Short noted.

"That's right," Jimmy said.

"How did you feel about killing people?"

"I didn't have much feeling. I didn't kill nobody who was innocent."

As the taping continued, Short asked about Sinatra's comments to the Gaming Board and his relationships with mobsters in the Premier Theatre photo.

"He's full of baloney. He thrives on this stuff; I'm telling you he thrives on it. He ain't gonna tell that to the president. I don't know how he covers that up."

After the taping session, Jimmy staged a private party for the film crew, his marshals, and lawyers at a nearby restaurant, Porta Fino, in Old Town Alexandria.

Afterward he called Akerman at home to brag about his courtly manner, picking up the tab for the crew.

"I'm telling you, Nick, these guys were really impressed," Jimmy was saying.

"More like scared to death," Akerman replied.

"What do you mean?"

"Well, you told Short to deliver the money in cash, in a paper bag, right? Well, he didn't quite know if that was all right. He called to ask me about it and he told me he felt like some kind of gangster."

Jimmy was laughing.

"How much did you finally get from them?" Akerman asked.

"Eleven thousand."

"Jeez. I thought you were looking to get five?"

"Yeah, that was my bottom line. But I told these guys I wanted 20,000—I told them I deserved that much because it was a risk to my security to be seen on TV. You know, no way I'm ever going to London, so I gave them a line of bullshit and then I let them talk me down to eleven."

Jimmy could still work a mark as well as anyone.

"No wonder Short was nervous. That's a lot of cash to be carrying in a paper bag," Akerman was saying between fits of laughter.

"Well, Nick, you know I have to work in cash. I can't deposit a check made out to my real name and I can't give them my other identities. And I got trouble with the tax people, you know."

"No, I didn't. What's the problem?"

"Well, Dennis insisted that I straighten out my back taxes because I'm making this legitimate money. So I met with this guy from the IRS here in Washington a few weeks ago. We spent like two days together at this hotel working out all my taxes, you know, like the money I've made from the book and everything. Well, after all that, he has me signing all these forms he's filled out and he asks for my social security number and I tell him I don't have one. See, until I'm relocated to a permanent location with a final identity, I don't get my social security. So this IRS guy just said 'forget about it,' as far as the IRS is concerned, I don't exist."

He went to Puerto Rico, staying at the Holiday Inn by the San Juan airport for a while and then at the Howard Johnson's Inn in Santurce as Jimmy Russo.

When a tourist from New Jersey stopped him at a hotel restaurant and asked for his autograph, Jimmy shrugged, mumbling "No comprendo Inglés." He then walked off to his room, packed his bags, and left San Juan for Ponce, on the other side of the island.

Each time he returned from a meeting in Washington or Miami he relocated to a new island, often fulfilling his wish to live outside the U.S., if only for a few days or weeks at a time. For a while, he was Jimmy Lombardo in the Dominican Republic and after that he was Jimmy Russell in several smaller islands.

He lived secluded in hotels, taking infrequent trips to the beach, pool, or shopping. When local marshals determined he was getting too well entrenched—risking someone recognizing him—they'd move him again.

At one point, after a late-night flight, he arrived in Martinique ready to check in and couldn't remember who he was supposed to be. When he finally got the new name right he gave the desk clerk a charge card under the wrong name. And when he finally got that straight, he signed the register as Jimmy Fratianno.

It was okay, though. He only stayed in Martinique a few days—just long enough to meet a thirty-two-year-old leggy French woman, despondent over her boyfriend's leaving her—and then returned to Washington to meet with Fox in preparation for the Todisco deposition.

The deposition was uneventful. The only memorable moment came when Todisco's lawyer, James Homola, arrived toting a shopping bag filled with copies of *The Last Mafioso* and asked Jimmy to autograph them. The signing ceremony, memorialized as part of the videotaped deposition, offered proof of Jimmy's acclaim—an interesting contrast to Homola's later efforts to discredit him.

Ultimately, the case would end in a draw: no money was paid and settlement was made before trial, with the *Bee* agreeing not to write any further articles about Todisco.

Jimmy departed Washington for Brunswick, Georgia, a coastal tourist town, where he would spend late spring and fall with Jean.

Jean loved it. Their life together settled into what she regarded as "normal." They had a modern, furnished condominium overlooking the water. They went out to dinner and the movies. When Jimmy had business to attend to, all he needed to do was drive to a government installation on nearby St. Simon's Island. He even attended church on Sundays.

Jean made friends—most through her church groups—and Jimmy suffered the dinner parties, entertaining the audience with tales of Los Angeles, Las Vegas, and Hollywood in the 1940s and 1950s. He boasted of his relationships with Sinatra and Johnny Roselli.

Jimmy never made any effort to cover up his past: where he had lived, who he had known, how he had "dabbled in a little illegal gambling" just after the war, and how he had become acquainted with some of the better-known West Coast mob luminaries. It was near to impossible for a man like Jimmy to entirely deny his history, and it had as much to do with pride as difficulty in living a complex lie. His only alteration of the facts came when asked what he did for a living, before retirement. Then he would say something like import-export businesses, and Jean would whisper that he did some secret work for the government.

Virtually no one was fooled. He would get knowing looks from their friends. Some would joke about Jimmy's silver tongue, his ability to "make an offer no one could refuse." When confronted, Jean confided Jimmy's true identity—no one ever asked Jimmy. After a while, their friends avoided what they thought were compromising questions.

Jean continued to be active in religious crusades, much of it on late-night TV with evangelical broadcasts. For the last few years, unknown to Jimmy, Oral Roberts had been a regular recipient of her tithing. She had also sent a few thousand to help in the construction of the Crystal Cathedral in Garden Grove, California. She eventually received a certificate for her donations: her name had been chosen as one of those to be inscribed into the crystal windows of the shrine. She was at once delighted and bemused: The name to be sanctified was Jean Lombardo. She recalled the biblical passage about receiving a new name when reborn and satisfied herself that St. Peter would be pleased.

But when Jimmy learned that a percentage of his income was being sent to these evangelists of the airwaves, he was outraged, but he controlled his temper, stopping short of calling them TV con men.

"Look, Jimmy," Jean cooed one night as they lay in bed, "your life has never been so good. You have money and a nice house and me to watch after you. And don't you think that my tithing, that God might have something to do with it? You're just so damned ungrateful. Do you ever thank him for all the bounty of our life together?"

Jimmy moaned and rolled over.

The next morning Jimmy left the condominium in silence, returning that afternoon with word that Ahearn's $50,000 check had been deposited into their account.

"Hey babe," Jimmy said, beaming with joy. "Ain't it great. Look what the Lord did for us today."

She knew Jimmy was mocking her, but she accepted whatever small victories she could.

Late one afternoon Jean pulled Jimmy away from the TV, where he was ahead three runs in the seventh inning on a $100 bet with Newt on a Braves-Mets game, insisting he take her out so she could buy a candy bar. A Seven-Eleven, walking distance from their condo, provided relief for Jean's sudden sweet desire.

As Jimmy waited in line to pay for Jean's Snickers bars, she wandered the store, stopping in front of the paperback book rack, where she found an unauthorized volume on Jimmy's life with his photo on the cover.

"Can they get away with that?" Jean asked, waving a copy of the book in Jimmy's face. "Can they just write about you without asking our permission or paying you anything?"

He tossed the book back on the shelf as he dragged her from the store. At home it was Jean who phoned Dennis McDonald demanding that he stop the sale of "that other book."

"I really don't see where anything can be done," McDonald told her, "not unless you show me where the book says something that isn't true."

"So there's nothing we can do about this stuff?"

"Not really, Jean. I don't think—"

Jean placed the receiver back in its cradle without giving Jimmy a chance to speak to McDonald.

"I have to get out of here," she said, grabbing her handbag and heading for the door.

Jimmy followed, racing to the driver's side of their Olds 98 and demanding to drive.

They traveled in silence for about an hour, staring from the car at Georgia's lush countryside.

Jean finally began talking: "The truth is that I'm upset about us, Jimmy. I know that this is only temporary, that pretty soon you're going to go back to traveling around the country and I'm going back to Texas."

"Hey babe, listen. This can't go on forever. Soon we'll settle down somewhere. Maybe another year. But while I'm testifying it just ain't safe for you to be with me."

Jimmy pulled the car to the side of the road.

"And besides, you don't want to be living the way I do, moving every few weeks from hotel to hotel, having to stay indoors most of the time," he continued, trying to console her.

"I don't believe that. You want to know what I think, Jimmy? I think you just can't live like normal people. It's like you can't deal with all the freedom of life. If you're free, you know you're going to get into trouble. You never learned the Lord's rules about how people are supposed to get along together. It's like you want to be in prison or something."

Jimmy didn't understand that. Who would want to be in prison? "It's nothing like that at all, babe. I'm just doin' what I have to do so we can have some money. Pretty soon this will all change."

"Is that a promise?" Jean asked.

"Yeah. Give me another year—no, give me eighteen months, and then we'll settle down somewhere. Even if I'm still testifying."

Jean wasn't convinced, but it was the closest she had come to getting a commitment from Jimmy since they'd entered WITSEC. She accepted it as a sign of hope.

They drove around until after dark, stopping to eat dinner at an Italian restaurant about 50 miles from Brunswick.

After ordering, a waitress approached Jimmy with a free drink, a menu, and a broad grin.

"The couple over there want to buy you this drink. They say they know you're that famous Mafia guy and would like your autograph," she said without any hesitation, extending the menu and a pen in front of Jimmy.

Jimmy broke into uncontrollable, childlike fits of giggles as he glanced across the room to where a well-dressed couple in their fifties sat smiling and waving sheepishly. Jean beamed with pride and gave a little nod of recognition.

"Tell them they must be mistaken," Jimmy said, declining the menu. "But thank them for the drink," he added, winking to the admiring couple.

They stayed in Georgia until late summer, when Jimmy flew to Cleveland to testify in a state case against Anthony Libatore, a Teamsters official accused of taking part in the FBI leak. Libatore had fled in December 1977 before he could be tried with the rest of the Cleveland gang. It was Marino's last hurrah. The jury came back hung.

Next was the Bufalino case, a one-week trial in which Akerman charged the aging Pittston, Pennsylvania, crime boss with ordering the murder of Jack Napoli, a government witness. Seated alongside Bufalino was Mike Rizzi, who had agreed with Jimmy in 1977 to arrange the never-completed Napoli execution. The charge was conspiracy to violate the civil rights of a government witness—the federal government's way of charging murder.

In a rare tactic, Bufalino took the stand in his own defense. He denied the charges. He insisted he was not involved in organized crime. He acknowledged attending the infamous 1957 mob conclave at Apalachin, New York, where local police stumbled into a meeting of several dozen mob leaders from across the nation. [Fratianno was supposed to have attended but was in jail at the time.] But, Bufalino claimed, he was there only to deliver soda.

Bufalino was convicted; Rizzi walked.

Jimmy spent the winter in the islands. Jean stayed in Texas. For the holidays, they met at the home of a retired agent outside of Richmond, Virginia.

"What's this bullshit?" Jimmy was screaming as he sat on his terrace overlooking the coral blue Caribbean in Mayaguez, Puerto Rico. "It was you guys got me into this thing, now someone in the government's goin' to straighten it out."

Henderson was struggling to explain what seemed an inexplicable situation even for a lawyer—especially for a government prosecutor.

"Jimmy, our hands are tied. Let me try making it as simple as I can. Marie Bompensiero is the wife of Frank Bompensiero—"

"Don't treat me like some fuckin' idiot, Jim. I know Marie nearly all my life. I woulda made a play for her when she was young except she was married to Momo Adamo, the L.A. underboss in them years. Anyway, so she's suing the government for getting Bomp into trouble with the Family, why do I get involved?"

Henderson picked up the story. "Yeah, and she's saying that by using Frank to draw the Family into the Forex sting operation we—uh, the FBI—caused him to be killed."

"Absolutely. Barron and that other agent, Armstrong, left him hanging out there, poor motherfucker. They used him and tossed him out. But how the fuck does she get off suing me for a million dollars?"

This is the part Henderson had been through five times already.

"The suit claims you took part in identifying Bomp as an informant and arranging his murder—all of which you've affirmed in testimony. Now she claims that because the others faced trial and were acquitted in the murder conspiracy, that leaves just you and the FBI who can assume responsibility for his death. What it comes down to is they're putting you on trial for Bomp's murder. Now the problem is that you're a private citizen and you're being sued for something you did as a private citizen before you joined witness protection, so the government can't provide you with a lawyer. You're on your own."

Henderson listened to the silence coming from the other side of the line as Jimmy considered the situation. "Hello? Jimmy?"

"I'm here. I'll tell you what these pricks are up to, Jim. Here's the thing: This isn't Marie behind this—this is the Family, Chris Petti and his lawyer [Nicholas] DePinto and the rest of them in San Diego. They're figuring either they take me for a million dollars or something, or they get me on their turf so they can set it up to clip me. Believe me, Jim, I know what I'm talking about. Marie has nothing to do with this."

Henderson had his own theory, which he wasn't sharing with Jimmy. In his view, Marie Bompensiero was being used, not to kill Jimmy, but rather to discredit him. If they could prove Jimmy was responsible for Bomp's murder, it would go a long way toward discrediting not only his past testimony, but would be a damning piece of evidence against Fratianno in future cases. It would also be a condemnation of the government's use of accomplice witnesses.

After another moment of silence Jimmy continued: "Here's what I'm doing. If the government isn't going to defend me, I'll defend myself. Shit, I've been through enough of these trials that I can do a better job than any lawyer. Besides, I'm not going to pay anyone to go into court on a sham charge like this."

"Jimmy, this isn't legal advice; I can't give you legal advice, okay. But why don't you talk to Phil Fox. He's a friend and maybe he can help you out. Maybe he'll have some ideas on how to deal with this thing."

"Okay, Jim. That's probably not a bad idea. I'll call him tonight. McPherson's flying in here next week to pick me up, I guess I'll see you then."

It was the same old routine. Jimmy was snuck into the darkened U.S. District Courthouse on February 17, 1982, in San Diego two nights before the trial by a half dozen marshals commanded by McPherson.

The entire thing gave Jimmy the jitters. He hated living in the marshals' custody, and San Diego was like a vile dream. Everyone he knew there wanted him dead. The whole trip evoked recollections of his earliest days in MCC. Given the option, he would rather have been in New York.

If there was any redeeming value to his trip it came the next morning when he walked into court surrounded by five armed marshals. Besides McPherson, seated in the courtroom was a host of friendly faces: McDonald, Henderson, Kelton, Newt, Lore, Ahearn, and other agents and prosecutors he'd worked with.

Fox hadn't made the trip, but he had spent several hours on the phone with Jimmy offering advice. He had provided him with a few legal briefs to submit in an attempt to have the case dismissed.

There were also some less friendly faces in the crowd: Agent John Armstrong, Bomp's FBI contact, who still blamed Jimmy for Bomp's murder; Chris Petti; DePinto; and Spilotro's lawyer, Oscar Goodman.

Wishing he could spit, Jimmy shot a look at Petti and, staring right at him, moved his lips to form the word *cocksucker*.

Marie Bompensiero, the frail, gray-haired widow, took the stand with the aid of her lawyer. She used a cane and wore a hearing aid. Her lawyer, Allen Charne, had her speak of being destitute since the death of her husband; how she had never known that he was a member of organized crime, and certainly nothing of his relationship with the FBI, until his death.

As Charne finished, Jimmy, clean shaven and dressed in a blue business suit, looking every bit the lawyer he wanted to play, stood up and walked toward Marie.

"Hello, Marie," he said in a familiar tone of voice.

Startled for a moment by the sense of friendliness, she stared hard through thick eyeglasses, and then said, "I don't think I've ever seen you before."

Charne instructed Jimmy, "Tell her your name."

Smiling, Jimmy leaned close to Marie: "Jimmy Fratianno."

"You're Jimmy?" she said, suddenly aglow with excitement. "You've been over there the whole time? I'm surprised to see you."

Jimmy could have sat down without another word—he had proven his point, Marie had no idea what this charade was all about.

Jimmy explained that he was going to have to ask her some questions, and Marie, smiling, told him to go right ahead. He asked about the Bomp, his connections to organized crime, and her previous marriage to Momo Adamo.

"You think Momo told me anything? You know better than that, Jimmy," she said with girlish glee.

As to Bomp, she said she had had suspicions, but never pushed too hard to know his business. "I used to kinda hint around about it. But he'd say, 'You take care of the house,' and he'd take care of the outside.

"I really don't know, Jimmy," she said, extending her hand for him.

Holding her frail right hand in his two hands, Jimmy sought to console her. "Marie, thirty-five years I've been in this organization and I've known many, many women like you."

Armstrong was next on the stand. He described how he had asked Bomp to inquire about Forex, the FBI front, knowing Bomp would instruct the L.A. Family to shake it down. It wasn't until after the indictments came out that Bomp was told the truth and asked to join witness protection.

"I was more worried than he was," Armstrong said.

He described his belief that it was Jimmy who lured Bompensiero to the phone booth—not Brooklier or Bonanno—to have him killed.

Jimmy was lost in his own thoughts. As he sat listening, he was suddenly struck by the entire set up. The way Jimmy figured it, Armstrong and Barron meant to shut down all of La Cosa Nostra's West Coast operations through the PORNEX sting operation. They would indict all the low- and middle-level guys for pornography and then, convincing Bomp that his life was in danger, get him to go into

WITSEC and testify against everyone else. Bomp was the only one who had direct dealings with the bosses of all three West Coast Families—L.A., San Francisco, and San Jose—as well as being an associate of Joe Bonanno's and the Chicago Family. What a coup it would have been for Marie and Barron.

For the first time, Jimmy understood why the two agents hated him so: It was Jimmy who ended up turning and Ahearn, not Armstrong and Barron, who got the glory.

It made having to sit through this case worthwhile.

As court adjourned for the day, Jimmy was led out, through the hallway, past Petti.

"Fuckin' squeal," Petti whispered as Jimmy passed.

Jimmy didn't hesitate. He turned on his heel and was ready to jump Petti. "You dirty little asshole—"

The marshals interceded, guiding Petti in one direction, Jimmy in the other.

On the other end of the corridor there was almost as heated a discussion, where Armstrong had cornered Ahearn. Standing eyeball-to-eyeball, toe-to-toe, Armstrong pointed toward Jimmy: "He's the one killed Bomp and why we're dealing with this guy, why we're letting him go into court and lie his ass off, I don't understand."

"Hey look, we're both agents, if there's something there, you tell me about it, show me a scrap of evidence that I can use to show he killed Bomp or lied on the stand, and we'll take him down," Ahearn said, turning and walking away.

The case lasted only three days. Jimmy testified about his limited role in the attempts on Bomp's life: the first, in 1975, before they suspected Bomp had set them up, when he was acting boss in L.A.; and the second, the evening he was called by Tommy Ricciardi, who asked what time Bomp was going out to the phone booth.

During his testimony, Jimmy complained to U.S. District Judge Howard Turrentine that the entire case was a sham: "She didn't even know I was in the courtroom. Who has this lawsuit, Mrs. Bompensiero or Mr. DePinto? I don't know what they're trying to pull."

When Charne rested the plaintiff's case, Judge Turrentine dismissed the suit against the FBI. He said that Bompensiero had never been forced to set up the L.A. mobster in the sting operation, that he apparently understood the risks of being an informant, and that he'd been warned well in advance of his murder that he should consider entering the protection program.

The case against Jimmy, however, continued for one more day, with Henderson taking the stand as the sole defense witness:

"As far as we could determine, Mr. Fratianno didn't know when or where Mr. Bompensiero might be killed and had no actual participation in the murder."

In his closing outburst, Jimmy charged, "This suit is an attempt by the mob to get me out in the open so they can kill me," and that "Nicholas DePinto is a mob attorney, who is part and parcel of the effort to get me along with Chris Petti, Tony Spilotro, and other members of La Cosa Nostra."

Turrentine reserved decision.

Outside the courtroom, DePinto called Jimmy's claims false and Petti's lawyer, Oscar Goodman, said, "The government knows he's a liar, and if there were any substance to Fratianno's charges my client would have been charged."

Three weeks after the trial, Judge Turrentine dismissed the case against Jimmy on a technicality. One of the petitions Fox had given Jimmy to file questioned why the case was being brought in federal rather than state court. Turrentine ruled that although Jimmy was in witness protection, and therefore forced to live elsewhere, he was still technically a resident of California and the case should have been brought in state court.

15

Making It for Penthouse

IT MAY HAVE BEEN the most costly piece of journalism ever to appear in the national press: a March 1975 article in *Penthouse* entitled "La Costa: The Hundred-Million-Dollar Resort with Criminal Clientele."

It was the story of Southern California's most opulent resort, Rancho La Costa, built on mob connections, $87 million in Teamsters loans, and a clientele that included such notables as Richard Nixon's cover-up team, Jimmy Fratianno, and Las Vegas mob overseer Tony Spilotro.

Freelance writers Lowell Bergman and Jeff Gerth were hardly the first to tackle the subject: virtually every major newspaper and magazine in the nation had taken a shot at the San Diego County resort and its founding fathers, one of which was Morris "Moe" Dalitz, a preeminent Prohibition mob rum-runner who later became one of Las Vegas's leading entrepreneurs.

But this time La Costa decided to fight back—first demanding *Penthouse* publisher Robert Guccione run a retraction, and then, weeks later, filing a $630 million libel action. It was the highest libel award ever sought in the U.S. It seemed their clear intent was to bankrupt Guccione; many saw it as a strong, chilling message to publishers throughout the United States that the mob's legitimate businesses were not to be made targets of reporting.

La Costa's executives hired the best legal team they could assemble, placing Louis Nizer at the head of the table.

Guccione wasn't going to be outgunned, fielding an equally impressive team of attorneys, with Roy Grutman, a self-possessed, arrogant, and enormously talented New York City lawyer, in charge. Grutman, an aggressive courtroom showman, hired the best support staff he could find, including Jack Barron, who became involved in the case before he had actually retired and was later accused of lifting confidential reports on La Costa from the FBI's Los Angeles office.

In its earliest days, Jimmy had been a party to the suit. Joey Aiuppa, Chicago's mob boss, ordered Johnny Roselli to have Jimmy file a separate libel action. The article had called Jimmy an "infamous hit man" and it seemed to most legal advisers, including McDonald, an easy task to show that the magazine had little foundation for such a brazen, unattributed statement.

When Jimmy turned government informant, his first private visitor at MCC San Diego was Guccione, who brought Jimmy a pile of *Penthouse* back issues. He also brought an offer: He would pay handsomely for Jimmy's testimony "when and if" the case ever got to trial.

When and if, indeed. After its initial filing in May 1975, the case had worked its way through the state and federal courts with little deliberate speed or direction. The primary pretrial issue was whether those named in the article as founders and operators of La Costa were public figures. The law holds a double standard for public figures— such as entertainers, politicians, and high-profile businessmen—and nonpublic figures. To win a libel action, a public figure must prove that untrue statements were produced with malice and knowledge that the statement was untrue, an enormous burden for a plaintiff; a nonpublic figure must prove only that the statement was untrue, placing the burden of proof on the defense. It's one of those interesting contradictions of American law: In libel trials involving nonpublic figures, the defendant is effectively guilty until proven innocent.

The courts determined that Dalitz and partner Allard Roen were public figures and, rather than setting out to prove the magazine knowingly printed untrue statements about them, they withdrew from the suit. Those left to press the case were La Costa part-owners Mervyn Adelson and Irwin Molasky, who are better known as the co-founders of Lorimar Productions, makers of TV's "The Waltons" and "Dallas." The courts held that they were not public figures and *Penthouse* would have to prove the truth of its article or face the damages, which had been trimmed to $522 million.

Just as the case was ready for trial, the authors, Bergman and Gerth, withdrew from the defense case, reaching settlement with

Nizer and writing a letter expressing their "regret" for the article. Grutman was outraged. He claimed Nizer and La Costa co-counsel Michael Silverberg had violated legal ethics and state law, going behind his back to cut a private deal with the writers. He argued to the court that during their discussions with Nizer, Bergman and Gerth may have disclosed defense strategy, compromising *Penthouse*'s case. For those reasons, Grutman argued, Nizer and Silverberg should be barred from the case. A lower court agreed, but the La Costa lawyers were reinstated by the appellate court.

Before the trial ever started, Grutman was overwhelmed. It was going to be tough enough to prove the article was true, but without the authors seated at the defense table it would be near to impossible. Grutman's strongest witness, the only person capable of delivering independent knowledge of organized crime's relationship to La Costa, was Jimmy. At the rate of $250 an hour, Jimmy sat for several days, weeks before trial, presenting a 1,000-page deposition in which he told of how he had been ordered by Roselli to file a suit—the one he later dropped—against *Penthouse*. He explained that he had lied in his first deposition when he denied any association with organized crime. And he explained about his membership in La Cosa Nostra.

Grutman's strategy was to have Jimmy testify about meetings he had attended at La Costa and Dalitz's connections to organized crime. Second, he would seek to have Jimmy testify as an expert witness, describing how guys "connected" to the mob could obtain Teamsters loans to start a business and the place legitimate "front men" in charge.

After nearly seven years of pretrial wrangling, the case came to trial—and was assigned to Los Angeles County Superior Court Judge Kenneth Gale, who sat in Compton, California, one of Los Angeles's worst slums. How the case got to Gale's courtroom remains unclear. It had something to do with random selection and the need to find a state judge who could spend four months to a year absorbed in a single action.

Judge Gale, a slight man with piercing dark eyes and a shock of white hair, had practiced trial law in Los Angeles and Las Vegas for more than thirty years, but was no match for the bitter confrontations resulting from courtroom egos the size of Nizer's and Grutman's.

Grutman, possessing the sharper tongue of the two lawyers, repeatedly drew Gale's ire. Twice Gale cited the *Penthouse* lead lawyer for contempt on minor indiscretions, and he constantly found fault with Grutman's ethics and legal interpretations, barring him from presenting most of the *Penthouse* case.

Gale prohibited the most basic elements of defense:

Documents assembled during a grand jury inquiry into La Costa, which were supposed to be turned over to the defense by Judge Gale, were never released;

Jerome Adler, who had provided a vast deposition on the legal editing and vetting he had done on the *Penthouse* article, was permitted only one hour to explain the care taken to document statements in the article;

And the jury was barred from reviewing a copy of the magazine containing the La Costa article.

Gale defended his withholding of the magazine from the jury on the grounds that it "is probably offensive to sixty percent of the population of this nation. The court's personal feeling is, in general, the magazine is so nauseous that most readers who read it wouldn't give too great a credence to the article in question."

Gale was only slightly more lenient with Nizer's team, but the burden of proof rested on Grutman, not Nizer.

Before Jimmy showed up, the intense rigors of the case had created such tensions that Grutman was suffering incapacitating back spasms—and the very worst was yet to come.

The case had been going on for five months when Jimmy arrived in Los Angeles on February 24, 1982, a few days before he was scheduled to testify. Carl Shapiro, Grutman's lead co-counsel, met Jimmy at Henderson's office to prepare his testimony.

"So how's it going for you guys? Pretty good or what?"

"Well, we got this judge—Jimmy, I'm telling you, if our evidence was the size of the Pacific, all this guy is letting us put in front of the jury would be a glass of water," Shapiro said.

"You think someone got to this prick or what?"

"Well, I can't say. We don't know much about this Judge Gale. He was assigned to the case just before trial and no one knows too much about him."

Jimmy stared in silence for a moment. "Gale. That wouldn't be Kenny Gale, would it? Thin little guy with thick white hair?"

"You know about him, huh?"

"Shit, know about him? I know him real well."

Shapiro was scared to ask the next question—the answer could make things worse than they already were if it turned out Gale had it in for Jimmy.

"Hey Jimmy, how do you know this guy? This could be important. He's really been screwing us over."

"Doesn't matter, I just know know him. Let's put it that way, okay. I know him from way back. He's a friend, Carl, just a friend. Forget about it."

"Look, Jimmy, I don't think he's a friend anymore in this trial. You got to tell us how you know him. This guy's been giving us a real hard time and it could really help to know something about him, something that could explain what his problem is."

"Well, I don't treat my friends like that. Just forget about it," Jimmy insisted.

Shapiro spent half an hour pushing and cajoling, but Jimmy was steadfast.

"Okay. Look, Jimmy, you're going to testify in a couple of days. If your evidence comes in the way you think it's going to come in, I won't ask you how you know him. But if he cuts you off the way I think he's going to cut you off, then you'll have to let us know how you know him. Are you willing to do that?"

"Sure, Carl. But don't worry about that, that's not going to happen. He's a stand-up guy. He's a friend."

Jimmy took the stand and nodded to Judge Gale. Gale, without any special sense of recognition, returned the nod.

And then it was circus time.

On average, for every one of Grutman's questions there was at least one objection. Gale generally allowed Jimmy to reply until he got to the substance of his testimony.

With some difficulty, Jimmy established that he could identify certain members of La Cosa Nostra because he had been introduced to them as *amico nostra*, but he was barred from offering details.

He was permitted to describe his associations with the Chicago mob and meetings they had had at the Desert Inn in Las Vegas, but he wasn't permitted to discuss the Desert Inn being owned by Dalitz.

He got so far as to describe a meeting at La Costa with Sam Giancana, at that time the boss in Chicago, but that's as far as they got:

MR. GRUTMAN: Mr. Fratianno, without telling us the contents of the conversation between you and Mr. Giancana, can you tell us what the subject discussed was.

A. The planning of killing Desi Arnaz.

Q. When was that—

On an objection from Silverberg the answer was stricken from the record as "nonresponsive" and the jury was instructed to disregard it.

The tale Jimmy didn't get to tell was how the mob, angered by the portrayal of the mob in Arnaz's TV series, "The Untouchables," had decided to have Arnaz killed.

After much argument, Jimmy was permitted a simple "yes" in reply to Grutman's asking if "any criminal activity" was discussed at his La Costa meeting with Giancana.

Similarly, he was prohibited from explaining that various mob figures were associated with Dalitz, or that La Costa was a regular meeting place for criminal discussions by mobsters, and that Jackie Presser and Rudy Tham met there on at least one occasion.

Grutman was getting cut off at every turn.

As he headed toward concluding his direct examination, Grutman tried to present an explanation of Jimmy's suit against *Penthouse*, the one that Roselli had ordered Jimmy to file.

Q. Mr. Fratianno, I asked you at the outset of this examination about the contents of this *Penthouse* article which called you an infamous hit man. Had you ever been called an infamous hit man before?

MR. SILVERBERG: Not relevant, your honor.

THE COURT: Sustained.

Q. Who brought the *Penthouse* article to your attention?

MR. SILVERBERG: Not relevant, your honor.

THE COURT: Sustained.

Q. Did you sue *Penthouse* magazine?

MR. SILVERBERG: Not relevant whether he sued, your honor.

MR. GRUTMAN: I think it's highly relevant.

THE COURT: I will sustain the objection.

Q. At or about the time that the March 1975 issue of *Penthouse* magazine appeared, did you have a conversation with Johnny Roselli?

The question was cut off and the lawyers proceeded to the bench. Grutman, red-faced, argued that Jimmy should be permitted to explain why he filed his suit against *Penthouse* and why he lied in his first deposition, inasmuch as La Costa's lawyers would be permitted to use the first deposition to discredit Jimmy.

Gale disagreed. He said Grutman would have to wait until later, until after La Costa used the material to discredit Jimmy, to get an explanation.

Shortly thereafter the case was recessed for the day.

As Jimmy stepped down from the stand, under escort of two federal marshals, he walked by the defense table, seizing Shapiro's shoulder in his large hand. "Okay, I got to talk to you. Now."

Jimmy led the way; his marshals followed. Shapiro signaled to Grutman, and the two men breathlessly tried to catch up with the entourage.

"What's going on here?" Grutman asked Shapiro as they headed toward the lock-up area, where Jimmy was kept under guard between appearances.

"I don't know yet," Shapiro began. "But Jimmy says he knows the judge."

It was the first Grutman had heard about it.

"I didn't tell you earlier because it seemed it would only muddy the waters while you had him on the stand."

"How does he know him?" Grutman demanded.

"Look, I don't know any more than that," Shapiro explained. "All he'd tell me was that he knew the guy and that he'd let us know more if Gale gave him any trouble."

After waiting a few minutes, Shapiro and Grutman were escorted to the lock-up by a marshal.

Before either of the lawyers could say a word Jimmy exploded.

"Let me tell you about this motherfucker. I'm going to tell you a couple of things about this prick that's gonna knock you on your ass.

"I've known this prick for years. He was my wife's father's lawyer. Jean knows him better than I do. She's known him since she was a kid. But he's been a lawyer for a whole load of made guys and union guys in Las Vegas. Believe me, I know what I'm talking about. He knows who I am and all about me. We've been out to dinner and Jean and I have had him over to the house. He even tried to get me an early parole one time.

"And I'll tell you one more thing. You remember I told you about my filing this suit against *Penthouse*, how Johnny told me to file it and how I talked to my lawyer about it?"

Shapiro and Grutman, unable to get a word in to respond to Jimmy's hysterical monologue, nodded in unison.

"Well, Gale was the one I went to with the case at first. I asked him if he would take the case and he said he thought I had a real good suit. He gave me all kinds of encouragement, but said he wasn't going to be able to represent me, so I took the case to Dennis McDonald.

"That's the game this prick's playing. He's scared to death, every time you ask about the *Penthouse* suit I brought, he thinks I'm going to say something about him. That's why he's sustaining all them fuckin' objections. He wants to shut me up and there ain't no way I'm shutting up now. I'm hot, man. I mean really mad.

"So what are we going to do about this prick?"

The two lawyers stood in amazement at what they were hearing. The case was in its fifteenth week of trial; it had been no secret that Jimmy would be called to testify, and Gale had not recused himself.

"Holy shit," Grutman said quietly, shaking his head. "What do I do now? 'Oh, excuse me your honor, but it seems you're an old friend of this witness, a killer, a Mafia boss, so will you please step down from this case?' Gale will never buy it."

"It wouldn't carry much weight for Jimmy to file an affidavit," Shapiro added. "That would only look like he had some ax to grind here. But his wife could do it. She could lay out the whole thing, how long she'd known him and how she and Jimmy and he were close friends for years and all."

"Yeah, Jean'd do it in a hot fuckin' minute if I told her to," Jimmy said.

"Okay then. How do we get ahold of her?"

That afternoon, Shapiro drove out to Palm Springs, where Jean, unknown to the marshals, was visiting with friends. She balked at first, but after speaking with Jimmy, she was convinced to tell the entire story, with certain embarrassing personal recollections redacted.

Jack Barron shifted gears from investigating La Costa and its connections to the mob, to investigating Gale, his connections to Fratianno and his former clients.

As Shapiro and Barron prepared a brief to have Gale disqualified, the trial continued.

Louis Nizer, a master of trial law, turned to Jimmy's original *Penthouse* deposition as a source of impeachment. Where Jimmy testified at trial that he had visited La Costa at least twice, including meetings with Giancana and Roselli, in his first deposition he said he had never been there.

Q. And do you recall whether you also said, "I don't know where that God damned place is"?
A. I don't recall saying that—I'd like to explain.
MR. GRUTMAN: May the witness be permitted to explain his answer?
MR. NIZER: Please answer my question, sir.
THE COURT: No, please.
THE WITNESS: Well, your honor, he is taking it out of the deposition. I know what he's doing.
THE COURT: Please, you have counsel that will represent you in respect to—
THE WITNESS: Well, I would like to explain some of the answers. I think they need some explaining.
THE COURT: You will get that opportunity.
MR. GRUTMAN: May he do so now, your honor?
THE COURT: No. One step at a time. The opportunity will come.
THE WITNESS: He can go through that whole deposition. There's maybe 150 lies in it. I will admit there are lies. What do you want from me? I admit ninety percent of it are lies.

Jimmy balked at every question relating to the deposition: "I don't recall what I said"; "Refresh my recollection"; "The record speaks for itself"; "I lied throughout that deposition."

Nizer did win one apparent concession: Jimmy said he never saw Mervyn Adelson or Irwin Molasky during his visits or meetings to La Costa, and that over the years he had visited many hotels on Cosa Nostra business and that those hotels didn't necessarily have any connections to the mob or the Teamsters.

But Nizer repeatedly came back to the deposition, or badgered Jimmy about his murders. And Jimmy continued to press for the opportunity to explain his answers, why he had lied and why he had killed.

Nizer was bearing down on Jimmy's role in the execution of Frank Niccoli:

Q. Did you invite him over to your house for a drink?
A. Yes, sir.
Q. And did you put a rope around his neck?
A. I would like to explain it, sir.
Q. No, before you explain it, sir, did you put a rope—
A. Now, wait a minute—

THE COURT: Wait a minute.

THE WITNESS: Well, your honor, there's an explanation to these cases.

THE COURT: I know, but—

THE WITNESS: I am forced to do what I do. He's getting away with murder.

The spectator-packed courtroom broke into laughter, and after a moment of surprise, Jimmy, too, saw the humor of his comment. But he still didn't get to put his explanation in.

As the day drew to a close, Grutman requested once more that Jimmy have the chance to explain his answers, and Gale replied: "He can make it tomorrow. He can make it tomorrow morning."

But the morning brought a new issue: Jimmy's qualifying as an expert witness.

Gale was, to say the least, reluctant to accept the notion of an expert witness on organized crime. Unlike the Marchiondo case, Jimmy's fee would be paid by *Penthouse* regardless of his "expert witness" status. But Grutman needed Jimmy to qualify as an expert to explain the linkage of the mob to the Teamsters, linkage vital to the theory that La Costa was a subsidiary of that unholy coupling.

Grutman made an "offer" of proof to show Jimmy was an expert— a legal discourse in which a witness normally describes credentials, degrees, memberships, and honors. In Jimmy's case, however, an offer of proof focused on his joining La Cosa Nostra, his involvement in crime—from bookmaking to extortion, pornography to murder— and a litany of the cases in which he had testified.

Although the exercise was performed in a closed hearing, outside the presence of the jury, Gale still prohibited any but the most cursory examination: barring Jimmy from describing his speaking on the phone to Presser and Tham during their meeting at La Costa; the L.A. mob's efforts to extort Dalitz; names of prominent mob bosses; how "connected guys" benefit from their relationship with La Cosa Nostra.

Gale wasn't buying Jimmy as an expert witness. Crime, he would say, was not a matter of expertise. Terms such as "connected" or "boss" were not to be regarded as having any special meaning in a court of law. What mattered was what Jimmy could testify to from personal knowledge and participation, not what he understood in terms of relationships.

As the jury returned to the courtroom, Jimmy, seated in the witness box, was in a blind rage.

Grutman picked up where they had left off the day before—

seeking to have Gale make good on his promise that Jimmy could explain the lies he told in his first *Penthouse* deposition in 1976.

It was a short exchange:

MR. GRUTMAN: Did you tell the truth in the answers that you gave to the questions that were put to you in the 1981 deposition in the case of La Costa against *Penthouse?*

MR. NIZER: The objection has been sustained to that earlier, your honor, it's for the jury to determine that.

THE COURT: Sustained.

Jimmy exploded: Wait a minute. He said sustain the answer. I never heard anything like that.

THE COURT: Mr. Bailiff, remove Mr. Fratianno.

THE WITNESS: I'm all right. You don't have to remove me. I just see what's going on in this courtroom. I just can't stand what's going on in the courtroom. I'm okay.

THE COURT: All right.

THE WITNESS: You don't have to remove me.

MR. GRUTMAN: Mr. Fratianno, yesterday when Mr. Nizer was asking you questions you said you wanted to give an explanation. Do you remember that?

A. That's correct, sir.

Q. Will you give us that explanation now?

MR. SILVERBERG: Objection, your honor.

THE COURT: Sustained.

There was some more argument, but that pretty much summed up Jimmy's participation—at least his role in the courtroom.

That evening Jimmy called Newt, who put him in touch with Denny Walsh. Jimmy got on the phone and broke into a long diatribe about Gale, offering Walsh "the story of your life."

In an interview weeks later, Walsh was the first to confront Gale about his association with Jimmy. Gale denied there was any such thing as a "personal relationship," he only knew him casually through Jean. Yet when pressed, Gale shrouded any additional contact with Jimmy in "attorney-client privilege."

It took a few more weeks, but Walsh scratched around and eventually came up with and published a memorandum from Jimmy's parole file describing a March 22, 1971, meeting Gale had with Manley Bowler, a state parole agency official:

Manley J. Bowler . . . was recently approached by an attorney named Kenneth Gale. Mr. Gale attempted to speak to him . . . in behalf of Mr.

Fratianno. The attorney had not been directly in contact with Mr. Fratianno, but had been in contact with Fratianno's girlfriend.

Mr. Bowler indicated that Mr. Gale made "a very slim pitch" in behalf of Fratianno but did not come out and make a direct request for leniency or release on parole. When pressed by Mr. Bowler, the attorney apparently indicated that Mr. Fratianno had done him some favors in the past. He was not specific as to what the favors were and Mr. Bowler expressed the opinion that the attorney was somewhat nervous and/or possibly embarrassed by even bringing the matter to Mr. Bowler's attention.

What followed was an exchange of legal hostilities at levels of ugliness usually reserved for divorce court.

A month after Jimmy's testimony, Grutman presented Gale with a motion for a mistrial—citing Jean and Jimmy's long-standing relationship with the judge as well as information Jack Barron had unearthed showing Gale had represented union racketeers while working as a lawyer in Las Vegas. Gale not only refused the motion, but he issued a gag order barring any discussion of the motion's contents.

Grutman, incensed, took his motion to the state's supreme court—charging Gale had "concealed his true past . . . has himself been involved in possible labor racketeering," and has "prejudiced the evidence in this case" in order to "orchestrate" a victory for La Costa—and asked that Gale be disqualified.

The state's high court sat on the motion as the jury, after six months of testimony, entered into three weeks of deliberations. The jury, finding their way through a mountain of evidence and obfuscation from both sides, returned a verdict on May 13, 1982, finding in favor of *Penthouse*, saying, in effect, that what had appeared in the article was the truth.

Grutman was stunned and elated. He had felt from the outset that his evidence was sufficient to bring victory, but he had never expected that the limited evidence Gale had permitted into the record would be sufficient.

The case should have ended there, but Gale, in a final act of defiance, invoked a rare contrivance of law, overturning the jury's verdict and ordering a new trial. He cited Grutman with using improper conduct and called the verdict "a miscarriage of justice."

Before the merits of the Grutman-Gale melee were decided, David Eagleson, presiding judge of the state superior court interceded, removing Gale from jurisdiction over the retrial. Eagleson offered no comment.

However, the California appeals courts later sided with Grutman, holding that Gale had erred by rejecting the *Penthouse* motion and not disqualifying himself.

After some ten years of legal jousting, the two sides had spent well in excess of $14 million. Jimmy collected a mere $40,000.

On December 5, 1985, as the court prepared once more to get a trial date, the two sides reached a settlement. There was no blame set and no hostilities vented—no wrong and no money damages. Just a statement, signed by the litigants:

Since May, 1975, we have been litigating what has become the longest, costliest, largest and probably most complex libel case that has ever been before the American courts. As the record now stands, a new trial has been ordered as to some plaintiffs. The toll which this litigation has exacted has been punishing and arduous on both sides.

Continued litigation will only further torture and cause more expense to all parties. Accordingly, we have now reached a point where it appears that if the case were to continue through yet additional court proceedings, whoever would ultimately win would enjoy only a pyrrhic victory at best.

During the course of the trial and subsequent thereto, we have learned things about each other which were not known to us before the litigation.

Penthouse, in the article which it published and about which the lawsuit was litigated, did not mean to imply nor did it intend for its readers to believe that Messrs. Adelson and Molasky are or were members of organized crime or criminals. In addition, *Penthouse* acknowledges that all of the individual plaintiffs, including Messrs. Roen and Dalitz, have been extremely active in commendable, civic and philanthropic activities which have earned them recognition from many estimable people. Furthermore, *Penthouse* acknowledges that among the plaintiffs' successful business activities is the La Costa resort itself, one of the outstanding resort complexes in the world.

The plaintiffs acknowledge that during the course of the litigation they have learned things about the defendants which were not known to them before they initiated the lawsuit. They have learned of many personal and professional awards and distinctions that have been conferred upon *Penthouse* and its publisher, Robert C. Guccione. After nearly a decade of seemingly endless litigation, all sides are agreed that there is no easy solution to the parties' concerns which are abiding problems in a democratic society in which people often hold strongly opposing beliefs about each other.

The parties have agreed to settle their differences by discontinuing further litigation. Each side has had an opportunity to set before the courts and the public its position with respect to the case and the public has been served by having these contentions publicly aired. It is the opinion of all parties that, notwithstanding their continuing differences of opinion, they are not obligated to litigate forever. Accordingly, each side will take those things that gratified it (and those things that constituted disappointments), disengage from the litigation, and go about their separate ways.

In effect, they spent more than $14 million for the right in a democratic society to say they disagreed and continued to disagree, but didn't want to pay any more to prove who was right.

Jimmy may have been the only one who came away from the melee fully satisfied, convinced that "I won that fuckin' case for Guccione."

After *Penthouse*, Jimmy went into semi-retirement for several months. He retreated, again with Jean, to Georgia where he awaited anxiously the outcome of the federal trial of the Cleveland mob.

It had taken more than four years, but all the players had finally fallen into place. All of the mob players in the FBI leak and the conspiracy to kill Danny Greene had been identified. And the U.S. Supreme Court had ruled that RICO could be applied to an illegal enterprise such as La Cosa Nostra.

Jimmy had expected to be called. He began making noises early on about how he shouldn't be forced to testify in Cleveland, how it would endanger his family and all the rest of the excuses he could find. But the prosecutors had no intention of calling him. Their case was complicated enough without the added confusion of having to review all of Jimmy's prior contradictory statements about the Cleveland case. It was decided early on that they would do this one without him.

The trial ran nearly four months, ending in July 1982 with across-the-board convictions—and heavy, multiple prison sentences, sixteen to eighteen years each, amounting to life without parole for all but the youngest of the gang.

Months later a second case developed from the GANGMURS probe, a narcotics case, which went to trial, ending in the conviction of every known remaining member of the Cleveland mob, including Angelo Lonardo, the Family's most recent underboss, who was sentenced to 103 years in federal prison.

The Cleveland Family, once one of America's proudest mob strongholds, was entirely eliminated. The only survivor was Maishe Rockman, Johnny Scalish's Jewish brother-in-law, who did what he could to hold the Family together.

16

Fighting the Program

SUNSET cast a broad, blazing streak across the water, stretching endlessly from his backyard to the horizon. Down a gentle hill from the house was the lawn, then a field of wildflowers competing with patches of ground-hugging, wind-beaten shrubs, and beyond a sheer cliff, small pine-dusted islands sprang up from the water.

To the north was a vast expanse of Canada; to the south the U.S.A.

This was no government hideout. Jimmy had bought the land and built this house, completing it in 1985 for just under $190,000. It was a custom-designed home, his palace—something a man could show with pride.

It was thoroughly modern, with 8-foot-high windows and sliding glass doors leading to a deck overlooking the water. The deck—about 12 feet wide, 50 feet long, and three stories above the ground—offered the sense of being on a sailing yacht.

Inside was a 55-by-20-foot living/dining room, divided by a stone fireplace, which rose two stories to the peak of a cathedral ceiling. There were four bedrooms, a den, and an exercise room. Every room had a color TV hooked to a satellite dish; there were usually two of them running at any given moment.

The furnishings were French provincial; the art was gentle pastels, original sketches of Boston harbor, nothing garish or too modern. Plush, wall-to-wall carpeting was covered at several central locations by richly detailed oriental rugs. In the center hallway hung a chandelier with no fewer than eighty hand-cut, golf-ball-size crystals.

From the street it looked like a modest, cedar-paneled house; Jimmy didn't want to attract too much attention. This wasn't a wealthy community; rather, it was a hard-working part of the American heartland, where people got by on far less than would be considered adequate in the cities.

Jean adored the house. She spent her days driving two hours each way to the nearest city on decorating sprees and her evenings attending nearby church functions, setting down roots in the community. Yet she couldn't work up any enthusiasm for the location: the winters were too cold, the summers too mild, and she was burdened by how desolate the surrounding woods made her feel.

Jimmy, however, was snug and secure.

"Even if they knew where I was they couldn't find me," Jimmy told Newt as they strolled the yard, admiring the lawn he had spent hours nourishing and grooming.

"This sure is a marvelous place you've got," Newt said in sincere admiration as he lit a cigarette.

Newt was the only person outside WITSEC who knew with any certainty who Jimmy was and where he was living. It was a violation of security to have Newt up there, but Jimmy always bent the rules a bit to satisfy himself. And besides, this wasn't solely a pleasure trip. Newt was now working exclusively for two clients: Denny Walsh and Jimmy. At Jimmy's insistence, Newt had been hired to investigate two libel suits filed against his publisher, Times Books, for statements made in *The Last Mafioso*. Neither case had gone to court, and Newt had developed impressive proof that the book was accurate in both instances.

"I'm thinking of putting in a pool over there, next year, for Jean," Jimmy said, pointing to the center of the yard. "I'm gonna have it covered and heated so she can use it in winter. The girl loves to swim."

Jimmy reached over and grabbed a Marlboro from Newt's shirt pocket. He looked over toward the house to be sure Jean wasn't watching before lighting it. On his last annual physical, the doctors at Johns Hopkins had told him he had to quit cigars. He had switched to chewing tobacco, but every so often took a taste of smoke. He hated doctors, but he did whatever they told him.

"But tell me, Jim, do you really think the wise guys are still looking for you? I mean, you really think you need to live all the way out here?"

"Hey, are you kidding me," he said, drawing on the cigarette. "Spilotro still has a crew looking for me—the FBI knows about that."

They pulled up a pair of lounge chairs and sat watching the summer sun set into the water; Jimmy toyed with the *TV Guide* crossword puzzle.

"Besides, these guys would love to take a whack at me before that Kansas City case. You know both Spilotro and Aiuppa are in that one and they hate me like poison." Jimmy started giggling. "Just wait, Newt. I'm going to stare that motherfucker Aiuppa right in the eye, just the way he stared me down after he killed Johnny. I'm going to settle that score all right."

King, a Siberian husky, and Jack, a long-haired German shepherd, came up alongside Jimmy's chair and nuzzled against his side. The dogs were constant companions, strays that Jimmy had adopted and trained to their new names. At night they roamed the yard howling at intruders; during the day they wandered miles from home, returning every few hours to look for Jimmy.

"You know, Newt, I've testified against four bosses now, every one of them has ended up in prison," Jimmy said. "And this program still treats me like shit. They still don't pay all my bills."

"I don't see what you're bitching about," Newt said, with a good-natured belly laugh and a sweep of his hand, pointing to their surroundings. "Looks kinda cozy to me."

"Oh, come on, man. This is all my money here, money I made in depositions or with interviews or the book. Some of it Dennis loaned me. You know when I'm on the road they pay the hotel bill, but they still give me only twenty-five dollars a day to live on. Shit, Newt, breakfast at a hotel costs you eight dollars and a steak at dinner is going to run twenty with a drink and a tip. And what about lunch? I'm telling you, these people are tighter than two coats of paint. And you know, they destroyed $8,000 worth of antique furniture when we moved here from Texas, and they haven't paid for that, and then there are the cars—you know, every time we move they make me sell the cars so they can't be traced. And do you think I get reimbursed for the losses I take on that? Hell, no.

"I'm a pain in the ass to them. I'm the one guy who tells them what they can go do with this program, and they don't like it. Safir's told me, 'If you don't like it then leave.' They want to get rid of me so bad they can taste it. Boy, if I knew then what I know today, I never would have gone with this program."

Jimmy was on automatic pilot. But Newt, who'd heard it all before, found Jimmy's delivery less forceful, his complaints less credible as they sat looking out on the water.

"Let me tell you something else about this program. They put this broad in charge of me. I mean, come on. A broad? Telling me what to do? That just shows you how little these motherfuckers understand about a guy like me."

The "broad"—as Jimmy put it—was Marilyn Mode, a slim blonde in her thirties who had the unenviable task of directing security for Jimmy and Jean, including speaking to them on an almost daily basis to act as their contact with the outside world. Generally, it was Mode who suffered with what she fondly called "Jimmy's daily scream," a morning ritual in which he would press one item from his long list of complaints about life and the program.

Despite his hysterics, Mode always played it by the book, knowing as well as anyone the special set of rules carved out for Jimmy.

After five years on the program, it had been decided in 1983 that Jimmy and Jean had to be permanently relocated. Jimmy had inspected the waterfront area he would later build on, and bought a house nearby. But when he learned that WITSEC intended to put him on minimum funding and require he find a job, he raised hell with Safir and, later that year, arranged a meeting in Washington with Stephen Trott, the assistant U.S. Attorney General in charge of the Justice Department's Criminal Division.

Jimmy packed the room with his supporters: McDonald, Henderson, Ahearn, Mike DeFeo (the L.A. prosecutor who had initially negotiated Jimmy's deal), Pat Foran (the agent who had directed the Cleveland leak case), as well as agents and prosecutors who were anticipating Jimmy's testimony in pending cases. Also attending were Mode, Safir, and Gerald Shur, Safir's superior at Justice.

After a round of introductions, Jimmy took control: "Look here, Trott, these guys want me to go out and expose myself, they want me to get a job. They think I'm like ninety-eight percent of the bums on this program. There were promises made to me when I got into this thing that me and my family would be taken care of. They made all sorts of promises that they're not living up to. Now they don't plan on treating me like a man, they don't intend to hold up their end. Well, I'll tell you something, you let them get away with this and you can go testify in these cases."

He presented a laundry list of things he wanted from the program—everything from paying to clean Jean's furs to new drapes for their home, and specific dollars and cents accounts of his needs for mortgage payments, local property taxes, insurance, and utilities.

Trott asked if Jimmy had any document showing that he had been promised he would be taken care of for the rest of his life.

"I don't have no paper, if that's what you mean, but I know what was said to me."

When it became Safir's and Shur's turns, they explained that they were applying standard WITSEC rules. "We're not treating you any different than any other witness," Shur explained.

Henderson, who had sat in silence, somewhat embarrassed that he would have to defend Jimmy's ravings, jumped in to the fray.

"I think that's the problem," he began. "Jimmy Fratianno isn't like any other witness. Forgetting for a moment the remarkable amount of testimony he's provided for us, he's an old man and you can't very well expect him to go out and start making a living in a legitimate manner at this point of his life. What are you going to ask a man of his age and experience to do? Become a waiter? Not to mention his notoriety and the likelihood that someone would make him if he was out hustling to make a living. You just can't expect a man like this to get legitimate employment.

"Now, as I see it, the bottom line is this: If he's forced to expose himself and he gets killed, no matter what excuses you make for public distribution, the reality will be that no one will ever again trust the program. It would be a devastating blow to the O.C. section. Because if we can't protect and provide for Fratianno, the most influential witness we've ever had, then who else is going to ever trust us?"

Trott agreed. Jimmy Fratianno shouldn't be treated like just any witness, but he adjourned the meeting without any promises.

Days later, McDonald received a letter from Trott outlining the special consideration that would be given to Jimmy:

The following amounts will comprise his monthly funding: house payments: $800; electric: $190; water: $50; furniture rentals: $197. $8,000 in a lump sum toward a car purchase and gasoline will be taken from his regular subsistence fund. He will further receive full funding for telephone calls relating to Mr. Fratianno's cooperation with law enforcement after he submits his statements. He will receive subsistence funding of $1,200 for one, subsistence for two of $1,350. In addition to monthly funding Mr. Fratianno will also receive the following additional funding: auto insurance, $1,400; household insurance, $1,100 per year; real estate taxes, $1,070; sewer assessment, $1,227; sewer connection, $400; sewer installation, $430; security draperies, $2,500. The department also agrees to continue to pay all necessary medical expenses for Mr. and Mrs. Fratianno, through Oct. 31, 1985.

It amounted to $33,477 a year, untaxed—plus $11,300 in one-time payments.

It was virtually everything he could expect—but he wanted more.

"You know, a doctor signed a letter for us saying Jean had to move out of our first house here because of her allergies, and they still wouldn't pay our moving expenses," he complained to Newt.

"Well, Jim, they do provide for your security—I mean your new identity and all," Newt offered.

"Security? Do you see any marshals around here? And now I've got this little appliance repair business in town just to make ends meet. I shouldn't have to go out to make a living and expose myself. The nearest marshal is 130 miles away. Security? I provide my own security.

"Well, that last agreement with the government expires at the end of this year, in October, and I'm going to have to go to Washington to renegotiate this thing. I'm just going to tell them what I want, and if I don't get it, fuck them. I'll leave this program cold turkey."

The dogs, who had been resting silently, one on each of Jimmy's feet, suddenly leaped up and ran toward the corner of the house, barking wildly. Jimmy watched carefully. A moment later, John Kasten, a neighbor from up the block, came around to the backyard, with the dogs falling over each other as they ran patterns around his legs.

Kasten, an affable fat man in his fifties, had retired from the Canadian commodities business several years earlier after double bypass surgery. As he approached, he broke into a series of bad jokes about President Reagan's recent colon cancer operation.

Jimmy recoiled, his body tightened, and he sent off an apparent chill as Kasten pulled up a chair. Jimmy made the introductions and then excused himself to make drinks.

"What's wrong, Jimmy boy, not amused by a little medical humor?" Kasten said, his voice trailing Jimmy into the house. "I'll tell you, Newt, this friend of yours can be a real tough audience. Now the lady of the house, that Mrs. Nichols, she's a fine lady, with a good sense of humor."

"Oh, yes sirree, Jean's a real fine girl," Newt replied.

"Yeah, I'll tell you, they're both real fine people. Everyone here has accepted them just like family, don't you know," Kasten said, his voice dropping a bit, his eyes focusing on Newt's.

"This isn't the easiest of places to settle, you know. I mean, being so far off the beaten path and all."

"Oh, but it sure is beautiful country," Newt injected.

"Yeah, sure it's gorgeous, but it's remote, Newt. Not many people come this far to settle or to visit, you know. It's the kind of place a man could come to if he never wanted anyone to find him," Kasten said, now staring at Newt for some reaction.

Newt kept smiling and nodding through Kasten's increasingly serious comments.

"But I'll tell you, I like him and all. Yeah, I sure like that Jimmy boy," Kasten said. "But there are just some times when I think the only way to get him to laugh is to make him an offer he can't refuse. You know what I mean, Newt?"

The Justice Department was on a rampage. It was out to crush La Cosa Nostra.

In the mid-1980s it seemed there wasn't a month that passed without some new revelation, indictment, or conviction of a major mob organization. Virtually every major U.S. city had a mob trial underway or pending against La Cosa Nostra's leaders. And if Jimmy wasn't testifying, at the very least he had been asked to offer his guidance in the investigation and prosecution.

The Kansas City trial, the largest mob case ever undertaken up to that time, would mark the beginning of a new round of testimony for Jimmy. It involved the leadership of the Midwest's major crime Families, fifteen men in all, including Spilotro, Aiuppa, and the entire leadership of the Chicago mob, Cleveland's Maishe Rockman, Milwaukee's mob boss Frank Balistrieri, and Kansas City mob leader Nick Civella. They were charged with using their control of Teamsters leaders to obtain $67 million in Teamsters Central States Pension Fund loans. The loans were turned over to Allen Glick, an unwitting mob front man, who purchased the Fremont and Stardust casino-hotels and permitted the mob loan brokers to plant their top men in the casino money rooms. At least $2 million was slipped out without Glick knowing about it.

Jimmy was scheduled to testify in Kansas City against Aiuppa, Spilotro, and Chicago mob *capo* Joey Lombardo and to explain how La Cosa Nostra controlled the Teamsters.

Next on Jimmy's itinerary was a round of testimony in New York City, which had fallen under the spell of Rudolph Giuliani.

Giuliani had won the hearts of New Yorkers. He was the handsome young prosecutor clearly doing battle with the most outright forces of evil in society. At thirty-eight, he came to a city where La Cosa Nostra operated openly and declared war, just as he had as the Justice Department's top gun in the war against narcotics. He declared war in grand juries, bringing in hundreds of mob indictments. He declared war in the courtroom, with a near-perfect conviction record. He declared war in the streets, touring some of the city's most notorious narcotics and mob neighborhoods. And he declared war, almost nightly, on the evening news—delivering his message in concise, staccato statements, perfect for network replay and *USA Today*–style leads.

Upon taking over as U.S. Attorney for the Southern District of New York in 1983, Giuliani promised and delivered a new focus; he wanted more indictments and he got a 23 percent increase within twelve months.

His staff of young assistants didn't always approve. Some saw white-collar cases they deemed important ending up on a back burner as Giuliani pursued the splashier prosecutions of corrupt politicians or mob bosses. Others disagreed with his press conference style of prosecution—heralding each indictment and conviction to a gathering of reporters. No one doubted that his ultimate aim was to become mayor or governor.

But no one argues with results.

By the summer of 1985, Giuliani had five major La Cosa Nostra cases at trial or pretrial simultaneously, every one of them initiated before he came to New York: Colombo Family boss Carmine "Junior" Persico and ten leaders of that family were up on RICO charges, involving extortion, bribery, gambling, and loan-sharking; in the so-called Pizza Connection case, twenty-three men were charged with operating an international heroin ring, using pizza parlors as import points in the U.S.; Paul Castellano was named along with twenty-four others in connection with twenty-six mob murders and operating an international car theft ring; Genovese mob financier Matthew "Matty the Horse" Ianiello was awaiting trial on RICO charges, involving his operation of bars and carting businesses; and lastly, the Commission case, just starting to make its way through the courts.

That case involved the bosses and underbosses of each of New York's Five Families, the nucleus of the national crime Commission, which arbitrated disputes and defined turf for La Cosa Nostra. It was also, according to the government, the body that controlled New York's vital construction industry.

And Giuliani was just beginning to formulate a civil RICO case designed to remove from office leaders of the Teamsters, seeking to have them replaced with a court-appointed trustee.

With the exception of the Pizza Connection case, Jimmy played a role in all of Giuliani's mob-busting proceedings either as a witness or with guidance for investigators.

The past two years leading up to this big push had been relatively slow for Jimmy. He had testified in a New York sentencing hearing against his erstwhile friend Frank "Skinny" Velotta, parlaying a seven-year narcotics sentence into sixteen years; the Pennsylvania Crime Commission had interviewed him once and the President's Organized Crime Commission had called on him twice, once for testimony on mob money laundering and another time on pornography operations; in Las Vegas he had testified against a Lake Tahoe extortionist; and he had made an appearance before a New York grand jury investigating a uranium mine fraud, in which Jimmy had invested at Marchiondo's suggestion.

He had been interviewed by Labor Department investigators looking into allegations that Jackie Presser, then Teamsters president, had made off with millions of dollars by keeping ghost employees on his payroll. He told them as much as he knew: Presser was a front for La Cosa Nostra in Cleveland.

But when pressed to explain the basis of his knowledge, Jimmy exploded: "Lookit, the bosses of Cleveland, Chicago, and Kansas City picked him. I wasn't there, if that's what you mean. But I know it, man. That's the way this thing works. Besides, he told me once he couldn't make a move without first checking with the Family."

He had also advised Doug Roller in the Chicago trial of mob *capo* Joey Lombardo, Teamsters president Roy Williams, and the union's financial conduit Allen Dorfman. They had all been convicted, along with several lesser Teamsters officials, of trying to bribe U.S. Senator Howard W. Cannon.

Immediately after Dorfman's conviction, Jimmy had tried to warn Roller, telling him that Dorfman would either have to start cooperating immediately or he would be killed: "It's only common sense, Doug. Aiuppa isn't going to wait around to see if this guy's going to start cooperating." Two weeks later, Dorfman, free on bail, was gunned down in a Chicago parking lot.

At the Williams-Lombardo sentencing hearing, Jimmy described how La Cosa Nostra controls the Teamsters—placing made guys in key union positions to control the election of Teamsters officials—

and identified Lombardo as his contact for meetings with mob boss Aiuppa. In setting the sentence, U.S. District Judge Prentice Marshall said he was largely disregarding Jimmy's testimony, but still found Lombardo was "an operative of organized crime." They each drew a ten-year sentence.

"I'm really quite concerned," Jean was whispering into the phone as she paced the kitchen, inadvertently wrapping herself in the phone cord. "Jimmy's been acting oddly, Marilyn, and I've been doing some reading and I think he's got Alzheimer's disease."

Marilyn Mode, at her desk in the WITSEC offices in suburban Tysons Corner, Virginia, rolled her eyes.

"Jean," she said, elongating the vowel. "Now really. The man has the most remarkable memory anyone has ever seen. He's been getting physical and psychological check-ups at least once a year—not to mention the various medical treatments he's had for cataracts and gum work. And except for a case of high blood pressure every time he gets anywhere near a doctor, no one has found anything wrong with him."

"Sure, Marilyn. But you people don't live with him. You don't see the wild mood swings and weird behavior. One moment he'll be calm and really sweet and the next he'll be ranting like a banshee. And he seems to be constantly distracted by something. I'm telling you, for the past few weeks he just hasn't been the same man. Something's going on with him."

Marilyn wasn't convinced. She had been witness to those odd mood swings for two years, and they always became worse when he was around Jean.

"Look, he's coming in here for meetings next month. I'll see what we can do. But I really think you're exaggerating."

"Maybe I am. But there's something wrong with that man, Marilyn. He walks around the house nervous all the time. And he does the oddest things. Like taking the *TV Guide* and ripping pages out of it. Not even articles, just pages of listings," she said. "Now don't tell me that isn't peculiar."

"Like I said, Jean, I'll do what I can."

In the top drawer of Jimmy's dresser, under his hair tint, brushes, nail files, and other grooming aids, was a hidden panel in which he kept a .22 automatic handgun. Atop the weapon were several pages of cable TV listings and ads. The only common element to each was the listing of a seven-part series, "Murder Inc."—the interview he had done with the British Thames Television crew three years earlier. Several of the ads carried Jimmy's photo.

He had called Akerman—who had joined a prestigious Park Avenue law firm—and complained that the show was never supposed to appear anywhere outside Britain. A small production company in the U.S. had purchased the syndication rights and was selling the show to nonnetwork-affiliated stations. There was nothing they could do now. The program was set to begin airing in mid-November.

Jimmy's problem was twofold: If his neighbors saw the program, it would blow his cover; and if WITSEC found out, they'd designate the area around his home a "danger zone" and force him to move.

Jimmy had his life's savings invested in this community. He didn't want to leave his house—there was no way he could ever make back his construction and decorating costs on the house. He had $20,000 invested in a nearby piece of land zoned for commercial use; $80,000 invested in their first house in the area; and another $50,000 in his appliance shop. All of it could be lost if he were forced to move again. He thought seriously about sticking it out, no matter what the dangers.

As the show's airing approached, Jimmy became increasingly on edge, exploding as Jean continued in her shop-till-you-drop decorating mode, ordering wallpaper, a baby grand piano, and additional rugs. It never occurred to him to confide in Jean; he knew she would run off at the mouth to Mode or someone at the church about it.

He was spending less time at the shop and more time at home, figuring the fewer people who knew his face, the better. When he did go to town he called ahead to have one of his repairmen waiting out front to take his car, so he could walk right in without looking for parking or walking around.

Mike Carelli, a local building contractor, had phoned the shop several times looking for Jimmy, but Jimmy hadn't returned the calls.

The two men, though three decades apart in age, had become friends after Carelli did some of the work on Jimmy's house. They had gotten into the habit of meeting at Jimmy's store a few times a week for lunch, sitting around talking like a couple of old "goombas" about hustling for money and women. Jean didn't like him.

"Just remember, Jimmy," Carelli would say, "us grease balls got to stick together."

Saturday afternoon Jimmy answered the phone at home to find Carelli on the line.

"Hey Jimmy, you been avoiding me or what?" Carelli asked.

"No, Mike, I've just been home, you know. Trying to take it easy for a few days."

"You feelin' all right? You sick or somethin'?"

"Fuck no. Feel strong as an ox. What's up?"

"Well listen pal, I want to see you about some things. I mean, I've got something here I think you'll be interested in looking at."

"What is it?"

"Never mind, just come by the house. I'll be here all afternoon. We'll have a few beers and talk."

"Ah, well, okay. I guess I've been cooped up in here long enough. I'll be by in about an hour."

Jimmy couldn't help feeling uneasy about the call. He trusted Carelli, but there was something in his secretiveness that didn't sit right. And it was unusual for Carelli to be home on a Saturday.

As he picked up his car keys from the dresser, Jimmy stopped and opened the drawer, removing the .22, fingering it for a few moments. "Fuck no," he muttered to himself, sliding the gun back to its compartment. "This guy ain't connected."

Jimmy pulled his Olds into Carelli's driveway, all the way back behind the house to the garage, and walked up to the open kitchen door, where Carelli was reading a newspaper.

"Hey Jimmy, come on in, let me get you a cold one," Carelli said, setting the paper down on the table.

After a few minutes of idle chatter—business, broads, and food—Jimmy asked what it was Mike wanted to show him. Carelli, smiling, began to lift the newspaper from the table. Jimmy hadn't noticed it at first, but there was something under the newspaper. Carelli was lifting the newspaper very purposefully, Jimmy thought. The object looked to be about the size of a book or, perhaps, a gun. He knew he was overreacting as every muscle tensed. There was no reason to be fearful, he told himself, but his instincts insisted otherwise. Carelli was talking, saying something about "trust" and everybody deserving "a second chance." But Jimmy wasn't hearing the words; he was just watching to see what was under the newspaper. It was a copy of *The Last Mafioso*.

"So like I said, Jimmy, I just wanted you to know that I'm proud to have you as a friend."

Carelli looked at Jimmy for some kind of response.

"Say Mike, is there anything we got to talk about here or what?" Jimmy said without moving his eyes from Carelli's for a moment.

"Not a fuckin' thing, Jimmy. Not unless there's something you got on your mind. I forgot what it was I wanted to talk to you about, you know."

Jimmy stood up, took another sip of beer, and walked out to his car without another word.

That evening he flew to Washington, where he would stay until the marshals completed a background check on Carelli.

But as he sat in his Alexandria hotel room the next night, Jimmy's fears of exposure were further heightened: "60 Minutes" did a segment about the Sicilian Mafia and, in comparing it to the U.S. La Cosa Nostra, showed a couple of pictures of Jimmy from the interview he had done with Mike Wallace.

The marshals decided Jimmy might as well stay a few extra days—ultimately for nearly two weeks—during which he would meet with agents from the Kansas City and New York City cases.

He never told anyone in Washington about the Thames TV program, and because it was only showing in a few isolated parts of Canada and the U.S., he figured WITSEC probably wouldn't hear about it. The odd part of it all was that for the first time since he had been in the program, Jimmy was fearing for his life. But instead of taking every possible precaution, he was treating WITSEC like an enemy, complaining to the FBI and prosecutors that WITSEC was giving him a hard time by not allowing him to go home. The agents were sympathetic. They complained to Justice that the marshals were disturbing their witness and he should be treated better.

"You know, Jimmy, we've got rules; rules designed to assure your security," Mode told him when word of his complaints filtered back to her. "No one told you to do an interview with '60 Minutes' or write a book; those were your decisions. And if your safety is now in jeopardy, well, you're just going to have to suffer the consequences."

Jimmy's response was predictable: "If you people gave me enough money to live on I wouldn't have to expose myself doing interviews."

Carelli passed the security screening and Jimmy was permitted to return home after twelve days in Washington.

"Murder Inc." aired its first segment on the Sunday night before Thanksgiving and ran for an hour every night for the rest of the week. In all but one episode Jimmy received prominent play. There was no point hiding it from Jean any longer; they watched the program together with a mixture of pride and fear.

"Well, honey. Maybe the marshals will buy the house from us and let us move someplace warm. You think?"

"Not a chance," Jimmy shot back.

Monday morning, Kasten showed up at the door.

"Sooo, we got a celebrity in the neighborhood, huh?" the fat man said with a wink.

By Friday, everyone knew. The phone was ringing steadily. Everyone was circumspect.

Jimmy began keeping the dogs in the house all day—much to Jean's distress—so they could listen for intruders.

Word of the program had gotten around to Washington, and two marshals were on their way to the house to pick Jimmy up and take him back to Washington.

Jimmy called Ahearn and brought him up to date.

"Well, this couldn't have come at a worse time, Jimmy," said Ahearn, who was now the special agent in charge of the Bureau's Omaha division.

"What do you mean by that?"

"Well, you know Roy Williams has turned. He's testifying in the Kansas City case next week. And you know already that Lonardo, your friend, the Cleveland underboss, also began talking after his narcotics conviction and will show up in Kansas City any day now."

"Yeah, so? What's that got to do with me?"

"Jimmy, you're slipping, boy. Look, if they've got those two to testify, from now on your value isn't as high as it once was," Ahearn said.

"You got to be kidding. These guys never left their hometowns, they don't know the bosses in New York or nothing like I do."

"Maybe not, maybe yes. I don't know what they've been saying, but it sure isn't going to help your cause any.

"In any case, here's what I'm doing. I've already arranged for Justice to pay you another fee after the Kansas City case—probably not as much as the 50,000 you got last time, but it will help. Now, what I think you've got to do, is get ahold of those New York prosecutors and agents in that Castellano case and anything else you've got going and get them to put some pressure on Safir to make your new deal go down real fast and easy."

Jimmy worked the phones enlisting support up to the moment

the marshals came through the door to take him off to Washington, where Mode and Safir were waiting.

Their talks went nowhere.

He sat in Mode's office and listened as Safir explained their position. His home was now a "danger zone." Too many people knew who he was. He had to move—to a location WITSEC deemed safe. They suggested the Gulf Coast of Florida or Georgia, near where he and Jean had lived before.

He would also have to take a cut in funding—$1,200 a month total.

Jimmy responded that they would have to buy him two new cars and keep up the mortgage and other payments on his house. They said they doubted it was possible, but they'd look into it.

The first session ended in a draw.

"They say they're going to throw me off the program if I don't go on their terms, Newt, and fuck them, 'cause I ain't going on their terms. I have some principles you know. It's their fault in the first place that I had to expose myself to make a buck. Now I go where I want or I don't go nowhere."

Through the phone, from 3,000 miles away, Newt could hear the desperation, and the onset of the flu, in his friend's voice.

"Well, Jim, I wish I had some better news for you. I did as you asked. I called Meese and left a message, but he never got back to me. Instead, this guy Trott called this morning. He told me that this was entirely in Safir's purview, and that I should try to get you to cooperate with Safir."

"Hey Newt," Jimmy exploded, with such force that his craggy voice burst into a coughing jag. "This Safir hates me, man. I told him that he'd have to be crazy to send me to Florida—they got a jillion made guys down there. And Georgia? There were like two dozen people there who knew who I was. I'm telling you, what they're trying to do is make it as tough as they can so I'll leave the program."

"Jimmy, I can't believe Meese would buy that," Newt said. "You know, he's just like Reagan. The two of them are loyal to a fault to anyone who's done them a service. I'm going to write him a letter."

"Yeah, McDonald said he was going to write to Meese, too. And I'll tell you something else, these FBIs and prosecutors are furious. They say that the program just fucks them all up, jerking their witnesses around. The program has no interest in us witnesses, you know. There's real bad blood between the FBI and this program. I'm talking to a few agents here about maybe quitting this thing and going with the FBI again, like I did when you met me in California."

"I can't believe Justice would permit the Bureau to do that, Jim."

"Well, they've done it for me before and this prosecutor in the New York case, Bruce Baird, he told me that five of the witnesses testifying in that Castellano case are all with the FBI, that they refused to go on the program. I'll tell you the way this program works: It preys on guys who are broke. A guy with his own money, like Lonardo or Williams, wouldn't go anywhere near this fuckin' thing."

"By the way, you see the paper today, about Williams?" Newt asked, trying to defuse Jimmy's tirade.

"Yeah, poor bastard. I can't believe that judge wouldn't cut him loose after he testified in Kansas City. Guy as sick as he is with emphysema and all having to do ten years. Shit, he'll die in there."

"And did you hear about DellaCroce?"

"What?"

"You didn't hear? Anielo DellaCroce died this morning. Or at least his lawyer, oh, you know him, the New York hot-shot, the one defended that Bernie Goetz guy—"

"You mean Barry Slotnick, sure."

"Yeah, Slotnick. He announced that the old man died in a hospital. Sounded like it was cancer, 'cause all they'd say is it was from natural causes."

Jimmy was silent as he calculated the meaning of DellaCroce's death.

DellaCroce, although never formally recognized as the boss of the Gambino Family, was regarded as the most powerful mobster in the United States. It was only with DellaCroce's blessing that Paul Castellano had ascended to leadership of the Gambino Family—and a civil war had been avoided between DellaCroce's and Castellano's supporters. Without DellaCroce to hold his band of young turks at bay, the balance of power was again in doubt.

"Without DellaCroce to back him up, I don't know how much longer Castellano's going to hold power," Jimmy offered as his analysis. "He's already indicted in this case I'm suppose to testify in, and the Commission case is built on wiretaps the FBI had in his house. Forget about it, this guy is becoming a real liability to the Five Families."

Over the next two weeks, as Jimmy waited in luxury motel rooms in and around Washington, his problems were discussed at meetings attended by the FBI, prosecutors, and WITSEC—generally ending in screaming bouts about whose interests were best served by forcing Jimmy to live by standard WITSEC regulations. Nothing was resolved, but then nothing ever was resolved between the FBI and WITSEC. The two agencies, both divisions of the Justice Department, were in constant competition to control witnesses.

Jimmy's stock dropped a few more points on December 16, when Paul Castellano was gunned down at dusk by three men as he stepped out of his Lincoln in front of a fashionable mid-Manhattan restaurant. Free on $2 million bail as his trial progressed, Castellano had spent the day at his lawyer's office and had dinner reservations at Sparks Steak House. The restaurant's managers were conducting a staff meeting in the back of the restaurant when the shooting occurred, so no one got a look at the incident. Official explanations for the slaying were the same as Jimmy's prophecy to Newt: "He'd become a liability." Before Christmas, John Gotti, a forty-four-year-old former member of DellaCroce's crew, emerged as the new Gambino strongman, and it was presumed that he had arranged Castellano's murder. At the time of his ascendancy, Gotti was awaiting trial in federal court on RICO charges stemming from the slaying of Tony "TP" Plate, the Florida loan shark who disappeared just before he and DellaCroce were to be tried for the murder of an FBI informant.

Castellano's death may have offered more credibility to Jimmy's expertise, and it certainly relieved him of one trial he would have had to testify in, yet it further reduced his negotiating strength, eliminating a set of agents and prosecutors who had been arguing with WITSEC in his behalf.

Jimmy left Washington for Kansas City with his future uncertain. At his insistence, he would return home after the completion of his testimony. He and Safir had agreed to use Christmas as a cooling off period, after which Jimmy would have to make up his mind whether to remain on the program on their terms or go off on his own.

In Kansas City, the defense lawyers were primed and ready for the man they had come to deride as "Jimmy the Witness."

The case had been initiated after Joe Agosto, a mob comptroller in Vegas, turned government witness, providing the testimony needed to win indictments. But Agosto died while serving time in the Valachi suite. The official diagnosis had been heart failure; Jimmy's diagnosis was that he died of stress. Both were correct.

Williams, Glick, Lonardo, and Jimmy collectively made up for Agosto's absence.

Williams described how he had risen to the top of the Teamsters with the backing of Kansas City crime boss Nick Civella, and had then been coerced by Civella, in 1974, to have the pension fund trustees approve a $62.7 million loan for the purchase of the Stardust and Fremont casino-hotels. Afterward, Williams said, he received $1,500 a month, skimmed from the casino's counting rooms, as a payoff for his cooperation.

Glick, who had made a small fortune in San Diego real estate during the 1970s while still in his thirties, explained how Milwaukee mob boss Frank Balistrieri had helped him get the Teamsters loan to purchase the casinos. After the purchases were completed, Glick testified, Balistrieri ordered him to "step aside" or else "my sons would be killed one by one."

Lonardo, at eighty-one, was the government's star witness. He described meetings he had attended leading up to the casino purchases and how packages of $40,000 to $100,000 a month began arriving in four Midwestern mob cities—Cleveland, Kansas City, Milwaukee, and Chicago—soon after the mob took control of the casinos. He also described his meetings with Aiuppa and Civella at which they chose Teamsters presidents Roy Williams and later Jackie Presser.

Jimmy's testimony focused on his knowledge of the Chicago outfit's members—the boss Joey Aiuppa, his underboss Jackie Cerone, and *capo* Joey Lombardo—charged in the case and their comments to him about mob holdings in Las Vegas.

He was barely on the stand for an entire day. The defense attacked his credibility, citing the money he had received from WITSEC— more than $500,000 at that point, including $88,689 for subsistence and $70,000 for medical—suggesting his testimony was bought by the government.

Jimmy replied that he had spent $150,000 of his own money while on the program. He protested that his testimony wasn't bought; it was the truth. And he tried to explain his views about WITSEC, but it was cut off by the defense.

His greatest disappointment was that Spilotro wasn't there. "Tony the Ant" was already on trial in Las Vegas on unrelated RICO charges involving the "Hole in the Wall Gang," which he was charged with directing in robberies, extortions, and arsons. He had been granted a separate trial in Kansas City, which wasn't scheduled to get underway for a year.

With his status as precarious as it was at that point, Jimmy could have made good on his threats and not testified at all. But this was one case he had been waiting a long time for. "This one's for Johnny," he kept mumbling to himself as he stared down at Aiuppa from the witness box.

And besides, there was Ahearn's promise of some more cash when the case was over.

The yard and driveway were buried in snow. It was the kind of snow that sets like concrete, creating a winter-long surface that squeaks when you walk on it.

In the month he had been gone, Jean had kept the business running and Kasten had come by regularly to help out with heavy household errands, such as dragging the Christmas tree into the living room.

Gustav and Hildie Shultz, who lived three doors away, had wrapped Jimmy's outdoor shrubs in burlap to protect them from the cold.

Mike Carelli arrived one morning with two of his men. They strung crystal-white holiday lights, tracing the outline of the house and the branches of the leafless trees.

And about an hour before Jimmy was expected that day-before-Christmas Eve, Carelli showed up with a two-quart jar of eggnog.

"It's a family recipe, Jeanie. I mean, uh, well, my mother used to make this stuff," Carelli said, blushing.

"I know what you mean, Mike," Jean said with a laugh, and a deep raspy cough she had developed in recent days. "Why don't you stay a while and wait for Jimmy. He'd be delighted to see you."

"Thanks, Jeanie, but I'd rather leave tonight to you guys. From what they say in the papers it sounds like Jim's been pretty busy," Carelli said, suddenly feeling odd at his open familiarity with who Jimmy was.

Jean just smiled and bid him a merry Christmas as he slipped out the door.

Jimmy wasn't exactly filled with the Christmas spirit when he came home. But with eggnog, a roaring fire, and a Christmas tree to adorn, he warmed up pretty quickly.

For two days Jimmy and Jean did little more than act like young lovers, whispering sweet phrases to each other and giggling on cue. He even attended Christmas Mass with her.

On Christmas morning they exchanged gifts. For Jean, a diamond that had belonged to his mother, which he had placed in a heavy gold pendant setting by a jeweler in Washington.

For Jimmy, a gold ID bracelet.

But the Christmas spirit couldn't linger very long.

Jimmy was effectively on his own in what everyone kept telling him was a "danger zone." The .22 automatic was more often in his pocket than in his dresser drawer. He never walked around outside the house—always entering and leaving the car through the garage. Jean had to tend the garbage. Carelli came by and added four more heavy-duty spotlights in the front and back yards. The curtains were drawn tight and the TV was turned down low.

Their bickering began again.

Just before New Year's Eve, Jean found the courage to ask what they were going to do about money if he dropped off the program. Jimmy's response was to brandish his gun and scream.

"That's my fuckin' problem. I'll deal with it and you keep your nose out of my business," he said, waving the gun toward her face.

"Jimmy, I have to know what you're thinking," she pleaded, sobbing in fear and desperation. "This can't continue. You're carrying on like a stranger, a crazy man. For God's sake Jimmy, if we have to leave all this we will. We'll start again, somewhere, I know we can."

She was collapsed on the floor, resting her head on the living room sofa, her body convulsed by hysterical sobbing. Jimmy stood motionless, staring, as if pulled back from a dream. He sat on the sofa, placed one hand on her head in comfort, the other hand rested open on the sofa cushion with the .22 flat on top of it.

They remained like that for almost half an hour before Jimmy spoke. "You're going to have to leave."

"But Jimmy—"

"Shit, don't interrupt me. Okay?"

Jean nodded, her face swollen, her eyes bloodshot.

"You're going to have to cut a separate deal with Safir. They can keep you on the program. They'll pay your way. And I'll keep fighting them until we get what we need to live decently."

"Okay, Jimmy, but what if they don't come around? What then?"

"Well, the way I figure it, they need me in these cases in New York. And Henderson has a set of indictments coming in L.A. that he'll need me in. So I think the FBI will have to take me."

"Jimmy, I don't like you here all by yourself. I'm willing to stay with you. I'm not scared."

"That's no good, babe. It's too cold for you up here. You're already coughing; you're going to end up with pneumonia again. And besides, if you go back on the program, with the house in your name, it means they'll have to pay at least a portion of the mortgage and bills here."

"Oh, shit, Jimmy," Jean said, realizing that his concern was for the house's well-being, not hers. "I always knew the time would come when you'd sell me to the Philistines."

On December 31, 1985, Jimmy was dropped from the program. He received his last subsistence funding a few days later. Protection would be provided if he had to travel somewhere on official business. Social security checks, which WITSEC had been processing under his assumed name, ceased. The phone, which had been his primary outlet for contact with friends, became a financial burden with which he had to deal on his own.

A week later, Jean packed her bags—fourteen in all—and was swept off to Washington, where she would negotiate her new location and funding. The first thing Mode told her was that she wasn't to give Jimmy any hint of where she was. That was all right. She felt that their marriage was over. She never expected to see him again.

The night Jean left, Jimmy sat in the kitchen and cried. He hadn't cried in a very long time. The dogs looked on in bewilderment.

Word came from Washington that Spilotro got a hung jury in Vegas. But the Kansas City case brought convictions against the top five defendants, including Aiuppa. Eight others pleaded guilty. Two defendants, John J. and Joseph P. Balistrieri, were acquitted.

Jimmy sat alone, holed up in the big house overlooking the water, waiting for the phone to ring, expecting good news any day from Ahearn or Newt or someone at the Justice Department.

Newt called to tell him Licavoli had died in prison.

Epilogue: Jimmy the Witness

Jimmy's riding lookout, slung low in the plush leather bench seat of his Cadillac. I'm at the wheel, guiding the silent, big blue machine through autumn darkness, golden-brown leaves shooting and swirling about the streets in its wake.

He says he doesn't like driving after dark these days; he says it's his age, his eyes. But peering through the tinted windows into these twisting, country roads he can warn of a rabbit frozen in the headlights 100 feet ahead.

We're returning from dinner, where he tried to set me up. He was urging that I get it on with a young woman he knows—"She's built nice, ain't she?" To his annoyance, I rejected the offer. Jimmy is always trying to do a favor for a friend. Is it goodwill or does he want me to be beholden to him?

I remind myself of the caution offered by Mace Ebhart when I met Jimmy three years earlier: "Jimmy's not so bad; just always remember who you're dealing with."

As we drive, he's talking about the past, refining tales of glory and desperation; telling me how to write about his confrontations with WITSEC and the law. He's especially proud of his most recent victory, in New York, where he testified against Carmine Persico, boss of the Colombo Family. He isn't so proud of his new deal with WITSEC and avoids talking about it.

"How does that go?" he asks, pausing for a moment. "I may have lost some battles, but I'm gonna win the war."

382

Jimmy reentered WITSEC after several months of arguments and failed efforts by his supporters, the FBI and prosecutors, to win everything he wanted. It was a compromise: They picked up partial payments on the house until it was sold, but they reduced his stipend and he had to live where they wanted.

"Yeah, but you've paid a price—I mean, your freedom, looking over your shoulder all the time, having to hide out and live where you're told," I say, trying to coax him into a little more philosophical mode of thought.

He shoots back without a moment's hesitation: "Hey man, it's not like I'm scared—just cautious. You know what I'm saying?"

There is some silence as I search for a way to corner the old fox with what seems such an obvious truth to me: He *is* scared.

Of course, his fears, if he would ever admit them, were substantially eased when Spilotro was found beaten to death, possibly buried alive, early in 1986, in a shallow grave in a corn field a few miles from Aiuppa's suburban Chicago home. The brutality of Spilotro's murder was a measure of the mob's anger. He had become too much of a liability to the Chicago Family: there had been too many murders, too much trouble in Las Vegas, which led to people getting upset, the feds having to crack down, a few people cooperating, and, ultimately, the convictions of Aiuppa and the rest of the Midwest bosses— "See, there was a reason for them old rules about not fuckin' around in Vegas." When Spilotro had disappeared some weeks earlier, Jimmy had predicted his demise.

"So then, there really isn't much chance anyone's out looking to clip you; Spilotro's dead and the others are in jail. So it's more trouble than it's worth. Is that the idea, Jimmy?" I say, pulling up to a stop sign.

"Are you fuckin' kidding?" he says, his voice reaching an indignant screech. "Lookit, these motherfuckers hate me like poison, you know what I'm saying? They'd kill me just for the message it'd send to other guys. Move this car will you," he says, sliding a little lower in his seat, aware of headlights illuminating the road behind us.

"Okay. So you returned to the program for your safety. I mean, you've told me a hundred times you're not doing it for the money; they don't pay you enough, right? It had to be for protection or money, or both."

"I did it because they owe me," he replies slowly. "Let's put it that way: They owe me."

That's not just a rationalization; he believes it. And even if he is less than entirely pleased with the terms, Jimmy Fratianno always collects whatever he can on a debt.

Even if it falls short of what he thinks he deserves, Jimmy appears satisfied with his deal. He gets more than most witnesses—perhaps more than any witness. And he really isn't completely opposed to living on their terms; he has never taken full responsibility for his life. It suits him to let someone else make decisions, which he can later rail against to reach a compromise. If you don't make decisions, you aren't responsible. He likes it that way.

"They owe me safety, and they owe me money. I've testified and I'm going to go on testifying, so they owe me. That's our deal, Mike. Shit, with all I've done for them, these cocksuckers could never come up even with what they owe me. Forget about it."

He pulls himself up erect in his seat, his arms crossed comfortably, looking out at the road ahead.

It's hard to argue with that assessment. In his time, Jimmy has been places and heard things no wiretap could ever hear—and understand. In his time on witness stands, he has proven things no one else could prove. His legacy—and he has never fully appreciated this—will be that he broke new ground, becoming the vehicle for proving that La Cosa Nostra is vulnerable.

But all he sees is a simple cumulative box score of how many bosses he has put away—Brooklier, Tieri, Bufalino, Aiuppa, Balistrieri, Persico—and when pressed, he admits to aiding in the downfall of his childhood friend Licavoli. Effectively, they were all sentenced to life terms.

"But what's left for you, Jimmy?"

"I don't know anymore. There ain't many cases where I know what these guys done. Most of the guys I knew good are dead or in jail, and I was the one put these motherfuckers away. It's like this case with Persico, all I done was go to New York and testify that I'd been introduced to him as boss of the Colombo Family. Now they want me, more or less, as an expert, you know, to come in and say this is how the organization operates. It ain't no big deal."

He will never really appreciate the unique value of that expertise.

At the time of this writing, the President's Commission on Organized Crime has just completed its three-year study of the secret societies— La Cosa Nostra and all its hues. What the distinguished jurists, lawmen, and officials divined were the specifics of what Jimmy Fratianno could have explained, if they had listened carefully, with a couple days in the witness stand: La Cosa Nostra has found its way into the everyday lives of every one of us through its corruption of unions, politicians, and businesses.

The commission, having set out to determine the dimensions of the problem, put its findings into real annual terms: control of 414,000 jobs, $6.5 billion in taxes, and $77.20 in added consumer costs for every American.

But the commission gave little in the way of analysis of how effectively the judicial system is coping with those problems, or where law enforcement could stand some improvement.

In many respects, Jimmy Fratianno's experiences as a government witness makes him a living laboratory for examining some aspects of the justice system's successes and failures.

The argument can be made that crime pays. Not petty ante crime, but big crime. The lesson to be learned is that if you do the crime, make it the biggest, be a leader, make it your business to know everyone's role—and then know a little more. That way, when the appropriate time comes, you have something to offer the government in return for an immunity bath. Look at the record: Angelo Lonardo, Licavoli's successor as Cleveland boss, had 103 years reduced to parole; Ray Ferritto got a trip to the gas chamber dropped to five years; the cavalcade of accomplice witnesses in the Premier Theatre case faced from five to twenty years each, and all ultimately walked away with light, if any, time; even Eliot Weisman, after two trials and a six-year prison term, got off easy after cooperating; Joe Hauser, the con man in the Brilab case, did some easy time in the Valachi suite; and, of course, Jimmy had a potential death sentence and/or a twenty-year RICO sentence reduced to twenty-two months.

Roy Williams was the only one here that got hammered, but his was an extreme case: head of the nation's largest union, trying to currupt a U.S. Senator, taking the government through a costly trial, and then, after his co-defendant is blown away, he suddenly decides to cooperate. It was far too little, far too late.

However, using the same evidence, it can be argued that the wages of crime are hardly worth the risk of being caught. None of those who signed on as a government witness—especially Fratianno—got an easy ride. They all had to surrender their former lifestyles to begin anew. Jimmy did what he regarded as his toughest prison time in the Valachi suite. He lived well for a couple of years, but was always dependent upon and controlled by the dole.

Oddly enough, and perhaps a point easily overlooked, the WIT-SEC program frequently does more to rehabilitate an offender than prison. Certainly there are a vast number of losers who ignore the opportunity to start over with a clean slate, but many do make it work for good.

Jimmy Fratianno may have been a cheap hood in a mob boss's clothing in his former life, but since he hooked up with the government he became a success. He was never a smooth operator—no high-power money broker, no kingmaker. His plan to put together Teamsters dental plans in Warren, Ohio, and San Francisco—through his contacts with Allen Dorfman, Rudy Tham, and Jackie Presser— fell flat; his shakedowns of big porno operators in L.A. never materialized; his big gun deal with Vincent Todisco came to nothing; his Knights of Malta benefit with Frank Sinatra never worked out; his investments with Billy Marchiondo fizzled. The only times it worked for Jimmy were his trucking business—a completely legit operation— and his deal with the government.

And his deal with the government has done more than provided protection and money. He came to feel he was part of a team which was, after all, a driving force in Jimmy's life, the need to belong to some order—smaller than society but larger than himself, which provided clear parameters. Not since his days in the trucking business had Jimmy owned a home, tended a yard, or cared about setting down roots in a community. Even in simple dollars and cents logic: It may cost the taxpayers plenty to keep Fratianno satisfied, but we have gotten value for our money in terms of prosecutions and not having to pay to keep him in prison.

Ultimately, there can be no question but that crime does, in some instances, pay, but only when you don't get caught. No matter how sweet Fratianno's deal, or anyone else's for that matter, may appear, getting caught still means paying a price higher than the value of the crime. Cutting a deal with the government after being caught may provide certain rewards—limited exposure to prison and some nominal income—but only rarely is it worth having done the crime.

Fratianno was not one of those rare cases where it paid. He avoided a potentially hefty prison term or the death sentence, but he was repaid with extraordinary services. And as a side benefit, the government has reformed a gangster, keeping him honest by threat of prosecuting him for his crimes if he lied.

But there's that question, once again: Did Jimmy Fratianno lie? Was that how he made and kept his deal with the government, by being an astute liar? And if they caught him lying, would the government really admit to it and prosecute him?

The last question is the easiest to answer: No. The government would never, unless forced through some highly unusual circumstance, prosecute one of its own witnesses for perjury. And certainly not a witness as valuable as Jimmy Fratianno. After speaking with several dozen prosecutors, I have not found one who recalls it ever happening. It probably has, a few times, in some obscure matters. But as a rule of thumb, it is fair to say it does not happen. There are plenty of reasons beyond the self-serving prosecutors' motives not to prosecute a cooperative witness. For one thing, it is hard to prove that a lie was more than a misunderstanding of terminology or a misstatement. And for another, to prove perjury, it is necessary to show the specific advantage the witness gained by the particular lie.

The government rarely even prosecutes those who double-cross them. Look at Ferritto: He testified once and when called to appear again, refused. The government could have challenged him, saying he broke his deal and prosecuted him for the Greene murder. But they gave him a pass. In the Don Bolles murder, the state did prosecute its witness when he refused to testify in a retrial, but only because, without his cooperation, the state had no one else to hold accountable for one of the most notorious murders of the decade.

Is Jimmy an astute liar? Not terribly. What he is very good at is avoiding getting hung up on specifics, such as dates or locations or precise identifications, which defense lawyers can use to discredit him. His best lie, if it can be called that, is to say he doesn't recall. Frequently, he has had some independent recollection of an event but uncertainty, and a degree of bullheadedness, has evoked a non-answer.

And as to the key question: Did Jimmy Fratianno lie his way through all those trials?

There is much reasonable doubt to review on this matter:

Did he actually have a greater hand in killing Frank Bompensiero than he lets on? Did he really have some firsthand knowledge of the Nardi and Greene slayings? There has never been anything to prove it, but everyone, including Ahearn and the FBI in Cleveland, believes he has always held something back on those murder cases.

His statements on Bomp's murder have been contradictory: first he says he set up Bomp, then he says it was Dragna's idea; he talks about the diligent efforts he and Dragna exercised toward Bomp's murder, and then says he really did not want to see him dead. On the Los Angeles porno shakedowns, he told Demaris he did not know who Cleveland sent out to shake down pornographer Reuben Sturman, and then at trial says it was Glenn Pauley. Is it conceivable that a greed-driven Jimmy Fratianno passed up the chance of shaking down Forex, which his friend Bomp had told him was making $200,000 a year?

And on the Cleveland case, there is nothing to suggest he had a direct hand in the Nardi and Greene murders, except possibly having introduced Ferritto to the mob, which he said occurred years before the gang wars got underway. But is it possible that he knew *nothing* of those murders despite his repeated visits, during the course of the gang wars, with the key conspirators, his closest friends, who shared with him details about their FBI mole?

And isn't it interesting that in many of the cases where he has no personal knowledge of the background of a conspiracy, there is always something he learned from another now-dead mobster. In the Premier Theatre case it was his involvement with Fat Dom Alongi; in Cleveland it was Dope DelSanter or Lips Moceri; in Los Angeles it was Bomp and Ricciardi. Maybe that's just the odds in La Cosa Nostra, that death frequently intercedes before trial. Or maybe he was cunning enough to recognize that dead men cannot deny his testimony.

I recently spoke with Norman Ostrow, Weisman's lawyer, about Fratianno's testimony. Ostrow railed at the notion that Fratianno arrived at the theater, as he testified, and was introduced to Weisman, DePalma, and Fusco, each as partners.

"Come on, now. You think that Marson went around that place saying, 'Jimmy-whatever-your-name-is-this-week, I'd like you to meet Eliot Weisman, he's one of the partners?'

"And do you think Weisman was an idiot? You think he didn't know who Fratianno was? Do you think Weisman poured his heart out to Fratianno about how he was a front, or pawn, or whatever it was Fratianno said he told him, and that he was the one who would take the fall for all the illegal activities at the theater? Is this a man who you would trust to tell secrets to? Give me a break," Ostrow said with a disgusted sweep of his hand.

Ostrow doesn't buy it. But then again, no matter how unlikely a scenario it may seem, no one could ever refute that it happened that way.

Howard Weitzman, Dragna's lawyer, similarly looked upon Fratianno as a stench in the nostrils of decency, but during an interview at his offices offered no clear insight to lies.

Barry Ivan Slotnick smiles and shrugs. "What can I tell you? He's probably the best prosecution witness I've ever dealt with. But is he lying? I think they all do. But I wasn't able to prove it."

William Marchiondo would not sit for an interview to try refuting Fratianno's testimony: "That man Fratello or Fratianno is a bold-faced fucking liar. And if you use my name in that book you had better be accurate," he said, adding his intention to sue me and my publisher.

I pointed out to Marchiondo how difficult it would be to offer a fully accurate picture without his point of view, but in two phone conversations he refused any requests for an interview.

Some defense lawyers claimed to have hard evidence of Fratianno's lies. Tony Brooklier, the mob boss's son, and Jay Goldberg, Tieri's lawyer, said they had a book or books cataloging Jimmy's past inconsistent statements. "Hard proof of his continuous lies, from one trial to the next," Brooklier said.

They each offered to share their book of lies with me, but Brooklier dropped from sight and never returned my calls after I replied with silence to his inquiries of Fratianno's current hide-out. And Goldberg balked upon learning that Jimmy was cooperating in this work. He said he would reconsider his denial if he could review some portion of the manuscript in order to assure that my approch was evenhanded. I refused the request.

The defense lawyers are not alone. Several judges have been skeptical of Fratianno's tales. In the Williams-Lombardo sentencing hearing, U.S. District Judge Prentice Marshall, a noted jurist, went so far as to say he was largely rejecting Fratianno's testimony about Lombardo's role in organized crime—and yet he handed down hefty sentences based on Lombardo's criminal history. And U.S. District Judge Terry Hatter, Jr., was widely believed to have been disgusted with Fratianno, one explanation for the light sentences in the Los Angeles case.

But did Fratianno lie about the substance of any of the charges he brought to court? What is my view, as a jury-of-one, after reviewing in excess of 15,000 pages of trial transcripts and FBI debriefings, after watching dozens of hours of videotaped depositions, and, most importantly, after spending hundreds of hours in his company?

Well, like any jury, corroboration is required before you can believe anything Fratianno says—and balancing that is the need for corroboration if it is to be proved that he lied.

The best example is the Los Angeles case. Just because the jury there did not convict on the Bompensiero murder does not mean Fratianno lied; it only means that there was insufficient corroboration to convict and sufficient reasonable doubt to acquit.

The verdict on Jimmy the Witness: I have found no proof that Fratianno ever lied on the substance of a criminal charge. Even taking into account all of the reasonable doubts listed above, there remains no hard proof—no documents or direct contradictory testimony—that Fratianno intentionally lied about the substance of a case.

As to personal belief—dealing in the realm of impression, beyond the cold facts—I believe Fratianno has told the truth, to the best of his ability, on the substance of criminal charges, with only one notable exception.

The one nagging doubt in my mind is in Fratianno's testimony in Los Angeles, the conversation in which he says Brooklier confessed making the phone call that sent Bompensiero to the phone booth and his execution. It just does not make sense to me that Brooklier would have made the call; the boss doesn't get involved in anything that messy. And even if he had, would he admit it to Fratianno, a man he entirely distrusted at that point?

That is not to say that I buy the argument that Fratianno made the call or was involved, with Joe Bonanno, in killing Bompensiero.

No, I believe the rest of his story about the L.A. Family killing Bompensiero—the pieces of independent evidence support his claims. I just wonder if he so badly wanted to assure that Brooklier was in the jackpot that he spiced up his story a bit.

But that is only one man's opinion; reasonable men may differ.

Only on some rare occasions—and those insignificant matters, not related to the substance of a criminal charge—can it be said with certainty that Fratianno was incorrect or lied. For example, in the theater trial he claimed to have seen the final cash split after the last Sinatra show, but Ostrow proved he departed before the last show; and F. Lee Bailey caught him at one point, questioning him about documents he claimed to have read but never had.

I believe Jimmy Fratianno believes he told the truth in all those cases. His enormous ego and sense of self-assurance leads him to speak in hyperbole, making what seems to him a logical extension of facts to a conclusion that may be flawed. For example: Weisman's complaining to him that "I'm the one gonna get in trouble over all this" and reading that as Weisman's confession of knowingly being the mob's front man; seeing money split up after a Sinatra performance and thinking that it must have been the last divvy; or having given a cursory glance to a set of documents in the Albuquerque case and saying he had read them. Like most of us, his memory is colored by personal perception, making it difficult to discern belief from fact.

One final area where I believe, but cannot prove, he lied was to avoid testifying in the Cleveland case, but then only to the FBI and prosecutor, not on the witness stand.

Does WITSEC work?

The program works about as well as it can under current conditions. The program's goal is twofold: first, to protect and care for its witnesses, and second, to protect society from a witness doing harm—hence the long list of rules and regulations that define witnesses' conduct and life-style.

But there are failings of the program, such as its inability—or unwillingness—to police witnesses who have gone astray. A witness who, under a new identity, commits crimes and is picked up by police in a suspicious situation will be readily released because he has no prior record or outstanding warrants listed in the federal crime computer.

And the program has failed in its ability to work well with prosecutors and the FBI. The FBI and WITSEC, both independent divisions of the Justice Department, seem to operate at cross purposes. There are regular battles over the proper treatment of a witness; Fratianno is far from alone in his complaints that the program fails to make special exceptions for special witnesses. And he is not the only one to threaten—or to make good on a threat—to walk away from the government program, denying prosecutors aid in a long-awaited trial because of a dispute with WITSEC.

If there are recommendations to be made here, it seems to me that the Witness Security Program should be incorporated as a division of the FBI, making the Bureau responsible for use and protection of witnesses, as well as responsible for protecting society from errant witnesses. It would certainly take some adjustment in FBI operations to secure the witness files from general access, but it would enable greater facility for law enforcement to know when a witness has run amok; help those responsible for a witness's testimony to have responsibility and authority in determining reasonable treatment for a witness; and would create a smoother interface between witnesses and prosecution teams in preparation for trial.

Does the justice system, wedded to the likes of Fratianno, work?

In the long view, sure. Justice is distilled from the process. The burden of proof-beyond-a-reasonable-doubt, shouldered by the government, seems to work well: The bad guys are usually put away and their enterprises crippled.

Especially helpful to law enforcement has been a decaying sense of order within La Cosa Nostra. *Omertà* is regularly violated—as in Los Angeles, where most of the mob's leaders were at one time or another talking to the FBI. And violations of the old taboos—narcotics dealing and violence in Las Vegas—have spurred law enforcement to action.

But the cost of winning convictions with accomplice witnesses like Fratianno and Ferritto—or Pruett, the one-man killing and raping machine, or Henry Hill, the "wise guy" hustler—remains a nagging question.

It seems to me that justice is at a critical stage, driven to near-excess and abuse in its desperation to eradicate the corrupt influence of La Cosa Nostra, the darkest edge of American society, where the only moral imperatives are greed and self-protection. To stop organized crime's toll of corruption, to cut through layers of mob insulation, justice may be perverted by a belief that the ends justify almost any means; but in the long haul, the cure could be as bad as the disease.

Some examples:

• The Jackie Presser case. Despite Jimmy's repeated testimony that Presser was a wholly-owned subsidiary of the Cleveland mob, the FBI never made a case against Presser. Instead, the U.S. Labor Department struggled from about 1983 to 1985, without success, to make a case against Presser for maintaining "ghost employees" on his Cleveland union local payrolls—employees who collected salaries for fictitious jobs. When Labor investigators got close enough to prove their case, agent Robert Friedrick stepped in, claiming Presser's illegal activities had been authorized as part of his efforts as an informant. It later came out that no such authority was—or could be—granted; rather, it appears, Friedrick was protecting Presser because he had been such a good informant. There were those in the FBI who viewed Presser's crimes as petty and not worth losing him as an informant. Friedrick was indicted simultaneously with Presser. Both await trial as of this writing: Presser for embezzlement of union funds and racketeering; Friedrick for lying to officials during the Presser investigation.

• Ahearn, the FBI, and local prosecutor Carmen Marino in Cleveland always doubted Fratianno's role in the Nardi and Greene killings. Yet they were willing to give him a pass, buying what they believed were his lies, in order to win his cooperation.

• The FBI clearly abused its relationship with Bompensiero, setting him up in the PORNEX sting. They knew and intended that the mob would learn that Bomp was the informant who had set them up, thereby jeopardizing his life, which Barron expected would make him run to the FBI for protection. Instead, he was killed.

• In the Premier Theatre case, most of those charged were criminals, but some were businessmen whose primary transgression had been to deal with some bad guys and to later refuse to cooperate with the government for fear of losing their lives or livelihoods. Akerman successfully used the case as a bludgeon to win their cooperation in other cases. Their initial failure to cooperate, in effect, became their crime.

• There remain doubts in my mind—and in the minds of others— whether there ever was a contract on Fratianno's life, or whether it was an invention of Ahearn's ambition.

• In Cleveland, local police and prosecutors long believed the feds were protecting Greene from local criminal charges in return for his information.

It's interesting to note that in Cleveland, where there appears to be, at least from this narrow perspective, the greatest abuses, there were also the greatest successes in prosecuting the mob. Is that a coincidence? Does the end justify the means?

Have we abandoned not the letter of the law, but the spirit and basic tenets underlying the concept of justice being blind to special needs or interests? Is this a process of decay, though well-intended, that may gradually erode the foundation of justice?

Unquestionably, as prosecutors have pointed out, there is no other way to win prosecutions against La Cosa Nostra and its colleagues except to engage the cooperation of other bad players.

"There are no swans in the sewer."

But must those entrusted to protect society also crawl into the sewer, tempting the immoral creatures that reside there with incentives? Wouldn't it make more sense to *demand* a criminal's cooperation rather than offering reduced sentences and a ride in witness protection? Shouldn't justice be meted out evenly to all those involved in criminal wrongs?

A case in point: In New York City, the last in a series of mob-busting RICO trials ended recently with a stunning defeat for prosecutors. A prosecutorial juggernaut—which had from 1985 into 1987 brought down the leaders of four of New York's crime Families, their top henchmen, and their international narcotics cartels—appeared destined to break the back of La Cosa Nostra. But the last of those cases, that against Gambino underboss Anielo DellaCroce and his cohorts, was forced to change its focus when DellaCroce died of cancer in November 1985 and Gambino boss Paul Castellano was gunned down days later. The new ruler of the nation's largest mob Family— or so observers insisted—was DellaCroce protégé John Gotti.

The DellaCroce case was reassembled in a hurry with Gotti as the new centerpiece. New evidence was collected and some quick deals were cut with some unsavory characters. The seven-month trial was less than neat: There were government witnesses unable to keep their stories straight and one defense witness who told a convincing story about federal efforts to buy his testimony with immunity baths and even drugs.

Gotti's acquittal—on Friday, the 13th of February, 1987—proved a dark day for the U.S. Justice Department. The jury focused its attention on a chart defense lawyers had assembled demonstrating the many crimes the government's witnesses admitted committing. The verdict, delivered after seven days of deliberation, was seen as a condemnation of a system which tempts immoral men with incentives—and threatens to corrupt our system of justice.

It seems to me that there is serious reason for concern—and need for an independent review to look more closely, on a nationwide basis, at potential problems. A commission, or congressional hearings, and/ or an in-depth study by the recently created investigative arm of Congress's General Accounting Office should review the long-term dangers of the justice system's struggle with organized crime, focusing on:

• The Witness Security Program, to determine not only how better systems of control can be exercised over errant witnesses, but whether the program would be more effectively run by the FBI.

- The use of sentencing as incentive, or as a bludgeon, to win defendants' cooperation.
- Use of immunity and the means by which prosecutors and agents of the law win the cooperation of informants and witnesses, as well as accounting the resulting prosecutions, to determine the veracity of those witnesses.
- The uses and abuses of sting operations, such as the one in which Bompensiero was set up, and, for good measure, a review of Title III wiretaps and RICO cases.

What I would hope this review could produce is some standards, or perhaps a permanent oversight group, a regulatory agency, or judicial panel with authority to rule on the government's methods in the nebulous arena of building cases—coercing informants to aid in the creation of sting operations, which lead to plea bargains, immunity deals, and admission to WITSEC for testimony at trial.

This is currently the unilateral domain of the Justice Department. The courts certainly deal with any obvious abuses that contravene the law, but there seems to be need for long-term, outside review; some way to safeguard the principles as well as the laws.

Does the system work? Does it generally rid society of the bad guys while preserving the rights of the innocent? Of course it does, for now. The courts continue to secure individuals' rights while La Cosa Nostra's members, as well as their enterprises, are under attack like never before.

As U.S. Attorney Rudolph Giuliani and others have suggested, if current trends continue, La Cosa Nostra will cease to exist in its current form by the mid-1990s. Certainly other groups will fill the void, or La Cosa Nostra will continue in a different form, but they, too, will in relatively short order be identified and contained.

A common complaint about these prosecutions has been that they too frequently succeed in convicting only the top guys, the old men who are ready to die—witness Fratianno's efforts against Tieri, Brooklier, and Licavoli, each of whom died soon after sentencing. But the process of prosecutions, removing those leaders before they are ready to die—by either natural causes or someone else's design—is forcing younger men to assume leadership, and they in turn will be prosecuted or removed by their colleagues; a process that will gradually challenge La Cosa Nostra's ability to field seasoned and wise leaders, and disrupt unity of the secret society.

Fratianno doesn't think in these long terms. He sees an immediate advantage, a quick buck or a simple score to be settled. Yet it is his testimony that established the precedents needed to destroy La Cosa Nostra, the organization that he believes consumed his life and then threatened to snuff it out.

He never will realize the extent of his vengeance.

Index